A·N·N·U·A·L E·D·I·T·I·O·N·S

Educating Exceptional Children

Sixteenth Edition

04/05

W9-ATK-636

EDITOR

Karen L. Freiberg

University of Maryland, Baltimore County

Dr. Karen Freiberg has an interdisciplinary educational and employment background in nursing, education, and developmental psychology. She received her B.S. from the State University of New York at Plattsburgh, her M.S. from Cornell University, and her Ph.D. from Syracuse University. She has worked as a school nurse, a pediatric nurse, a public health nurse for the Navajo Indians, an associate project director for a child development clinic, a researcher in several areas of child development, and a university professor. Dr. Freiberg is the author of an award-winning textbook, *Human Development: A Life-Span Approach*, which is now in its fourth edition. She is currently on the faculty at the University of Maryland, Baltimore County.

McGraw-Hill/Dushkin

530 Old Whitfield Street, Guilford, Connecticut 06437

Visit us on the Internet
http://www.dushkin.com

Credits

1. **Inclusive Education**
   Unit photo—© 2004 by PhotoDisc, Inc.
2. **Early Childhood**
   Unit photo—© 2004 by Cleo Freelance Photography.
3. **Learning Disabilities**
   Unit photo—United Nations photo.
4. **Speech and Language Impairments**
   Unit photo—United Nations photo.
5. **Developmental Disabilities**
   Unit photo—United Nations photo.
6. **Emotional and Behavioral Disorders**
   Unit photo—© 2004 by Cleo Freelance Photography.
7. **Vision and Hearing Impairments**
   Unit photo—United Nations photo.
8. **Multiple Disabilities**
   Unit photo—United Nations photo.
9. **Orthopedic and Health Impairments**
   Unit photo—United Nations photo.
10. **Giftedness**
    Unit photo—Courtesy of Pamela Carley.
11. **Transition**
    Unit photo—© 2004 by PhotoDisc, Inc.

Copyright

Cataloging in Publication Data
Main entry under title: Annual Editions: Educating Exceptional Children. 2004/2005.
1. Educating Exceptional Children—Periodicals. I. Freiberg, Karen L., *comp.* II. Title: Educating Exceptional Children.
ISBN 0–07–287448–1   658'.05   ISSN 0198–7518

Sixteenth Edition

Cover image © 2004 PhotoDisc, Inc.
Printed in the United States of America   1234567890BAHBAH54   Printed on Recycled Paper

Editors/Advisory Board

Members of the Advisory Board are instrumental in the final selection of articles for each edition of ANNUAL EDITIONS. Their review of articles for content, level, currentness, and appropriateness provides critical direction to the editor and staff. We think that you will find their careful consideration well reflected in this volume.

EDITOR

Karen L. Freiberg
University of Maryland, Baltimore County

ADVISORY BOARD

Elizabeth Begley
Ithaca College

Erin Brumbaugh
Marietta College

MaryAnn Byrnes
University of Massachusetts, Boston

Lorna Catford
Sonoma State University

Jozi De Leon
New Mexico State University

Sheila Drake
MidAmerica Nazarene University

Colleen Finegan-Stoll
Wright State University

Robin I. Herman
Central State University

Thomas J. Long
Catholic University of America

Carla J. Manno
George Mason University

Mack McCoulskey
Angelo State University

Sharon A. Merrill
Xavier University

Susan M. Munson
Duquesne University

Marcia J. Reinholtz
Greensboro College

Joyce M. Smith
SUNY College, Oswego

Linda A. Svobodny
Minnesota State University, Moorhead

Ruth Thompson
Edinboro University

Kathleen S. Whittier
SUNY at Plattsburgh

Steve L. Williams
California State University, Hayward

Staff

Jeffrey L. Hahn, Vice President/Publisher

EDITORIAL STAFF

Theodore Knight, Ph.D., Managing Editor
Roberta Monaco, Managing Developmental Editor
Dorothy Fink, Associate Developmental Editor
Addie Raucci, Senior Administrative Editor
Robin Zarnetske, Permissions Editor
Marie Lazauskas, Permissions Assistant
Lisa Holmes-Doebrick, Senior Program Coordinator

TECHNOLOGY STAFF

Richard Tietjen, Senior Publishing Technologist
Marcuss Oslander, Sponsoring Editor of eContent
Christopher Santos, Senior eContent Developer
Janice Ward, Software Support Analyst
Angela Mule, eContent Developer
Ciro Parente, Technology Developmental Editor
Joe Offredi, Technology Developmental Editor

PRODUCTION STAFF

Brenda S. Filley, Director of Production
Charles Vitelli, Designer
Mike Campbell, Production Coordinator
Eldis Lima, Graphics
Nancy Norton, Graphics
Juliana Arbo, Typesetting Supervisor
Julie Marsh, Project Editor
Jocelyn Proto, Typesetter
Cynthia Powers, Typesetter

To the Reader

In publishing ANNUAL EDITIONS we recognize the enormous role played by the magazines, newspapers, and journals of the public press in providing current, first-rate educational information in a broad spectrum of interest areas. Many of these articles are appropriate for students, researchers, and professionals seeking accurate, current material to help bridge the gap between principles and theories and the real world. These articles, however, become more useful for study when those of lasting value are carefully collected, organized, indexed, and reproduced in a low-cost format, which provides easy and permanent access when the material is needed. That is the role played by ANNUAL EDITIONS.

The new millennium has been wrenched by unexpected expenses: terror alerts, rebuilding after terrorist attacks, fighting a war against weapons of mass destruction, constructing more military might, repairing after nature's misfortunes, and coping with downsizing, unemployment, and recession. Among the losers: our children, education, and reforms aimed at a kinder, gentler world.

A comment heard from an incoming school superintendent recently shed light on the movement afoot for the education of our children: "My schools will have no students requiring special services." Is such an egalitarianism stance covering a hidden agenda to save money or a desire to defy the Individuals with Disabilities Education Act (IDEA), with its principle of education in the least restrictive environment (LRE), or to acquire power? Perhaps the superintendent believes that educating every child equally will challenge and motivate every child to achieve equally?

Some radio and television talk show hosts describe the provision of special educational services to some children as pampering, or perpetuating dependency, or, worse yet, to pandering to the tastes and desires of decadent, left-wing, effete (depleted of effectiveness) intellectuals. How do you feel about this description?

This compendium of articles about children who need, and benefit from, special educational services may serve as a counterbalance against the voices calling for reactionary reform. Is the elimination of any kind of so-called favored treatment (supportive assistance) for children with exceptionalities a correction of past misguided education? Where do you stand on this issue? Our current lack of funds for education will require some changes. To what extent will more efficient use of financial resources necessitate the elimination of services? What services should go first? Will belt tightening have any positive effects?

A new and burgeoning field, biotechnology, may have an answer for our future: no children born with exceptionalities. Is this science fiction or a real possibility?

The Human Genome Project's completion enabled us to decode the human genome. This means that we have knowledge of the sequencing of CATG (cytosine, adenine, thymine, guanine), the chemicals that form DNA. It means that we can replace strands of DNA (genes) with altered CATG sequences. It means that we can alter human development.

Should twenty-first-century scientists be allowed to alter genes? Who will pay for resequencing of CATG to bring about new behaviors? Will human cloning be allowed to prevent the birth of any human with a disability? Will test-tube fertilization, genome inspection, and genetic correction be used as an alternative means of preventing the birth of so-called "imperfect" beings? These and other questions are likely to lead to contentious debates for many years to come.

A near-future answer to individuals with exceptionalities will be to replace dysfunctional body parts with new body parts generated from stem cells. In the United States, the Bush administration, with its strong pro-life stance, has infuriated many scientists by suggesting that a stem cell (a fertilized egg a few days old) is already a human life. If a stem cell is a human life, can it be transformed into some type of replacement tissue to cure diabetes, autism, asthma, epilepsy, or attention deficit disorder? Many are arguing that an embryo on a Petri dish is not a human life, while the same embryo attached to a woman's uterine lining is a life. This thorniest of human ethical dilemmas is yet to be resolved.

In homes where families are raising children with disabilities or conditions of exceptionality, the above questions have special poignancy. Where should the balancing fulcrum be placed between challenges and cautions?

Annual Editions: Educating Exceptional Children 04/05 includes articles discussing the pros and cons of educational reform and special education. It explains how IDEA provisions are being implemented in all areas of special education. Selections have been made with an eye to conveying information, giving personal experiences, offering suggestions for implementation, and stimulating meaningful discussions among future parents and teachers.

To help us improve future editions of this anthology, please complete and return the postage-paid *article rating form* on the last page. Your suggestions are valued and appreciated.

Karen Freiberg

Karen L. Freiberg
Editor

Contents

UNIT 1
Inclusive Education

Four articles present strategies for establishing positive interaction between students with and without special needs.

Unit Overview   xviii

UNIT 2
Early Childhood

Three unit articles discuss the implementation of special services to preschoolers with disabilities.

Unit Overview   22

The concepts in bold italics are developed in the article. For further expansion, please refer to the Topic Guide and the Index.

UNIT 3
Learning Disabilities

The assessment and special needs of students with learning disabilities are addressed in this unit's four selections.

The concepts in bold italics are developed in the article. For further expansion, please refer to the Topic Guide and the Index.

UNIT 4
Speech and Language Impairments

In this unit, three selections examine communication disorders and suggest ways in which students can develop their speech and language.

UNIT 5
Developmental Disabilities

Three articles in this section discuss concerns and strategies for providing optimal educational programs for students with developmental disabilities and Down syndrome.

The concepts in bold italics are developed in the article. For further expansion, please refer to the Topic Guide and the Index.

UNIT 6
Emotional and Behavioral Disorders

Ways to teach emotionally and behaviorally, disordered students are discussed in the unit's four articles.

UNIT 7
Vision and Hearing Impairments

Two selections discuss the special needs of visually and hearing impaired children within the school system.

The concepts in bold italics are developed in the article. For further expansion, please refer to the Topic Guide and the Index.

UNIT 8
Multiple Disabilities

The implications of educational programs for children with multiple impairments are examined in this unit's three articles.

UNIT 9
Orthopedic and Health Impairments

In this unit, three articles discuss how health problems and mobility impairments have an impact on a child's education.

The concepts in bold italics are developed in the article. For further expansion, please refer to the Topic Guide and the Index.

The concepts in bold italics are developed in the article. For further expansion, please refer to the Topic Guide and the Index.

The concepts in bold italics are developed in the article. For further expansion, please refer to the Topic Guide and the Index.

Topic Guide

This topic guide suggests how the selections in this book relate to the subjects covered in your course. You may want to use the topics listed on these pages to search the Web more easily.

On the following pages a number of Web sites have been gathered specifically for this book. They are arranged to reflect the units of this *Annual Edition.* You can link to these sites by going to the DUSHKIN ONLINE support site at *http://www.dushkin.com/online/.*

ALL THE ARTICLES THAT RELATE TO EACH TOPIC ARE LISTED BELOW THE BOLD-FACED TERM.

World Wide Web Sites

The following World Wide Web sites have been carefully researched and selected to support the articles found in this reader. The easiest way to access these selected sites is to go to our DUSHKIN ONLINE support site at *http://www.dushkin.com/online/*.

AE: Educating Exceptional Children 04/05

The following sites were available at the time of publication. Visit our Web site—we update DUSHKIN ONLINE regularly to reflect any changes.

General Sources

Consortium for Citizens With Disabilities

http://www.c-c-d.org

Included in this coalition organization is an Education Task Force that follows issues of early childhood special education, the president's commission on excellence in special education, issues of rethinking special education, 2001 IDEA principles, and many other related issues.

ERIC Clearinghouse on Disabilities and Gifted Education

http://www.ericec.org

This ERIC clearinghouse has information on everything important to special education professionals. It links also to The Council for Exceptional Children and the National Clearinghouse for Professions in Special Education.

Family Village

http://www.familyvillage.wisc.edu/index.htmlx

Here is a global community of disability-related resources that is set up under such headings as library, shopping mall, school, community center, and others.

National Information Center for Children and Youth With Disabilities (NICHCY)

http://www.nichcy.org/index.html

NICHCY provides information and makes referrals in areas related to specific disabilities, early intervention, special education and related services, individualized education programs, and much more. The site also connects to a listing of Parent's Guides to resources for children and youth with disabilities.

National Rehabilitation Information Center (NARIC)

http://www.naric.com

A series of databases that can be keyword-searched on subjects including physical, mental, and psychiatric disabilities, vocational rehabilitation, special education, assistive technology, and more can be found on this site.

President's Commission on Excellence in Special Education (PCESE)

http://www.ed.gov/inits/commissionsboards/whspecialeducation/

The report stemming from the work of the PCESE, *A New Era: Revitalizing Special Education for Children and Their Families,* can be downloaded in full at this site.

School Psychology Resources Online

http://www.schoolpsychology.net

Numerous sites on special conditions, disorders, and disabilities, as well as other data ranging from assertiveness/evaluation to research, are available on this resource page for psychologists, parents, and educators.

Special Education Exchange

http://www.spedex.com/main_graphics.htm

SpEdEx, as this site is more commonly known, offers a wealth of information, links, and resources to everyone interested in special education.

Special Education News

http://www.specialednews.com/disabilities/disabnews/povanddisab031200.html

This particular section of this site discusses the problems of coping with both poverty and disability. Explore the rest of the site also for information for educators on behavior management, conflict resolution, early intervention, specific disabilities, and much more.

UNIT 1: Inclusive Education

Consortium on Inclusive Schooling Practices

http://www.asri.edu/cfsp/brochure/abtcons.htm

The Consortium represents a collaborative effort to build the capacity of state and local education agencies to provide inclusive educational services in school and community settings, focusing on systemic reform rather than on changes in special education only.

Institute on Disability/University of New Hampshire

http://iod.unh.edu

This site includes Early Childhood, Inclusive Education, High School and Post-Secondary School, Community Living and Adult Life, Related Links, both state and national, and information on technology, health care, public policy, as well as leadership training and professional development.

Kids Together, Inc.

http://www.kidstogether.org

Based on the IDEA law about teaching children with disabilties in regular classrooms, this site contains all the information on inclusion you might need to know.

New Horizons for Learning

http://www.newhorizons.org

Based on the theory of inclusion, this site is filled with information on special needs inclusion, technology and learning, a brain lab, and much more, presented as floors in a building.

UNIT 2: Early Childhood

Division for Early Childhood

http://www.dec-sped.org

A division of the Council for Exceptional Children, the DEC advocates for the improvement of conditions of young children with special needs. Child development theory, programming data, parenting data, research, and links to other sites can be found on this site.

Institute on Community Integration Projects

http://ici.umn.edu/projectscenters/

Research projects related to early childhood and early intervention services for special education are described here.

National Academy for Child Development (NACD)
http://www.nacd.org

The NACD, an international organization, is dedicated to helping children and adults reach their full potential. Its home page presents links to various programs, research, and resources into such topics as learning disabilities, ADD/ADHD, brain injuries, autism, accelerated and gifted, and other similar topic areas.

National Early Childhood Technical Assistance System
http://www.nectas.org

An exceptionally complete site on children with special needs, NECTAS explores many areas, including the IDEA and inclusion, and includes a projects database.

Special Education Resources on the Internet (SERI)
http://seriweb.com

SERI offers helpful sites in all phases of special education in early childhood, including disabilities, mental retardation, behavior disorders, and autism.

UNIT 3: Learning Disabilities

Children and Adults With Attention Deficit/Hyperactivity Disorder (CHADD)
http://www.chadd.org

CHADD works to improve the lives of people with AD/HD through education, advocacy, and support, offering information that can be trusted. The site includes fact sheets, legislative information, research studies, and links.

The Instant Access Treasure Chest
http://www.fln.vcu.edu/ld/ld.html

Billed as the Foreign Language Teacher's Guide to Learning Disabilities, this site contains a very thorough list of resources for anyone interested in LD education issues.

Learning Disabilities Association of America (LDA)
http://www.ldanatl.org

The purpose of the LDA is to advance the education and general welfare of children of normal and potentially normal intelligence who show handicaps of a perceptual, conceptual, or coordinative nature.

Learning Disabilities Online
http://www.ldonline.org

This is a good source for information about all kinds of learning disabilities with links to other related material.

OHSU Center on Self Determination
http://cdrc.ohsu.edu/selfdetermination/education/moving/communitysolutions.html

The community solutions project described at this site focused on the unique needs of minority adolescents with disabilities as they transitioned from high school to adulthood.

Teaching Children With Attention Deficit Disorder
http://www.kidsource.com/kidsource/content2/add.html

This in-depth site defines both types of ADD and discusses establishing the proper learning environment.

UNIT 4: Speech and Language Impairments

Issues in Emergent Literacy for Children With Language Impairments
http://www.ciera.org/library/reports/inquiry-2/2-002/2-002.html

This article explores the relationship between oral language impairment and reading disabilities in children. The article suggests that language impairment may be a basic deficit that affects language function in both its oral and written forms.

Speech and Language Disorders Fact Sheet
http://www.nichcy.org/pubs/factshe/fs11txt.htm

This online publication of the National Dissemination Center for Children With Disabilities offers much useful information, including resources, organizations, and discussions of incidence, characteristics, educational implications, and how technology can help children with speech and language disorders.

Speech Disorders WWW Sites
http://www.socialnet.lu/handitel/wwwlinks/dumb.html

A thorough collection of Web sites, plus an article on the relationship between form and function in the speech of specifically language-impaired children, may be accessed here.

UNIT 5: Developmental Disabilities

Arc of the United States
http://www.thearc.org

Here is the Web site of the national organization of and for people with mental retardation and related disabilities and their families. It includes governmental affairs, services, position statements, FAQs, publications, and related links.

Disability-Related Sources on the Web
http://www.arcarizona.org/dislnkin.html

This resource's many links include grant resources, federally funded projects and federal agencies, assistive technology, national and international organizations, and educational resources and directories.

Gentle Teaching
http://www.gentleteaching.nl

Maintained by the foundation for Gentle Teaching in the Netherlands, this page explains a nonviolent approach for helping children and adults with special needs.

UNIT 6: Emotional and Behavioral Disorders

Educating Students With Emotional/Behavioral Disorders
http://www.nichcy.org/pubs/bibliog/bib10txt.htm

Excellent bibliographical and video information dealing with the education of children with emotional and/or behavioral disorders is available at this site.

Pacer Center: Emotional Behavioral Disorders
http://www.pacer.org/ebd/

Active in Minnesota for 8 years in helping parents become advocates for their EBD children, PACER has gone on to present workshops for parents on how to access aid for their child, explain what a parent should look for in a child they suspect of EBD, prepare a behavioral intervention guide, and link to resources, including IDEA's Parnership in Education site, and much more./

Resources in Emotional or Behavioral Disorders (EBD)
http://www.gwu.edu/~ebdweb/

At this page, link to a collection of Web resources for teachers of students with serious emotional disturbances.

UNIT 7: Vision and Hearing Impairments

Info to Go: Laurent Clerc National Deaf Education Center
http://clerccenter.gallaudet.edu/InfoToGo/index.html

Important for parents and educators, this Web site from Gallaudet University offers information on audiology, communication, education, legal, and health issues of deaf people.

www.dushkin.com/online/

The New York Institute for Special Education
http://www.nyise.org/index.html

This school is an educational facility that serves children who are blind or visually impaired. The site includes program descriptions and resources for the blind.

UNIT 8: Multiple Disabilities

Activity Ideas for Students With Severe, Profound, or Multiple Disabilities
http://www.palaestra.com/featurestory.html

The Fall 1997 issue of the *Palaestra* contains this interesting article on teaching students who have multiple disabilities. The complete text is offered here online.

Severe and/or Multiple Disabilities
http://www.nichcy.org/pubs/factshe/fs10txt.htm

This fact sheet offers a definition of multiple disabilities, discusses incidence, characteristics, medical, and educational implications, and suggests resources and organizations that might be of help to parents and educators of children with severe impairments.

UNIT 9: Orthopedic and Health Impairments

Association to Benefit Children (ABC)
http://www.a-b-c.org

ABC presents a network of programs that includes child advocacy, education for disabled children, care for HIV-positive children, employment, housing, foster care, and day care.

An Idea Whose Time Has Come
http://www.boggscenter.org/mich3899.htm

The purpose of community-based education is to help students in special education to become more independent. Here is an excellent description of how it is being done in at least one community.

Resources for VE Teachers
http://www.cpt.fsu.edu/tree//ve/tofc.html

Effective practices for teachers of varying exceptionalities (VE) classes are listed here.

UNIT 10: Giftedness

The Council for Exceptional Children
http://www.cec.sped.org/index.html

This page will give you access to information on identifying and teaching gifted children, attention-deficit disorders, and other topics in gifted education.

National Association for Gifted Children (NAGC)
http://www.nagc.org/home00.htm

NAGC, a national nonprofit organization for gifted children, is dedicated to developing their high potential.

UNIT 11: Transition

Building Partnerships Between Centers for Independent Living and Schools
http://cdrc.ohsu.edu/csd1/home/Projects_at_the_Center/Networks/BUILDING_PARTNERSHIPS

This article overviews the Take Charge approach to transitioning young people with disabilities into their future. The model uses coaching to assist youth to learn self-determination and transition planning skills.

National Center on Secondary Education and Transition
http://www.ncset.org

This site coordinates national resources, offers technical assistance, and disseminates information related to secondary education and transition for youth with disabilities in order to create opportunities for youth with disabilities to achieve successful futures.

We highly recommend that you review our Web site for expanded information and our other product lines. We are continually updating and adding links to our Web site in order to offer you the most usable and useful information that will support and expand the value of your Annual Editions. You can reach us at: *http://www.dushkin.com/annualeditions/.*

UNIT 1
Inclusive Education

Unit Selections

1. **Standards for Diverse Learners**, Paula Kluth and Diana Straut
2. **Trends in the Special Education Teaching Force: Do They Reflect Legislative Mandates and Legal Requirements?** Elizabeth Whitten and Liliana Rodriguez-Campos
3. **What's Good? Suggested Resources for Beginning Special Education Teachers**, Sharon A. Maroney
4. **An Interview With Dr. Marilyn Friend**, Mary T. Brownell and Chriss Walther-Thomas

Key Points to Consider

• What conditions are needed to teach using a standards-based curriculum?

• How have professional teaching preparation practices been altered by IDEA?

• What can beginning teachers do to succeed in inclusive education?

• How important is collaboration between regular education and special education teachers? Defend your answer.

 Links: www.dushkin.com/online/
These sites are annotated in the World Wide Web pages.

Consortium on Inclusive Schooling Practices
http://www.asri.edu/cfsp/brochure/abtcons.htm

Institute on Disability/University of New Hampshire
http://iod.unh.edu

Kids Together, Inc.
http://www.kidstogether.org

New Horizons for Learning
http://www.newhorizons.org

A huge strength of American schools is the dedication and motivation of its professional teachers. Weaknesses include inadequate social, emotional, and financial support, lack of inservice education, and decreasing wherewithal for continuing education. Teachers need all the help they can get to be the best they can possibly be and to feel appreciated!

This unit on Inclusive Education highlights what's good in special education and includes some suggestions for ways it can be improved.

Regular education teachers are expected to know how to provide special educational services to every child with an exceptional condition in their classroom, despite not having had course work in special education. The numbers of students with exceptionalities who are being educated in regular education classes are increasing annually. During its 28 years in existence, the Individuals with Disabilities Education Act (IDEA) has reduced the numbers of special needs students being educated in residential centers, hospitals, homes, or special schools to less than 5 percent. Children who once would have been turned away from public schools are now being admitted in enormous numbers. Without adequate preparation and support, regular education teachers feel overwhelmed. Their abilities to educate all of their students, those with and those without disabilities, suffer grave consequences.

The trend toward inclusive education necessitates more knowledge and expertise on the part of all regular education teachers. Educating children with exceptionalities can no longer be viewed as the job of special education teachers. This trend also mandates knowledge about collaboration and advisory activities on the part of all special educators. Teamwork is essential as special education and regular education are becoming more and more intertwined.

Public schools have an obligation to provide free educational services in the least restrictive environment possible to all children who have diagnosed conditions of exceptionality. Although laws in Canada and the United States differ slightly, all public schools have an obligation to serve children with exceptional conditions in as normal an educational environment as possible. Inclusive education is difficult. It works very well for some students with exceptionalities in some situations and marginally or not at all for other students with exceptionalities in other situations.

For inclusion to succeed within a school, everyone must be committed to be part of the solution: superintendent, principal, teachers, coaches, aides, ancillary staff, students, parents, and families. Special education teachers often find that their jobs involve much more than instructing students with special needs. They serve as consultants to regular education teachers to ensure that inclusion is meaningful for their students. They collaborate with parents, administrators, support personnel, and community agencies as well as with regular education teachers. They plan curriculum and oversee the writing of Individualized Family Service Plans (IFSPs), Individualized Education Plans (IEPs), and Individualized Transition Plans (ITPs). They schedule and make sure that services are provided by all team-involved persons. They keep up with enormous amounts of paperwork. They update parents even when parents are too involved or not involved enough. They keep abreast of new resources, new legal processes, and new instructional techniques. They make projections for the futures of their students and set out ways to make good things happen. They also struggle to be accountable, both educationally and financially, for all they do.

The term "least restrictive environment" is often mistakenly understood as the need for all children to be educated in a regular education classroom. If students can learn and achieve better in inclusive programs, then they belong there. If students can succeed only marginally in inclusive education classrooms, some alternate solutions are necessary. A continuum of placement options exists to maximize the goal of educating every child. For some children, a separate class, or even a separate school, is still optimal.

Every child with an exceptional condition is different from every other child in symptoms, needs, and teachability. Each child is, therefore, provided with a unique individualized education plan. This plan consists of both long- and short-term goals for education, specially designed instructional procedures with related services, and methods to evaluate the child's progress. The IEP is updated and revised annually. Special education teachers, parents, and all applicable service providers must collaborate at least this often to make recommendations for goals and teaching strategies. The IEPs should always be outcomes oriented with functional curricula.

The first article in this unit discusses standards-based curriculum. The inclusion education movement has contributed to some very diverse classroom climates, where standards-based curricula must be flexible and developmental. There is no longer such a thing as a "grade" where one lesson plan fits all, even in rural areas. Teaching to standards requires careful assessments, access to different levels of meaningful content, and assistance from all stakeholders in education—parents, teachers, and community members.

The second selection, "Trends in the Special Education Teaching Force: Do They Reflect Legislative Mandates and Legal Requirements?" describes the changes in preparation of teachers between 1987 and 2000 to comply with the demands of IDEA and its aftermath.

The third article included in this unit suggests resources for beginning special education teachers. Experienced educators have given their expertise to Sharon Maroney to pass on to novice teachers. Advice is included on developing professionalism, instructing effectively, managing behavior, and using special techniques. The author also counsels readers to try new things and have fun in their chosen professions. Educating exceptional children is challenging. It should also be exciting and fun.

The last selection in this inclusive education unit is an interview with an expert on inclusive education for students with disabilities. Dr. Marilyn Friend discusses what it takes to make the collaboration of regular education and special education work. She answers questions about the challenges as well as the resources for success.

Standards for Diverse Learners

Standards-based lessons create rich and challenging learning experiences for all students.

Paula Kluth and Diana Straut

Education standards receive much attention these days from political leaders, parents, and educators. Many of these stakeholders are concerned about what the standards movement means for the pluralistic classroom.

What kind of diversity exists in U.S. classrooms? Every kind.

- Students are no longer either Catholic, Jew, or Protestant; in fact, the fastest growing religion in the United States is Islam (Hodgkinson, 1998).
- Most of the 5.3 million U.S. students with disabilities spend some part of their day in classes with nondisabled students (Kaye, 1997).
- By 1995, bilingual programs were operating in nearly 200 U.S. schools (Rethinking Schools, 1998).
- At least one-third of the school-aged population in the United States is nonwhite (Marlowe & Page, 1999).
- 43 million people in the United States move every year (Hodgkinson, 1998), creating an increasingly mobile student population.

In addition, trends such as multicultural education, antitracking pedagogy, inclusive education, dual bilingual programs, magnet schools, and multi-age classrooms are contributing to the rich diversity of U.S. schools.

The standards movement will have little meaning if it cannot respond to the needs of all these students. Can we develop standards *and* make curriculum, instruction, and assessment responsive to learning differences?

Five Conditions

Doing so is not only possible, but vitally important; every student must be able to participate in standards-based education. To make standards inclusive, however, educators must support and cultivate five conditions.

- *Standards are developmental and flexible*. Standards should not be a one-size-fits-all approach to education. A student cannot and should not be expected to know and do exactly the same things as his or her peers. Developmental and flexible standards provide different students in the same classroom with opportunities to work on a range of concepts and skills according to individual abilities, needs, and interests (Reigeluth, 1997).

By adopting a personalized approach, teachers can use standards to "allow a range of acceptable performance" so that

> all students may continue to work toward student-outcome goals such as graduation or literacy, but within each goal area knowledge and skill standards may vary based on student-ability levels. (Geenen & Ysseldyke, 1997, p. 222)

For example, students can share how to solve an arithmetic problem in many ways. Some students may use sign language or communication boards to show understanding, others may write a paragraph explaining the process, and still others may express their knowledge through drawings. In addition, students in the same classroom can focus on problems that range in complexity, with some students describing the process for reducing frac-

tions and others designing and explaining binomial equations.

To teach standards effectively in a diverse classroom, educators need to adapt the curriculum to meet the individual needs of learners and make alternatives available for instructional materials, teaching strategies, curricular goals, learning environments, instructional arrangements, and lesson formats (Udvari-Solner, 1996). For example, some students might use protractors and a compass to study obtuse and acute angles, whereas others may need to use a geometry software program. Experiential projects that encourage vocalizing and moving can meet the needs of active students who like to get out of their seats, investigate problems, and manipulate materials.

Some teachers believe that implementing adaptations in a standards-based classroom will diminish curriculum and instruction. The opposite is true. Creative adaptations can make curriculum more relevant, make abstract concepts more concrete, and connect the instructor's teaching style more effectively to students' different learning styles (Udvari-Solner, 1996). The following lesson illustrates how rich and challenging standards-based lessons can be for students with various learning profiles.

> Mr. Lee drafted daily lessons based on the standards he was teaching. For example, Mr. Lee decided to read every other chapter of [a historical novel] aloud to the students. They would read the opposite chapters in partners. He also decided to use learning centers with cooperative groups. Each center focused on an aspect of World War II and engaged students via one of the multiple learning styles. For example, one

of the centers involved journal writing, based on actual diaries from the Holocaust. Another center focused on geography and involved mapping the progress of war based on listening to actual radio broadcasts recorded during World War II. (Fisher & Roach, 1999, p. 18)

Mr. Lee's careful planning and conscientious design of the curriculum and instruction invites all learners to participate in an engaging and age-appropriate curriculum and also responds to a variety of learning styles. Mr. Lee's classroom does not expect one size to fit all students.

- *Standards require a wide range of assessment tools.* Professional literature and the popular media have linked standards with high-stakes testing. Standards and testing, however, are not the same. Educators must separate testing from the standards in conversations, in the design of curriculum, and in classroom instruction.

We believe that high-stakes assessment models are harmful and exclusive. Under the guise of accountability, several U.S. states and some individual school districts have implemented standardized testing programs that sort, eliminate, or stratify students from kindergarten through 12th grade. When students struggle with standardized tests, we only find out that they cannot perform effectively with such an assessment tool. When students do achieve high test scores, we do not necessarily know that they have learned more, learned better, or become more skilled or knowledgeable. These tests provide plenty of information about how skilled students are at taking standardized tests on a given day, but the tests do not provide much information about whether students have actually met the standards.

Standards do need some type of consistent and comprehensive assessment system, however. The most effective way to gather information about what students know and are able to do is to use a range of data collection strategies, including portfolios, interviews, observations, anecdotal records, self-evaluation questionnaires, journals, and learning logs (Lopez-Reyna & Bay, 1997; Pike & Salend, 1995). Students charged with explaining the ideas embodied in the Declaration of Independence, for example, could demonstrate their understanding by interviewing a peer, participating in a group skit, or writing an essay on the topic.

Kentucky has resisted high-stakes testing and has found a way to include all students in the formal assessment process (Kearns, Kleinert, & Kennedy, 1999). Most students in Kentucky undergo both traditional and alternative assessments. Students with significant disabilities participate in the statewide assessment by working on alternative portfolios that are tailored to their needs and strengths. Kentucky designed this range of assessments because many students struggle with traditional assessments and, more important, because a reliance on one kind of assessment does not provide a meaningful analysis of any student's abilities or progress.

In contrast to standardized measures, authentic assessments offer a fuller picture of student learning because they relate directly to what students are learning, are continuous and cumulative, occur during actual learning experiences, are collaborative, and clearly communicate proficiency to all stakeholders (Pike, Compain, & Mumper, 1994; Pike & Salend, 1995; Valencia, 1990). And because standards ask students to perform a range of competencies, we need a range of assessments to measure the learning of these competencies.

- *Standards allow equitable access to meaningful content.* If there were some alternative to standards that could ensure that all students—regardless of learning profile, race, ethnicity, or proficiency in English—had access to challenging academic content, then perhaps we could dismiss the standards movement. The truth is that we have not done a good job of giving all students—particularly those students with unique learning characteristics—access to an appealing, thought-provoking, and stimulating curriculum.

For example, Reese, a student with significant disabilities, works in an inclusive general education 4th grade classroom. While the general education students work in small groups to investigate fossils, Reese sits in the corner of the classroom and completes a counting worksheet with a paraprofessional.

Had Reese been expected to participate in a standards-based curriculum, he could be meeting his individual goals of "interacting appropriately with peers" and "classifying objects by at least three different characteristics." At the same time, he would have the opportunity to use interesting materials, work with peers, and learn about geography and history. Sorting fossils into categories or building a model di-

nosaur with a cooperative group would be both more meaningful and more content-based than filling in a worksheet that taught no science and did nothing to include Reese in the classroom community.

A set of standards, articulated across the state or district, can give parents, teachers, and administrators a common language for talking about student goals and progress. More crucial, attention to a set of common outcomes can serve as a challenge to view students as capable and to respect them with an appropriately rigorous curriculum.

- *It takes a community to implement standards.* Teaching to the standards is part of classroom teachers' responsibilities, but it is not their job alone. Teachers should receive assistance from all stakeholders in the school and community.

Collaboration among general and special educators can provide students with more opportunities to address the standards and to practice related skills. All students benefit from the different teaching approaches, instructional styles, and perspectives offered by two or more educators working in the same classroom (Cook & Friend, 1995).

The standards movement can provide teachers with a compass for crafting a rich curriculum and appropriate instruction.

Teaming across classrooms can also bring students closer to mastering the standards. For example, one physical education teacher helps kindergarten students recognize shapes by asking students to name the shapes of tumbling mats, hula-hoops, and floor scooters. While students learn new skills like hopping, galloping, and following rules, they are also engaged in an impromptu, cross-curricular, standards-based lesson with almost no up-front planning from the classroom teacher.

Teachers are not the only adults who can support a standards-based curriculum. The school secretary, recess monitor, lunchroom aides, teaching assistants, and family visitors can help. In one school, a custodian practices spelling words with students as they wait in line for lunch. Imagine the benefit of this fun exchange.

Students, the most important stakeholders in the standards movement, often know the least about implementing standards. Teachers should share information about standards in ways that students can understand; students are more likely to hit targets when they can see them (Strong, Silver, & Perini, 1999). Acting as allies in their own learning, students can develop personal strategies for meeting standards, and older students can even assist in developing standards-based lessons.

• *Standards are a catalyst for other reforms.* Some proponents of standards market them as the savior of public education, and many hope that this singular initiative will solve a wide range of educational and societal ills. At the same time, misconceptions about standards—as one-size-fits all, inequitable monsters that subject students and teachers to high-stakes tests—are creating a backlash that could reduce educators' commitment to designing learning opportunities for all students.

Standards are not the only route to educational excellence, but they can help us address the most pressing issues that stand in the way of students having a quality educational experience. For standards to work, schools need caring learning communities; skilled and responsive teachers; adequate financial, human, and material resources; effective partnerships with families; and concerned and visionary leadership. The standards movement should motivate political leaders to work for increased funding, smaller class sizes, better staff development opportunities, increased teacher planning time, and more social supports in schools, such as counselors and family liaisons.

The standards movement can provide teachers with a compass for crafting a rich curriculum and appropriate instruction, offering new opportunities and setting high expectations for all students in the multicultural, heterogeneous, dynamic classrooms of the 21st century.

References

Cook, L., & Friend, M. (1995). Coteaching: Guidelines for creating effective practices. *Focus on Exceptional Children, 28*(3), 1–15.

Fisher, D., & Roach, V. (1999). *Opening doors: Connecting students to curriculum, classmates, and learning.* Colorado Springs, CO: PEAK Parent Center.

Geenen, K., & Ysseldyke, J. E. (1997). Educational standards and students with disabilities. *The Educational Forum, 61*(1), 220–229.

Hodgkinson, H. L. (1998). Demographics of diversity for the 21st century. *The Education Digest, 64*(1), 4–7.

Kaye, H. S. (1997). Education of children with disabilities. *Disability Statistics Abstracts, 19.* San Francisco: Disability Statistics Center.

Kearns, J. F., Kleinert, H. L., & Kennedy, S. (1999). We need not exclude anyone. *Educational Leadership, 56*(6), 33–38.

Lopez-Reyna, N. A., & Bay, M. (1997). Enriching assessment: Using varied assessments for diverse learners. *Teaching Exceptional Children, 29*(4), 33–37.

Marlowe, B. A., & Page, M. L. (1999). Making the most of the classroom mosaic: A constructivist perspective. *Multicultural Education, 6*(4), 19–21.

Pike, K., Compain, R., & Mumper, J. (1994). *New connections: An integrated approach to literacy.* New York: Harper Collins.

Pike, K., & Salend, S. J. (1995). Authentic assessment strategies: Alternatives to norm-referenced testing. *Teaching Exceptional Children, 28*(1), 15–20.

Reigeluth, C. M. (1997). Educational standards: To standardize or to customize learning? *Phi Delta Kappan, 79,* 202–206.

Rethinking Schools. (1998). Number of language-minority students skyrockets. *Rethinking Schools Online, 12.* Milwaukee, WI: Rethinking Schools. Available: www.rethinkingschools.org/Archives/12_03/langsid.htm

Strong, R., Silver, H., & Perini, M. (1999). Keeping it simple and deep. *Educational Leadership, 56*(6). 22–24.

Udvari-Solner, A. (1996, July). Examining teacher thinking: Constructing a process to design curricular adaptations. *Remedial and Special Education, 17,* 245–254.

Valencia, S. (1990). A portfolio approach to classroom reading assessment: The why, whats, and hows. *The Reading Teacher, 43*(4), 338–340.

Authors' note: An expanded version of this article will appear in *Access to Academics for ALL Students* by P. Kluth, D. Straut, & D. Biklen (Eds.) (Mahwah, NJ: Lawrence Erlbaum Associates Publishers, in press).

Paula Kluth (pkluth@syr.edu) and **Diana Straut** (dmstraut@syr.edu) are Assistant Professors of Teaching and Leadership, Syracuse University, 150 Huntington Hall, Syracuse, NY 13244.

Trends in the Special Education Teaching Force: Do They Reflect Legislative Mandates and Legal Requirements?

by Elizabeth Whitten and Liliana Rodriquez-Campos

Introduction

Over the past decade several changes have evolved in special education teacher education, as well as reform movements throughout all aspects of the field of education, requiring appropriate and effective curriculum and instruction for students with disabilities in inclusive environments.[1] This type of movement has created the need to redefine the roles of special education teachers and prepare them to assume different roles. Although the Individuals with Disabilities Education Act (IDEA) of 1997 requires schools to include students with disabilities in the general education classroom to the maximum extent possible with appropriate support, teacher-preparation programs are struggling to keep up with the increasing need for special education teachers who reflect "best teaching practices" in educating students with disabilities. To be successful in least-restrictive settings, students need professionals prepared to provide the necessary support.[2] To meet these challenges teacher-preparation programs across the nation are modifying and redeveloping their programs.[3]

Although many researchers have made observations and predictions regarding the trends for special education in the next century, this article, based on a national survey, investigated trends across the nation in the special education teaching force.[4] The survey was administered in four waves (1987–88, 1990–91, 1993–94, and 1999–2000). The data were analyzed to determine if there were specific trends in the special education teacher population over the past decade. The identified trends include type of teaching assignments, diversity, training, certification, service delivery, and collaboration among personnel.

Teaching Assignment. Educational trends in special education teaching assignments reflect current legislation mandating inclusive education. An increasing number of students with disabilities are receiving their education in the general education classroom.[5] Teaching in isolation is rapidly coming to a close, and general education teachers are finding more and more students with disabilities in their classrooms for a larger portion of the day.[6] Special education teachers find themselves less often in segregated classrooms and more frequently in support roles to the general education classroom and teacher. Inclusive service-delivery models have been credited with decreasing the number of special education referrals.[7] If this trend continues, fewer students will be identified with disabilities because their needs will be met in the general education setting with special education support.

Teacher Diversity. The diversity in today's classroom is steadily increasing.[8] African, Hispanic, and Asian Americans comprise one-third of the U.S. population, and one-third of total school enrollment will be culturally diverse as well.[9] Substantial evidence shows overrepresentation of racial and ethnic groups in special education. Harry found a higher percentage of African American, Hispanic, and Asian American students in special education than in general education.[10] Regardless of student diversity in special education, the vast majority of special education teachers are Anglo American and speak only English.[11] In 1995 the percentage (14%) of special education teachers representing diverse backgrounds was less than half the percentage (32%) representing the diversity of students receiving special education services.[12] One of the barriers to addressing the needs of multicultural students receiving special education services is the lack of multicultural special education teachers.[13] Teachers from diverse cultural backgrounds provide students of diversity with role models as well as translators. Thus, special education personnel preparation programs will ideally recruit more teachers from culturally diverse backgrounds to provide students of diversity with an "intercultural understanding and communication."[14]

Teacher Preparation. Given the increasing demand for special education teachers, personnel preparation programs have found it necessary to intensify their use of time and resources. As a result many alternative programs now encourage teachers to complete certification requirements while they are employed, and distance education personnel preparation programs are available for teachers living in remote areas.[15] Such innovative preparation programs have increased the number of degrees and certified special education teachers and will most likely continue to provide career opportunities for potential special education teachers. Such programs include those operating at the University of West Virginia, the University of Kentucky, Fayetteville State University, the University of North Carolina, and Western Michigan University.[16]

Service Delivery. For many decades students with disabilities have received educational instruction in segregated settings, ranging from self-contained classrooms to resource rooms. The underlying assumption for specialized instruction has been that students with disabilities cannot be successfully instructed in the general education classroom, even with appropriate support.[17] Federal mandates, however, require schools to include students with disabilities in instruction with their nondisabled peers to the maximum extent possible.[18] Several researchers have found that teachers are not adequately prepared for inclusion.[19] Additionally, general and special education teachers are not certain of their roles in fully including students with disabilities. As a result the trends do not reflect the demands of federal laws mandating inclusive environments for students with disabilities. Lombardi and Ludlow suggest that special education may be the answer to many of our school problems.[20] Individual instruction significantly reduces documented school problems such as truancy, behavior problems, and low student achievement.[21] Teachers and teacher educators will need preparation and retooling to stay abreast of the needed changes in service delivery.

Collaboration among Personnel. Educators face significant challenges in today's diverse classroom.[22] To meet the educational needs of students with disabilities and those at risk academically or behaviorally, educators need to collaborate and to share their expertise. Collaborative skills require training and practice. Teacher preparation programs in general education typically require pre-service teachers to take a three-credit course on working with students with disabilities, and such a course does not involve preparation in collaboration or teaming.[23] Nevertheless, most general educators are teaching students with disabilities with minimal or no special education support in their classrooms.[24] General education teachers are well aware of the traditional practice of pulling students with disabilities from the general education classroom and providing them instruction in a segregated classroom with special education teachers. General educators are now expected to accept these same students into their classroom without receiving adequate preparation on how to instruct them or how to collaborate with support personnel. Nevertheless, special education teachers are expected to provide supportive services to general education so that students with disabilities can be successfully included in general education classrooms. Likewise, special education teachers infrequently have training in collaboration that would allow them to provide supportive services.

Purpose of the Study. This study of four waves of surveys conducted by the NCES describes how the characteristics of the special education (SPED) teaching force have evolved over the years. The details of the survey will be explained below. The survey data collected by NCES offer an excellent opportunity for determining whether the trend characteristics of SPED teachers are aligning with federal legislation regarding students with disabilities.

Sample, Data Source, and Weighting. The data for this study were extracted from the Schools and Staffing Survey (SASS) conducted by the NCES. The SASS is a national survey of school principals, schoolteachers, and local educational authorities. Given the nature of this article, the study used data collected from special educators who worked in public schools.

The data were analyzed from four SASS surveys conducted in 1987–88, 1990–91, 1993–94, and 1999–2000. Therefore, this study is a particular kind of longitudinal study called a *trend study.* In other words, by analyzing the national data from four rounds of the survey, we are able to discuss the trend of the relationship between the rhetoric and reality related to expectations for SPED teachers.

Actual and weighted samples for regular and special education teachers are shown in Table 1. The actual sample sizes of SPED teachers were 4,307 for SASS 1987–88; 5,054 for SASS 1990–91; 5,288 for SASS 1993–94; and 4,753 for SASS 1999–2000. Again, the subsamples of SPED teachers were not representative; hence, weights were applied in order for weighted samples to be representative of SPED teachers at the national level. As a result, the weighted samples of SPED teachers were 239,786 for SASS 1987–88; 273,956 for SASS 1990–91; 270,101 for SASS 1993–94; and 329,167 for SASS 1999–2000.

Results: Teaching Assignment. Data related to the special educator's current teaching assignment and school level are displayed in Table 2. The SPED teachers assigned to teach students with learning disabilities have shown the highest percentage throughout the years studied in this article. However, this percentage dipped from 47.3 in 1987–88 to 27.4 in 1990–91 to 27.2 in 1993–94, and then rose again to 28.9 in 1999–2000. Between the 1987–88 and 1999–2000 school years, the percentage of special educators assigned to teach students with mental retardation decreased from 19.4 to 6.3. The percentage of special educators assigned to teach students with emotional disturbance dipped from 9.4 in 1987–88 to 6.7 in 1993–94, and then rose to 8.6 in 1999–2000. For teachers assigned to work with speech- or hearing-impaired students, the percentage decreased from 12 in 1987–88 to 7.3 in 1993–94, and then increased to 8.7 in 1999–2000. The percentage of special educators assigned to teach general special education rose from 29.6 in 1990–91 to 33.6 in 1993–94 and decreased to 31.7 in 1999–2000. Furthermore, the percentage of special educators assigned to teach other types of special education options decreased from 11.9 in 1987–88 to 3.5 in 1999–2000.

Teacher Diversity. The longitudinal national data displayed in Table 3 indicate that the population of special

Table 1

Actual and weighted sample sizes:
A comparison across 1987–88, 1990–91, 1993–94, and 1999–2000

	1987–88		1990–91		1993–94		1999–2000	
	Regular	SPED	Regular	SPED	Regular	SPED	Regular	SPED
Actual sample	40,593	4,307	46,705	5,054	47,105	5,288	42,086	4,753
Weighted sample	2,323,204	239,786	2,559,488	273,956	2,561,293	270,101	2,984,781	329,167

Table 2

Special education teaching assignment:
A comparison across 1987–88, 1990–91, 1993–94, and 1999–2000 (in percentages)

	1987–88	1990–91	1993–94	1999–2000[3]
Current teaching assignment				
Learning disabilities[1]	47.3	27.4	27.2	28.9
Mental retardation	19.4	9.8	9.5	6.3
Emotional disturbance	9.4	8.3	6.7	8.6
Speech and hearing impairment[2]	12.0	8.7	7.3	8.7
Special education, general	NA	29.6	33.6	31.7
Deaf and hard-of-hearing	NA	2.3	2.1	1.2
Visually handicapped	NA	1.0	0.6	0.2
Orthopedically impaired	NA	1.0	0.5	0.4
Mildly handicapped	NA	2.2	2.8	5.0
Severely handicapped	NA	3.1	2.4	2.3
Autism	NA	NA	NA	1.0
Developmentally delayed	NA	NA	NA	0.9
Early childhood special education	NA	NA	NA	1.2
Traumatically brain-injured	NA	NA	NA	0.0
Other special education	11.9	6.7	7.3	3.5
Total	100.0	100.0	100.0	100.0
School level[4]				
Pre-kindergarten	13.5	16.5	5.9	4.6
Elementary	76.4	77.3	47.8	48.0
Middle/junior high	57.2	60.1	42.0	35.3
Senior high	43.3	49.5	29.2	28.1

[1] For the years 1987–88 and 1999–2000, this item was called "Learning disabled." However, for the years 1990–91 and 1993–94, this item was called "Specific learning disabilities."

[2] For the years 1987–88 and 1999–2000, this item was called "Speech and hearing impairment." However, for the years 1990–91 and 1993–94, this item was called "Speech/Language impaired."

[3] For the years 1999–2000 the term "Visually handicapped" was called "Visually impaired," the term "Mildly handicapped" was called "Mildly/moderately disabled," and term "Severely handicapped" was called "Severely/profoundly disabled."

[4] Since it is possible for a respondent to check two or more options (e.g., both kindergarten and elementary), the total percentage across the four school levels do total more than 100%.

educators has become more diversified by race. Therefore, the results reveal the general expectation that educators should reflect the increasingly diversified student population. Specifically, the data indicate an increasingly higher percentage of minority special educators in our schools. Accordingly, special educators of Hispanic origin showed the highest percentage of increase, from 2.2 in 1987–88 to 3.8 in 1999–2000. This increase was small in comparison to the expectation and the trend of diversity in student body.

Between the 1987–88 and 1999–2000 school years, the percentage of Asian or Pacific Islander special educators rose from 0.9 to 1.5. The combination of special educators who are American Indian, Aleut, or Eskimo first dipped in percentage from 1.2 in 1987–88 to 0.7 in 1990–91 and then rose to 1.3 in 1999–2000. However, the percentage of black special educators increased from 9.5 in 1987–88 to 9.6 in 1990–91 and then decreased to 9.2 in 1999–2000. Furthermore, the percentage of special educators of white origin rose from 88.4 in 1987–88 to 89.9 in 1993–94, and

Table 3

Special education teacher diversity:
A comparison across 1987–88, 1990–91, 1993–94, and 1999–2000 (in percentages)

	1987–88	1990–91	1993–94	1999–2000
Race				
Asian or Pacific Islander	0.9	1.0	1.0	1.5
American Indian, Aleut, Eskimo	1.2	0.7	0.8	1.3
Black	9.5	9.6	8.2	9.2
White	88.4	88.7	89.9	88.0
Hispanic origin				
Yes	2.2	2.5	3.2	3.8
No	97.8	97.5	96.8	96.2

Table 4

Special education teacher preparation:
A comparison across 1987–88, 1990–91, 1993–94, and 1999–2000 (in percentages)

	1987–88	1990–91	1993–94	1999–2000
Educational attainment by SPED teachers				
Bachelor's degree	99.8	99.9	99.3	99.7
Master's degree	54.1	55.6	54.0	53.9
Ed. specialist/professional diploma	10.3	7.8	7.5	4.7
Doctorate degree	0.6	1.2	1.0	0.5
Concentration in SPED				
Major	41.5	44.5	43.1	42.7
Minor	18.0	18.9	8.1	7.4
Certification	97.1	96.0	96.5	93.3

decreased to 88 in 1999–2000. In summary, the data on race show that the population of SPED teachers has become slightly more diversified.

Teacher Preparation. The results shown in Table 4 indicate that SPED teachers are a highly educated group. Between the 1987–88 and 1999–2000 school years, more than 99% of the population of special educators had earned bachelor's degrees. The percentage of special educators who had master's degrees rose from 54.1 in 1987–88 to 55.6 in 1990–91 and decreased to 54 in 1993–94 to 53.9 in 1999–2000. In addition, results show that the percentage of special educators who have educational specialist or professional diplomas decreased from 10.3 in 1987–88 to 4.7 in 1999–2000. Furthermore, the percentage of special educators who have doctoral degrees rose from 0.6 in 1987–88 to 1.2 in 1990–91 and decreased to 0.5 in 1999–2000.

Between 1987–88 and 1999–2000 almost all the special educators had certification in the SPED field, although this percentage decreased from 97.1 to 93.3 (see Table 4). However, the percentage of special educators with a major in the SPED field rose from 41.5 in 1987–88 to 44.5 in 1990–91 and decreased to 43.1 in 1993–94 to 42.7 in 1999–2000. Furthermore, the percentage of special educators with a minor in the SPED field increased from 18 in 1987–

88 to 18.9 in 1990–91, and then decreased to 8.1 in 1993–94 to 7.4 in 1999–2000. While more than half the special education teachers did not identify majors in special education, the overwhelming majority holds state-level special education certification. This is due to the varying requirements regarding degrees and certifications held by each state and university.

Table 5 shows the types of certification held by special educators from the 1987–88 to the 1999–2000 school years. Particularly, the regular or standard state certification displayed the highest percentage across the years studied in this article. This percentage rose from 86.1 in 1987–88 to 86.9 in 1990–91 and decreased to 85 in 1999–2000. For temporary, provisional, or emergency certification, the percentage of special educators decreased from 7.5 in 1987–88 to 5.8 in 1999–2000. Additionally, the percentage of special educators with probationary certification increased from 3.2 in 1987–88 to 3.3 in 1990–91 and then decreased to 2.5 in 1999–2000.

Service Delivery. The results in Table 6 display service delivery for elementary and secondary special educators. For the elementary level, results show that the percentage of special educators in collaborative teaching classes rose from 2.0 in 1987–88 to 11.2 in 1993–94 and decreased to 8.5 in 1999–2000. The percentage of special ed-

Table 5

**Type of certification held by special education teachers:
A comparison across 1987–88, 1990–91, 1993–94, and 1999–2000 (in percentages)**

	1987–88	1990–91	1993–94	1999–2000
Type of certification				
Regular/standard state certification	86.1	86.9	86.1	85.0
Temporary/provisional/emergency certification	7.5	5.8	7.3	5.8
Probationary certification	3.2	3.3	1.8	2.5
Other	0.3	0.0	1.3	0.0
Missing	2.9	4.0	3.5	6.7
Total	100.0	100.0	100.0	100.0

Table 6

**Special education teacher service delivery:
A comparison across 1987–88, 1990–91, 1993–94, and 1999–2000 (in percentages)**

	1987–88	1990–91	1993–94	1999–2000
Elementary				
Collaborative teaching	2.0	4.1	11.2	8.5
Resource room or pull-out class	46.8	48.0	42.1	46.8
Departmentalized instruction	4.2	3.4	7.0	5.6
Self-contained class	47.0	43.6	38.9	38.4
Elementary enrichment class	NA	1.0	0.8	0.7
Total	100.0	100.0	100.0	100.0
Secondary				
Collaborative teaching	5.9	7.9	8.4	10.3
Resource room or pull-out class	19.3	24.9	22.0	23.9
Departmentalized instruction	37.5	33.8	35.6	39.4
Self-contained class	37.3	33.3	34.0	26.4
Elementary enrichment class	NA	0.1	0.1	NA
Total	100.0	100.0	100.0	100.0

ucators in resource rooms increased from 46.8 in 1987–88 to 48.0 in 1990–91 and then decreased to 46.8 in 1999–2000. The percentage of special educators in departmentalized instruction classes rose from 4.2 in 1987–88 to 7.0 in 1993–94 and decreased to 5.6 in 1999–2000. Furthermore, the percentage of special educators in self-contained classes decreased from 47.0 in 1987–88 to 38.4 in 1999–2000.

In service delivery for the secondary level, the results in Table 6 show that between the 1987–88 and 1999–2000 school years, the percentage of special educators in collaborative teaching classes rose from 5.9 to 10.3. Additionally, the percentage of special educators in resource rooms increased from 19.3 in 1987–88 to 23.9 in 1999–2000. On the other hand, the percentage of special educators in departmentalized instruction classes decreased from 37.5 in 1987–88 to 33.8 in 1990–91 and then increased to 39.4 in 1999–2000. Further, the percentage of special educators in self-contained classes dipped from 37.3 in 1987–88 to 26.4 in 1999–2000. Although the service-delivery options for students with disabilities reflect the legis-

lative changes toward inclusion, the data clearly show that schools are using separate settings for the majority of instruction to students with disabilities.

Collaboration among Personnel. Data in Table 7 indicate how special educators perceive collaborative efforts among personnel, as well as the shared beliefs and values among colleagues. Special educators were asked to rate their perceptions on a 4-point scale, with 1 meaning *strongly agree* and 4 meaning *strongly disagree*. Only the percentages of those who responded *strongly agree* were reported on the tally. In regard to collaborative efforts among personnel, the results show that special educators' positive perceptions on this issue went down for all three certifications. Specifically, for special educators with regular or standard state certifications, the percentage decreased from 30 in 1987–88 to 4.3 in 1999–2000. For special educators with a probationary certification, the percentage dipped from 1.2 in 1987–88 to 0.1 in 1999–2000. Furthermore, from the 1987–88 to the 1999–2000 school years, the percentage of special educators with temporary, provisional, or emergency certification decreased from 2.5 to 0.1.

Table 7

Percentage of SPED teachers who strongly agreed that there was collaboration among staff:
A comparison across 1987–88, 1993–94, and 1999–2000

	1987–88	1993–94	1999–2000
Collaborative effort among personnel			
Regular/standard state certification	30.0	22.0	4.3
Probationary certification	1.2	0.5	0.1
Temporary/provisional/emergency certification	2.5	1.2	0.1
Shared beliefs and values among colleagues			
Regular/standard state certification	28.3	20.0	3.0
Probationary certification	0.9	0.5	0.1
Temporary/provisional/emergency certification	1.9	0.8	0.1

In regard to shared beliefs and values among colleagues, the data indicate that special educators' positive perceptions on this issue also went down for teachers of all three types of certification. The percentage of special educators with regular or standard state certification decreased from 28.3 in 1987–88 to 3.0 in 1999–2000. For special educators with probationary certification, the percentage decreased from 0.9 in 1987–88 to 0.1 in 1999–2000. Furthermore, from 1987–88 to 1999–2000, the percentage of special educators with temporary, provisional, or emergency certification dipped from 1.9 to 0.1. This data indicate that with increased inclusion, collaboration between general education teachers and special education teachers is no longer merely an option. Teachers should be adequately prepared to engage in effective collaboration.

Conclusion

The data presented in the results section indicate that trends found in the special education teaching force in recent years reflect changes in federal mandates and society in general. Although the process of retooling our special education personnel preparation programs and preparing teachers in-service is slow and arduous, the data indicate movement toward more inclusive service delivery. The percentage of special education teachers in today's schools has increased while assigning teachers to specific disability areas has decreased. These data reflect that schools are taking a more noncategorical approach to meeting the needs of students with disabilities as well as those students at risk academically or behaviorally. Additionally, delivery of services to students with disabilities is more inclusive: higher percentages of students receive services in resource rooms than in any other situation, and collaborative teaching has increased while self-contained classrooms have decreased. Nevertheless, teachers are not responding favorably to the need to collaborate with other school staff, which may indicate the limited training they have received in collaboration as well as the additional time needed for effective collaboration.

Although the diversity of the special education teaching force has increased slightly, it has not equaled the diversity of the students receiving special education services. The data indicate an increase in Asian American and Eskimo teachers, with the highest increase in teachers of Hispanic origin. We cannot be satisfied with the current state of diversity in our multicultural special education teachers.

The overwhelming majority of special education teachers have bachelor's degrees and more than half hold master's degrees. Eighty-five percent report that they have special education certification, and only 6.1% are on temporary or probationary certification. These data are inconsistent with state reports of increased demand for qualified special education teachers.

In summary, the data of the study reveal predictable trends in the special education teaching force. Throughout the years, special education teachers have: (a) maintained high levels of educational attainment; (b) slightly increased the diversity of the teaching force; (c) moved to more inclusive teaching; (d) focused increasingly on individual instruction rather than disability; and (e) increased the need to engage in continuous collaboration with general education teachers. Educators should not be satisfied with the current state of special education until they have established a climate that seamlessly supports inclusive teaching, mulitculturalism, and collaboration among staff.

Notes

1. D. P. Britzman, "Teacher Education in the Confusion of Our Times," *Journal of Teacher Education* 51 (May/June 2000): 200–205.
2. Individuals with Disabilities Education Act (IDEA) of 1997, P.L. 105–17, 20, U.S.C. SS 1400 ed seq.
3. B. Bateman, "Learning Disabilities: The Changing Landscape," *Journal of Learning Disabilities* 25 (1992): 29–36; and C. Walter-Thomas, L. Korinek, V. McLauglin, and B. Williams, *Collaboration for Inclusive Education: Developing Successful Programs* (Needham Heights, Mass.: Allyn and Bacon, 2000).
4. T. P. Lombardi and B. L. Ludlow, *Trends Shaping the Future of Special Education* (Bloomington, Ind.: Phi Delta Kappa

Educational Foundation, 1996); J. McLeskey, D. Henry, and M. Axelrod, "Inclusion of Students with Learning Disabilities: An Examination of Data from Report to Congress," *Exceptional Children* 66 (1999): 55–66; and S. Vaughn, S. Moody, and J. Schulman, "Broken Promises: Reading Instruction in the Resource Room," *Exceptional Children* 64 (1998): 211–225.

5. U.S. Department of Education. *The Condition of Education 2000, in Brief* (Washington, D.C.: Author: 2001).

6. N. Reinhillar, "Co-teaching: New Variations on a Not-so-new Practice," *Teacher Education and Special Education* 19 (1996): 37–47.

7. Walter-Thomas et al., *Collaboration for Inclusive Education.*

8. G. Cartledge and S. A. Loe, "Cultural Diversity and Social Skill Instruction," *Exceptionally 9*, nos. 1 and 2 (2001): 33–46; and A. G. Leasvell, M. Cowart, and R. W. Wilhelm, "Strategies for Preparing Culturally Responsive Teachers," *Equity and Excellence in Education* 32 (1999): 64–71.

9. C. A. Utley, K. C. Delquadri, F. E. Obiakor, and V. A. Mims, "General and Special Educators' Strategies for Multicultural Students," *Teacher Education and Special Education* 23 (2000): 34–50.

10. B. Harry, "Making Sense of Disability: Low-income Puerto Rican Parents' Theories of the Problem." *Exceptional Children* 59 (1992): 27–40, and B. Harry, *The Disproportionate Representation of Minority Students in Special Education: Theories and Recommendations* (Alexandria, Va.: National Association of State Directors of Special Education, 1994).

11. Utley et al., "General and Special Educators' Strategies."

12. L. H. Cook and E. E. Boe, "Who Is Teaching Students with Disabilities?" *Teaching Exceptional Children* 28 (1995): 70–72.

13. Utley et al., "General and Special Educators' Strategies."

14. Ibid.

15. T. Berkeley and B. Ludlow, "Meeting the Needs of Special Student Populations in Rural Locales," in A. J. DeYoung (ed.), *Rural Education: Issues and Practice* (New York: Garland, 1991), and S. Howard, M. Ault, H. Knowlton, and R. Swall, "Distance Education: Promises and Cautions for Special Education," *Teacher Education and Special Education* 15 (1992): 275–283.

16. R. L. Ludlow and J. S. Platt, "Developing Practicum Supervision Skills in Colleague Teachers," in *Alternative Futures for Rural Special Education* (Proceedings of the National Rural Special Education Conference 1988) (ERIC Document Reproduction Service No. ED 299 749); D. Cross, B. Collins, and J. Schuster, *Training Rural Educators in Kentucky* (Lexington, Ky.: University of Kentucky, Department of Special Education, 1991); V. J. Dickens and C. J. Jones, "Regular/Special Education Consultation: A Teacher Education Training Strategy for Implementation," *Teacher Education and Special Education* 13 (1990): 221–224; E. Whitten and J. Dynak, *Transdisciplinary Collaboration Preparation Program* (Kalamazoo, Mich.: Western Michigan University, Department of Special Education, 1998); and W. Wiener and E. Whitten, *Visual Impairments and Orientation and Mobility Training Preparation Program* (Kalamazoo, Mich.: Western Michigan University, Department of Special Education and Department of Blind Rehabilitation, 2000).

17. M. Will, "Educating Children with Learning Problems: A Shared Responsibility," *Exceptional Children* 53 (1986): 411–415.

18. Individuals with Disabilities Education Act (IDEA) of 1997.

19. Britzman, "Teacher Education."

20. Lombardi and Ludlow, "*Trends Shaping the Future.*"

21. T. P. Lombardi, D. L. Nuzzo, K. D. Kennedy, and J. Foshay, "Perceptions of Parents, Teachers, and Students Regarding an Integrated Education Inclusion Program," *High School Journal* 77 (April/May 1994): 161–168.

22. M. W. Bahr, E. Whitten, L. Dieker, C. E. Kocarek, and D. Manson, "A Comparison of School-Based Intervention Teams: Implications for Educational and Legal Reform," *Exceptional Children* 66 (1999): 67–83.

23. C. K. Ormsbee and K. D. Finson, "Modifying Science Activities and Materials to Enhance Instruction for Students with Learning and Behavior Problems" *Intervention in School and Clinic* 36, no. 1 (2000): 10–14.

24. R. Coombs-Richardson and J. Mead, "Supporting General Educators' Inclusive Practices," *Teacher Education and Special Education* 24 (2001): 383–390.

Elizabeth Whitten, Ph.D., is chair of the Department of Educational Studies and a faculty member in special education at Western Michigan University.

Liliana Rodríguez-Campos, Ph.D., is a faculty member in evaluation at Western Michigan University.

What's Good?
Suggested Resources for Beginning Special Education Teachers

"What's good?" "What do I need?" "What will I actually use?"
"What should I buy with my limited budget?"

Sharon A. Maroney

These are the questions most often asked by beginning teachers when seeking advice on acquiring materials and locating resources for classroom use. Faced with too many responsibilities and too little time, wanting to be fully prepared but not knowing exactly how, seeing catalogs filled with teaching materials but having no experience with any, and having limited financial resources, beginning teachers need assistance in selecting teaching resources. Teachers need strategies that are effective, efficient, easy to use, practical, and adaptable. Information must reflect current best practices in education.

> SPECIAL EDUCATION TEACHERS CAN DEVELOP PROFESSIONALISM THROUGH MEMBERSHIP IN PROFESSIONAL ORGANIZATIONS AND KNOWLEDGE OF THE LEGAL REQUIREMENTS OF THE FIELD.

This article includes a set of classroom resources identified by experienced teachers as recommended resources for beginning teachers. The resources are grouped into six areas of priority for beginning special education teachers: (a) developing professionalism, (b) basics for effective instruction, (c) academic instruction, (d) cognitive-behavioral instruction, (e) behavioral management, and (f) classroom extras.

Developing Professionalism

We need to view teaching as a profession, not just a job. Teachers continually work to become true professionals by obtaining access to information, keeping current with the developments in the field, and being knowledgeable of what it means to be a professional special educator. Special education teachers can develop professionalism through membership in professional organizations and knowledge of the legal requirements of the field.

As newly established special education professionals, beginning teachers should become members of a professional organization that advocates for special educators, special education, and the students and families who receive special educa-

tion services. With membership in The Council for Exceptional Children (CEC), teachers have access to high-quality, timely information and the CEC Web site (http://www.cec.sped.org); reap the benefits of CEC's advocacy activities; and receive the following publications: *TEACHING Exceptional Children* (6 issues/year), *Exceptional Children* (4 issues/year), *CEC Today* (10 issues/year), and *Research Connections in Special Education* (2 issues/year). Membership in the CEC offers opportunities to become involved in the profession at the local, state, national, and international levels through professional development, leadership, advocacy, publications, and networking activities. Membership is also available in the 17 divisions of CEC, representing areas of interest within special education.

Special education teachers should be proficient in using the resources of the federally-funded Educational Resources Information Center—the ERIC system. This includes knowing how to search the ERIC database and use the resources of the ERIC Clearinghouses. The ERIC Clearinghouse on Disabilities and Gifted Education is located at The Council for Exceptional Children in Reston, VA.

All special education teachers should have copies of current district, state, and federal rules, regulations, and policies for special education. This is especially important for beginning teachers, who are expected to be knowledgeable of and adhere to rules and regulations immediately. As soon as beginning teachers accept positions, they should contact the director of special education within the school district, the intermediate special education agency, and the state department of special education to request and obtain this information. All teachers need to have their own copy of the rules and regulations so [as] not to rely on others for the interpretation of or access to these documents.

THE WEB SITE OF THE
U.S. OFFICE OF SPECIAL
EDUCATION PROGRAMS
PROVIDES ACCESS TO
INFORMATION ON FEDERAL
INITIATIVES, LEGAL ISSUES,
AND NATIONAL RESOURCES
IN SPECIAL EDUCATION.

The book, *IDEA 1997: Let's Make It Work* (1998) uses a question-and-answer format to present the content of the Individuals with Disabilities Education Act (IDEA) of 1997. Recently a first-year special education teacher shared that although she had prepared for and completed several individualized education program (IEP) meetings, she still felt that the other professionals on the IEP team understood the IEP process much better than she did. This teacher found *IDEA 1997: Let's Make It Work* (1998) to be especially useful, understandable, and full of the information she needed.

The compact disk, *Discover IDEA CD '99* (1999), allows teachers to access the actual text of the IDEA 1997, in addition to providing a frequently asked questions (FAQs) section and

keyword search capability. This resource is especially useful for locating exact wording and references to specific topics throughout the law. Teachers can visit the IDEA Practices Web site (http://www.ideapractices. org) to preview this CD and learn about the IDEA Partnerships Projects of the U.S. Department of Education.

Several Web sites devoted to special education currently exist on the Internet. The National Center for Children and Youth with Disabilities (NICHY) Web site (http://www. nichy.org) and Special Education Resources on the Internet (SERI; http// www.hood.edu/seri) are two teacher- and parent-friendly Internet resources for information on special education and people with disabilities. The NICHY site distributes numerous publications and information sheets on different disabilities and topics in special education. SERI posts information and links to several other Web sites on special education and related topics. The Web site of the U.S. Office of Special Education Programs (http://www.ed.gov/ offices/OSERS/OSEP/index.html) provides access to information on federal initiatives, legal issues, and national resources in special education.

The *Survival Guide for the First Year Special Education Teacher* (Cohen, Gale, & Meyer, 1994) is a teacher-friendly book that many beginning teachers have found extremely helpful. Teachers especially liked the use of lists and the good basic advice and information. Survival topics include shunning the need to be superman or superwoman, preparing emergency lesson plans for when all else fails, the dos for working with general educators, and hints for positive report card comments. This resource can provide an informal approach to address the responsibilities required of special education teachers.

Effective Instruction

Research has identified several strategies that constitute effective teach-

ing that can be applied to academic and behavioral instruction; special education and general education classrooms; and individual, small-group, and large-group instruction. Because students currently identified as needing special education services typically experience severe deficits in several academic and behavioral skills, teachers need to be knowledgeable of and able to implement effective teaching strategies.

The First Days of School: How to Be an Effective Teacher (Wong & Wong, 1998) is an excellent resource for first-year teachers and one that experienced teachers will use throughout their careers. The authors identify three characteristics of effective teachers: holding positive expectations for student success; being good classroom managers; and designing lessons to help students teach mastery. The book presents comprehensive, almost step-by-step information to enable teachers to attain all three characteristics. Sections titled "Your very first priority when class starts is to get the students to work" and "Are you an invitational or disinvitational teacher?" are examples of the common sense approach of this book.

An extensive collection of research-based techniques is presented in *Strategies and Tactics for Effective Instruction* (Algozzine, Ysseldyke, & Elliott, 1997) and *Time Savers for Educators* (Elliott, Algozzine, & Ysseldyke, 1997). The strategies are presented to address four components of effective instruction: planning instruction, managing instruction, delivering instruction, and evaluating instruction. Teachers will especially appreciate the reproducibles provided so strategies can be used immediately and with little preparation. An additional resource on research-based teaching strategies is the Educational Resources Information Center Clearinghouse on Teaching and Teacher Education (ERIC—on the Web: http://www.ericsp.org). The ERIC Clearinghouse, a program of the National Library of Education, U.S. Department of Education, is the largest database on teaching and teacher education.

THE MOST IMPORTANT ACADEMIC RESOURCES SPECIAL EDUCATION TEACHERS MUST HAVE ARE THE CURRENT GENERAL EDUCATION CURRICULAR MATERIALS, INCLUDING ALL STUDENT MATERIALS, TEACHER'S MANUALS, AND ANCILLARY MATERIALS.

Effective instruction also requires the effective use of time. As many special education teachers know, the time students spend waiting (wait time) can easily turn into disruption time. Beginning teachers can review resources such as *Five-Minute Warm-ups for the Middle Grades: Quick and Easy Activities to Reinforce Basic Skills* (Green, Schlichting, & Thomas, 1994) and create an index card file of activities that can quickly engage students during those 5–10 minutes of wait time. Although the title indicates application to the middle grades, the activities in this book can be adapted easily for other ability levels, grade levels, or content. This is a helpful resource for any teacher looking to decrease waiting time, increase student engagement, and prevent disruptive behavior.

Academic Instruction

Unfortunately for some beginning teachers, teacher training programs in special education often include limited course work in teaching methods and materials in academic curricula areas, especially science, social students, language arts, and the general education curricula. As a result, special education teachers frequently feel unprepared to teach all the academic content areas they are required to teach. Therefore, many beginning teachers must prepare themselves for this teaching responsibility.

The most important academic resource special education teachers must have are the current general education curricular materials, including all student materials, teacher's manuals, and ancillary materials. These materials are invaluable for beginning teachers in that they include a scope and sequence of skills to be taught, comprehensive lesson plans, and a variety of assessment tools. Many current curricula also include instructional strategies and accommodations for students with special needs. As mandated by IDEA 1997, all students receiving special education must have access to the general education curriculum. Special education teachers need to approach their school administrators and request their own copies of these materials. Limited access to these resources will decrease the effectiveness and efficiency of instruction.

TeachNet.com (http://www.teachnet.com) and Education World (http://www.education-world.com) are two Web sites suggested for teachers interested in accessing teaching resources on the Internet. These interactive sites are designed for classroom teachers and provide a variety of resources for teachers with varying interests and needs. TeachNet.com offers lesson plans, how-to information sheets, and a teacher-to-teacher message center. Education World offers resources and information in general education and special education, across curriculum areas, and links to related sites. Both of these sites are easy to navigate, and the information is clearly presented.

Motivating students is a challenge for all teachers, especially when students have had a history of academic difficulty. *If You're Going to Teach Kids to Write, You've Gotta Have This Book* (Frank, 1995) is an extremely entertaining approach to teaching and motivating students to write. This book is filled with creative, fun, motivating writing activities and illustrations while at the same time presenting a sound process for developing writing skills. A second re-

source to help motivate students to write is the *Scholastic Rhyming Dictionary* (Young, 1994). Some teachers have commented that after some of their students were introduced to this book, the students couldn't wait to use this dictionary to write rap lyrics in their free time.

TEACHERS NEED STRATEGIES THAT ARE EFFECTIVE, EFFICIENT, EASY TO USE, PRACTICAL, AND ADAPTABLE.

Cognitive-Behavioral Instruction

Cognitive-behavioral instruction involves teaching students to think before they act and to become aware of the role their thoughts play in determining their behavior. Many special education teachers successfully change student behavior by rewarding desired behavior, and many students demonstrate certain types of behavior in efforts to earn rewards. But what happens when there isn't someone available to reward behavior? Cognitive-behavioral instruction, on the other hand, enables students to control their own behavior independently and throughout their lives. The following are four cognitive-behavioral instruction curricula. Beginning teachers are advised to select one of these curricula and to use it earnestly. Cutting and pasting activities from different curricula is not recommended.

1. Clear Thinking (Nichols, 1998) is an instructional curriculum designed to teach adolescents and young adults cognitive restructuring for clearer and more logical thinking, as based on the rational emotive therapy model. Teachers of students with behavioral disorders have been pleased with this program and with how well students have received it. This program includes an instructor's guide, *Clear Thinking: Talking Back to Whispering Shadows* (Nichols, 1998) and a student text, *Whisper-*

ing Shadows; Think clearly & Claim Your Personal Power (Nicholas & Shaw, 1998).

2. For the elementary grades, *Thinking, Feeling, Behaving* (Vernon, 1989a, and 1989b) is a curriculum also based on rational emotive therapy. It is designed to teach students the connections between their thoughts, feelings, and behavior, and that rational thoughts lead to rational feelings and rational behaviors. This curriculum is available at two grade levels: *Thinking, Feeling, Behaving: An Emotional Education Curriculum for Children* (Vernon, 1989b) and *Thinking, Feeling, Behaving: An Emotional Education Curriculum for Adolescents* (Vernon, 1989a).

3. *I Can Problem Solve: An Interpersonal Cognitive Problem-Solving Program* (Shure, 1992), is an instructional curriculum containing 77 lessons designed to teach students how to think and to use thinking to solve their own problems. This program is available at three grade levels: pre-school, kindergarten and primary, and intermediate elementary grades.

4. The skillstreaming curriculum by Goldstein and McGinnis (1997) is a complete prosocial skills curriculum following a direct instruction approach involving teacher modeling and student role playing. Each curriculum provides teachers with assessment tools, strategies for conducting group lessons, and activities for generalization. This curriculum is available at three grade levels: *Skillstreaming the Elementary School Child* (McGinnis & Goldstein, 1997), *Skillstreaming the Adolescent* (Goldstein & McGinnis, 1997); and *Skillstreaming in Early Childhood* (McGinnis & Goldstein, 1997).

Behavior Management

When asked to identify the most important factor related to the success or failure of beginning teachers, school administrators frequently cite behavior management. Beginning special education teachers must be prepared with classwide and individual behavior management techniques that they can effectively and efficiently use. Teachers have found these resources helpful:

- *The Tough Kid Book* (Rhode, Jenson, & Reavis, 1993) materials provide beginning teachers with the basics in behavior management in a teacher-friendly, ready-to-use format. Both beginning and practicing teachers have found these materials extremely useful. *The Tough Kid Book* (Rhode, Jenson, & Reavis) presents several practical strategies to increase or decrease student behavior, as well as strategies for academic instruction. *The Tough Kid Tool Box* (Jenson, Rhode, & Reavis, 1994) provides the reproducibles for the implementation of the strategies presented in *The Tough Kid Book*.

- *The Teacher's Encyclopedia of Behavior Management: 100 Problems and 500 Plans* (Sprick & Howard, 1995) presents in-depth descriptions of three or more interventions for each of 100 kinds of common problem behavior. The step-by-step descriptions, with sample recording and evaluation materials, provide beginning teachers with the information they need to implement each intervention. The book serves as a model of the comprehensive application of several behavioral change strategies.

- *The Pre-referral Intervention Manual: The Most Common Learning and Behavior Problems Encountered in the Educational Environment* (McCarney & Cummins, 1988) is a book of ideas for classroom interventions. It can be extremely helpful when brainstorming ideas for prereferral interventions, classroom accommodations, and behavioral interventions for students. Included in this book are 193 academic and social behavior problems with approximately 20 or more intervention suggestions for each.

Internet Addresses for Suggested Web Sites

The Council for Exceptional Children (CEC): www.cec.sped.org
ERIC Clearinghouse on Disabilities and Gifted Education: www.ericec.sped.org
ERIC Clearinghouse on Teaching and Teacher Education: http://www.ericsp.org
Education World: http://www.education-world.com
IDEA Practices: http://www.ideapractices.org
National Information Center for Children and Youth with Disabilities (NICHY): http://www.nichy.org
Special Education Resources on the Internet (SERI): http://www.hood.edu/seri
TeachNet.com: http://www.teachnet.com

TEACHER TRAINING PROGRAMS IN SPECIAL EDUCATION OFTEN INCLUDE LIMITED COURSE WORK IN TEACHING METHODS AND MATERIALS IN ACADEMIC CURRICULA AREAS, ESPECIALLY SCIENCE, SOCIAL STUDENTS, LANGUAGE ARTS, AND THE GENERAL EDUCATION CURRICULA.

Classroom Extras

School should be academically focused, challenging, supportive, exciting, and fun. With the never-ending demands faced by beginning teachers and the uncertainty that goes along with beginning a career, some teachers forget to have fun in the classroom or feel they don't have the time to try something new. On the other hand, some very enthusiastic teachers quickly burn out by trying to do something new and different each day. Here's a more re-

Recommended Resources for Beginning Teachers

Clear Thinking: Talking Back to Whispering Shadows: Instructor's Guide (Nichols, 1998). ISBN 0-9649142-2-0, $30.

The Council for Exceptional Children (CEC). Membership information, 1-800-232-7733, annual fee $75–$85.

Discover IDEA CD '99 (1999). Available from IDEA Partnerships Projects, http://www.ideapractices.org, $10.

The First Days of School: How to Be an Effective Teacher (Wong & Wong, 1998). ISBN 0-9629360-0-0-6, $30.

Five-Minute Warmups for the Middle Grades: Quick and Easy Activities to Reinforce Basic Skills (Green, Schlichting, & Thomas, 1994). ISBN 0-86530-263-4, $10

I Can Problem Solve: An Interpersonal Cognitive Problem-Solving Program for the Intermediate Elementary Level (Shure, 1992). ISBN 0-87822-340-1, $40.

I Can Problem Solve: An Interpersonal Cognitive Problem-Solving Program for the Kindergarten and Primary Level (Shure, 1992). ISBN 0-87822-339-8, $40.

I Can Problem Solve: An Interpersonal Cognitive Problem-Solving Program for the Preschool Level (Shure, 1992). ISBN 0-87822-338-X, $40.

IDEA 1997: Let's Make It Work (1998). ISBN 0-86586-303-2. Available from CEC, 1-800-232-7733, $15.

If You're Going to Teach Kids to Write, You've Gotta Have This Book (Frank, 1995). ISBN 0-86530-317-7, $15.

Instructor, published by Scholastic Inc., 1-800-544-2917, $15 per year.

The Laughing Classroom: Everyone's Guide to Teaching with Humor and Play (Loomans & Kolberg, 1993), ISBN # 0-915811-44-8, $15.

The Pre-referral Intervention Manual: The Most Common Learning and Behavior Problems Encountered in the Educational Environment (McCarney & Cummins, 1988). ISBN 1-87837-211-4, $30.

Scholastic Rhyming Dictionary (Young, 1994). ISBN 0-590-49461-9, $13.

Skillstreaming the Adolescent (Goldstein & McGinnis, 1997). ISBN 0-87822-369-X, $18.

Skillstreaming in Early Childhood (McGinnis & Goldstein, 1997). ISBN 0-87822-321-5, $14.

Skillstreaming the Elementary School Child (McGinnis & Goldstein, 1997). ISBN 0-87822-372-X, $18.

Strategies and Tactics for Effective Instruction (Algozzine, Ysseldyke, & Elliott, 1997). ISBN 1-57035-119-8, $30.

Survival Guide for the First Year Special Education Teacher (Cohen, Gale, & Meyer, 1994). ISBN 0-86586-256-7. Available from CEC, 1-800-232-7733, $12.

The Teacher's Encyclopedia of Behavior Management: 100 Problems and 500 Plans (Sprick & Howard, 1995). ISBN 1-57035-031-0, $40.

Teaching Tolerance, available from Teaching Tolerance, 400 Washington Avenue, Montgomery, AL 36104, at no cost.

Thinking, Feeling, Behaving: An Emotional Education Curriculum for Adolescents (Vernon, 1989). ISBN 0-87822-306-1, $26.

Thinking, Feeling, Behaving: An Emotional Education Curriculum for Children (Vernon, 1989). ISBN 0-87822-305-3, $26.

Time Savers for Educators (Elliott, Algozzine, & Ysseldyke, 1997). ISBN 1-57035-118-X, $20.

The Tough Kid Book (Rhode, Jenson, & Reavis, 1993). ISBN 0-944584-55-1, $20.

The Tough Kid Tool Box (Jenson, Rhode, & Reavis, 1994). ISBN 1-57035-000-0, $20.

Whispering Shadows: Think Clearly & Claim Your Personal Power: Student Text (Nichols & Shaw, 1998). ISBN 0-9649142-1-2, $15

Note: All costs are approximate.

---

alistic plan for using the resources described in this section: First, plan one night each month to read one magazine, book chapter, or other resource; second, select one new idea or activity to try that month. Selecting, planning for, and implementing one new idea each month is a reasonable and achievable goal for a beginning teacher.

SCHOOL SHOULD BE ACADEMICALLY FOCUSED, CHALLENGING, SUPPORTIVE, EXCITING, AND FUN.

Of all the teacher-oriented magazines, *Instructor* consistently has much to offer beginning teachers: high-quality content, noteworthy educators as authors, and attractive and teacher-friendly presentation. *Instructor* magazine, available at the primary or intermediate level, includes monthly feature articles, posters for classroom use, student activity sheets, and information related to teachers and teaching. *Teaching Tolerance* magazine includes many articles on teacher and school developed programs to promote tolerance toward all types of diversity. Of special interest are the articles describing actual teachers and their projects, programs, and student activities. Beginning teachers find the activities and resources especially helpful for gathering ideas for culturally diverse classrooms.

The Laughing Classroom: Everyone's Guide to Teaching with Humor and Play (Loomans & Kolberg, 1993) is a collection of the authors' teaching experiences and reflections with several ideas for classroom activities. After an experienced special education teacher described how her attitude toward laughter and fun in classroom had changed as a result of this book, several other teachers purchased *The Laughing Classroom* and had similar positive experiences. This resource encourages teachers to reflect on their teaching and offers suggestions for change.

Final Thoughts

This article has described many useful resources for beginning teachers;

but these teachers will find themselves inundated with additional resources they will be *required* to use in the classroom. These materials will include curricula, benchmarks or standards, discipline plans, and other resources established by the school, district, or state. Beginning teachers should first consult building administrators, directors or coordinators of special education, and teaching colleagues to obtain these required resources and implementation information.

As beginning teachers obtain and use various resources, they should remember that *more is not always better*. It is preferable to have a few excellent resources and to study and use them completely and correctly, rather than to have several resources and become overwhelmed or confused by all the ideas presented.

References

Algozzine, B., Ysseldyke, J. E., & Elliott, J. (1997). *Strategies and tactics for effective instruction.* Longmont, CO: Sopris West.

Cohen, M. K., Gale, M., & Meyer, J. M. (1994). *Survival guide for the first year special education teacher* (Rev. ed.) Reston, VA: The Council for Exceptional Children.

The Council for Exceptional Children. (1998). *IDEA 1997: Let's make it work.* Reston, VA: Author.

Elliott, J., Algozzine, B., & Ysseldyke, J. E. (1997). *Time savers for educators.* Longmont, CO: Sopris West.

Frank, M. (1995). *If you're going to teach kids to write, you've gotta have his book* (2nd ed.). Nashville, TN: Incentive Publications.

Goldstein, A. P., & McGinnis, E. (1997). *Skillstreaming the adolescent* (2nd ed.). Champaign, IL: Research Press.

Green, B., Schlichting, S., & Thomas, M. E. (1994). *Five-minute warmups for the middle grades: Quick and easy activities to reinforce basic skills.* Nashville, TN: Incentive Publications.

Jenson, W., Rhode, G., & Reavis, H. K. (1994). *The tough kid tool box.* Longmont, CO: Sopris West.

Loomans, D., & Kolberg, K. (1993). *The laughing classroom: Everyone's guide to teaching with humor and play.* Tiburon, CA: H. J. Kramer Inc.

McCarney, S. B., & Cummins, K. K. (1988). *The pre-referral intervention manual: The most common learning and behavior problems encountered in the educational environment.* Columbia, MO: Hawthorne Press.

McGinnis, E., & Goldstein, A. P. (1997). *Skillstreaming the elementary school child* (2nd ed.). Champaign, IL: Research Press.

McGinnis, E., & Goldstein, A. P. (1997). *Skillstreaming in early childhood* (2nd ed.). Champaign, IL: Research Press.

Nichols, P. (1998). *Clear Thinking: Talking back to whispering shadows.* Iowa City, IA: River Lights Publishing.

Nichols, P., & Shaw, M. (1998). *Whispering shadows: Think clearly & claim your personal power.* Iowa City, IA: River Lights Publishing.

Rhode, G., Jenson, W., & Reavis, H. K. (1993). *The tough kid book.* Longmont, CO: Sopris West.

Shure, M. B. (1992). *I can problem solve: An interpersonal cognitive problem-solving program.* Champaign, IL: Research Press.

Sprick, R. S., & Howard, L. M. (1995). *The teacher's encyclopedia of behavior management: 100 problems and 500 plans.* Longmont, CO: Sopris West.

Vernon, A. (1989a). *Thinking, feeling, behaving: An emotional education curriculum for adolescents.* Champaign, IL: Research Press.

Vernon, A. (1989b). *Thinking, feeling, behaving: An emotional education curriculum for children.* Champaign, IL: Research Press.

Wong, H. K., & Wong, R. T. (1998). *The first days of school: How to be an effective teacher* (Rev. ed.). Sunnydale, CA: Wong Publications.

Young, S. (1994). *The Scholastic rhyming dictionary.* New York: Scholastic Inc.

Sharon A. Maroney *(CEC Chapter #682), Professor in Special Education, Western Illinois University, Macomb, Illinois.*

Address correspondence to the author at Western Illinois University, Special Education Department, 25 Horrabin Hall, Macomb, IL 61455 (e-mail: SA-Maroney1@wiu.edu).

An Interview With... **Dr Marilyn Friend**

Mary T. Brownell and Chriss Walther-Thomas, Dept. Editors

Dr. Marilyn Friend is a leading expert in the areas of professional collaboration, coteaching, and inclusive education for students with disabilities. She began her educational career with a dual degree in special education and general education. Her first teaching job was as a fifth-grade teacher in a large urban school district where many tensions existed within the school among the teachers and between the teachers and principal. The disagreements extended to the community, and several lawsuits had been filed by parents naming the principal and the school district. Because of the problems, teachers tended to keep to themselves. It was a hostile environment for a beginning teacher, and Dr. Friend felt very isolated there, reluctant to ask colleagues for much-needed advice.

In contrast, she spent her last year of public school teaching working as a special education teacher in a highly collaborative, small urban school. The teachers worked well together in both formal (e.g., curriculum committee) and informal (e.g., problem solving about students at risk for failure) situations to maximize their limited resources. At this school, Dr. Friend collaborated in a variety of instructional activities, including coteaching with a sixth-grade teacher at a time when such an arrangement was not even considered an option for delivering services to students with disabilities. Students with disabilities and typical learners succeeded in this setting, and the teachers supported and learned from each other. Because of these dramatically different experiences, Dr. Friend recognized the critical importance of collaboration in public school environments.

She decided to pursue the study of collaboration as a doctoral student at Indiana University, and in addition to special education, she included study in psychology because of its rich history of theory, literature, and practice related to collaboration. After graduating, she served as a faculty member at the University of Oklahoma, Northern Illinois University, and Indiana University–Purdue University at Indianapolis. Currently, she is the chairperson of the Department of Specialized Education Services at the University of North Carolina at Greensboro. Throughout her academic career, Dr. Friend has focused on effective collaboration, inclusive practices, and related areas such as teaming and consultation. She has written numerous articles and produced several videotapes on these topics that are widely used by teachers, teacher educators, and staff developers. She is the co-author of two best-selling texts on these topics, Including Students with Special Needs: A Practical Guide for Classroom Teachers (2002, authored with Dr. William Bursuck) and Interactions: Collaboration Skills for School Professionals (2000, authored with Dr. Lynne Cook). Additionally, Dr. Friend has been active in teacher education efforts, serving in a variety of national leadership positions in

the Council for Exceptional Children (CEC), including president of the Teacher Education Division (TED). Through her writing, research, teaching, staff development, and advocacy efforts, Dr. Friend has been a leading voice on the importance of preparing preservice and inservice teachers as well as administrators and related services personnel for roles as effective collaborators.

Q: Why is collaboration important in schools?

At the broadest level, collaboration is important in schools because it has become a defining characteristic of society in the 21st century. If you examine publications in business, health, social services, technology, and other major disciplines, you will find that collaboration is a unifying theme. In fact, Bennis and Biederman (1997) proposed that all the most societally defining inventions of the 20th century were the result of collaboration. Lisbeth Schorr's (1997) book about creating healthy communities and overcoming poverty is another example: The overriding theme is collaboration. Collaboration has become the primary contemporary strategy to foster innovation, create effective programs, and sustain them over time. Since schools reflect the society in which they exist, it is becoming a tenet that they must, too, rely on collaboration.

The importance of collaboration for schools is also a pragmatic matter: In this day and age there is simply too much for any one educator to know in order to effectively meet the needs of all his or her students. If in schools we would act in the understanding that some professionals should be experts in instructional strategies, some in the use of cooperative learning approaches, some in responding to troubling student behavior, some in assessment practices, and some in building students' self-esteem and social skills, we could draw on each others' knowledge and skills and collectively create more effective schools for our students. Too often, though, educators seem uncomfortable with this type of culture of sharing expertise. While we talk a lot about collaboration in education, in many schools each teacher seems to feel responsible for addressing academic and behavior concerns until the problems are so serious that the teacher is convinced that someone else should assume responsibility for solving them. We use the word *collaboration*, and some shared efforts do occur, but the culture of schools still fosters isolated, individual professional problem solving.

One other reason that collaboration is important for today's schools comes from a legislative and legal impetus. The expectation in the Individuals with Disabilities Education Act of 1997 concerning the least restrictive environment and the assumption that the general education classroom is that environment for many students with disabilities leads almost inevitably to increased attention on collaboration. Likewise, the law's provision for participation by parents in their children's education and by general education teachers sets the stage for the growing centrality of collaboration in schools.

But even beyond law concerning special education services, collaboration is being recommended as a way for schools to operate—in middle school teams, in site-based leadership teams, in collegial staff development, and so on. Collaboration is a means to accomplish the complex goals of schools, a way to build community while responding to the many pressures of the contemporary education system. We need collaboration to ensure that schools are positive, supportive, and effective places for students to learn and teachers to teach. Classroom teachers and other educators (e.g., special education teachers, reading specialists, Title I teachers) are working with increasingly diverse students; all school personnel are under tremendous pressure to ensure that all students achieve higher academic standards. In this context, collaboration is not a luxury; it is a necessity.

Q: What does it take to make collaboration work effectively in schools?

Although I could make many recommendations about specific ideas and strategies for promoting collaborative practices in schools, the very first and most fundamental one would be to raise teachers' and administrators' understanding of and commitment to collaboration as a critical part of school functioning, and then to extend that understanding to the general community. A disposition for collegiality is essential because of the elusive nature of collaboration: Unlike some trends in education, collaboration is a sum of subtleties and thus more difficult to build support for and give attention to. Maybe an example would help. If you asked any group of citizens about important trends in schools, technology would probably be mentioned. Many initiatives exist to ensure that all schools have adequate computer resources and that access to the Internet is available. Significant funding is committed to technology goals, and the private sector is helping schools become technologically up-to-date. However, if you asked that same group of citizens about collaboration in schools, it is likely that you would receive little response or support or possibly an assertion that teachers certainly should learn to work together. Without the concrete evidence of hardware and software and with the dilemma that collaboration requires time away from students for educators to interact, it is more difficult for collaboration to become a prominent issue in terms of public support, funding, or private sector attention. How common is it for a business to offer schools funding to build teams or opportunities to participate in staff development to become more effective at interpersonal communication skills? Collaboration is unlikely to receive the attention it deserves without increased understanding.

After that general notion of a commitment to collaboration, I would say that the most important factor in making collaboration a reality in schools is the principal. An expectation set at the district level certainly is helpful, but it seems that collabora-

tion can be accomplished without such a central mandate if the principal not only desires a collaborative culture but also is willing to express that expectation and devote resources to reaching it. This moves collaboration far beyond a laudable approach that some teachers use informally because they see its value as a standard for a school. One outstanding principal I know worked in a school in which teachers tended to stay in their classrooms, where small cliques existed but little collaboration occurred. He decided a change was in order, and he took specific steps to recreate the school culture. He created lunch-hour study groups where teachers read about and debated various issues related to collaboration. He created working committees assigned to make important decisions concerning the school, and he taught committee members strategies for working effectively during meetings and for group problem solving. He asked an external consultant to meet with staff to identify concerns and resolve them, including interpersonal issues. After 2 years, teachers and other professionals in the school worked closely together, and they saw collaboration as an essential element of all aspects of their jobs. This all happened because someone in the school set the standard and led staff to it; the someone who can do this is the principal.

Q: What do teachers need to learn about working with others?

After the disposition supportive of collaboration that I mentioned before, all preservice and inservice teachers should have knowledge and skills that contribute to effective collaboration. For example, preservice teachers should learn and experience in their initial training the concept that "effective teachers work together." Thus, they should work with partners and in small groups in their methods classes, and they should reflect on the advantages and potential problems of working with colleagues. In field experiences and student teaching, they should have opportunities to watch effective collaboration among experienced educators, and they should discuss what makes the interactions effective and how they could do the same. For example, they might observe planning meetings in which coteachers set priorities and make decisions for the upcoming week. They might also participate in intervention assistance meetings during which professionals problem solve for students experiencing persistent serious academic or behavior problems. A third example would be to observe teacher interactions with parents. Experiences such as these can assist preservice teachers in developing an appreciation for the value of collaboration and in building a knowledge base for successful professional interactions. This approach also recognizes the importance of identifying collaboration skills. Expecting preservice teachers to learn about collaboration simply by being together in schools is not enough; proximity is a necessary but insufficient condition for collaboration.

Both preservice and inservice teachers should also learn and practice specific skills, especially communication skills. Here is one small example: Sometimes I hear teachers interacting in ways that are not particularly respectful of others' perspectives. If a teacher says, "Don't you think it would be better if we…," that professional is actually expressing his or her own opinion but trying to assign it to the other person in the interaction. That type of comment doesn't encourage colleagues to voice their opinions and may be perceived as a tactic to avoid hearing anyone else's opinion. A better way to interact might be to say, "My preference is that we…. What do you think?" In this case the speaker has owned and offered an opinion, not assigned it to the other person, and has invited the other person to express an opinion, too. In addition to appropriate communication skills, educators need to understand how to complete a process of working together. Most importantly, they need skills for engaging in a problem-solving process with others to reach a shared goal.

Third, teachers need to demonstrate through their actions that collaboration is not about working with best friends or, necessarily, with like-minded people. Collaboration is about trust and respect. It's about working together to create better outcomes for all students. If teachers learn to like each other in the process, that is a bonus, but it is not a prerequisite. I mention this because in some schools, the professionals who collaborate are those who are most comfortable with each other; others are not part of the culture. Educators collaborate because doing so benefits students. They sometimes work together, even if they would not socialize and sometimes even if they have rather opposing views of teaching and learning. Collaboration is not a personal preference; it is a strategy to do what is best for students.

Finally, experienced teachers need to understand how to work effectively with new teachers and with new partners who may have less experience in collaboration. When veteran teachers have built a strong background of interacting with others in consultative, teaming, or co-teaching relationships, they sometimes, consciously or unconsciously, think that their own experiences comprise the best way to collaborate. When their partners change, they are tempted to keep doing things the old way without allowing the new partnership to develop a character of its own. In addition, they may not understand that inexperienced colleagues do not have the same level of skills, experience, or confidence in the process. Effective collaboration is always about lifelong learning. Successful collaborators believe that there is still more to know, and they are respectful of their colleagues' level of understanding and comfort in working together.

Q: What are the biggest challenges that collaborators face? (14)

Principals and teachers must first address pragmatic barriers in order to make collaboration work. By far, the biggest such barrier is time, not just time to work together but time for constructive communication. Time is such a precious resource in school environments. Teachers need time for planning and preparation, they need time for joint teaching, they need time to share their perspectives on the success of their efforts. Given the amount of time that professionals typically are expected to work alone with students and to spend on preparing reports and completing other responsibilities, not much time is left for collaborating with colleagues unless collaboration is viewed as a priority. In both large and small schools, in urban, suburban, and rural schools, teachers often find it nearly impossible to arrange common planning

time. Overcoming this barrier requires creative thinking. In one high school where I recently worked, teachers regularly used technology to facilitate their collaboration. This school was so large that finding common planning time was not realistic. As a result, teachers used e-mail to share ideas, plan lessons, communicate concerns, and jointly problem solve. For them, e-mail is an efficient communication approach, and although the teachers would like more opportunities for face-to-face interactions, they decided to be constructive about the constraints instead of succumbing to the temptation to complain about it.

Some institutional barriers to collaboration also seem to be emerging, possibly because of reform and accountability initiatives. Some teachers fear that collaborating to meet the needs of a diverse group of students may result in slowing the progress of typical learners. Some also fear that students with disabilities will not achieve high enough outcomes and that teachers will unjustly be held accountable for this. Additionally, some principals are hesitant to support adults working together when it appears that such time is taken away from instruction. They mistakenly see collaboration as less important than direct teaching, forgetting that teaching could be significantly more effective as the result of the collaboration. It is interesting that in schools that overcome this kind of thinking, many students who struggle to learn are making significant educational progress, and other students are not being held back.

As I noted earlier, some teachers and principals also have mindsets that can work against collaboration. For example, some teachers are territorial about classroom space and teaching procedures. They resent any indication that alternatives to their practices could also be effective. I hear from special education teachers that their role in some classrooms is that of assistant; it is such a waste of valuable teaching resources. But I am also upset when classroom teachers describe special educators who are reluctant to do anything other than work with small groups. Again, so many teaching and learning options are being overlooked.

Another "mindset" challenge has to do with administrators and their understanding of collaboration. Administrators sometimes do not understand the complexities of collaboration, and consequently, they are not sure how to nurture it, assess it, and determine the type of professional development needed to make it happen. Even when administrators are well intentioned, they do things that create hurdles for collaboration. For instance, a set of coteachers recently explained with frustration that their principal told them that coteaching was a great idea but that each teacher was to teach only her "own" students in the shared classroom! Principals need to know how to create a vision for collaboration as well as how to create structures and processes for collaboration.

Q: In addition to the strategies we've already discussed, what else can effective school leaders do to facilitate collaboration in their schools?
#(6)

Principals can help their faculty members develop technical skills involved in collaboration. They need to know what the skills are, model them appropriately, and provide professional development opportunities that will enable people to develop new skills and enhance existing ones. It is also important for school leaders to stay involved in collaborative efforts to ensure that participants have the support they need to address challenging issues that are bound to arise. As teachers become more comfortable working with one another, tensions often develop as they become aware of differences in their philosophies and approaches to instruction. Principals can point out commonalties that exist and help teachers keep thinking about the main goals for their students. Effective principals serve as facilitators and problem solvers by sending the message that they are not afraid of difficult issues and that they don't give up when conflicts arise. They work effectively to bring people together to problem solve and get past the rough spots. For example, on one intervention team, members agreed with a highly vocal reading specialist to complete an extensive assessment of a student's skills. Outside the specialist's presence, though, other team members expressed regret at the decision and grumbled that they had gone along with the specialist just so that she would quit repeating her preference for the assessment. The principal called the team to a meeting to discuss how members were participating in decision making, how disagreements were being addressed, and how to express dissatisfaction during team interactions. The somewhat painful but tremendously honest conversation resulted in a huge improvement in the team's functioning, and it was the principal's ability to facilitate the breakthrough to a new level of collaborative skill that made the difference. I believe that collaboration is not about how big the school budget is or the size of classrooms or the number of personnel. Once you have healthy safe schools, it is more about people, expectations, and ways to work together.

Q: What if an administrator is not a strong supporter of collaboration?

Teachers can help administrators understand the importance of collaboration by providing information, discussing its importance, undertaking collaborative initiatives that are a result of their own efforts. They also can participate in collaborative endeavors if they are personally satisfying. However, having said that, I also want to make it clear that individual teachers can only go so far. It is not realistic to think that an individual teacher can be expected to set the standard for the entire school. Teachers can be a strong positive influence and enthusiastic participants and spokespeople for collaboration; principals are the ones who have to create the standard for it. If a principal is not supportive or is actively opposed to collaborative efforts, teachers may have to adjust their own expectations, at least temporarily. I have a cartoon that explains it well: One character explains to the other, "They say the secret of success is to be in the right place at the right time... But since you never know when the right time is going to be... I figure the best strategy is to find the right place and just hang out!" For teachers anxious to collaborate in nonsupportive atmospheres, the advice seems apt.

Q: What are some resources that teachers, teacher educators, and administrators can use to improve their knowledge of collaboration?

Many authors are now addressing the topic of collaboration. Here are some of the materials that teachers and administrators may find useful:

Bennis, W., & Biederman, P. W. (1997). *Organizing genius: The secrets of creative collaboration.* Reading, MA: Addison-Wesley.

Brownell, M. T., Yeager, E., Rennells, M. S., & Riley, T. (1997). Teachers working together: What teacher educators and researchers should know. *Teacher Education and Special Education, 20,* 340-359.

Burrello, L. C., Lashley, C. L., & Beatty, E. E. (2001). *Educating all students together: How school leaders create unified systems.* Thousand Oaks, CA: Corwin.

Daane, C. J., Beirne-Smith, M., & Latham, D. (2001). Administrators' and teachers' perceptions of the collaborative efforts of inclusion in the elementary grades. *Education, 121,* 331-338.

Fishbaugh, M. S. E. (2000). *The collaboration guide for early career educators.* Baltimore: Brookes.

Friend, M. (2000). Perspectives: Collaboration in the twenty-first century. *Remedial and Special Education, 20,* 130-132, 160.

Friend, M., Burrello, L., & Burrello, J. (Co-Producers). (2001). *Leading a district to scale: Access to the general education curriculum for every student* [videotape]. Bloomington: Indiana University, Elephant Rock Productions.

Friend, M., Burrello, L., & Burrello, J. (Co-Producers). (2001). *Successful high school inclusion: Making access a reality for all students* [videotape]. Bloomington: Indiana University, Elephant Rock Productions.

Friend, M., Burrello, L., & Burrello, J. (2000). *Complexities of collaboration* [videotape]. Bloomington: Indiana University, Elephant Rock Productions.

Friend, M., & Bursuck, W. (2002). *Including students with special needs: A practical guide for classroom teachers* (3rd ed.). Needham Heights, MA: Allyn & Bacon.

Friend, M., & Cook, L. (2000). *Interactions: Collaboration skills for school professionals* (3rd ed.). White Plains, NY: Longman.

Friend, M. (Co-Producer with L. Burrello & J. Burrello). (1995). *The power of two: Including students through coteaching* [videotape]. Bloomington, IN: Elephant Rock Productions. (Distributed by the Council for Exceptional Children, Reston, VA)

Martin, A. K., & Hutchinson, N. L. (1999). *Two communities of practice: Learning the limits to collaboration.* Paper presented at the annual meeting of the Educational Research Association (Montreal, Quebec, Canada). (ERIC Document Reproduction No. ED 435 732)

Schorr, L. B. (1997). *Common purpose: Strengthening families and neighborhoods to rebuild America.* New York: Anchor Books/Random House.

Walther-Thomas, C., Korinek, L., & McLaughlin, V. L. (2000). Collaboration to support students' success. *Focus on Exceptional Children, 32*(3), 1-18.

Walther-Thomas, C., Korinek, L., McLaughlin, V. L., & Williams, B. T. (2000). *Collaboration for inclusive education: Developing successful programs.* Boston: Allyn & Bacon.

From *Intervention in School and Clinic*, March 2002, pp. 223-228. © 2002 by Intervention in School and Clinic.

UNIT 2
Early Childhood

Unit Selections

5. **Music in the Inclusive Environment**, Marcia Earl Humpal and Jan Wolf
6. **Language Flowering, Language Empowering: 20 Ways Parents and Teachers Can Assist Young Children**, Alice S. Honig
7. **The Itinerant Teacher Hits the Road: A Map for Instruction in Young Children's Social Skills**, Faith Haertig Sadler

Key Points to Consider

- How does music benefit preschoolers with special needs in inclusive settings?

- Why is language fundamental to early childhood interventions?

- Describe the requirements that must be met by itinerant teachers who perform special educational services.

 Links: www.dushkin.com/online/
These sites are annotated in the World Wide Web pages.

Division for Early Childhood
http://www.dec-sped.org

Institute on Community Integration Projects
http://ici.umn.edu/projectscenters/

National Academy for Child Development (NACD)
http://www.nacd.org

National Early Childhood Technical Assistance System
http://www.nectas.org

Special Education Resources on the Internet (SERI)
http://seriweb.com

Public law 99-457 has been called one of the most important educational decisions of the United States. It was a 1986 amendment (Part H) to PL94-142 (the Education for All Handicapped Children Act), which the U.S. Congress established as a grant incentive aimed at providing services for young children at risk of disability beginning at the age of 3. By 1991 this amendment to the now-renamed Individuals with Disabilities Education Act (IDEA) was reauthorized. It operates through "Child Find" organizations that look for babies, toddlers, and preschoolers with conditions of obvious disability (such as blindness, deafness, or orthopedic handicap). These young children can receive special educational services according to IDEA's mandate, "a free and appropriate education for all in the least restrictive environment." Many infants and young children are being found who are at "high risk" of developing educational disabilities (for example, low vision or hearing impairments) unless education begins before the age of 6. This outreach is having a profound impact on the care of families and children.

The United States is faced with multiple questions about the education of its future citizens—its young children. Many American babies are born preterm, small for gestational age, or with extremely low birth weight. This is a direct result of the United States' high rate of teenage pregnancy (nearly double that of most European countries and Canada) and its low rate of providing adequate prenatal care, especially for the young, the poor, or recent immigrant mothers. These infants are at high risk for developing disabilities and conditions of educational exceptionality. Early intervention can help these babies.

All services to be provided for any infant, toddler, or preschooler with a disability, and for his or her family, are to be articulated in an individualized family service plan (IFSP). The IFSP is to be written and implemented as soon as the infant or young child is determined to be at risk. IFSPs specify what services will be provided for the parents, for the diagnosed child, for siblings, and for all significant caregivers. Children with pervasive disabilities (such as autism, traumatic brain injuries, blindness, deafness, orthopedic impairments, severe health impairments, or multiple disabilities) may require extensive and very expensive early childhood interventions.

IFSPs are written in collaboration with parents, experts in the area of the child's exceptional condition, teachers, home-service providers, and other significant providers. They are updated every 6 months until the child turns 3 and receives an individualized education plan (IEP). A case manager is assigned to oversee each individual child with an IFSP to ensure high-quality and continuous intervention services.

In the United States, Child Find locates and identifies infants, toddlers, and young children who qualify for early childhood special education and family services. An actual diagnosis, or label of condition of exceptionality, is not required. Assessment is usually accomplished in a multidisciplinary fashion. It can be very difficult, but as much as possible, it is conducted in the child's home in a nonthreatening fashion. Diagnosis of exceptionalities in children who cannot yet answer questions is complicated. Personal observations are used as well as parent reports. Most of the experts involved in the multidisciplinary assessment want to see the child more than once to help compensate for the fact that all children have good days and bad days. In cases where the parents are non-English-speakers and a translator is required, assessment may take several days.

Despite the care taken, many children who qualify for, and would benefit from, early intervention services are missed. Child Find associations are not well funded. There are constant shortages of time, materials, and multidisciplinary professionals to do assessments. Finding translators for parents who speak uncommon foreign languages adds to the problems. Occasionally the availability of funds for early childhood interventions encourages the overdiagnosis of risk factors in infants from low-income, minority, immigrant, or rural families.

A challenge to all professionals providing early childhood special services is how to work with diverse parents. Some parents welcome any and all intervention, even if it is not merited. Other parents resist any labeling of their child as "disabled" and refuse services. Professionals must make allowances for cultural, economic, and educational diversity, multiple caregivers, and single parents. Regardless of the situation, parental participation is the sine qua non of early childhood intervention.

At-home services may include instruction in the educational goals of the IFSP, and in skills such as discipline, behavior management, nutrition, and health maintenance. At-home services also include counseling for parents, siblings, and significant others to help them deal with their fears and to help them accept, love, and challenge their special child to become all he or she is capable of being. A case manager helps ensure that there is cooperation and coordination of services by all team members.

Most children receiving early childhood services have some center-based or combined center- and home-based special education. Center care introduces children to peers and introduces the family to other families with similar concerns. It is easier to ensure quality education and evaluate progress when a child spends at least a part of his or her time in a well-equipped educational center.

The first article in this unit addresses the importance of rhythm and music in early childhood. New research suggests that music and math stimulate development of neurons in the same brain areas. Music not only helps organize and promote neuronal growth, it also enhances socialization between children and stimulates language and creative production.

The second article explains why language is fundamental to all early childhood interventions and how it becomes a critical factor in later school success. Preschool teachers and outreach programs need to expand their concern and expertise to families. Alice Honig gives specific suggestions for 20 learning activities to empower young children with language arts.

The last article in unit 2 discusses the benefits of early intervention using itinerant teachers who travel from place to place to perform their special educational services. The extension of services from birth to the age of 3 in homes and local communities has given impetus to indirect service delivery models. An itinerant teacher can provide technical assistance in many ways.

Music in the Inclusive Environment

Five-year-old Sam uses a wheelchair. Due to a difficult birth, he has little motor development or control and no spoken language. He understands but can't speak.

Twice a week, I [Jan] am the music teacher for 22 kindergartners, including Sam. His level of participation is that of an observer, and at times I am not sure what he feels about our time together. The children accept his level of ability and when we put his wheelchair in the center of the circle for "Ring around the Rosy," his squeals of delight give it all away. He laughs and bobs his head back and forth, eyes sparkling all the while as we circle his chair, fall down, and bounce back up only to play the game one more time.

Marcia Earl Humpal and Jan Wolf

What did Sam gain from this musical experience? Pure joy! At first I felt I was slighting him. Wasn't there a way to make his experience more active and inclusive? We tried pushing the wheelchair in the circle, but Sam's response was not the same. He became withdrawn. The experience of sharing the joy from his pivotal center position evoked the most expression.

Music in the early childhood environment offers varying levels of engagement ranging from simply listening or observing to joining in as an active participant.

To onlookers Sam may appear passive, but all of us who know him well are aware of his participation. The music reaches him, as it does all of us, in his way and at his time and place. His squeals and screeches, sparkling eyes, and smiling face communicate his delight to everyone in the room.

Music in the early childhood environment does not depend on specific skills or competence. It offers varying levels of engagement ranging from simply listening or observing to joining in as an active participant. Music stimulates the senses and involves children at many levels, reaching them aesthetically and appealing to their emotional sense. It is playful, soothing, and joyful! It promotes literacy growth by engaging children in experiences involving language; new vocabulary in an engaging context; print; and rhymes, chants, and songs that may inspire higher-level thinking concepts. It con-

> ### Music lets everyone participate
>
> **Six-year-old Anthony** has a diagnosis of autism. He has little tolerance for musical sounds. Every time we sing, he moans as though in pain from the sound. I [Jan] try to remember that maybe for Anthony our music is too loud.
>
> One day the other children and I gather in the front of the room with drums, triangles, shakers, and sand blocks. I play my guitar. Anthony crawls under his desk and makes every effort to stay there. At the end of each repetition of our song, we switch instruments so everyone can have a chance to play something new.
>
> As we near the end of the song, I nod to Emily, the teaching assistant. Emily understands my unspoken suggestion. She gets up and quietly offers Anthony her drum. As we continue singing and playing, Emily and I peek over to see Anthony playing the drum. He is still under the desk and perhaps is still somewhat bothered by the sounds, but he has found his own sense of pleasure in playing the instrument with us.
>
> Anthony has found a way to join us, on his own time and his own terms. The music that so upset him has become an ally. He is now willing to play with the class, just from a distance.

tributes to a feeling of community as children come together through shared songs, rhymes, chants, and singing games.

Music enhances an inclusive classroom by leveling the playing field so everyone can be a participant. Whether a

Music calms and focuses the mind

I hurry into the school to get to my assigned first grade classroom. The children love music, and I [Jan] look forward to working with them. I crash nose-to-nose with a teaching assistant who works with the youngest children in the school district who have severe behavioral disabilities—the children in my assigned class. Many of them come to school with concerns that would make most of us stagger.

This is a particularly difficult Monday. The assistant quickly summarizes the turmoil. George has had a horrible weekend at home. Alexis has not taken her medication. Justin has spent the weekend away from the consistency of home with Mom and is in a spin as a result. Perhaps, I think, I can find a way to help.

In the classroom I find the teacher sitting in the rocking chair humming, rocking, and holding a child. Two other children are listening through headsets to Baroque music. Soft music comes from the CD player on the shelf. The music's power of relaxation fills the room. The teacher has found solutions on her own. It had been an overwhelming 90-minute beginning to the day, but now, with understanding and change of mood, the atmosphere is calm. The music speaks to the children's emotions. They can now leave their homeroom, go to their inclusive environments, and learn and play with their friends. Music has met the children's need for peace. It has elicited a sense of calm in all of them.

Music teaches social skills

Ariel has difficulty adjusting to the social demands of the classroom. She screams when her mother leaves in the morning and refuses to sit with the group during circle time. Sometimes she throws instruments against the wall or hits children who approach her. Because of this behavior, the children no longer try to be her friend. She plays and works alone. Within her established routine, she seems to be happy.

I [Marcia] come to Ariel's preschool class for 30 minutes each week to conduct music sessions. As a music specialist who is also a music therapist, I not only teach music concepts, but also help the classroom staff and specialists adapt activities and use music to reinforce goals such as sharing, learning concepts, and refining fine and gross motor movements. Often I suggest songs and strategies staff can use throughout the day to meet a variety of needs.

The classroom teachers and I have noticed that Ariel stops and looks when anyone sings a cleanup song. We discover that if we keep the song going and guide her to the toy shelves, Ariel will help with the cleanup. Barney's ditty, "Clean up, clean up, everybody everywhere, clean up, clean up, everybody do your share" really works if we keep singing it over and over until all the children complete the task.

Because music works to encourage Ariel to put toys away, we decide to try it for other tasks. I write simple messages to accompany familiar tunes. The teachers post these throughout the classroom and use them regularly during transitions. After cleaning up, it is time for snacks. "Mmmmm, good, mmmmm, good. Now it's time to have our snack, mmmmm good." When sung to the Campbell's Soup theme, these words round up the children, including Ariel.

As time passes Ariel learns to say good-bye to her mother and join the group for a short time when she hears specific songs. Near the end of the year, she begins to share instruments with a friend when the instructions are given in the context of music: "I'll pass the sticks from me to you; I'll pass the sticks, and you can do it too." Music helps Ariel be an involved member of the class.

child is a listener or a player, music is accessible and partial participation does not detract from its positive effects.

The essence of music is joyful, nonjudgmental, noncompetitive, and predictable.

For all aspects of music making, children can respond in a range of ways. Some children may be able to sing complete songs with the group or make up their own songs while playing. For others, imitating vocal sounds or playing with their voices is "singing" (Johnson 1996). As an aesthetic expression, the essence of music is joyful, nonjudgmental, noncompetitive, and predictable. Everyone joins in at his or her own level of comfort.

Music activities can encourage interaction among all children in nonthreatening and enjoyable ways.

Musical activities can include all children in meaningful ways when they are designed to offer varied levels of participation. Music can engage all children as collaborators, participants, and community members in activities ranging from group singing and instrument playing to movement games. Individually, music allows children to personalize experiences through listening and bonding with recorded music, moving in expressive ways, entering into song dialogues with a friend, or creating sound segments on drums.

Research supports the value of music in learning. Music releases endorphins that provide feelings of happiness and energy. It helps to organize the firing patterns in the cerebral cortex, strengthening creativity and spatial-temporal reasoning (Campbell 1997). A study by Colwell (1994) indicates that using music with a whole language approach to reading facilitates greater text accuracy. Music can also enhance print concepts and prewriting skills (Standley & Hughes 1997) as well as receptive and expressive language (Harding & Ballard 1983; Hoskins 1988; Birkenshaw-Fleming 1997). Music acts as a catalyst to calm listeners, improve special perceptions, and encourage focused, clear thinking (Campbell 1997).

Music can open doors and allow children to join in classroom routines with their friends. Music activities can encourage interaction among all children in nonthreaten-

Start the Music

In 2000 the National Association for Music Education (MENC), Texaco Foundation, NAEYC, and the U.S. Department of Education developed Start the Music, a series of projects and events designed to help bring age-appropriate music education to every child in America. These organizations solicited the expertise of early childhood music educators, music therapists, education association administrators, early childhood educators, and health care providers to identify best practices for early childhood music education and to develop strategies to implement those practices.

Developmentally and individually appropriate musical experiences are guided by these beliefs (MENC 1995):

- All children have music potential. They
  —bring their own unique interests and abilities to the music learning environment;
  —can develop critical thinking skills through musical ideas;
  —come to early childhood music experiences from diverse backgrounds;
  —should experience exemplary musical sounds, activities, and materials.
- Young children should not be expected to meet *performance* goals.
  —Their play is their work.

—They learn best in pleasant physical and social environments.
—They need diverse learning environments.
—They need effective adult models.

Start the Music recognizes the role adults play in assisting young children in their musical development. Families, caregivers, and teachers can all help children grow musically (Neelly, Kenney, & Wolf 2000, 1) by

- **immersing children in musical conversations** while singing, speaking rhythmically, moving expressively, and playing musical instruments. By doing these things, we stimulate children's initial awareness of the beauty and the structure of musical sound.
- **encouraging children's musical responses** by smiling, nodding, and responding with expressive sounds and movements. We thus show children that music making is valuable and important.
- **finding ways to encourage and motivate children's playful exploration,** interpretation, and understanding of musical sound.

Start the Music recognizes that all children are individuals and that music experiences should be a part of *every* child's world.

---

ing and enjoyable ways. In fact, music can actually teach social skills.

Inclusion has become the norm in preschool classrooms throughout the United States, and in some cases has been facilitated by early childhood inclusive music pilot programs (Davis 1990; Hughes et al. 1990; Humpal 1991; Furman & Furman 1996; Humpal & Dimmick 1996). Hughes and colleagues (1990) note that peer acceptance is often viewed as the most serious obstacle to successful inclusive programming and that acceptance can be successfully reached through structured musical interactions. Further, since the brain processes music in both hemispheres, music can stimulate cognitive functioning and may allow for understanding when the spoken word fails (Campbell 1997). Music may provide a cue for an upcoming event or may act as a gentle reminder of what is expected in a group situation.

Conclusion

Music should be a part of *every* young child's day (see "Start the Music"). Music's power to reach *all* children is driven by the sense of community originating from shared songs, rhymes, chants, singing games, and musical books. These activities serve as gateways to involving

individuals and groups of young children. Music creates joy through aesthetics. Music creates inspirational moments and opportunities to make sense out of chaos. Music *belongs* in the inclusive classroom.

References

Birkenshaw-Fleming, L. 1997. Music for young children: Teaching for the fullest development of every child. *Early Childhood Connections* 3 (2): 6–13.

Campbell, D. 1997. *The Mozart effect.* New York: Avon.

Colwell, C. 1994. Therapeutic application of music in the whole language kindergarten. *Journal of Music Therapy* 31 (4): 238–47.

Davis, R. 1990. A model for the integration of music therapy within the preschool classrooms for children with physical disabilities or language delays. *Music Therapy Perspectives* 8: 82–84.

Furman, A., & C. Furman. 1996. Music therapy for learners in a public school early education center. In *Models of music therapy interventions in school settings: From institution to inclusion,* ed. B. Wilson, 258–76. Silver Spring, MD: American Music Therapy Association. [Monograph]

Harding, C., & K. Ballard. 1983. The effectiveness of music as a stimulus and as a contingent reward in promoting the spontaneous speech of three physically handicapped preschoolers. *Journal of Music Therapy* 20 (2): 86–101.

Hoskins, C. 1988. Use of music to increase verbal response and improve expressive language abilities of preschool language-delayed children. *Journal of Music Therapy* 25 (2): 73–83.

Hughes, J., B. Robbins, B. MacKenzie, & S. Robb. 1990. Integrating exceptional and nonexceptional young children through music play: A pilot program. *Music Therapy Perspectives* 8: 52–56.

Humpal, M. 1991. The effects of an integrated early childhood program on social interaction among children with handicaps and their typical peers. *Journal of Music Therapy* 28 (3): 161–77.

Humpal, M., & J. Dimmick. 1996. Music therapy for learners in an early childhood community interagency setting. In *Models of music therapy interventions in school settings: From institution to inclusion*, ed. B. Wilson, 271–311. Silver Spring, MD: American Music Therapy Association. [Monograph]

Johnson, F. 1996. Models of service delivery. In *Models of music therapy interventions in school settings: From institution to inclusion*, ed. B. Wilson, 48–77. Silver Spring, MD: American Music Therapy Association.

MENC (National Association for Music Education). 1995. *Prekindergarten music education standards*. Reston, VA: MENC.

Neely, L., S. Kenney, & J. Wolf. 2000. *Start the Music strategies*. Reston, VA: MENC.

Standley, J., & J. Hughes. 1997. Evaluation of an early intervention music curriculum for enhancing prereading/writing skills. *Music Therapy Perspectives* 15 (2): 79–86.

For further reading

American Music Therapy Association. 1999. Music therapy and the young child fact sheet. Silver Spring, MD: AMTA.

Boston, B.O. 2000. Start the Music: A report from the Early Childhood Music Summit. Online: http://www.menc.org/guides/startmusic/stmreport.htm

Campbell, D. 2000. *The Mozart effect for children*. New York: HarperCollins.

Miranda, L., A. Arthur, T. Milan, O. Mahoney, & B. Perry. 1998. The art of healing: The CIVITAS Healing Arts Project. *Early Childhood Connections* 4 (4): 35–39.

A Special Book for Children Ages 4–8

Millman, I. 1998. *Moses goes to a concert*. New York: Frances Foster.

Moses and his school friends are deaf. They communicate through American Sign Language (ASL). Today Moses and his classmates are going to a concert. Their teacher, Mr. Samuels, has two surprises in store for them to make this particular concert a special event. At the end of the book are two full conversations in sign language and a page showing the hand alphabet.

Marcia Earl Humpal, M.Ed., MT-BC, is a music therapist in the early childhood division of the Cuyahoga County Board of Mental Retardation and Developmental Disabilities in Cleveland, Ohio. Her model for early childhood inclusive music programs has been the topic of published research and numerous conference presentations.

Jan Wolf, M.S.Ed., is an adjunct instructor in early childhood education at Kent State University and music teacher at The Kindergarten Center, Medina City Schools, Ohio. Jan is a frequent presenter at conferences and is the author of articles on music and young children and the book *Teaching Music*.

From *Young Children*, March 2003, pp. 103-107. Reprinted with permission from the National Association for the Education of Young Children.

Language Flowering, Language Empowering: 20 Ways Parents and Teachers Can Assist Young Children

By Alice S. Honig

Parents, home visitors, and teachers in early childhood settings need tools for empowering young children to flourish in many domains. The domain of language development is fundamentally critical to later school success, social ease, and abstract thinking skills. To be wise mentors who use teaching tools and techniques well, we need understandings and insights about developmental progressions in each special child development area.

In some U.S. communities, as many as 45% of youngsters are "failing" kindergarten because their prereading language skills are not at a level that can prepare them for successful beginning reading in first grade. Some parents need far more help if they are to provide rich language support for their children's early school success (Payne, Whitehurst, & Angell, 1994). In many communities, such outreach supports are in rare supply. Fortunately, preschool teachers are gatekeepers into the rich territories of literacy. They need to expand their concern and expertise to families. Together the adults serve as primary guides who introduce children to the delights, byways, signposts, and fruitful gardens of the land of language learning.

What Do We Need To Know?

First, we need to know the *norms and windows* of language growth (Honig, 1989). How do language and competence in reading and writing grow from the infant/toddler period through the nearly school-age period? Knowledge of the normative *stages* of language development grounds our work (Cazden, 1981; Harris, 1990; Honig, 1983). For example, holophrasis (one-word speech) appears somewhere near the end of the first year, amid baby jargon and babbling sounds with intonations. Two-word (telegraphic) speech usually comes in before 24 months ("Want dat!" "Doggie dere." "My toy!" "Daddy fix." "Big moo-moo!"). The ability to form adult negatives ("I don't want meatballs" rather than "No me want dat") and to form full questions ("How do I draw that, teacher?") appear during the third year. During the later preschool years, children learn to interpret passive questions ("Was the car hit by the truck?") and to decode and answer "Why" questions accurately.

Some children find coordinating their tongue, lips, palate, and other language production parts difficult, while others have an easier time, even with consonant clusters, such as *str* in *street*. As for pronunciation, usually by 4 years of age, about three fourths of child articulation is clear and intelligible.

Second, we need strong *research "ammunition"* to defend our developmentally appropriate practices (Committee on the Prevention of Reading Difficulties, 1997). Researches illuminate the quality of early support for literacy that caregivers *and* parents must provide to boost young children's language learning. Moerk, Snow, Tizard, Berko-Gleason, McQueen and Washington, the de Villiers, and many other researchers help us appreciate *how* adults facilitate and promote early passions for communication in turn-taking talk and conversations, passion for stories, and skills for spelling, writing, and reading (Greenberg, 1998).

Third, we need to consider how *language skills are special socially* for making friends and getting along well. Promoting early language competency during the infancy years could even serve to lessen the probability of harsh discipline with children. Families may be more frustrated and stressed in interactions with children who have receptive and expressive language delays. With teacher support for early child language skills and support for family language enrichment games with young children (Honig, 1982), some folks may then find it more appropriate to discipline with words rather than physical force.

Prisons are filled with adults who never learned to read or can read only at rudimentary levels. Thus, a fourth major emphasis must be on helpful *curriculum ideas* to enhance and promote early language competence from early infancy onward and to prevent school reading failures (Fowler, 1990; Honig, 1982; McCabe, 1992; Van Allen & Van Allen, 1982).

Girded with ideas, techniques, and reading materials, adults can effectively implement a language-rich curriculum to boost early literacy and motivation for early reading activities. More children will be likely to read fluently and read for pleasure in elementary grades. When networks of parents and professionals—caregivers, teachers, home visitors, and speech therapists—work together, then young children have seen greater chances for early language flowering. Effective teachers capitalize on the strengths and unique learning styles of each child, his/her special story interests, and oral fluency, to engage each youngster in book learning and book loving.

Techniques for Parents and Teachers

1. Offer Turn-Taking Talk with Babies. As you tenderly carry out daily routines with infants, verbally and responsively in "turn-taking talk," express your pleasure for their cooing and babbling with you (Devine, 1991; Honig, 1985).

2. Provide Prompts. Adults create early verbal *scaffolding* for emerging language (Bruner, 1983). Be particularly aware of the level at which a child is functioning. Some children use multiword sentences clearly by age 2. Others exhibit many articulatory substitutions (*bunny wabbit, shishy, or lellow* [for yellow], *dar* [for car]) and communicate mostly with two-word phrases. Tuned-in teaching adults know just how to *lure* little ones forward into further language competence by working in what Vygotsky called the "Zone of Proximal Development" (Brunner, 1984). With a teacher's insightful support, a child

reaches further understandings and learns more.

As you care for and talk with a child under 3, provide pauses to entice little ones to "finish" your phrases:

- Mary had a little ____.
- You need your toothbrush to brush your ____.
- I know a little gray mouse. He lives in a little gray ____.
- We go see saw up and down. We go up and ____.
- Baa baa, black sheep, have you any ____?
- Row row row your ____.
- First we put on your socks; then we put on your ____.

3. Be a Generous Word Giver. Label objects, actions, feelings, facial emotions, and events. If a toddler is now walking alone pretty well, exclaim admiringly: "You are walking, really getting up and walking now. You must be so proud of yourself!"

Use encouraging words and specific praise for new accomplishments, as when baby uses a spoon in self-feeding or wrinkles her nose to sniff a flower. When toddlers eagerly point out a barking doggy walking beyond the playyard gate, affirm cheerfully, "That doggy is going woof, woof, woof. Doggy is walking right by our yard!"

"The gerbil is twitching his whiskers" confirms for your preschoolers just what the animal is doing as each child reaches out to pet the gerbil gently. Your naming of events and things anchors reality in words and increases a young child's power to use linguistic symbols. How triumphant a 4-year-old on a museum trip feels as he looks up at the huge skeleton and informs you, "That's Tyrannosaurus Rex!"

When your toddlers and preschoolers are very sure of a label, play silly games on occasion. For example, hold up a green checker and say, "Is this purple?" Or pat a child's knee and say, "Oh, I'm patting your elbow!" Preschoolers love to catch a teacher making an absurd mistake once in a while!

4. Model and Expand on Infant/Toddler Language. Suppose a baby in bathtub exclaims "Wawa." Then cheerfully confirm: "Yes, that's water in your tub. You go splish splash in the water. You go swimmy swim in the water." All this while you "swim" the baby while holding her under her tummy. Suppose an infant says, "Ju!" Father then asserts, "You're right! Juice.

Orange juice. You love to drink orange juice, honey." Such tiny tidbits of language interactions expand and enrich an infant's language world.

5. Use Parallel Talk. Provide words to accompany child gestures (Honig, 1989). For example, as your 8-month-olds vigorously respond to music with their bodies, rejoice with them and exclaim, "You really like bouncing up and down to the music! Bounce, bounce, bounce!"

Your words *describe* what is going on, what children are doing or feeling. During parent group meetings, encourage family members to provide words for whatever they see their infant or toddler doing or trying to do. As a preschooler fills her pail with wooden beads, say clearly, "You are filling up the tub with those wooden beads. You are piling up the wooden beads in your tub."

If a child is lugging a basket of blocks, exclaim, "Those blocks sure are heavy to carry. The basket feels so heavy!" Keep on using parallel talk during outdoor playtime, as well as indoors. "You are taking turns climbing up the stairs of the slide" gives word power and reminds children of playground rules.

6. Use Self-Talk. Talk about *what* you are doing for a child or for the group and *how* you are doing it: "I am setting out a large piece of collage paper for every child. Now I will give you some pieces to paste on your collage paper. Here are some sprinkly glittery letters for you, Jo. Here are some tiny aluminum foil shapes, Kwanghee. You decide how you want them to go as you paste them down on your collage paper."

This principle is especially important in working with infants. For example, "I need to go get some clean diapers. So I'll carry you over to the diaper supply box. Here we go walking over to get some clean diapers." As you reach to get a jar of baby food down for a meal, say, "I am getting down some yum yum applesauce for your lunch."

7. Arrange for Children to Act Out Familiar Tales. Once preschoolers become deeply comfortable with a well known story, such as *Goldilocks and the Three Bears* or *The Three Billy Goats Gruff*, then they will be ready to act out the characters. Toddlers with few words can use pantomime at first to act out the characters. Sometimes children want to act out violent behaviors of favorite TV-show characters, such as Ninja Turtles. How can you keep your classroom peaceful and yet encourage dramatic story acting? Perhaps at circle time you can have a dialogue with your preschoolers about what kinds of stories are safe to act out in the class and which ones are more likely to end in someone feeling hurt or getting hurt.

8. Encourage Children to Create Easy Funny Rhymes. Language can be playful and fun and a vehicle for creativity if children are encouraged to be imaginative. At group time, challenge children to chime in with a rhyme:

I like my cat; she's not skinny or FLAT,
But she is round and FAT;
She likes baseball and a BAT;
She wears a jacket and a HAT;
She doesn't like me to yell "SCAT!";
She curls up on her MAT;
She's not a BAT or a RAT;
She never acts like a BRAT;
Now, what do you think of THAT!

Each child can contribute a rhyme to add to the giggles. Sometimes their rhymes will be silly sounds but not "real" words. Perhaps that is why children delight particularly in Dr. Seuss books that emphasize humorous rhymes—"McGrew Zoo" or "Star-Bellied Sneetches" or "Yertle the Turtle." Humor enhances language pleasure (Honig, 1988). Even babies rhyme nonsense syllables to themselves in their cribs. Preschoolers will giggle and try to imitate Prelutsky's (1983) refreshing rhymes, such as

Whatever one toucan can do
is sooner done by toucans two.
And three toucans (it's very true)
can do much more than two can do!

9. Converse Frequently With Children. Talk with children individually as well as in group time all through the day during classroom and childcare routines and especially during snack and meal times (Honig & Brophy, 1997). Even with babies, act as if their strings of babbles have real meaning and are important communications genuinely interesting to you.

10. Teach Children to Give Themselves Verbal Planning Cues. Language has an executive function. Children can use words to guide their own behaviors and to reflect on their plans and actions (Vygotsky & Luria, 1994). When there are social scuffles, encourage *future-oriented thinking* and divergent thinking by asking, "What else can you think of to try?" What

verbal cues might help a child remember his promise to give the tricycle to a friend with whom he is "taking turns"?

Verbal rehearsal is important. In the wooden blocks and train track corner, children need to go over plans to proceed in building train tracks and bridges together with peers. What materials will a group of preschoolers need to gather? How are they planning on sharing the different jobs to be done while creating together a long mural about sea activities, including sailing boats, sea turtles, sharks, coral, and fishes?

Teach babies and toddlers self-control words. As they reach toward something forbidden, such as a sugar bowl on a table, some murmur to themselves "No touch dat" and then draw the hand back.

11. Use Convergent Questions to Find Out What Children Do Know. Research reveals that over 80% of teacher questions to toddlers are convergent. These "closed" questions, of course, help us find out exactly what children do know or have learned. Such questions are answered with either a yes or no response or just one correct response (Honig, 1983). "How many bananas does the monkey eat all together if he eats two bananas from this basket and then eats one more banana from the other basket?" "What do we call the house that a birdie lives in?" Or probably a frequent convergent question of toddler parents or teachers: "Do you have to go potty?"

12. Use Socratic Questions to Encourage Reasoning and Creativity. Asking Socratic, open-ended questions is a powerful technique by which adults can stimulate children's thinking as well as show genuine respect for their reasoning abilities. Socratic questions are tools to help children "distance" from concrete experiences and they encourage more abstract thinking (Blank, 1973). Vygotsky's work reveals that only with the adult tutor's help can children reach deeper or more complex levels of understanding and reasoning. Adult careful crafting of Socratic questions in a personalized language interaction with a child provides the impetus for the child to reach actively into memory and to stretch thinking skills to reason syllogistically, to explain, to plan, to predict, and to hypothesize.

The brain develops amazingly rapidly during the first years of life. Socratic questions help grow brain connections as children are challenged to think up answers!

Socratic questions encourage choices, promote children's recall from memory,

sharpen observation skills, and encourage planning and if-then syllogistic reasoning skills:

What could you do with a paper towel roll when all the towels are used up?

Why is it a good idea to eat soup with a spoon and not a fork?

How could you comfort a baby who is crying?

What stuff would you need to gather together if you wanted to bake cookies?

Which of my two pencils is longer? How could I find out which of these two pencils is longer; tell me how I can do that?

I know you really wish you could have that toy right now. Jamie is using it. What will happen next if you grab that toy from Jamie? How will he feel? What do you think he'll do then? What is our classroom rule about sharing?

How come in this picture (of a tropical storm) all the trees seem to be bending down and swaying back and forth? What do you think is making that happen?

The cooked chocolate pudding looks so thick and creamy. Can you remember how it looked before we started cooking? How did it look when we opened the package? What do you like best to spread on top of your pancakes?

Challenge yourself to create more Socratic questions every day and to tailor those questions to each individual child's language level.

13. Restate Meanings in Simple Words.

Children are sometimes puzzled by our explanations or our requests. If children look puzzled by what you are saying, then repeat and vary your words so that the children are sure to catch your meaning. In turn, listen carefully for child meanings and puzzlements, worries and wonders. Preschoolers who ask "Why" questions a lot may be struggling to understand a difficult concept. Your creative skills help you to formulate simple yet satisfying explanations.

14. Read Books Galore! Muster up all your dramatic flair as you turn the pages sharing pictures of barn animals with babies. Teach book skills to babies: how to turn pages, how to point to and label animals and make their sounds, how to chime in with repetitive words in a book where the same chorus or phrase turns up over and over again. (Think of *Horton Hatches the Egg* [Seuss, 1966], for example: An elephant's faithful 100%!) *Picture-book* *sharing* is a powerful language tool for teachers and parents of infants.

Make books so precious that your little ones will absolutely hunger for book reading (Fontaine, 1985; Honig, 1985; Honig & Brophy, 1997). Start early, read with expression, share picture books with babies, and promote a pleasureful, intimate ambiance as you read daily with children. At school, provide pillows and mats so that children can stretch out and turn book pages for themselves and go through their favorite books.

Writing is often sparked by children's enjoyment of the "writing" in books. Cheer on children who begin to invent their own spelling. One kindergarten child illustrated his picture of horses grazing on a prairie with the title, "Hrs lv hr" (horses live here). Writing with invented spelling is an early way children begin the process of connecting heard sounds with letters and their pride is enriched as they finish a drawing or sign a story dictated to the teacher/parent (Fields & Lee, 1987).

Remember that your primary goal is to create a positive passion for books. Make book sharing a socially satisfying activity for very young children. Read in varied ways. At school, sometimes children are in a more formal setting in a circle on a rug. Sometimes one child is cuddled in your lap, while others are leaning on you, listening intently (and maybe sucking hard on a thumb to help them concentrate on what happens as the little engine chugs up the mountain to bring toys to boys and girls). Be sure to vary your voice tones to enhance children's emotional pleasure with the pictures and tales. Show your own joy as a child chimes in, comments, points to a picture, takes off on a story theme (such as picking apples) and relates it to a home experience (helping mom make applesauce).

Choose books with internal rhythms and rhymes that enchant the children's ears while colorful pictures enchant their eyes.

Choose as many prosocial books as you can, such as *Hiawatha's Kind Heart, Two Good Friends* (Delton, 1990), *Something From Nothing* (Gilman, 1993), and Dr. Seuss's (1954) *Horton Hears a Who*. These stories emphasize caring, sharing, and helpful kindness toward one another.

15. Sing! Music and song offer possibilities for emotional connections that words alone cannot accomplish. Use songs to accompany gestures and actions. A habitually silent toddler with a grave face may well light up as he sways to "The Eentsy Weentsy Spider" song. Hand out large squares of colorful sheer nylon so children can sway and create personal dances to slow, romantic music. Play waltz music to fingerpaint by.

Sing songs with simple tonal progressions, such as

Do, a deer, a female deer,
Re, a drop of golden sun,
Mi, a name I call myself,
Fa, a long, long way to run....

Sing lullabies to soothe little ones into relaxation (Honig, 1995). Teachers can ask parents to contribute a lullaby from their own family or from their ethnic heritage. Nap time is easier when lullabies gently relax children into sleep.

Try major and minor scale progression singing as with the "Pussy Willow" song, where each line is on one note and the next line starts one note higher than the previous line:

I have a little pussy,
Her coat is soft and gray,
She lives out in the meadow,
She'll never run away.
She'll always be a pussy,
She'll never be a cat
'Cause she's a pussy willow,
Now what do you think of that!

Toddlers enjoy the brief vignettes of verses when there are gestures to accompany a song:

The wheels on the bus go round and
    round,
Round and round, round and round,
The wheels on the bus go round and
    round,
All through the town.

Narrative story-songs fascinate children and hold their attention even when some of the words are archaic or a bit difficult. The melody helps sweep children along into the story:

The fox went out on a chilly night.
And he prayed for the moon for to give
    him light.
For he had many a mile to go that night,
Before he reached the town-O,
Town-O, town-O.
He had many a mile to go that night,
Before he reached the town-O!
Or:
Hush little baby, don't say a word,
Papa's going to buy you a mocking
    bird.
If that mocking bird won't sing,
Papa's going to buy you a diamond
    ring.

16. Enliven Spontaneous Dramatic Play. Actively, but not intrusively, help young children to *extend their dramatic play themes* and ideas for roles so that no children are excluded or marginalized (Smilansky & Shefatya, 1990). For social role-plays, provide lots of props. Dolls, blankets, toy kitchen furniture, empty food cartons and boxes, juice cans, dress-up clothes, and toy telephones promote more elaborations on themes during pretend play.

Be alert if a preschooler carries out only limited rigid roles (monster play every day, for instance) rather than imaginative, creative roles. Provide multicultural dolls, assorted teddy bears, toy beds and blankets for tender, nurturing play. Encourage expansion of familiar role-playing of family scenarios. Guide and support early interactive role-play between friends. Even 1-year-old friends giggle and say "run, run" (often with hardly decipherable articulation, of course!) as they delightedly take turns chasing one another in and out of a cardboard playhouse. Think about how you will handle repetitive play that uses violent TV superhero themes. How can you encourage imagination and fantasy play and yet discourage "pretend" violence at home or in the classroom?

Children in the early grades can creatively construct extraordinary scenarios. One small group of first graders pretended they were the different parts of an old, broken-down washing machine which made noise and wobbled and rattled as it washed. The pantomime play revealed sophisticated prior planning and elaboration on the theme, even though in the finished pantomime the children acted out noises and movements rather than "words."

17. Help Children Use Words as Social Mediators. Teach children politeness words that calm down fusses and struggles between children: "I'm sorry I bumped into you." "You can have your turn now to play with the cars." "Please may I use your blue crayon?" "Thank you." [The Montessori "grace and courtesy" exercises are good models.] Friendly words and phrases help ease the transition from social squabbles to more peaceful peer play, even for toddlers with limited telegraphic speech.

Words serve as mental tools that facilitate a child's concept learning (Vygotsky & Luria, 1994). Adults can provide manageable challenges in eliciting words from young children:

What animal is that? What sound does it make?

How many mittens do you need for your hands? Well, first show me and tell me how many hands you have. Yes. You surely do have two hands. Now tell me how many mittens you will need for your two hands.

When a toddler is working with assorted blocks or a toy such as a ring stack set, use labels such as *big* and *little*. These contrast or *polar opposite* words help toddlers become aware of differences. They can concentrate better on the different ring sizes as they try pushing them down on the ring stack pole. Toddlers love learning polar opposites. Learning will be easier if the adult provides props [again, Montessori materials are good models]. At home, parents can find opportunities to present contrasts, such as a sopping *wet* washcloth and a *dry* one, a *sour* taste (lemon) and a *sweet* taste (honey), a picture of a freezing *cold* day and a *warm* sunshiny day, a *heavy* object (a rock) and a *light* object of similar size (a koosh ball). At the level of movement, the children can act out moving *slowly* or going *fast*, drawing a line with a crayon either slowly or quickly.

Preschoolers enjoy verbal games of thinking up the opposite to such concepts as sweet, heavy, dark, wet, quiet, cold, skinny, bumpy, hard, short, above, in front of, tall, empty, and so forth.

18. Teach Time, Space, and Number Words. Physics and math are integral parts of an early childhood curriculum. Young children love to measure, pour, compare, and count (even when they count out of numerical order, as they so frequently do).

Talk about what you will do with the children *after* lunch, or *before* naptime, or *soon, tomorrow,* or *when you have finished* a particular activity.

At home, set up cubes or checkers into a long pretend choo-choo train on a table and talk about the *first* car, the *middle* car, the *last* car or caboose. Which car becomes the last one if you decide to start from the opposite end of the line?

19. Recite Poetry. Art, dance, music, poetry! The ancient Greek muses still offer their gifts of esthetic beauty to all of us and their gifts of beauty propel children into language. Watch the awe and joy on a toddler's face as he squeals "Shishy!" in delighted homage to the graceful fanning, flicking tail of a large goldfish swimming

in a tank. Poetic language weaves an ecstatic sense of the magic of words. Little children feel the magic in cadences, metric schemes, and poetic rhythms and rhymes. Sometimes, read poems where the exquisite cadence will reach children's esthetic sense even though they may not understand all of the poet's exact words. Poetry kindles an esthetic appreciation of language that some basal readers certainly do not. Perhaps that is why Dr. Seuss's absurd rhymes provide such a listening delight for youngsters.

Poetry's tongue-twisting turns delight and capture the fancy of very young children as in Pooh Bear's poem.

The more it SNOWS,
Tiddley-pom,
the more it GOES on SNOWing!

Poems that use a lot of onomatopoeia (think of the *buzzy busy bees*) appeal to children. Create your own sound-clashing, sonorous poetic fragments (Gable, 1999). For example, share a picture of a large, green frog and poetically chant

Look at the slippery wet, slithery,
squirmy, squishy frog!

Absurdities in poems such as the quirky rhymes in "The Sheriff of Rottingham" tickle children's sense of humor. Absurdities abound in familiar songs, such as

The sun so hot I froze to death.
Suzannah, don't you cry.

Then there is the rhyming song about the old woman who swallowed a fly, which has absurd verses:

I know an old woman who swallowed a cat;
fancy that, to swallow a cat!

20. Teach Finger Plays and Chants. Play finger games that accompany chants such as "Pat-a-cake, pat-a-cake, baker's man" and "Open, close them!" Finger plays and chants capture children's attention because of the cadence of your voice, the cumulative word repetitions, and the accompanying interesting, simple, slow gestures.

Use repetitive numerical chants with hand gestures:

Five little monkeys jumping on the bed,
One fell off and bumped his head…
Four little monkeys jumping on the bed,
One fell off and bumped his head (etc.)

Toddlers love the naughtiness of the monkeys and they chime in for the verbal

countdown progression as each monkey in turn jumps on the bed and falls off.

Conclusions

Tailor your assistance to each child's individual level in language enrichment programming. Promote the use of language as a rich and integral accompaniment to play; to routine chores, such as diapering, feeding, toileting, shepherding, soothing, choosing materials; and to daily living experiences, as well as in special learning experience sessions. Conjure the joys of book reading time, the love of singing songs, the pleasure in social talk. The language mastery experiences you provide will ensure that your children become language lovers as well as eloquent language learners.

References

Blank, M. (1973). *Teaching learning in the preschool: A dialogue approach.* Columbus, OH: Merrill. (Superb illustrations of how a teacher can use the Socratic method in tutorial work with a preschooler.)

Bruner, J. (1983). *Child's talk: Learning to use language.* New York: Norton.

Bruner, J. (1984). Vygotsky's zone of proximal development: The hidden agenda. *New Directions for Child Development, 23,* 93–97.

Cazden, C. (Ed.). (1981). *Language in early childhood education.* Washington, DC: National Association for the Education of Young Children.

Committee on the Prevention of Reading Difficulties in Young Children. (1998). *Preventing reading difficulties in young children.* Washington, DC: National Academy Press.

Delton, J. (1990). *Two good friends.* New York: Bantam Doubleday.

Devine, M. (1991). *Baby talk: The art of communication with infants and toddlers.* New York: Plenum.

Fields, M. V., & Lee, D. (1987). *Let's begin reading right: A developmental approach to beginning literacy.* Columbus, OH: Merrill.

Fontaine, D. (1985). *Reading aloud to your child: A parent's guide.* Saratoga, CA: R & E Publishers. (Available from the publisher at P. O. Box 2008, Saratoga, CA 95070-0008).

Fowler, W. (1990). *Talking from infancy: How to nurture and cultivate early language development*. Cambridge, MA: Brookline.

Gable, S. (1999). Promote children's literacy with poetry. *Young Children, 54*(5), pp. 12–15.

Gilman, P. (1993). *Something from nothing*. New York: Scholastic.

Greenberg, P. (1998). Warmly and calmly teaching young children to read, write and spell: Thoughts about the first four of twelve well-known principles. Part 2. *Young Children, 53* (5), pp. 68–82.

Harris, J. (1990). *Early language development*. London: Routledge. (This fine textbook also offers teachers a variety of remediation strategies for young children with difficulties.)

Honig, A. S. (1982). *Playtime learning games*. Syracuse, NY: Syracuse University Press.

Honig, A. S. (1983). Research in review: Language environments for young children. *Young Children, 38* (1), pp. 56–57.

Honig, A. S. (1985). The art of talking to a baby. *Working Mothers, 8* (3), pp. 72–78.

Honig, A. S. (1988). Research in review: Humor development in children. *Young Children, 43* (4), pp. 60–73.

Honig, A. S. (1989, Summer). Talk, read, joke, make friends: Language power for children. *Day Care and Early Education*, pp. 14–17.

Honig, A. S. (1995). Singing with infants and toddlers, *Young Children, 50* (5), pp. 72–78.

Honig, A. S. & Brophy, H. *Talking with your baby: Family as the first school*. Syracuse, NY: Syracuse University Press.

McCabe, A. (1992). *Language games to play with your child*. New York: Plenum.

Payne, A. C., Whitehurst, G. J., & Angell, A. L. (1994). The role of the home literacy environment in the development of language ability in preschool children from low-income families. *Early Childhood Research Quarterly, 9*, 427–440.

Prelutsky, J. (1983). *Zoo doings*. New York: Scholastic.

Seuss, Dr. (1954). *Horton hears a who*. New York: Random House.

Seuss, Dr. (1966). *Horton hatches the egg*. New York: Random House.

Seuss, Dr. (1988). *The sneetches and other stories*. New York: Random House.

Smilansky, S., & Shefatya, L. (1990). *Facilitating play: A medium for promoting cognitive, socioemotional, and academic development in young children*. Gaithersburg, MD: Psychosocial & Educational Publications.

Van Allen, R., & Van Allen, C. (1982). *Language experiences and activities*. Epston, MA: Houghton Mifflin. (This book is chock-full of excellent curricular ideas for creating a rich classroom language environment with preschoolers.)

Vygotsky, L. S., & Luria, A. R. (1994). Tool and symbol in child development. In R. van der Veer & J. Valsiner (Eds.) *The Vygotsky reader* (pp. 99–176). Oxford, UK: Blackwell.

DR. ALICE STERLING HONIG is professor emerita of Child Development at Syracuse (NY) University and a member of the Montessori Life *editorial advisory board.*

The Itinerant Teacher Hits the Road

A Map for Instruction in Young Children's Social Skills

Faith Haertig Sadler

Early childhood special educators will be expected to adopt new roles with resect to indirect service delivery models (e.g., collaboration, consultation, technical assistance, and training).... The impetus for new professional roles comes primarily from legislation supporting community inclusion of infants and preschoolers with disabilities and their families. (Buysse & Wesley, 1993, p. 418–420.)

The approaching identity crisis is here. For many teachers, "the former teaching role—working and interacting with individual children and their parents—takes a back seat to the themes of logistics, consulting, and relationship issues" (Gallagher, 1997, p. 384). This article is written by one of these new itinerant special education teachers.

What Do Itinerant Teachers Do?

In many large metropolitan school districts, families of young children are offered a continuum of inclusion options, ranging from classes with a few peer models; to blended team-taught classes; and, finally, to full inclusion in community early childhood programs. Frequently children with milder delays receive their early intervention services at the most inclusive end of this continuum. They remain in the general preschools or day-care settings that their parents have chosen for them.

"The former teaching role—working and interacting with individual children and their parents—[now] takes a back seat to the themes of logistics, consulting, and relationship issues"

The diversity of these settings reflects the diversity of families in the community, thus providing intervention settings likely to be culturally and linguistically appropriate. Members of an early childhood itinerant team typically travel weekly to these settings to facilitate the delivery of appropriate special education services. Itinerant staff might provide direct services; consultation; or, in most cases, a combination of the two.

What Do Itinerant Teachers Need?

One of the biggest frustrations for many itinerant teachers has been the lack of resources available to guide them in this new role. Not only do itinerant teachers need an actual map of the city; they also need a theoretical "map" to provide a framework for stepping into this new job description. Many materials are being developed for training child care personnel to include children with disabilities in their programs, as well as materials for training new special education teachers to function in

consulting roles. The latter typically focus on relating issues such as active listening, team building, and problem-solving at meetings (see box, "Online Resources" for examples of the materials available).

Little is available, however, in the way of practical tools to help itinerant teachers organize and implement their job. These materials could provide insight into the nuts and bolts of choosing and embedding interventions into natural environments or could provide tips for dealing with the logistics of scheduling both time to consult and time to provide direct services.

What Do Itinerant Teachers Need to Know and Do to Provide Social-Skills Instruction?

When addressing delays in students' social skills, itinerant teachers need to
• Understand the continuum of social-skills interventions identified in the literature.
• Have a collection of resources reflecting this continuum.
• Match types of interventions to children, given their social settings, and organize these into a schedule.
• Understand the special challenges of this model.

Gallagher's (1997) findings support this. Gallagher followed a group of teachers during their first year in the itinerant role and noted: "Although the importance of the consulting role for teachers moving into new roles is often addressed, the specifics needed for day-to-day implementation of the lofty goals of inclusion are seldom discussed in the literature" (p. 384).

Not only do itinerant teachers need an actual map of the city; they also need a theoretical "map" to provide a framework for stepping into this new job description.

School staff often call on itinerant teachers to address one important area of child development—social skills. It is disconcerting to note, however, that many teachers report discomfort with this new consulting role, especially in supporting children displaying poor social skills (Wesley, Buysse, & Keyes, 2000). The purpose of this article is to suggest a nuts-and-bolts type of framework for addressing social skills instruction within the itinerant model. This article discusses in less detail the relationship issues of this model and instead provides practical information that is currently missing from the literature. I hope these ideas will help teachers who are uncomfortable in this new role and spark a trend in the development of resource materials addressing the day-to-day implementation of this model. The first thing itinerant teachers need to do is build their understanding (see box, "What Do Itinerant Teachers Need to Know and Do?").

Understand the Continuum of Social-Skills Interventions

First, as the itinerant teacher, you need to have a knowledge base of the continuum of interventions identified within the research literature for addressing delays in social skills. One book that provides a concise summary of this is *Integrating Young Children with Disabilities into Commu-*

nity Programs. In the chapter "Social Interaction Skills Interventions for Young Children with Disabilities in Integrated Settings," Odom and Brown (1993) ranked interventions from low intensity (which usually require low consultation time) to high intensity (which usually require high consultation time). Following is a discussion of four levels of their continuum as each might apply to the itinerant model.

Look for naturally occurring social situations where the child's objectives can be purposely taught and practiced.

Level A: Activity-Based Intervention. This is a naturalistic approach and the least intensive level of instruction. It also requires the least amount of preparation time for the itinerant teacher. Bricker (1998) noted: "Activity-based intervention is a child-directed, transactional approach that embeds children's individual goals and objectives in routine, planned, or child-initiated activities and uses logically occurring antecedents and consequences to develop functional and generative skills" (p. 11). When using this model to teach social skills, look for naturally occurring social situations where the child's objectives can be purposely taught and practiced. When this strategy is applied only to situations that are child initiated, it is referred to as "incidental teaching." According to Brown, McEvoy, and Bishop (1991), "Incidental teaching is different from more structured instruction in that it is conducted during unstructured activities for brief periods of time and typically when children show an interest in or are involved with materials, activities or other children" (p. 36).

When providing direct services at this level, you should remain in the vicinity of the student as he or she moves through classroom activities. This way, you can spontaneously embed instruction on social skills

into the natural course of the child's participation. "During an incidental teaching episode, a teacher can provide an adult model or encourage a peer to model appropriate social behavior, as well as prompt and shape appropriate social responding" (Brown et al., 1991, p. 36). When acting in a consulting role, you help the classroom staff examine a typical schedule, looking for opportunities to coach social interactions and then train staff in a few prompting techniques.

Cooperative learning games could include "pairs of children playing different roles: blower and popper with bubbles, hider and seeker in the sand with hidden toys, filler and dumper with buckets and assorted materials, and chooser and gluer with art supplies and glue."

Because this intervention is so natural and easy to implement, it is likely to be embraced positively by classroom staff. This is a good intervention to start with while you get better acquainted with the child and the preschool program. It also works well in combination with other more intensive approaches. When using this intervention, you should schedule weekly sessions during free-choice time. The disadvantage to this approach is that instruction may be too sparse and indirect for some children.

Social skills for young children might include signs of affection, such as giving a high-five, hugging, or shaking hands—which can be incorporated in traditional childhood songs or games,

Level B: Affection Training. This approach provides mildly intensive instruction and does not require much preparation time. It involves collecting or creating songs and games for opening "circle time" that require children to interact affectionately (usually nonverbally) with one another. These signs of affection might include giving a high-five, hugging, or shaking hands and are included as part of traditional childhood songs or games, such as the song "If You're Happy and You Know It" or the game "Duck, Duck, Goose" (Cooper & McEvoy, 1996).

When providing direct services, you lead the "affection" activities at opening circle time. Cooper and McEvoy (1996) recommended:

Before the activities begin, discuss the importance of being friends.... Then ask the children to demonstrate ways to show friendship, such as shaking hands, smiling, or telling people that you like them. Explain to the children that they are giving each other signs of friendship. (p. 67)

When consulting with staff, you support site staff in creating and leading affection activities themselves. Because this type of intervention is fairly simple and introduces only minor changes into the classroom, classroom staff will probably welcome it. The interactions are basic and thus work well when classmates vary greatly in their developmental skills. These activities raise the comfort level among classmates and thus facilitate an increased number of peer interactions during the rest of the school day.

Level C: Structured Social-Skills Groups.
DeKlyen and Odom (1989) found that rates of peer interaction between preschool children with and without disabilities were related to the level of activity structure employed by teachers. In structured social-skills groups, you manipulate the social environment of the classroom by providing specially designed social integration activities for brief periods of time during the day (Odom & Brown, 1993). These activities are structured in ways that require either social interaction (on a more complex level than the affection activities) or social cooperation. These activities could include simple board games, dramatic play themes with specific interactive roles, group art projects, assembly line cooking, or cooperative games.

Activities that apply concepts and structures from cooperative learning (Curran, 1990; Johnson, Johnson, & Holubec, 1988) would fall into this category. As Fad, Ross, and Boston, (1995) stated:

Cooperative learning has been proven to be an effective way to bring children with disabilities and their peers into an inclusive classroom structure.... Even very young children can learn social skills through cooperative learning—beginning with pairs of children playing different roles: blower and popper with bubbles, hider and seeker in the sand with hidden toys, filler and dumper with buckets and assorted materials, and chooser and gluer with art supplies and glue. (p. 28)

Adding a structured, peer-interaction play center as an option during free play is another way to apply this level of intervention. For example, a classroom may have a block center, home center, book center, art center, and the P.A.L.S. center. In the P.A.L.S. center, the staff "**P**air children, **A**rrange adult behavior, **L**imit materials, and **S**tructure the activity" (Chandler, 1998, p. 15).

This type of intervention is particularly useful for students who are fairly verbal and of normal intelligence but are outcasts from the group. These children may be affected by attention deficit disorder, a learning disability, Asperger's syndrome, or sensory integration disorder. They may be withdrawn, socially clumsy, or aggressive. If the preschool already has some structured instructional times in their program, then this type of intervention is usually accepted by the daily teaching staff. There are quite a few activity books on the market for this type of intervention. Searching an online bookstore with search words such as "preschool" plus "friendship," "social skills," and "cooperation" will lead teachers to current titles.

This type of intervention involves a fair amount of time sifting through materials and hand picking those that match the child's needs and the program's styles. When using a direct-service approach, you lead these activities. When in a consulting role, you encourage and train site staff to plan and lead the activities themselves. When using this approach, you should schedule the weekly visit during free-choice, small-group, or circle time, depending on the nature of the activities chosen.

Level D: Direct Social-Interaction Interventions.
These activities are the most direct type of instructional approach to teaching social skills. They are also the least naturalistic requiring more direct changes to the typical early childhood classroom. They usually come as kits or instructional manuals and outline a step-by-step format for teaching play skills or problem-solving skills (conflict resolution). In addition to the costs of purchasing the curriculum, there is usually training required. As the itinerant teacher, you should implement this level of intervention directly. Because the instruction is systematic, it involves a lot of preparation time—at least during the first year while learning to use the curriculum. Once learned, however, it can be a great resource for many years.

This type of intervention can be lengthy or, if necessary, shortened to a few lessons on specific target skills. One way to do this is outlined in "Come and Play: Developing Children's Social Skills in an Inclusive Preschool" by Collins, Ault, Hemmeter, and Doyle (1996). They recommend collecting a baseline, targeting specific skills, and teaching the skills using role-plays during group instruction. Following group instruction, the teacher observes skills and prompts the children in the skills during free play. This is followed

Resources for Social Skills Interventions

Activity-Based Intervention

Bricker, D. (1998). *An activity-based approach to early intervention*. Baltimore: Paul H. Brookes.

Brown, W., McEvoy, M., & Bishop, N. (1991). Incidental teaching of social behavior. *TEACHING Exceptional Children, (24)* 1, 35–38.

Segal, M., & Adcock, D. (1993). *Play together grow together: A cooperative curriculum for teachers of young children, New edition*. Ft. Lauderdale, FL: Family Center of Nova Southeastern University.

Affection Training

Cooper, C. S., & McEvoy, M., (1996). Group friendship activities. *TEACHING Exceptional Children, (28)* 3, 67–69.

McEvoy, M. A., Twardosz, S., & Bishop, N. (1990, May). Affection activities: Procedures for encouraging young children with handicaps to interact with their peers. *Education and Treatment of Children, 13*(2), 159–167.

Structured Social Integration Groups

Chandler, L. (1998). Promoting positive interaction between preschool-age children during free play: The PALS center. *Young Exceptional Children (1)* 3, 14–19.

Fad, K. S., Ross, M., & Boston, J. (1995). We're better together: Using cooperative learning to teach social skills to young children. *TEACHING Exceptional Children (27)* 4, 28–34.

Orlick, T. (1978). *The cooperative sports & games book*. New York: Pantheon Books.

Sher, B. (1998). *Self-esteem games: 300 fun activities that make children feel good about themselves*. New York: Wiley.

Smith, C. A. (1993). *The peaceful classroom: 162 easy activities to teach preschoolers compassion and cooperation*. Beltsville, MD: Gryphon House, Inc.

Direct Social Interaction Interventions

Collins, B. C., Ault, M. J., Hemmete, M. L., & Doyle, P. M. (1996, September/October). Come and play: Developing children's social skills in an inclusive preschool. *TEACHING Exceptional Children, (29)*, 1, 16–21.

Committee for Children. (1991). *Second Step: A violence prevention curriculum, level pre-K*. Seattle, WA: Author. (ERIC Document Reproduction Service No. ED 365 739)

McGinnis, E., & Goldstein, A. P. (1990). *Skills streaming in early childhood: Teaching prosocial skills to the preschool and kindergarten child*. Champaign, IL: Research Press.

Odom, S. L., & McConnell, S. R. (1997). *Play time/social time: Organizing your classroom to build interaction skills*. Minneapolis: University of Minnesota, Institute on Community Integration. (ERIC Document Reproduction Service No. ED 412 705/EC 305 924)

Rosenthal-Malek, A. (1997, January/February). Stop and think! Using metacognitive strategies to teach students social skills. *TEACHING Exceptional Children, (29)* 3, 29–31.

then by collecting more data, evaluating, and making modifications. Skills that might be taught this way include inviting a friend to play, sharing toys, asking for a turn, and responding to friends.

Curriculum kits that teach problem-solving may be designed to cover an entire school year. Many preschools do not want to take this much time away from their general curriculum. In this situation it is helpful to teach just the basic problem-solving steps. These self-interrogation strategies are also referred to as "metacognitive strategies." In the article "Stop and Think!" Rosenthal-Malek (1997) described

one way to do this. The self-interrogation strategies are taught in a group format just before free play. Then, the strategies taught at group are immediately promoted and practiced in free-play situations. *The Second Step Curriculum* (Committee for Children, 1991) teaches children to ask themselves: "What's the problem?" "What can I do?" "What would happen if… ?" "What should I try first?" and "Is it working?"

For this intervention, you should schedule the weekly visit during either a large- or small-group instructional time. This type of intervention works best if the classroom teacher remains with the group during the

lessons and reinforces the concepts during the rest of the week.

Gather Resources

The second thing an itinerant teacher must do is collect resources reflecting this continuum. Because you will have little time to spend preparing or hunting down materials, the resources must be kept right at hand. A typical day could include visiting three or four students at different schools, with the time in between spent in your car: driving or doing paperwork, making calls on a cell phone, and eating lunch to avoid an additional drive to the office.

One good resource would be professional books that review and summarize the research literature. These can be helpful because the itinerant teacher must be able to articulate what he or she does and, in most cases, train others to do it. If you have been in the self-contained classroom for a long time, much of your decision making has become intuitive. Sometimes terminology or the rationale behind certain techniques has gotten buried, along with the class notes from graduate school. Professional books can help you review the language of current best practices. One book that provides a brief overview of the research is: *Including Children with Special Needs in Early Childhood Programs* edited by Mark Wolery and Jan S. Wilbers (1994). This book is published by NAEYC and is very reasonably priced.

Activity books are also helpful for generating ideas for lessons, especially because planning time is so limited. Kits are another good resource; however, they are expensive and usually lengthy to implement. Teacher-made handouts are nice because they can be tailored to each situation; but they are time-consuming to create.

Articles from back issues of *TEACHING Exceptional Children* are a great resource. These articles were created for teachers; they are concise, easy to locate by topic, and inexpensive to obtain. It is particularly helpful that these articles may be copied up to 100 times for non-profit use. Articles such as these can be used to help you quickly organize ideas before meetings; when appropriate, they can be left behind for classroom staff to read (for helpful materials, see box, "Resources for Social Skills Interventions").

Match Types of Interventions to Children and Settings

Third, as the itinerant teacher, you must know how to match interventions to children, given their individual situations. This is where you need strong skills in observing and relating to others. Start by asking the parents what they value about this setting and what their expectations and hopes are for how their child will do here socially. Next, you observe the child in the natural environment, study the child's assessment results, and ask the classroom staff about their concerns. As an itinerant teacher, you must

- Become familiar with the program's philosophy and curriculum.
- Notice the program's cultural and linguistic characteristics.
- Look at the daily schedule, the number of students in the class, and the number of teachers and their skill level.

This information gathering helps you get a feel for this particular social "climate." You need to understand how the child is currently functioning within this environment, how peers and teachers feel about him or her, and how the staff feel about the presence of a special education itinerant teacher.

Obviously, you can't just assess all these things and then tell the parents plus site staff what you have "decided" to do. At this point, you must draw on your knowledge of collaboration and teaming models. One resource on this topic is *Partnership in Family-Centered Care: A Guide to Collaborative Early Intervention* (Rosin et al., 1996).

To meet legal timelines, you need to move fairly quickly to facilitate a meeting where the individualized education program (IEP) can be developed with the classroom staff and parents. At the end of the IEP meeting, you can propose that you could come and "float" during several weekly visits, after which a meeting can be held to plan how the team will teach the IEP objectives. This keeps you within the legal timelines for conducting the meeting but allows more time for assessing the situation and building rapport before recommending any specific level or type of intervention.

To prepare for the second meeting, consider one more piece of information: your weekly schedule. In some systems a full-time itinerant special education teacher sees each student 1 hour per week (plus often additional time spent meeting with staff) and 16–20 students in a week. That means some students are seen during circle time, some during free-choice time, some during small-group time, and so on. Teachers must implement some interventions, however, within certain types of activities. Thus, before recommending a particular type of intervention, ask yourself these questions:

- What level of intervention will meet the child's objectives as described on the IEP?
- Will this level be embraced by parents and by classroom staff?
- How can I fit this type of intervention into my schedule?

Understand the Special Challenges of This Model

Finally, as the itinerant teacher, you must understand the challenges you will face. You will be working in someone else's classroom, a classroom most likely chosen by the parents. That classroom's teaching staff, plus the parents, have much more contact time with the student than you do. For interventions to be really effective, classroom staff and parents must embrace them.

How can you motivate staff and parents to work with you?

- Start your work with the student at the low end of the continuum by modeling the incidental teaching techniques in the classroom. Odom, McConnell, and Chandler (1994) found that teachers are more inclined to use naturalistic interventions to teach social interaction, instead of intensive individual interventions. You can also suggest that parents use these incidental teaching techniques at home during play-dates with classmates or relatives. Starting on the lowest level of the continuum shows the classroom teachers and parents that specialized instruction doesn't have to severely change the way they interact with the child. This can help establish trust.

- Be familiar with the continuum of interventions and be able to articulate it in everyday terms. This capability will help parents and classroom staff view you as a useful resource.

- Encourage families and site staff to plan activities that reflect their own character at any level of intervention.

- Keep in mind that this model is primarily an indirect one when planning ways to monitor progress. Even if you are providing direct services once a week, you are also hoping to facilitate change in the daily behavior of classroom staff and parents.

- Measure student progress by collecting data on IEP objectives; but also be watching for signs that the classroom staff and parents are addressing the objectives. One tool for such communication is a traveling notebook that goes everywhere with the child in a backpack. Classroom teachers, parents, therapists, and the itinerant teacher all use this notebook to jot down their anecdotal notes about the child's activities; and they read one another's entries.

Final Thoughts

Because weekly instruction by the itinerant teacher is sparse and because it takes time to effect change in classroom staff and parents, the impact of this service delivery model is slow at first. The continuous modeling provided by a classroom of peers without disabilities, however, can be powerful for many children. It is also an enabling experience to have early childhood teachers and special education teachers working side by side. This coteaching experience slowly

increases the capacity of the community to meet the needs of children with disabilities.

This article has provided a map to assist the itinerant teacher in addressing student delays in social skills. As more teachers become familiar with this new role, they may draw even more maps providing practical information for the itinerant teacher. Some day we will no longer be in an identity crisis, but be confidently navigating our way in early childhood settings everywhere.

References

Bricker, D. (1998). *An activity-based approach to early intervention* (2nd ed.). Baltimore: Paul H. Brookes.

Brown, W., McEvoy, M., & Bishop, N. (1991). Incidental teaching of social behavior. *TEACHING Exceptional Children, (24)* 1, 35–38.

Buysse, V., & Wesley, P. W. (1993). The identity crisis in early childhood special education: A call for professional role clarification. *Topics in Early Childhood Special Education, 13* (4), 418–429.

Chandler, L. (1998). Promoting positive interaction between preschool-age children during free play: The PALS center. *Young Exceptional Children, (1)* 3, 14–19.

Collins, B. C., Ault, M. J., Hemmeter, M. L., & Doyle, P. M. (1996, September/October). Come and play: Developing children's social skills in an inclusive preschool. *TEACHING Exceptional Children, (29)* 1, 16–21.

Committee for Children. (1991). *Second Step: A violence prevention curriculum, level pre-K.* Seattle, WA: Author.

Cooper, C. S., & McEvoy (1996). Group friendship activities. *TEACHING Exceptional Children, (28)* 3, 67–69.

Curran, L. (1990). *Cooperative learning lessons for little ones: Literature-based language arts and social skills.* San Juan Capistrano, CA: Resources for Teachers.

DeKlyen, M., & Odom, S. L. (1989). Activity structure and social interaction with peers in developmentally integrated play groups. *Journal of Early Intervention, 13,* 342–351.

Fad, K. S., Ross, M., & Boston, J.(1995). We're better together: Using cooperative learning to teach social skills to young children. *TEACHING Exceptional Children, (27)* 4, 28–34.

Gallagher, P. A. (1997). Teachers and inclusion: Perspectives on changing roles. *Topics in Early Childhood Special Education, 17,* 363–386.

Johnson, D. W., Johnson, R., & Holubec, E. (1988). *Cooperation in the classroom* (Rev. ed.). Edina, MN: Interaction Book Company.

Odom, S. L., & Brown, W. H. (1993). Social interaction skills interventions for young children with disabilities in integrated settings. In C. A. Peck, A. L. Odom, & D. D. Bricker (Eds.), *Integrating young children with disabilities into community programs* (pp. 39–64). Baltimore: Paul H. Brookes.

Odom, S. L., McConnell, S. R., & Chandler, L. K. (1994). Acceptability and feasibility of classroom-based social interaction interventions for young children with disabilities. *Exceptional Children, 60,* 226–236.

Rosenthal-Malek, A. (1997, January/February). Stop and think! Using metacognitive strategies to teach students social skills. *TEACHING Exceptional Children, (29)* 3, 29–31.

Rosin, P., Whitehead, A., Tuchman, L., Jensien, F., Begun, A. & Irwin, L. (1996). *Partnership in family-centered care: A guide to collaborative early intervention.* Baltimore: Paul H. Brookes.

Wesley, P. W., Buysse, V., & Keyes, L. (2000). Comfort zone revisited: Child characteristics and professional comfort with consultation. *Journal of Early Intervention, 23* (2), 106–115.

Wolery, M., & Wilbers, J. S. (Eds.). (1994) *Including children with special needs in early childhood programs.* Washington DC: National Association for the Education of Young Children.

Faith Haertig Sadler *(CEC Chapter #28), Team Leader and Teacher, Early Childhood Itinerant Team, Seattle Public Schools, Washington.*

Address correspondence to the author at Seattle Public Schools, Wilson Room 104, 1130 N. 90th, Seattle, WA 98103 (e-mail: fsadler@at@;uswest.net).

From *Teaching Exceptional Children,* September/October 2001, pp. 60–66. © 2001 by The Council for Exceptional Children. Reprinted by permission.

UNIT 3
Learning Disabilities

Unit Selections

Key Points to Consider

- Describe scaffolded instruction. What is the goal of scaffolding for the learning disabled student?

- How do graphic organizers benefit students with LDs? Can teachers introduce graphic organizers into inclusive regular education classrooms?

- How has the high school program called LEAD helped LD students? How does it work?

- How can unit organizer routines keep high school students motivated to achieve and improve their performance in regular education classes?

 Links: www.dushkin.com/online/
These sites are annotated in the World Wide Web pages.

Children and Adults With Attention Deficit/Hyperactivity Disorder (CHADD)
http://www.chadd.org

The Instant Access Treasure Chest
http://www.fln.vcu.edu/ld/ld.html

Learning Disabilities Association of America (LDA)
http://www.ldanatl.org

Learning Disabilities Online
http://www.ldonline.org

OHSU Center on Self Determination
http://cdrc.ohsu.edu/selfdetermination/education/moving/communitysolutions.html

Teaching Children With Attention Deficit Disorder
http://www.kidsource.com/kidsource/content2/add.html

Learning how to learn is one of life's most important tasks. For students with disabilities of learning, it is a most critical lesson. Today general education teachers and special educators must seriously attend to the growing numbers of students who have a wide range of different learning disabilities (LDs). LD enrollments in inclusive, regular education classes have skyrocketed. They are the fastest-growing and largest category of exceptionalities in elementary, middle, and high schools. Children with LDs now make up more than 50 percent of those receiving special educational services.

The ways in which students with LDs are identified and served have been radically transformed with the reauthorization of PL94-142 in 1997 as PL105-17, or IDEA (Individuals with Disabilities Education Act). New assessment methods have made the identification of students with LDs easier and far more common. Many lawmakers and educators, however, feel that students who have other problems (for example, behavior disorders, poor learning histories, or dysfunctional families) are erroneously being diagnosed with LDs. IDEA requires states to place students with disabilities in regular classrooms as much as possible or lose their federal funding. A landmark U.S. Supreme Court case in November of 1993 (*Carter v. Florence Co., S.C.*) ruled that public schools must give appropriate educational services to students with LDs or pay the tuition for private schools to do so. This ruling opened a floodgate of new litigation by parents. IDEA has turned out to be much more expensive than Congress envisioned when it enacted this celebrated (and decried) education bill 25 years ago.

Is the rapid increase in students assessed to have learning disabilities really an artifact of misdiagnoses, exaggeration, and a duping of the system that makes funding available for special needs? Neonatal medical technology and achievements in preventive medicine and health maintenance have greatly reduced the numbers of children who are born deaf, blind, severely physically disabled, or with multiple exceptional conditions. The very same medical technology has greatly increased the numbers of children kept alive who are born prematurely, small for gestational age, with low birth weight, and "at-risk" for less severe disabilities such as LDs.

A learning disability is usually defined by the lay public as difficulty reading or calculating. IDEA defines it as a disorder in the processes involved in understanding or in using language, spoken or written, that may manifest itself in an imperfect ability to listen, speak, read, write, spell, or do mathematical calculations. Learning disabilities are identified differently outside of education. The *Diagnostic and Statistical Manual of Mental Disorders* (4th edition) divides LDs into academic skills disorders (reading, mathematics, written expression) and attention deficit hyperactive disorder (ADHD). The National Joint Committee for Learning Disabilities (NJCLD) separates LDs into specific problems related to the acquisition and use of listening, speaking, reading, writing, reasoning, or mathematical abilities. Attention deficit hyperactive disorder, if not accompanied by any specific learning problem or any specific behavioral/emotional disorder, can be assessed as a health disability by both IDEA and NJCLD especially if it can be ameliorated with medication. Due to parental

pressures, the IDEA definition of LDs has been amended administratively to include ADHD if the deficit in attention leads to difficulty in learning. In this compendium, ADHD is treated as a health disability.

The rest of the definition of an LD is an exclusionary definition. It helps clarify the nature of LDs. They are not developmental disabilities. They are not deficiencies in any of the sensory systems (vision, hearing, taste, touch, smell, kinesthetics, vestibular sensation). They are not problems associated with health or physical mobility. They are not emotional or behavioral disorders. They are not disabilities of speech or language. They can be assessed as true LDs only if there is a discrepancy between the child's ability to learn and his or her actual learning.

IDEA's strong emphasis on a free and appropriate educational placement for every child with a disability has forced schools to be more cautious about all assessments and labeling. Increasing numbers of children are now being assessed as LD who once might have been labeled developmentally disabled or disabled by speech, language, emotions, behavior, or one of the senses. A child with an LD may concurrently have a disability in any of these other areas, but if this occurs, both the LD and any other disabilities must be addressed in an individualized education plan (IEP) designed especially for that unique child.

Recent research suggests that reading disabilities may affect about 15 percent of elementary school–aged children. If this is accurate, many LD children are not yet being identified and serviced. The causes of LDs are unknown. Usually some central nervous system dysfunctions are believed to underlie the disabilities, even if their existence cannot be demonstrated. Other suspected causes include genetic inheritance, poor nutrition, or exposure to toxic agents. The NJCLD definition of LD presumes biological causation and lifetime chronicity.

This unit on learning disabilities addresses both the successes and the frustrations of educating children with LDs. The first article discusses the importance of a supportive environment. It describes scaffolded instruction, the systematic sequencing of prompted content, materials, and tasks, and teacher and peer support to optimize learning. The goal of scaffolding is to support students until they can carry out tasks or skills independently. The careful sequencing helps control frustration and assists students to clear their minds of the word "can't." Guidelines for effective scaffolding are given by Martha Larkin.

The second article makes practical suggestions for effecting curriculum changes that will assist with the education of students with LDs in inclusive regular education classes in neighborhood schools. Graphic organizers really help students learn.

The third article describes methods used by one school's LEAD (Learning and Education About Disabilities) group. It has multiple components that help students with LDs gain confidence and self-esteem. The LEAD group helps prepare them for all of life.

The last selection depicts the problems faced by high school teachers who struggle to give appropriate educational challenges to students with a vast range of mental abilities. The authors argue that students should not be allowed to slip through the cracks.

Providing Support for Student Independence Through Scaffolded Instruction

Martha J. Larkin

Students with learning disabilities need a supportive environment to function successfully in school—and later in the workplace. A supportive environment enables them to capitalize on their strengths and minimize or cope effectively with their weaknesses. Gerber, Ginsberg, and Reiff (1992) noted characteristics of successful adults with learning disabilities:

- Having the desire to excel.
- Reframing their disability in a positive manner.
- Setting explicit personal goals.
- Being willing to take risks.
- Taking advantage of strengths.

If students with learning and other disabilities are to exhibit characteristics of successful adults, they need appropriate support in school. Such support includes "scaffolding," or providing steps that lead to achievement (see box, "What Is Scaffolded Instruction?").

In this article, we visit a special education teacher who practiced effective scaffolding. This teacher shares her thoughts about the challenges she faced in assisting a student to achieve independence. Several other teachers provide guidelines for effective scaffolding.

Breaking the Failure Cycle

Many students who receive special education services as early as second and third grades already have become well immersed in a "failure cycle." These students are not identified to receive special educational services until the number of their failures well exceeds the number of their successful experiences. Melanie (not her real name), a third grader identified with a learning disability, lost all hope that she could be successful in school until Anna Davis (again, not her real name), a special education teacher, provided her a supportive environment (see box, "Meet Melanie").

Through scaffolded instruction, Anna Davis provided Melanie with the support she needed to become a successful reader and to begin developing confidence in her abilities. As Anna's comments indicated, ensuring a supportive environment for Melanie and her peers with disabilities is a substantial challenge. It is labor intensive and time consuming, and success is measured in small increments. As Melanie performs tasks with less teacher assistance, she gains more self-confidence and is more likely to take risks (e.g., attempting to perform a portion or even entire tasks independently). A measure of success for Melanie and many of her peers with learning disabilities is achieving the independence in at least some academic areas.

Educators can learn much from teachers like Anna who facilitate a caring, supportive environment for their students—to help them strive for independence.

How Can Teachers Provide Effective Scaffolded Instruction?

In a summary of the literature, Hogan and Pressley (1997) listed eight essential elements of scaffolded instruction: pre-engagement; establishing a shared goal; actively diagnosing the understandings and needs of the learners; providing tailored assistance; maintaining pursuit of the goal; giving feedback; controlling for frustration and risk; and assisting internationalization, independence, and generalization to other contexts. Teachers need not follow these elements in lockstep succession, but use them as general guidelines for dynamic, flexible scaffolding. Let's examine each, as it applies to the example of Melanie.

Pre-engagement with the Learner and Curriculum. During pre-engagement, the teacher considers curriculum goals and student needs to select an appropriate task (Hogan & Pressley, 1997). Anna Davis selected appropri-

What Is Scaffolded Instruction?

Scaffolded instruction is "the systematic sequencing of prompted content, materials, tasks, and teacher and peer support to optimize learning" (Dickson, Chard, & Simmons, 1993, p. 12). Scaffolding provides students with the help they need and allows them to complete a task with assistance before they are able to complete it independently (Pearson, 1996). The goal of scaffolding is to support students until they can apply the new skills and strategies independently. This means a gradual decrease in supports and a gradual increase in student responsibility with the responsibility for learning shifting from the teacher to the student (Rosenshine & Meister, 1992). In other words, scaffolded instruction means that teachers make sure that their students have the necessary support to complete a task successfully. When learning something new or difficult, students may need more assistance; and as they begin to demonstrate task mastery, the support is removed gradually. Through appropriately scaffolded instruction, students accept more responsibility for their learning and become more independent learners.

Dixon (1994) provided an example of scaffolded instruction as it might be used to teach a child with physical disabilities or a young child how to use a playground slide. An adult might begin by carrying the child up the steps to the slide and holding the child while both adult and child slide together. After a few times of sliding together, some of the scaffolding or adult support may be removed by placing the child low on the slide, allowing him or her to slide independently for a short distance. Gradually the scaffolding would be removed as the child assumed more responsibility toward sliding the entire distance independently.

Dixon (1994) cautioned against removing the scaffolding all at once or prematurely. Doing so— on a playground slide—could cause serious physical injury to the child. Likewise, removing scaffolding prematurely or never providing students with any supports in academic subjects could result in "serious intellectual injury." Physical injuries can heal, but achievement injuries may be difficult to rehabilitate (Dixon).

Ensuring a supportive environment for students with disabilities is a substantial challenge.

Establishing a Shared Goal. Mutual goal setting for Melanie and Anna was not difficult. Unlike some students who say that they don't want to learn to read, Melanie did want to read. Like many teachers of third-grade students with disabilities, Anna devoted a large portion of the day to teaching her students to read. As noted by Hogan and Pressley (1997), motivating students toward establishing a shared goal is providing a delicate balance between allowing the student to lead and following the traditional path of teacher-directed instruction.

Actively Diagnosing the Understandings and Needs of the Learners. The teacher must be sensitive to the learner and be knowledgeable of content matter to compare student performance to external standards for growth (Hogan & Pressley, 1997). Anna was sensitive to Melanie's need to feel successful and comfortable with the reading process. Anna reminded Melanie of her recent successful reading experiences when Melanie was convinced that she could not perform a similar reading task. In addition, Anna frequently questioned her students to determine their understanding of a task.

Providing Tailored Assistance. Hogan and Pressley (1997) suggested that assistance could take the form of cueing or prompting, questioning, modeling, telling, or discussing. Although Anna used all these forms of assistance, most of the examples provided will focus on cueing. The following illustrates how she used cueing to help Melanie with letter reversals.

> In reading, we used the rabbits [small plastic counters] for phonemic awareness. We were practicing spelling words. When you have *b* and *d*, if you turn the rabbits in that direction [the stomach of one rabbit counter points in the direction of the round part of the letter *b*, and another points in the opposite direction for the letter *d*], they're getting a pictorial cue again of which way [the letter should be turned]. I noticed that when Melanie wrote *bud*, she reversed her *b*s and *d*s. I said to her, "Remember the rabbits." She looked down and said, "Oh yeah," erased it, and put it the correct way. I think it's better to use little clues rather than saying, "Oh, you reversed that letter, or that letter is wrong." All I had to do is say, "Remember the rabbits," because I think that is a far more positive way of saying it.

Maintaining Pursuit of the Goal. Students who have been immersed in the "failure cycle" may have trouble maintaining pursuit of the goal. Particularly for compli-

ate reading tasks for Melanie, as guided by Melanie's individualized education program (IEP) goals. Anna was aware of the difficulties that Melanie had with reading and her lack of self-confidence in her reading ability.

Meet Melanie

Melanie said she wanted to be able to read. She didn't realize that she could read and that was a goal she desired. She said, "If I can only read like everyone else."

Then I said, "Well, you can."

She said, "No, I can't. I don't know how."

I said, "Yes, you do; but you don't know you do." I basically showed her that she could read. She is one of the stronger readers of the group.

I showed her that she knew how to do word-attack skills because she didn't think that she did. I showed her how to look for the small word in the big word and how to leave out a word she didn't know by reading the whole sentence and then figuring out the word. She learned to understand what she read just by asking the *who, what, where,* and *why* questions. She never asked herself those questions before because she never knew that was something you did. So she feels pretty good about herself.

Melanie attempts to pass over areas in which she is uncertain, rather than shut down and say she can't do it. I say, "Now, look how well you did there. Look how well you read and understood what you read. Now, let's try this. It is a little bit harder, but let's try it."

I will keep saying, "Look, remember what you did before? Think about how you used the techniques that you were using at that time to read that passage. Now let's try this one." If you don't make her feel that she has succeeded in one place, Melanie would tend to shut down and not want to try.

—*Anna Davis*

cated tasks, teachers may need to provide more support for students to be persistent and focused (Hogan & Pressley, 1997). Anna gave Melanie extra praise and encouragement to increase her level of motivation. Notice how Anna bolstered Melanie's confidence at the slightest indication that Melanie was slipping into failure.

Giving Feedback. Hogan and Pressley (1997) noted that the teacher who uses scaffolding summarizes student progress and highlights behaviors that lead to success in anticipation that students eventually will self-monitor their own learning. Anna provided feedback appropriately to Melanie by summarizing the progress that she had made in reading; Anna mentioned particular behaviors (i.e., Anna called them "techniques") that led to Melanie's success. Anna was keen on giving immediate feedback (i.e., as soon as possible following a behavior or task completion, usually within the same class period) to

her students and giving feedback in a way that students could have opportunities to correct their errors.

As a student performs tasks with less and less teacher assistance, she gains more self-confidence and is more likely to take risks.

Controlling for Frustration and Risk. The teacher needs to create an environment in which students are free to try alternatives without being penalized and in which mistakes are considered part of learning (Hogan & Pressley, 1997). Anna's classroom environment was one in which students could feel safe in taking risks with their learning. Students like Melanie knew that errors were part of the learning process. Anna described her classroom as

easy-going, relaxed, a place where learning is fun, where success if far more important than failure. Feedback is positive, so that there is no negativism. These kids have come from classes where they've been put down all of their life, three years of school.... They have been just miserable, and they hurt. They think they are dumb and can never learn. My job is to tell them, "Yes, you can learn, and you will, and this is how we are going to do it. It's easy. It's fun. Let's get on with it." I teach to make them succeed.

Assisting Internalization, Independence, and Generalization to Other Contexts. This means helping students to become less dependent on the teacher's extrinsic signals for what to do next and providing students with the opportunity to practice the skills in different contexts (Hogan & Pressley, 1997). Successful instruction is defined by the degree to which the student uses the information learned to meet the demands of natural settings (Ellis & Larkin, 1998). Anna wanted her students to become independent learners; she recognized that once the students left her classroom and the elementary school, there would be fewer opportunities for teacher assistance. Students would have to become more independent, or run the risk of failure. Anna valued student independence but realized that it would have to occur gradually for some:

I'm hoping I can find some small tiles where I can put letters on the tiles instead of using the rabbits. We are going to start moving the tiles so that I can see where there's awareness of the vowel sounds. Now we have done vowels for two years and [mastery] is still not there. I'll have to use the tiles where they [the students] place them. They're going to get a visual as well as a kinesthetic [cue], so when they write the word, I'm hoping it transfers.

Guidelines for Effective Scaffolding

- *Identify what students know.* Effective scaffolding requires that teachers are cognizant of what a student already knows (background or prior knowledge), the student's misconceptions, and the student's current zone of proximal development (i.e., which competencies are developing and which are beyond the student's current level of functioning; Pressley, Hogan, Wharton-McDonald, Mistretta, & Ettenberger, 1996). For example, Anna was aware that some of her students "think in terms of money." When she taught "rounding" to those students, Anna used the familiar concept of money.

- *Begin with what students can do.* Laura (not her real name), another special education teacher, was aware of individual student ability levels. When Laura began reading lessons, she gave the students with learning disabilities an opportunity to read something that could be read independently or with little teacher assistance. This enabled students to begin the reading lesson successfully.

- *Help students achieve success quickly.* Laura found that writing and penmanship tasks were laborious for some of her students with written expression disabilities. When she assisted her special education students in the general education classroom for a lesson on storytelling, Laura asked the students to dictate their ideas while she wrote them on paper. This accommodation enabled the students who had difficulty with written expression to generate ideas without worrying how to convey them on paper. Also, Laura served as an adult listener to reinforce the notion that storytelling and written expression is an act of communication and shared experience.

- *Help students to "be" like everyone else.* Miller and Fritz (1998) interviewed a successful adult with learning disabilities about his school history and found that a major theme was the individual's desire to be regarded like other students. These researchers suggested that as much as possible, teachers orient classroom tasks for students' work to be perceived as being like that of their peers. For example, Anna suggested that Mark (not his real name), a struggling student, be moved into a third-grade text like that of his peers. She informed Mark of his responsibility to work hard, but also let him know that she would be there to give him the assistance he needed. Anna noted that when Mark was placed in the third-grade math book with her assistance, he was still struggling with math, but was holding his own. She was confident that she made the right decision to place him in a more difficult math book, with assistance, because Mark felt good about using the same book as his third-grade peers.

- *Know when it's time to stop.* Anna learned from experience that continued drill and practice may not always be effective. She stated, "Overkill erases." Anna found that once her students had demonstrated mastery of a skill, continued practice may result in the students' refusing to work or students' producing work with numerous errors. For example, when some of Anna's students with learning disabilities were asked to complete a general education math assignment with 50 problems, she noticed that the students completed the first three rows of problems without an error. Students began making numerous errors on the final three rows. Anna found that employing systematic review and purposeful practice with a limited number of math problems was effective. She also noted that a just a few written or spoken questions regarding reading or language arts assignments provided needed review without overkill.

- *Help students be independent when they have command of the activity.* Effective scaffolding means that teachers need to listen and watch for clues from their students as to when teacher assistance is or is not needed. Obviously, teachers do not want students to fail, but they should not allow students to become too dependent on the teacher. As special education teacher Beverly (not her real name) noted, achieving independence is different for individual students. Some students may be at identical skill levels, but emotionally may be at different levels regarding the amount of frustration they can tolerate. Students may not be able "to be weaned" from teacher assistance at the same time. In other words, some students will need more teacher support while learning to perform a task; others will demonstrate task mastery more quickly. Like the mother bird that helps her chicks leave the nest to become independent birds, teachers need to help their students gradually move from teacher assistance to student independence as students demonstrate command of the task or activity.

By expressing that she hopes the visual and kinesthetic cues from the use of the tiles will aid transfer, Anna recognized how difficult the generalization of learned skills may be for some students with learning disabilities. Students first must acquire and maintain skills at a proficient level before they can be generalized to other contexts. Although much of her instructional time was spent helping students with skill acquisition and maintenance, Anna fostered independence and generalization in the area of student self-monitoring for errors. Just like she cued her students when they made letter reversals in reading, Anna also used cues to call students' attention to number reversals in math

> For number reversals like 5, 3, 6, and 7, I usually will say something like, "You really have to discipline your 3. It keeps jumping around on you." The kids laugh and they go, "Oh, yeah!"

Students who have been immersed in the "failure cycle" may have trouble maintaining pursuit of the goal.

Anna's sense of humor not only made the students feel at ease with error monitoring and correction, but also gave them opportunities to practice these skills when the teacher made a error.

> I usually tell them it is safe to make mistakes in here, because your teacher makes them every day.... I allow them to catch me on mistakes.... Yesterday, I couldn't get that word spelling right, s-c-r-a-t-c-h. The students were laughing and having a wonderful time, but I turned that into learning. "You tell me how to spell it, because I'm having a terrible time with this word."

Anna tried to provide cues only when students needed them (e.g., struggling with a familiar task in a new context, or making an error). To lessen teacher dependence gradually, Anna cued students to use "error monitoring" strategies when she gave the directions for an assignment. "When you do your sentences on page 86, please read them to yourself. Sometimes, when you read them to yourself, you find what you left out." Another way Anna used cues was to help students to verbalize how they recognized their own errors (e.g., "How did you recognize your mistake, Randy?"). Anna seized this opportunity to help Randy (not his real name) identify the naturally occurring events that alerted him to his error. Although Anna's students needed more assistance with generalization of skills, they were making progress on the road to independence.

In addition to the eight essential elements of scaffolded instruction, teachers like Anna have developed their own guidelines for effective scaffolding (see box, "Guidelines").

Final Thoughts

Students with learning disabilities need a supportive classroom environment that can help them recognize their strengths and feel confident about their abilities in order to achieve at least some degree of independent functioning. Through carefully scaffolded instruction, special education and general education teachers can take proactive paths of moving their students towards independence and achieving success. This path will be challenging for teachers and students. To provide effective scaffolding for some or all students in the classroom across several content areas may require an enormous amount of time and energy from the teacher (Pressley et al., 1996). Teachers must tailor scaffolding to meet individual student needs. Also, effective scaffolding requires the provision of "calibrated assistance" (Wong, 1998). Teachers must be cognizant of the kinds and degrees of assistance provided to individual students (for more about scaffolded instruction, see box, "Resources"). Support or assistance must be removed gradually (Rosenshine & Meister, 1992).

Finally, teachers need to pay attention to clues from their students as to when teacher support is or is not needed. As noted by Beed, Hawkins, and Roller (1991). "Independence must somehow be achieved through the daily interaction between teachers and children" (p. 648).

Although the examples in this article have focused on elementary school students and teachers, scaffolding principles and techniques can guide teachers to assist students on any grade level to become more independent learners.

References

Beed, P. L., Hawkins, E. M., & Roller, C. M. (1991). Moving learners toward independence: The power of scaffolded instruction. *The Reading Teacher, 44*, 648–655.

Dickson, S. V., Chard, D. J., & Simmons, D. C. (1993). An integrated reading/writing curriculum: A focus on scaffolding. *LD Forum, 18* (4), 12–16.

Dixon, R. (1994). Research-based guidelines for selecting a mathematics curriculum. *Effective School Practices, 13* (2), 47–61.

Ellis, E. S., & Larkin, M. J. (1998). Strategic instruction for adolescents with learning disabilities. In B. Y. L. Wong (Ed.), *Learning about learning disabilities* (2nd ed.; pp. 585–656). San Diego, CA: Academic Press.

Gerber, P. J., Ginsberg, R., & Reiff, H. B. (1992). Identifying alterable patterns in employment success for highly successful adults with learning disabilities. *Journal of Learning Disabilities, 25*, 474–487.

Hogan, K., & Pressley, M. (1997). Scaffolding scientific competencies within classroom communities of inquiry. In K. Hogan & M. Pressley (Eds.), *Scaffolding student learning: Instructional approaches & issues* (pp. 74–107). Cambridge, MA: Brookline Books.

Miller, M., & Fritz, M. F. (1998). A demonstration of resilience. *Intervention in School and Clinic, 35*, 265–271.

Pearson, P. D. (1996). Reclaiming the center, *The first R: Every child's right to read* (pp. 259–274). New York: Teachers College Columbia University.

Pressley, M., Hogan, K., Wharton-McDonald, R., Mistretta, J., & Ettenberger, S. (1996). The challenges of instructional scaffolding: The challenges of instruction that supports student

Resources for Scaffolded Instruction

Beed, P. L., Hawkins, E. M., & Roller, C. M. (1991). Moving learners toward independence: The power of scaffolded instruction. *The Reading Teacher, 44*, 648–655.

Dickson, S. V., Chard, D. J., & Simmons, D. C. (1993). An integrated reading/writing curriculum: A focus on scaffolding. *LD Forum, 18* (4), 12–16.

Dixon, R. C., & Carnine, D. (1993). Using scaffolding to teach writing. *Educational Leadership, 51* (3), 100–102.

Gambrell, L. B., Morrow, L. M., Neuman, S. B., & Pressley, M. (Eds.). (1999). *Best practices in literacy instruction.* New York: The Guilford Press.

Graves, M. F., & Braaten, S. (1996). Scaffolded reading experiences: Bridges to success. *Preventing School Failure, 40* (4), 169–173.

Graves, M. F., Graves, B. B., & Braaten, S. (1996). Scaffolded reading experiences for inclusive classes. *Educational Leadership, 53* (5), 14–16.

Hiebert, E. H., & Raphael, T. E. (1998). *Early literacy instruction.* Fort Worth, TX: Harcourt Brace College Publishers.

Hogan, K., & Pressley, M. (Eds). (1997). *Scaffolding student learning: Instructional approaches & issues.* Cambridge, MA: Brookline Books.

Kameenui, E. J., & Carnine, D. W. (1998). *Effective teaching strategies that accommodate diverse learners.* Upper Saddle River, NJ: Merrill.

Meichenbaum, D., & Biemiller, A. (1998). *Nurturing independent learners: Helping students take charge of their learning.* Cambridge, MA: Brookline Books.

Palincsar, A. S. (1991). Scaffolded instruction of listening comprehension with first graders at risk for academic difficulty. In A. McKeough & J. L. Lupart (Eds.), *Toward the practice of theory-based instruction* (pp. 50–65). Hillsdale, NJ: Erlbaum.

Pressley, M., Hogan, K., Wharton-McDonald, R., Mistretta, J., & Ettenberger, S. (1996). The challenges of instructional scaffolding: The challenges of instruction that supports student thinking. *Learning Disabilities Research & Practice, 11* (3), 138–146.

Rosenshine, B., & Meister, C. (1992). The use of scaffolds for teaching higher-level cognitive strategies. *Educational Leadership, 49* (7), 26–33.

Soderman, A. K., Gregory, K. M., & O'Neill, L. T. (1999). *Scaffolding emergent literacy: A child-centered approach for preschool through grade 5.* Boston: Allyn & Bacon.

Wollman-Bonilla, J. E., & Werchadlo, B. (199). Teacher and peer roles in scaffolding first graders' responses to literature. *Reading Teacher, 52*, 598–608.

Wong, B. Y. L. (Ed.). (1998). Scaffolding. (Special issue). *Journal of Learning Disabilities, 31* (4).

thinking. *Learning Disabilities Research & Practice, 11* (3), 138–146.

Rosenshine, B., & Meister, C. (1992). The use of scaffolds for teaching higher-level cognitive strategies. *Educational Leadership, 49* (7), 26–33.

Wong, B. Y. L. (1998). Analyses of intrinsic and extrinsic problems in the use of the scaffolding metaphor in learning disabilities intervention research: An introduction. *Journal of Learning Disabilities, 31*, 340–343.

Martha J. Larkin (CEC Chapter #356), Assistant Professor of Special Education, State University of West Georgia, Carrollton, Georgia.

Address correspondence to the author at Department of Special Education and Speech Language Pathology, 1600 Maple Street, State University of West Georgia, Carrollton, GA 30118 (e-mail: mlarkin@westga.edu).

This research was supported by a grant from the Donald D. Hammill Foundation. The author would like to thank the special education teachers in Alabama and Virginia who opened the doors to their classrooms and gave so willingly of their time, expertise, and perspectives.

Graphic Organizers to the Rescue!

Helping Students Link—
and Remember—
Information

Gloria A. Dye

How do we remember things?

How do we take advantage of our short-term memory?

How does information get stored for the long term?

Do people remember things in different ways?

What can help students improve their memory of content?

What can teachers do to support students with disabilities in storing long-term memory?

Psychologists and neuroscientists are working on these questions as we read this article, and many answers are ready and waiting for savvy teachers to grab and use with their students.

Students with mild to moderate disabilities need strategies to help them achieve success in their content-area classes. As special education teachers, one of our goals is to ensure, to the best of our ability, that students are achieving success in all classes. If students are to become successful in content-area classes, we must present information in a manner that is clear and organized. A clear, organized style will assist students in the note-taking process and will help them link the new information to their existing schema of knowledge. Graphic organizers may help as we present new information to students and as we review previous lessons.

What Are Graphic Organizers?

Graphic organizers are "visual displays teachers use to organize information in a manner that makes the information easier to understand and learn" (Meyen, Vergason, & Whelan 1996, p. 132). Here are some examples of graphic organizers:

- Venn diagrams.
- Semantic webs.
- Genealogical trees.
- Frames.

Some of these examples can be found in works by Lazear (1991) and Staton (1991). The frame is a more detailed type of graphic organizer; Ellis (1998) described its use in the Content Enhancement Series entitled *The Framing Routine*. The frame is a "two-dimensional graphic organizer that allows the teacher to display in an organized manner important information related to the targeted key topic" (p. 5).

The graphic organizer has its roots in schema theory. In effect, schema theory states that *new information must be linked to preexisting knowledge*. The teacher's task is to ensure that the child has prior knowledge related to the concept and to provide a means to assist the child in making the necessary connections between what is being taught and the child's prior knowledge. When people learn something new, they must retain it for later use. Our knowledge is stored in a scaffold-like hierarchy, which includes our way of organizing the information. According to Slavin (1991), we encode, store, and retrieve information based on this system. Schema

theory can be better understood when we examine the cognitive approach to learning.

Cognitive Approach to Learning

"The cognitive approach to learning seeks to understand how incoming information is processed and structured into memory" (Weinstein & Mayer, 1986, p. 316). Figure 1, a graphic organizer, illustrates how information is processed through the short-term memory and the long-term memory.

According to cognitive theory, a student is bombarded with a great deal of information. This is what happens (imagine arrows showing choices and processes):

- All this information enters the sensory register and is held there for only a few seconds.

- The information is either processed immediately or is forgotten.

- If the student chooses to process the information, it then moves from the sensory register to short-term memory.

- At this point, the student must rehearse this newly received information or it will be lost. The rehearsal is important because the longer a piece of information remains in short-term memory and is actively used, the greater the chance that this information will move from short-term memory to long-term memory.

Figure 1. Graphic Organizer: Information Processing

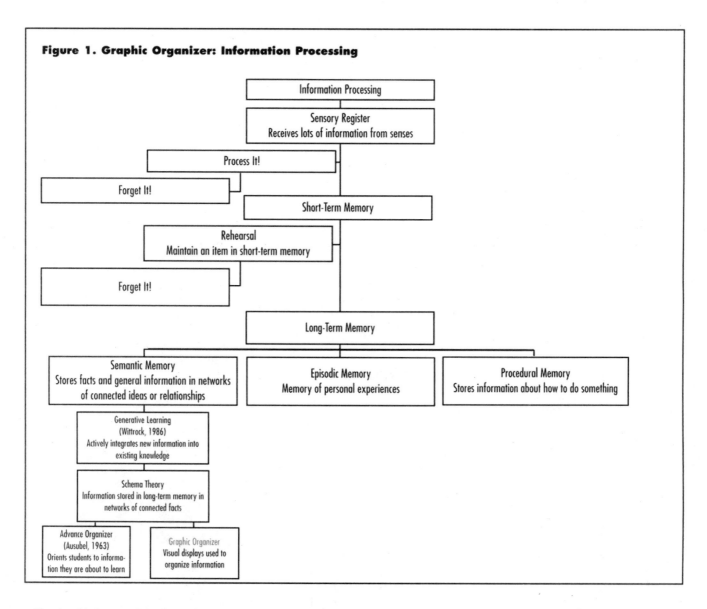

Clearly, this is one of the key points in teaching—helping the student move pertinent information into long-term memory.

According to Slavin (1991) and Mercer (1997), long-term memory can be divided into three parts: procedural memory, episodic memory, and semantic memory.

- Procedural memory stores information about how to do something.
- Episodic memory stores information about personal experiences.
- Semantic memory is organized in a different fashion. Semantic memory stores facts and general information in networks of connected ideas or relationships. This concept of semantic memory is grounded in *generative-learning* (Wittrock, 1986), which states that if learners are to discover or truly

understand the new information, they must actively integrate this new information into their existing knowledge.

Schema Theory

Schema theory explains this integration even further. Schema theory states that a person takes this new information and stores it in preexisting hierarchies or channels. Clearly, schema theory sets the groundwork for advance organizers (Ausubel, 1963), which, when presented at the beginning of a lesson, orient the students to information that the teacher is about to present. The graphic organizers are visual displays used to organize information (Meyen et al., 1996). These processes help students integrate the new knowledge into their scaffolds.

Theory Comparison

Let's compare this approach to the behaviorist approach:

- The *behaviorist* approach "focuses on observable behaviors, and views learning as the establishing of functional relationships between a student's behavior and the stimuli in the environment" (Bos & Vaughn, 1998, pp. 55–56).

- The *cognitive* approach "focuses on what happens in the mind, and views learning as changes in the learner's cognitive structure" (Bos & Vaughn, 1998, p. 56).

Simply stated, the behaviorist approach focuses on the behaviors of the teacher and the student; and the cognitive approach focuses on the internal thinking processes of the student.

Application of Schema Theory to Children

The most critical component of schema theory to remember is as follows: "Information that fits into a (student's) existing schema is more easily understood, learned, and retained than information that does not fit into an existing schema" (Slavin, 1991, p. 164). If, for example, a student with a disability has difficulty learning information in a content-area class, one might ascertain, based on this schema theory, that the student may have a problem fitting the information he or she has learned into his or her existing scaffold of knowledge. Although there are many reasons for this, one explanation could be that the student may not have the proper background knowledge. As Ausubel (1963) explained it: "Potentially meaningful material is always learned in relation to an existing background of relevant concepts, principles, and information which provide a framework for its reception" (p. 76).

Early Childhood Uses

Here are some ways you may use graphic organizers with children at the early childhood level:

1. Teaching children about animals and helping them classify the animals.
2. Explaining the connection between characters in a story.
3. Developing language skills by including pictures along with the words within the graphic organizer to explain a certain concept.

We know that most students with learning disabilities have difficulties processing information; thus, "the most fundamental characteristic of students with learning disabilities is their lack of academic achievement in one or more areas" (Turnbull, Turnbull, Shank, & Leal, 1999, pp. 126–127). Given the lack of background knowledge and the inability to organize the information, it may be difficult for a student with learning disabilities to retain this newly learned information.

Elementary Uses

Here are some ways you might use graphic organizers with children at the elementary level:

1. Helping children remember or understand the specific parts of a story.
2. Using phonological awareness activities, teaching the children how and when to spell the various /s/ sounds, for example.
3. Helping the children remember the states and capitals and where they are located in the United States. For example, the eastern states, the western states, the midwestern states.

Helping the student link new information to an existing knowledge base is one way teachers can assist students in learning new information in content-area classes. The use of a graphic organizer is an underlying premise of schema theory. Understanding this theory can assist teachers in their presentation of the material and may help students make the necessary linkages for learning to occur (U.S. Department of Education, 1987).

If, for example, you were conducting a lesson about flight, you might use the graphic organizer shown in Figure 2. You could help students link concepts of flight to their existing knowledge base by orga-

nizing the relationships among topics in the graphic organizer.

Using this graphic organizer to present information about flight, you can help students compare some of the early attempts at flight made by people in the United States with the early attempts at flight made by Europeans. You can also add additional spaces for students to fill out, as seen by the blank spaces in Figure 2 under North Carolina, Germany, Montgolfier, and Bleriot. Students might add information about the Wright Brothers, for example, in the North Carolina box, to continue to develop the lesson about flight.

By using a graphic organizer like the "flight" organizer, students can have a copy of the information and can add to it as the instruction progresses. Similarly, you might add additional blanks under various levels to extend the amount of information you wish to present to the students on that topic. This also would assist the student in linking prior knowledge with the new information you present.

Middle School Uses

Here are some ways to use graphic organizers with middle school students:

1. Illustrating science concepts, such as how and when various types of clouds form.
2. Understanding history concepts, such as the key issues leading to the Civil War.
3. Associating the instruments in an orchestra with the particular section that instrument might be in. One section of the graphic organizer might be entitled "woodwind instruments," with the specific instruments noted.

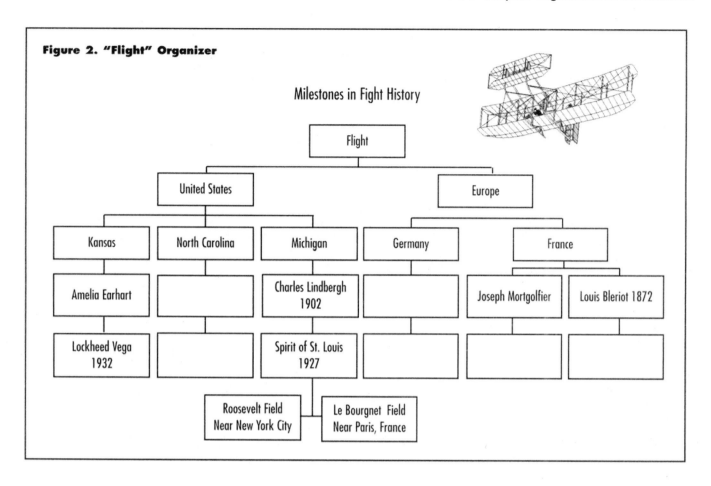

Figure 2. "Flight" Organizer

Milestones in Fight History

Creating Your Own Graphic Organizer

Graphic organizers are relatively easy to create; they can enhance a student's understanding of many lessons. Here are four basic steps to follow:

1. Select the information you intend to present to the students. This may be a chapter, or a story, or a certain concept.
2. Decide what key components are necessary for the students to learn.
3. Create a graphic representation of that information, such as those illustrated in Figures 1 and 2. Your graphic chart should identify the key concepts of components and help illustrate the linkages among the key elements of the concept.
4. Help the students see the connections by examining the information in the graphic organizer.

Graphic organizers lend themselves to many different kinds of content and to uses with all age levels of students (see boxes on Early Childhood, Elementary, Middle, and High School uses).

Final Thoughts

Graphic organizers can benefit teachers, students, and parents. By using graphic organizers, teachers can have a clear understanding of what they want to address in their classes. Graphic organizers provide students with a road map to follow as they expand their schemas by linking them to existing knowledge. When looking at a graphic organizer, like the "Flight" organizer, parents can have a clearer view of what their children will learn or what they have learned in a content-area class. By serving as a means of helping students link the new information with their existing knowledge base, graphic organizers can contribute to our ultimate goal—student learning.

References

Ausubel, D. P. (1963). *The psychology of meaningful verbal learning.* New York: Grune & Stratton.

Bos, C. S., & Vaughn, S. (1998). *Strategies for teaching students with learning and behavior problems* (4th ed.). Needham Heights, MA: Allyn & Bacon.

Ellis, E. S. (1998). *The framing routine.* Lawrence, KS: Edge Enterprises.

Lazear, D. (1991). *Seven ways of teaching.* Palatine, IL: Skylight.

Mercer, D. C. (1997). *Students with learning disabilities.* Upper Saddle River, NJ: Prentice Hall.

Meyen, E. L., Vergason, G. A. & Whelan, R. J. (1996). *Strategies for teaching exceptional children in inclusive settings.* Denver, CO: Love.

High School Uses

Here are some ways to use graphic organizers with high school students:

1. Comparing two stories in literature.
2. Explaining the key components from a chapter in the history text.
3. Describing the key concepts from a chapter in the science text.

Slavin, R. E. (1991). *Educational psychology* (3rd ed.). Needham Heights, MA: Allyn & Bacon.

Staton, H. N. (1991). *The content connection: How to integrate thinking and writing in the content areas.* Glenview, IL: Goodyear Books.

Turnbull, A., Turnbull, R., Shank, M., & Leal, D. (1999). *Exceptional lives: Special education in today's schools* (2nd ed.). Upper Saddle River, NJ: Merrill, Prentice Hall.

U.S. Department of Education. (1987). *What works* (2nd ed.). Washington, DC: U.S. Government Printing Office.

Weinstein, C. E., & Mayer, R. E. (1986). The teaching of learning strategies. In M. C. Wittrock (Ed.), *Handbook of research on teaching* (pp. 315–327). New York: Macmillan.

Wittrock, M. C. (1986). Students' thought processes. In M. C. Wittrock (Ed.), *Handbook of research on teaching* (3rd ed.). New York: Macmillan.

Gloria A. Dye *(CEC Chapter #816), Assistant Professor, Secondary Special Education, Washburn University, Topeka, Kansas.*

Address correspondence to the author at Washburn University, 1700 S.W. College Avenue, Topeka, KS 66621 (e-mail: zzdye@washburn.edu).

From *Teaching Exceptional Children*, January/February 2000, pp. 72–76. © 2000 by The Council for Exceptional Children. Reprinted by permission.

Successful Strategies for Promoting Self-Advocacy Among Students with LD: The LEAD Group

Students with learning disabilities (LD) often need to be taught self-determination skills to be better prepared for life after high school. This article describes the methods used by one school district to promote self-advocacy and self-awareness skills for students with LD. Through multicomponent group activities, students learned about their strengths and disabilities and how to advocate for their educational needs and rights. Advocacy skills were also applied to leadership roles, monitoring, and community education activities. Important features that contributed to the success of the program are described.

AL POCOCK, STAN LAMBROS, MEAGAN KARVONEN, DAVID W. TEST,
BOB ALGOZZINE, WENDY WOOD, AND JAMES E. MARTIN

Self-determination has been increasingly recognized as a critical outcome for students with disabilities as they prepare to transition to the adult world (Field, Martin, Miller, Ward, & Wehmeyer, 1998b). The U.S. Department of Education, Office of Special Education Programs, has funded numerous projects to develop self-determination conceptual models, assessments, and interventions (Ward & Kohler, 1996). Research demonstrates that self-determination is associated with greater quality of life (Wehmeyer & Schwartz, 1998) and more positive adult outcomes (Wehmeyer & Schwartz, 1997). Field, Martin, Miller, Ward, and Wehmeyer (1998a) conceptualized self-determination as follows:

> *a combination of skills, knowledge, and beliefs that enable a person to engage in goal directed, self-regulated, autonomous behavior. An understanding of one's strengths and limitations together with a belief in oneself as capable and effective are essential to self-determination. When acting on the basis of these skills and attitudes, individuals have greater ability to take control of their lives and assume the role of successful adults.*

A recent review of research literature shows that self-advocacy skills and self-awareness are the subsets of self-determination most often taught to individuals with learning disabilities (LD; Algozzine, Browder, Karvonen, Test, & Wood, 2001). Techniques used to promote self-awareness in students with LD often include the use of interest inventories, learning style assessments, and experiential activities designed to allow students to "try out" different activities (e.g., careers), as well as gain knowledge about LD.

Self-advocacy instruction for high school students often focuses on knowledge about rights and responsibilities, effective communication and negotiation skills, identifying and requesting accommodations and modifications, and instruction on participating in and even directing one's own Individualized Education Program (IEP) meeting. Some programs help students generalize their self-advocacy skills and knowledge to other environments, such as college or the workplace.

The next level of self-advocacy for individuals with disabilities is learning to apply those skills to a larger, systemic level: ensuring that society honors the rights of *all* individuals with disabilities. Creating a society that is responsive to the needs and rights of individuals with disabilities requires that self-advocates develop leadership skills, as well as other self-advocacy skills (Field et al., 1998b).

Many resources exist that teachers can use to help students with disabilities develop self-advocacy skills. In a literature review on self-advocacy instruction, Merchant and Gajar (1997) determined that self-advocacy is most often taught through the use of

- role play (Durlack, Rose, & Bursuck, 1994);
- strategies such as I-PLAN (*Inventory* strengths and areas of improvement, *Provide* information, *Listen* and respond, *Ask* questions, *Name* your goals; Van Reusen, Deschler, & Schumaker, 1989); or
- Direct instruction, including a description of the target behavior, demonstration, rehearsal, practice, feedback, and practice in a natural environment.

Numerous published curricula also include lessons that target self-advocacy skills:

- *Self-Directed IEP* (Martin, Marshall, Maxson, & Jerman, 1996);
- *Choicemaker Self-Determination Curriculum Series* (Martin & Marshall, 1995);
- *Next S.T.E.P.* (Halpern, Herr, Wolf, Doren, Johnson, & Lawson, 1997); *Steps to Self-Determination* (Field & Hoffman, 1996);
- *Take Charge for the Future* (Powers et al., 1996); and
- *Whose Future is it Anyway?* (Wehmeyer & Kelchner, 1995).

This article describes a program called Learning and Education About Disabilities (LEAD) implemented in one school district that uses a number of research-supported practices to successfully promote self-advocacy and other self-determination skills for students with LD. LEAD was selected as one of six exemplar sites as part of the Self-Determination Synthesis Project, a comprehensive research synthesis project funded by the Office of Special Education Programs, Department of Education. (More information about the exemplary sites and the entire project is available on the project Web site at http://www.uncc.edu/sdsp)

LEAD

Background

LEAD began in 1996 in response to concerns expressed by high school students with LD. Students and parents had reported that some general education teachers were re-

luctant to provide accommodations and modifications. Some students were having difficulty coping with their disability, and a guidance counselor who worked with several students with LD noticed that they lacked the self-awareness and disability awareness necessary to effectively explain their needs to teachers. The guidance counselor formed a support group with the intent of helping students better understand their learning disabilities and more effectively advocate for their academic needs. Since its inception, the group has grown from 4 to include as many as 17 students each academic year. LEAD participants meet during a class period and receive course credit that counts toward graduation. The group is co-led by the guidance counselor and a special education teacher. While the majority of LEAD students are diagnosed with LD, students with attention deficit disorder and hearing impairments have also been members.

Philosophy and Content

The primary tenet of the LEAD group is that of student ownership. Students determined the group's mission statement, which includes "increasing the level of understanding and awareness of the social, academic, and emotional aspects of learning disabilities.... We focus on not allowing disabilities to become liabilities." The group includes four elected officers who meet weekly to determine the group's upcoming activities. The group's coleaders share the philosophy of student ownership of the educational process and believe in promoting leadership opportunities.

To accommodate the needs of a growing group with varied backgrounds, LEAD now consists of two separate groups: one for ninth graders and one for an advanced group. Both groups have a weekly schedule that includes two days devoted to educational activities, one day for mentoring, and a fourth day for a support group meeting (see Figure 1). All members of both groups participate in community presentations. There is some flexibility in the schedule in order to plan for community presentations and address unexpected issues that arise. Each of the main content areas of LEAD is described in the following sections.

SELF-AWARENESS AND DISABILITY KNOWLEDGE. The LEAD group discovered early that although students had developed an awareness of their feelings about having a learning disability, they did not know themselves educationally. Because self-awareness is a critical foundation for being able to advocate effectively for oneself, the coleaders decided to focus on helping students first become more aware of themselves academically. In order to help students understand themselves better, students' cumulative folders, with IEPs, test results, and other data, became the class's textbook, for use in discussing academic strengths and weaknesses. A psychologist taught

Ninth-grade group				
Monday	**Tuesday**	**Wednesday**	**Thursday**	**Friday**
No class	Education day • The referral process	Support day • Informal discussion led by counselor	Education day • Begin new unit: Evaluation and interpretation of testing	Mentoring • Mentor pairs at other schools

Advanced group				
Monday	**Tuesday**	**Wednesday**	**Thursday**	**Friday**
Officers meet • Plan for next academic year • Plan mentoring activities	Education day • Review video of previous presentation, evaluate performance • Discuss classroom accomodations that can prevent students from needing to go to the resource room	Support day • Informal discussion led by counselor	Education day • Revise community presentation to include more about what LEAD membership entails	Mentoring • Mentor pairs at other schools

Figure 1. Sample week of LEAD activities.

the students about intelligence and achievement testing and how to understand their own IQ test results. Students not only benefited from learning that they were highly intelligent, but they also learned how their learning strengths and weaknesses were reflected in the IQ subtest scores. Students who had also taken personality inventories learned to interpret their information as a means of better understanding their strengths and areas in which they needed support. The unit on the evaluation and interpretation of test data (see sidebar, Sample LEAD Lesson Plan Outline), which spans six class sessions, has been extremely well received by LEAD students and their parents.

Equipped with knowledge about their strengths and needs, LEAD participants decide which additional topics they wish to cover; the coleaders determine how best to deliver the information and promote the related skills. Using a combination of personal knowledge and published resources (e.g., Sousa, 2000), the coleaders have created their own curriculum to include topics such as brain differences, the definition and diagnosis of different types of learning disabilities, accommodations and modification, legal rights under the Individuals with Disabilities Education Act and the Americans with Disabilities Act legislation, facilitating IEP and 504 meetings, learning styles, multiple intelligences, and other similar topics. Adults with LD serve as guest speakers, providing students with information about how they have learned to navigate the adult world.

The disability-related knowledge and self-awareness that LEAD students develop is then used as a basis for their self-advocacy. By knowing what accommodations

or modifications they require, students can brainstorm as a group how to best approach specific teachers with a request for an accommodation. Group members often talk through an entire scenario or use role-playing to practice their self-advocacy skills. One of the group's coleaders often accompanies freshmen on their first visit with a teacher to discuss accommodations. If a request is not successful, the coleaders and group members will help the student develop other ideas for negotiating with the teacher. As students gain experience in negotiating with their teachers, the coleaders remove themselves from those conversations, and the group members serve as a sounding board for problematic requests. The special education teacher who coleads the group works individually with teachers to develop the supports necessary for students' accommodations; however, the students are responsible for negotiating accommodations that do not significantly increase teachers' responsibilities.

LEAD students further refine their communication skills using an exercise in which one of the group's coleaders plays the role of a "non-believer," often a skeptical teacher or community member who claims not to believe in LD or the need for accommodations. In this "devil's advocate" role, the coleaders offer objections, stereotypes, misinterpretations, and other challenges to the students as they develop counterpoints and enhance their ability to articulate their disability. For example, a statement about the students looking "normal, not handicapped" might prompt a response about students' specific learning problems and how they impact the quality of their academic work. The coleader might then make further objections based on the quality of students' responses that then require the students to explain themselves more effectively or add details that they omitted from their previous responses.

SUPPORT GROUP. Through support group meetings, LEAD students discuss the challenges they face in coping with their disabilities. The support group component of LEAD has many of the common characteristics of effective group therapy (Corey & Corey, 1997). Group members provide a level of empathy that they believe individuals without disabilities are incapable of providing. They help each other cope with feelings such as shame and anxiety and build the confidence they need to approach teachers about accommodations. Group members also challenge each other at times when individuals try to hide their disability or do not take opportunities to self-advocate. The group relies less on the coleaders as facilitators for support group discussions compared with educational activities.

COMMUNITY PRESENTATIONS. The LEAD group frequently makes presentations to parents, students, preservice special education teachers, and teachers in nearby school districts. The group has also presented at state and national learning disabilities conferences and to their own high school faculty. The purpose of the presentations is to educate others about learning disabilities, but the scope of each presentation varies according to the audience. For example, group members can respond to questions from teachers about what teachers can do if they suspect a student has a learning disability, or how teachers can help their students become better self-advocates. The sidebar Sample Format of LEAD Group contains a sample format for a presentation to teachers.

Presentations to the business community include general information about young adults with LD and a panel discussion in which business leaders ask students about issues such as disclosure and confidentiality. LEAD participants also ask business representatives about how they compensate for weaknesses and accentuate their strengths in the workplace.

The disability-related knowledge and self-awareness that LEAD students develop is ... used as a basis for their self-advocacy.

One particularly dramatic element of most LEAD presentations is a poem written by one of the LEAD group students (see Figure 2). Audience members are given a handwritten copy [of] the student's first draft of a poem, followed by a later version of that poem after accommodations (e.g., use of computer spelling and grammar check features) were provided. This exercise helps audience members understand how a student with LD views the world; the poem's author speaks about how he real-

izes his mistakes but is unable to correct them. Students typically spend a few minutes during LEAD class prior to each presentation determining the schedule and priorities for that presentation. Continuing the philosophy of student ownership, the group's coleaders do not participate in the planning session, nor do they participate in the presentation itself.

Sample LEAD Lesson Plan Outline: Evaluation and Interpretation of Test Data

Testing background

1. Reliability
2. Validity
3. Percentiles

WJ

1. Subtests
2. What do they measure?
3. How would it apply to school subjects?
4. What do the scores mean?

WISC-III/WAIS-R

1. Full scale score
2. Performance subtests
   • Discussion of each subtest
   • How do the performance subtests indicate strengths and weaknesses?
3. Verbal subtests
4. Discussion of each subtest
5. How do the verbal subtests indicate strengths and weaknesses?

Review of what testing means

1. How important are the tests?
2. Do the tests determine your success or failure?
3. How is eligibility determined?
4. Is it worth the time?
5. Appropriate accommodations based on test data (lead-in to next unit)

Note. WJ = Woodcock-Johnson Psycho-Educational Battery (1977); WISC-III = Wechsler Intelligence Scale for Children–Third Edition (1991); WAIS-R = Wechsler Adult Intelligence Scale–Revised (1981).

Community presentations also serve as teaching opportunities as each presentation is videotaped and reviewed in subsequent LEAD class meetings. Students have an opportunity to critique their performance by identifying the strengths of the presentation, brainstorming ways to more effectively communicate answers to unexpected or complex questions from the audience, and reflecting on things that they wished they had said. Even in those cases where students believe they have answered well, the group reviews segments of the videotape and discusses ways in which they might have made their point more effectively.

MENTORING.   Beginning in LEAD's third year, students decided they wanted to help elementary and middle school students benefit from their own experiences in navigating the educational system. LEAD members worked with coleaders to develop ideas for building rapport with younger students and age-appropriate methods for delivering materials and messages. In the current mentoring approach, two LEAD members, a ninth grader and an upperclassman, are paired with small groups of students with LD in two elementary schools and one middle school.

While mentoring activities initially emphasized structured educational activities about disabilities, LEAD students discovered that a "big sibling" approach was a more effective way to informally educate younger students. Increased emphasis has been placed on building rapport and enhancing younger students' self-esteem. The LEAD mentors meet with younger students for an hour each week at the younger students' assigned schools for conversations about issues raised by the younger students. Mentors take opportunities to normalize the younger children's experiences and point out their strengths in the course of discussion. For example, if an elementary student says he is embarrassed about needing extra help in reading, the mentor might say that she also needed extra help when she was in elementary school, that she was still a "normal" person, and that she was glad she had received help because now she relied on those reading skills in high school. Middle school mentors start talking about the LEAD group in the second semester so that ninth graders can decide whether they want to join the group the next year.

Implementation Issues

Although the LEAD group has enjoyed strong administrative support from the beginning, a few barriers were encountered in the process of starting the LEAD group. The primary difficulty was student scheduling; numerous conflicts made it difficult to find time for the group to meet. Instead of being structured as a club or part-time seminar, the class was turned into a full-time elective course that students could choose as an alternative to other electives often chosen by students with LD.

Another roadblock encountered by LEAD early in the process was the disbelief among some general education teachers that learning disabilities even exist and that LEAD would be a beneficial class. As teachers have retired from the school, students from LEAD have met with the new teachers to help them understand the group's purpose. The emphasis placed on student responsibility for accommodations has also minimized the impact of accommodations on general education teachers' workload, dispelling one of the myths held by some teachers.

Sample Format of LEAD Group Presentation to Teachers

Introduce agenda

Read LEAD mission statement

Definition of learning disability

Individual introductions: name, type of problem or deficit, and a specific area of strength or a skill

Poem (see Figure 2): handout and discussion

Example accommodations

Question and answer session, with group president or leader acting as moderator

Original poem

Aloene loste wakling down the steert of this urben jungele. Whatein fore the love of my life not whet nowen too call me from behinded
It's not no colldnot sher if it day or night just whored wher I an going Alon and lost walking in the erbine jungle on to a road off inlitamet
An intlitament of sperit to become more than it is nowe too grwe past the brondres that logec has in slaved it in.
I her the bet of the stepe as my feet shelf me along the street of the jungle 1, 2, 3 the Bat of the hert as it is awankend with now relization of the futer and the past.
What Ive inconted and hop to incotedr on joner of lefe not wheat past it forst mark of trumph.

Poem with accommodations provided

Alone, lost walking down the streets of this urban jungle
Waiting for the love of my life not yet known
To call me from behind.
It's hot, not cold, and not sure if it's day or night
Just worried where I am going alone and lost.
Walking in the urban jungle on a road to enlightenment.

An enlightenment of the spirit
To become more than it is now.
To grow past the boundaries that logic has enslaved it in.
I hear the beat of the steps as my feet shuffle me along
The streets of the jungle.

One, two, three, the beat of the heart
As it is awakened with new realizations
Of the future and the past.
What I have encountered and hope to encounter on a
    journey of life not yet past its first marker of triumph.

Figure 2. Poem used to illustrate the impact of accommodations on a student's writing.
Used with permission.

Effective Practices

LEAD students, parents, and teachers all agree that LEAD has helped students become effective advocates, both for themselves, as well as all individuals with LD. Some of the critical factors that have helped LEAD be successful follow:

• **INTRODUCING SELF-DETERMINATION COMPONENT SKILLS IN AN EFFECTIVE SEQUENCE.** LEAD students first need to understand their strengths, challenges, learning styles, and interests before explaining them to others. As students become more self-aware, self-advocacy skills such as communication and negotiation are introduced. The additional skills of communicating to large groups and mentoring younger students build upon the LEAD students' earlier self-awareness and self-advocacy skills.

• **MAINTAINING A PHILOSOPHY OF STUDENT OWNERSHIP, WITH AN APPROPRIATE BALANCE OF SUPPORT, GUIDANCE, AND INDEPENDENCE.** Student ownership of the LEAD group's tasks and objectives has been of primary importance since day one. The coleaders help students enhance their self-awareness and self-advocacy skills within the context of the students' interests. At the same time, younger students are not expected to immediately grasp the concepts and develop effective advocacy skills without some guidance and coaching. One of the group's coleaders described the process of transferring ownership to students in the following way:

> For ninth graders, we hold both their hands while they're here. By the time they're in tenth grade we have released one [hand]. By the time they're in eleventh grade we're not holding them anymore. By the time they're in the twelfth grade we're patting them on the back and telling them, 'good luck'.

The LEAD group members have adopted a similar philosophy as they help students in nearby districts develop their own groups. LEAD students do not give the other students the "answers" about what accommodations they can ask for because they believe each student has to determine that for himself or herself.

• **EFFECTIVE MODELING OF SELF-ADVOCACY SKILLS.** Modeling functions in several different ways for LEAD. The group's coleaders, each of whom has a disability, are models for the LEAD students. Within the group, upperclassmen with better-developed self-awareness, leadership, and self-advocacy skills serve as models for the underclassmen. All of the LEAD group members serve as models for the elementary and middle school students that they mentor, as well as for students with LD in their high school who do not participate in LEAD.

• **OPPORTUNITIES FOR IMPROVING SELF-ADVOCACY SKILLS EMBEDDED IN ACTIVITIES OUTSIDE THE CLASSROOM.** When invited to present to the National Learning Disability Association Conference in Washington DC, LEAD participants had to present their plan to the local Board of Education in order to receive approval for the trip. Graduating seniors who expressed interest in attending college visited campuses and talked with representatives from the Disability Services offices. The group's coleaders observed and videotaped these interactions in order to help the students improve their ability to assess the availability of necessary supports at the colleges they were considering. Creativity is required of the group's coleaders as they identify these teachable moments for a group that determines their own curriculum.

• **CREATING A SCHOOL CULTURE THAT SUPPORTS SELF-ADVOCACY.** School and district administrators have become increasingly supportive of LEAD as they have visited with the students during class and observed their presentations to community groups and teachers. The district superintendent became a strong advocate for the group after accompanying them to the conference in Washington DC; now he helps them form relationships with the local business community. The principal's support of the group led him to allow the students to make a presentation to the high school's entire faculty during an inservice day. The group's coleaders also work one-on-one with general education teachers to explore how to support students' self-advocacy and respond to students' requests for accommodations. The special education teacher who coleads the group also coteaches mainstream English classes. The coleader models methods that promote students' self-advocacy within the classroom, and the two teachers have also collaborated to develop instructional methods that benefit students with and without LD. For example, they simultaneously deliver instruction differently based on students' learning styles and allow all students in the class to choose which method they prefer.

Implications for Practitioners

The LEAD group has successfully improved self-awareness, self-advocacy, and leadership skills among high school students with LD and other disabilities. While developing their own skills, they have also had a significant impact on others.

> What I've gotten out of LEAD, out of the kids...is that self-examination, that self-assessment, and it's forced me at 55 years old, I'm sitting down re-looking at my strengths and weaknesses through the eyes that they look at themselves with—through tough eyes. (School District Superintendent)

The students in LEAD have raised the community's consciousness about individuals with LD and helped younger students understand their own disabilities and how they can affect their educational experiences.

Implementing this innovative program has required ambition and creativity on the part of the students and coleaders, and support from administrators and parents. Students who participate in LEAD must have some degree of willingness to be open and acknowledge that they have a disability for the supportive and educational parts of the program to be effective. Even without all of these successful elements in place, certain parts of LEAD could apply to any program designed to enhance students' self-advocacy skills. Changes to the LEAD group structure and content could be modified depending on the students who participate. The LEAD group students expressed a definite bias against using prepared lesson plans and published curricula, but students at other schools may be more comfortable with the use of formal instructional materials. LEAD students have decided to write one participant's 504 Plan as a group; the same exercise could be used to help members develop their IEPs. Younger students who enter LEAD with less knowledge about learning disabilities could participate in a semester-long, intensive education component before integrating fully with the older students. The leadership structure of the LEAD group could also be adapted from a traditional four-officer structure to one based on the group's functions to allow students the opportunity to assume leadership roles within the group.

Although it may be challenging for educators to allow students to have control over the curriculum, student-directed work on self-awareness, leadership, and self-advocacy will ultimately be more effective in promoting those skills than will teachers providing instruction in what they *presume* to be students' needs. Teachers can still determine how to deliver instruction based on students' self-identified needs and preferences. Ultimately, LEAD has succeeded in helping students develop not only the critical skills of self-advocacy and self-awareness, but also fostering an altruistic philosophy that, when combined with leadership skills, can be effective in changing society's views of individuals with LD.

ABOUT THE AUTHORS

Al Pocock, MA, has been a special education teacher at Cheyenne Mountain High School for 19 years. **Stan Lambros**, MEd, is a counselor at Cheyenne Mountain High School in Colorado Springs, Colorado. He has been counseling students for 15 years, including 7 years in the school setting. **Meagan Karvonen**, MA, is the coordinator of the Self-Determination Synthesis Project. Her research interests include school-based health and mental health intervention, and self-determination. **David W. Test**, PhD, is a professor and graduate coordinator for the Special Education Program at UNC Charlotte. His research interests include transition, promoting self-determination, and applied behavior analysis. **Bob Algozzine**, PhD, is a professor in the Department of Educational Administration, Research, and Technology at UNC Charlotte. His recent research has been published in the *High School Journal*, the *Journal of Educational Research*, and *Teacher Education and Special Educa-*

tion. **Wendy Wood**, PhD, is an assistant professor of special education at UNC Charlotte. Her interests include self-determination, supported employment, and transition. **James E. Martin**, PhD, is the Zarrow Endowed Professor in Special Education and director of the Zarrow Center for Learning Enrichment at the University of Oklahoma. He is a co-developer of the *ChoiceMaker Self-Determination Curriculum Series* and author of many articles on self-determination. Address: David W. Test, Special Education Program, UNC Charlotte, 9201 University City Blvd., Charlotte, NC 28223-0001; e-mail: dwtest@email.uncc.edu

AUTHORS' NOTES

1. The LEAD Group at Cheyenne Mountain High School was one of six exemplar sites nationwide identified and studied as part of the Self-Determination Synthesis Project (SDSP). The SDSP is a research synthesis project conducted with support from the U.S. Department of Education, Office of Special Education Programs (Grant No. H324D980069), awarded to the University of North Carolina at Charlotte. The opinions expressed do not necessarily reflect the position or policy of the Department of Education, and no official endorsement should be inferred.

2. For more information about LEAD, contact Cheyenne Mountain High School at 719/475-6110.

3. The authors wish to thank Diane Browder for her comments on an earlier version of this manuscript.

REFERENCES

Algozzine, R. F., Browder, D. B., Karvonen, M., Test, D. W., & Wood, W. M. (2001). Effects of self-determination interventions on individuals with disabilities. *Review of Educational Research, 71*(2), 49–108.

Corey, M. S., & Corey, G. (1997). *Groups: Process and practice* (5th ed.). Pacific Grove, CA: Brooks/Cole.

Durlak, C. M., Rose, E., & Bursuck, W. D. (1994). Preparing high school students with learning disabilities for the transition to post-secondary education: Teaching the skills of self-determination. *Journal of Learning Disabilities, 27*, 51–59.

Field, S., & Hoffman, A. (1996). *Steps to self-determination.* Austin: PRO-ED.

Field, S., Martin, J., Miller, R., Ward, M., & Wehmeyer, M. (1998a). *A practical guide to teaching self-determination.* Reston, VA: Council for Exceptional Children.

Field, S., Martin, J., Miller, R., Ward, M., & Wehmeyer, M. (1998b). Self-determination for persons with disabilities: A position statement of the division on career development and transition. *Career Development for Exceptional Individuals, 21*, 113–128.

Halpern, A. S., Herr, C. M., Wolf, N. K., Doren, B., Johnson, M. D., & Lawson, J. D. (1997). *Next S.T.E.P.: Student transition and educational planning.* Austin: PRO-ED.

Martin, J. E., & Marshall, L. H. (1995). Choicemaker: A comprehensive self-determination transition program. *Intervention in School and Clinic, 30*, 147–156.

Martin, J. E., Marshall, L. H., Maxson, L., & Jerman, P. (1996). *Self-directed IEP.* Longmont, CO: Sopris West.

Merchant, D. J., & Gajar, A. (1997). A review of literature on self-advocacy components in transition programs for students with learning disabilities. *Journal of Vocational Rehabilitation, 8*, 223–231.

Powers, L. E., Sowers, J., Turner, A., Nesbitt, M., Knowles, A., & Ellison, R. (1996). TAKE CHARGE: A model for promoting self-determination among adolescents with challenges. In L. E. Powers, G. H. S. Singer, & J. Sowers (Eds.), *On the road* to autonomy: *Promoting self-competence for children and youth with disabilities* (pp. 291–322). Baltimore: Brookes.

Sousa, D. A. (2000). *How the brain learns: A classroom teacher's guide* (2nd ed.). Thousand Oaks, CA: Corwin.

Van Reusen, A. K., Deshler, D. D., & Schumaker, J. B. (1989). Effects of a student participation strategy in facilitating the involvement of adolescents with learning disabilities in the Individualized Education Program planning process. *Learning Disabilities, 1*(2), 23–34.

Ward, M. J., & Kohler, P. D. (1996). Teaching self-determination: Content and process. In L. E. Powers, G. H. S. Singer, & J. Sowers (Eds.), *On the road to autonomy: Promoting self-competence for children and youth with disabilities* (pp. 275–290). Baltimore: Brookes.

Wechsler, D. (1981). *Wechsler adult intelligence scale—Revised.* San Antonio, TX: Psychological Corp.

Wechsler, D. (1991). *Wechsler intelligence scale for children—Third edition.* San Antonio, TX: Psychological Corp.

Wehmeyer, M. L., & Kelchner, K. (1995). *Whose future is it anyway?* Arlington, TX: The Arc of the United States.

Wehmeyer, M. L., & Schwartz, M. (1997). Self-determination and positive adult outcomes: A follow up study of youth with mental retardation or learning disabilities. *Exceptional Children, 63,* 245–255.

Wehmeyer, M. L., & Schwartz, M. (1998). The relationship between self-determination and quality of life for adults with mental retardation. *Education and Training in Mental Retardation and Developmental Disabilities, 33,* 3–12.

Woodcock, R. W., & Johnson, W. B. (1977). *Woodcock-Johnson psycho-educational battery.* Allen, TX: DLM Teaching Resources.

Don't Water Down!
ENHANCE

Content Learning Through the Unit Organizer Routine

If it weren't for students impeding our progress in our race to the end of the term, we could certainly be sure of covering the material. The question, however, is not whether we as teachers can get to the end of the text or the end of the term, but whether our students are with us on that journey.

(P. Cross, personal communication, 1994)

Daniel J. Boudah • B. Keith Lenz • Janis A. Bulgren • Jean B. Schumaker • Donald D. Deshler

These remarks are an accurate and thoughtful response to some of the greatest challenges facing secondary teachers today as they attempt to meet their students' needs.

- The volume of information teachers are expected to teach is expanding dramatically, while the amount of instructional time remains constant.
- The community's expectations for improved student performance on local, state, and national competency exams are constantly increasing.
- Much of the information teachers are expected to teach is extremely complex, abstract, and often of little interest to students.
- Today's classes are becoming increasingly diverse and frequently include students who are high, average, and low achieving, as well as students who are considered gifted, students with disabilities, and those who are at risk for school failure. Thus, meeting the varying needs of students from each of these groups while fulfilling the other

demands related to content coverage poses an enormous task for the secondary classroom teacher.

To meet these challenges, we need instructional techniques that do not simply water down content learning, but are effective—and also acceptable to both teachers and students. This article translates one research-based teaching technique into practice. We describe and illustrate the instructional procedures, offer practical tips, and cite additional resources to support teachers.

Content Enhancement and the Unit Organizer Routine

Content Enhancement is a strategic approach to planning for and teaching content to academically diverse groups of students. It involves making decisions about what content to emphasize in teaching, transforming that content into learner-friendly formats, and presenting this content in memorable ways. In short, through

application of sound instructional principles and techniques, teachers can enrich the learning of all students without sacrificing important content. Moreover, teachers carry out instruction in an engaging partnership with students.

We have developed and validated several Content Enhancement instructional techniques, or "routines," in cooperation with teachers (e.g., Bulgren, Schumaker, & Deshler, 1993; Lenz, Marrs, Schumaker, & Deshler, 1993). These routines are commercially available with training (see "Additional Resources"). One Content Enhancement routine is called the Unit Organizer Routine. This routine focuses on how a teacher introduces, builds, and gains closure on the critical ideas and information in a content area unit. A unit is any "chunk" of content that a teacher selects to organize information into lessons and that ends in some type of test or closure activity. Typically, a content area course (e.g., science, history, math, English) is divided into several such units that may or may not conform to the organization of a textbook. Teachers and students often benefit from use of a routine designed to organize and enhance understanding of these chunks of content information.

The Unit Organizer Routine can help teachers plan for, introduce, and build a unit so that *all* students can do the following:

- Understand how the unit is part of bigger course ideas or a sequence of units.
- Understand the "gist" or central idea regarding the unit through a meaningful paraphrase of the unit title.
- See a structure or organization of the critical unit information.
- Define the relationships associated with critical information.
- Generate and answer questions regarding key unit information.
- Monitor their progress and accomplishments in learning.
- Keeping the "big ideas" and structure of the unit in mind as they learn the unit content.

In general, teachers can use the Unit Organizer to help students understand where they have been, where they are, and where they are going on their journey through the content.

The Unit Organizer enables teachers to present the content of a unit in an interactive way to students.

To introduce and teach the information in a unit, teachers use a visual device, called the *Unit Organizer*. During the interactive presentation of the Unit Organizer, teachers follow a set of instructional steps, called *Linking Steps*, that are imbedded within an instructional sequence—the *Cue-Do-Review Sequence*. Thus, successful use of the Unit Organizer Routine is based on three critical components: the Unit Organizer device, the instructional Linking Steps, and the Cue-Do-Review Sequence.

The Unit Organizer Device

To help teachers present their "vision" of a unit's information, they can use a visual device, called the Unit Organizer. Serving as the "centerpiece" of the Unit Organizer Routine, the Unit Organizer graphically organizes and depicts the content of the unit and related information.

The Unit Organizer consists of two pages:

- Page 1 presents an overall organization for the unit information, relationships, questions, and tasks.
- Page 2 provides an ongoing structure for effective note-taking.

Typically, the teacher and students construct Page 1 together at the introduction of a unit, when they simultaneously construct information on blank Unit Organizer forms. Figures 1 and 2 show templates for Pages 1 and 2, respectively; Figures 3 and 4 show examples of the completed pages. As the teacher and the students progress through the unit, they co-construct Page 2 as they add and connect relevant and important details that support the key information presented on Page 1.

The completed examples in Figure 3 and 4 show what the teacher and students created for a unit on the causes of the Civil War in a high school U.S. history class. As illustrated, a Unit Organizer does not depend on a textbook. Teachers and students can use the device to tie together information in a unit for which there is no textbook or to pull multiple textbook sections, chapters, or sources together to create a unit.

The Unit Organizer Sections

Each section of the Unit Organizer contains a specific type of information related to the unit.

1. *Current Unit.* In this section, students write the title of the new unit. This may be the name of the section of a textbook on which you are basing the unit or the name you give the unit. In Figure 3, the name of the current unit is "Causes of the Civil War."

2. *Last Unit/Experience.* The information in this space includes the name of the last unit that was covered or the last experience the students had relating to the current unit. In Figure 3, the name of the last unit was "Growth of the Nation."

3. *Next Unit/Experience.* In this section, students write the name of the unit or experience that will follow the cur-

rent unit. In Figure 3, the name of the next unit is "The Civil War."

4. *The Bigger Picture.* This section contains the name of the theme of larger category that holds several units together. In general, the name of this section, "The Bigger Picture," helps students understand how multiple units are related. In Figure 3, for example, the theme or larger category into which the last, current, and next units fit is "The Roots and Consequences of Civil Unrest."

5. *Unit Map.* The unit map—the heart of the Unit Organizer—includes two sources of information, as follows:

Unit Paraphrase—a "gist" statement, written in the oval at the top of the map, along with the page numbers of the text related to it. The unit paraphrase captures the central point or meaning of the current unit. Students write this paraphrase in words that they can easily understand and relate to, or as in the Figure 3 example, in words that reveal the central meaning of the unit title. Students can use a horizontal dotted line to separate the paraphrase from the text page numbers where they can find relevant information. In Figure 3, the unit paraphrase translates the name of the current unit, "Causes of the Civil War," into the central idea of "Sectionalism."

Graphic Organizer—a type of flow chart or "semantic" map showing the organization of the unit content. Students write key words within geometric shapes, such as ovals, to indicate the parts of the unit to be learned. In Figure 3, the unit map illustrates the four parts of the unit on the Civil War; "Areas of the U.S.," "Differences Between the Areas," "Events in the U.S.," and "Leaders Across the U.S." As a rule, the unit map should include no more than seven parts.

Within the unit map, students should draw lines between the geometric shapes and the unit paraphrase and include "line labels" on each line to indicate the relationships between the parts and the main idea of the unit. Students write the line labels in such a way that the words in the unit paraphrase, the line label, and the words in a connected geometric shape then form a complete sentence. The lines and line labels are critical elements in the map that help students understand how the parts of the unit are connected or related. When you include lines and line labels, you enable students to remember substantially more about unit information (Novak & Gowin, 1984).

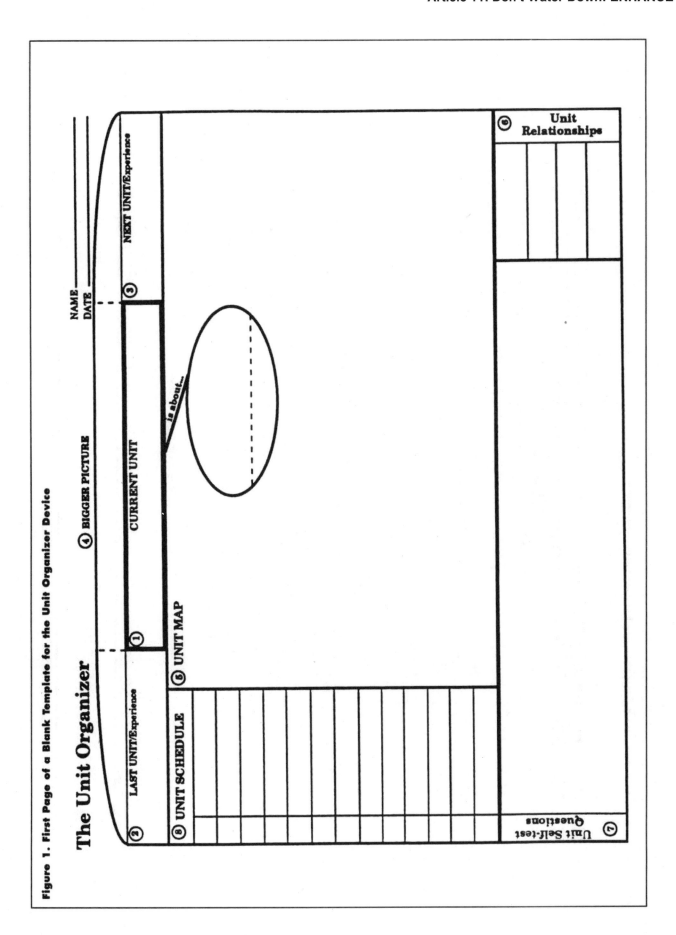

Figure 1. First Page of a Blank Template for the Unit Organizer Device

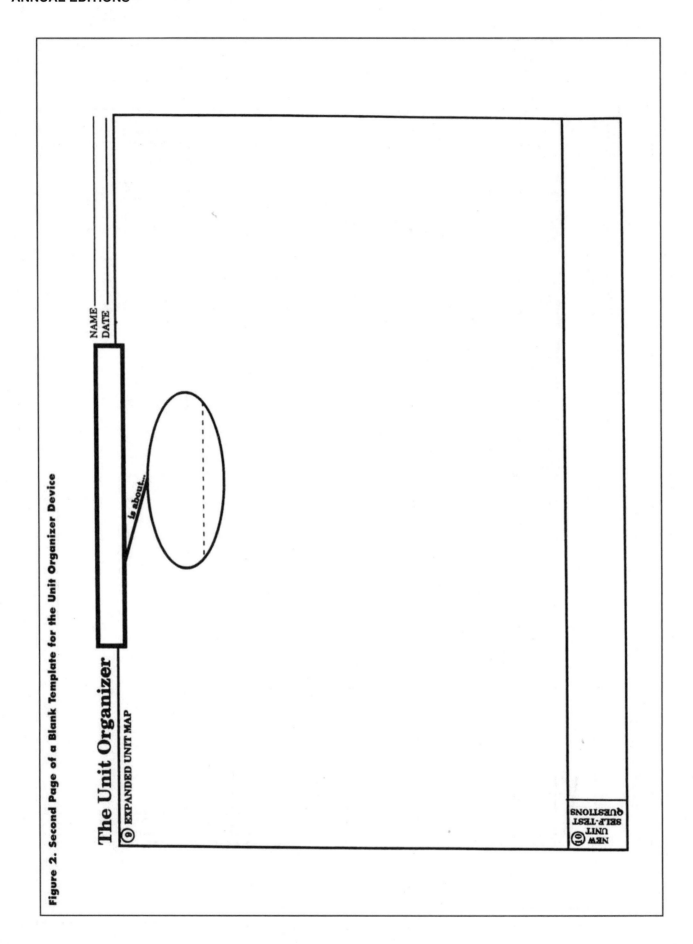

Figure 2. Second Page of a Blank Template for the Unit Organizer Device

Figure 3. First Page of a Completed Unit Organizer Device

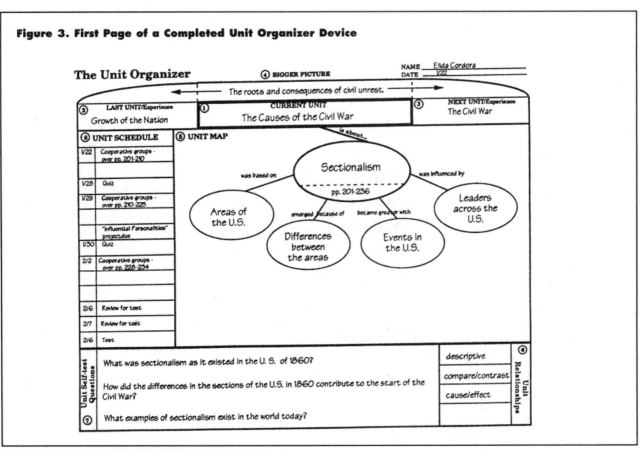

Figure 4. Second Page of a Completed Unit Organizer Device

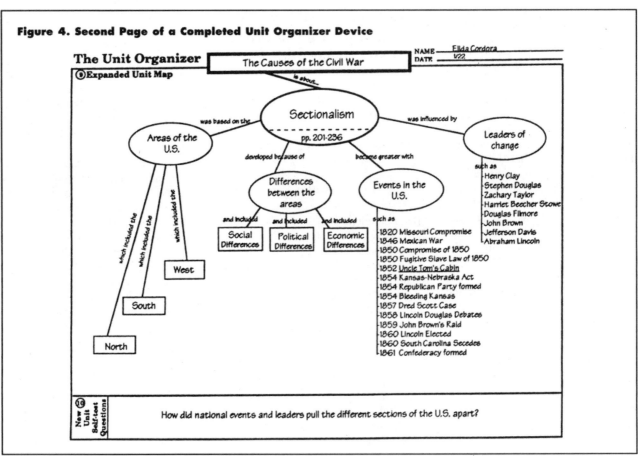

6. *Unit Relationships.* Students use this section to write the names of relationships that might be important to look for and the kinds of thinking required to learn the unit information. In Figure 3, for example, the teacher and students noted that the various areas of the nation must be described and then compared and contrasted to understand how their differences led to the Civil War.

7. *Unit Self-Test Questions.* Students use this section to generate and write questions related to different parts of the unit that they should be able to answer when the unit is complete. Later, when preparing for the unit test, students can ask themselves these questions to review the content of the unit. Figure 3 shows one of the questions that students generated about the Civil War: "What was sectionalism as it existed in the U.S. of 1860?"

8. *Unit Schedule.* The information in this section summarizes the schedule of required tasks, activities, or assignments that students must complete during the course of the unit. In this section, students write down their list of projects, homework assignments, and tests, rather than lesson topics for the unit. Figure 3, for example, shows dates in the square boxes and associated tasks and assignments in the adjacent rectangular boxes. Students should leave spaces in the schedule for items you or the students decide to add later during the unit.

9. *Expanded Unit Map.* After you introduce the unit, and you and your students complete the first page of the Unit Organizer, you can use the second page throughout and at the end of the unit to expand the unit map by adding critical subtopics, details, and key vocabulary in note form. Together, you and your students can identify and add these details daily to the expanded unit map as extensions of the original parts of the map. Students can use the expanded map as a note-taking device during daily lessons or during review at the end of each lesson. Figure 4 shows the expanded unit map for the unit on the "Causes of the Civil War."

10. *New Unit Self-Test Questions.* Use the space below the expanded unit map to write questions that you and your students identify as you explore the unit. For example, Figure 4 shows a question the teacher and students added to the expanded unit map: "How did national

events and leaders pull the different sections of the U.S. apart?"

Content Enhancement involves making decisions about what content to emphasize in teaching, transforming that content into learner-friendly formats, and presenting this content in memorable ways.

An Abbreviated Example of How to Use the Unit Organizer Routine

Using the Cue-Do-Review sequence (see box, above), lead students through the content of the unit by engaging them in the Unit Organizer Routine.

Cue

Hand out blank copies of the Unit Organizer device and explain that the class will be beginning a new unit, using the Unit Organizer. Show a blank Unit Organizer on an overhead projector and explain that you will complete that one as students complete their own. This should take only a few minutes. In addition, the first time the Unit Organizer is used, spend a few minutes talking about what it means to be organized at home, organized with schoolwork in a binder, and then talk about the value of the Unit Organizer for organizing class information. Each subsequent time that a Unit Organizer is used, it would still be valuable to review the benefits of using

the device and your expectations for student participation.

Do

Engage students in completing the Unit Organizer, using a set of Linking Steps. Linking Steps refer to the procedures a teacher uses to present the content of a unit in an interactive way to students. Linking Steps guide the way the Unit Organizer is used when introducing the unit (using Page 1 of the Unit Organizer), expanding the unit (using the Expanded Unit Organizer), and gaining closure on the unit. Although it would take less time to simply tell students what to write in each of the sections of the Unit Organizer, prompt student responses with questions that will enable them to actively use the device and will enhance their learning at each step.

First, help students to see the overall context of the unit and how the new unit is related to previous and future learning. Ask students to recall the name of the previous unit, prompt them to look at a text for the name of the current unit, and hypothesize the name of the next unit. Then ask them how the three units fit together, what they have in common, or the name of a larger category to which they might belong. Students seldom may be asked to think and respond to questions at that level, but even upper elementary students are able to provide reasonable responses when asked. With any group of students, it may be necessary to paraphrase a student's response to clarify the bigger picture. Complete Sections 1–4 of the Unit Organizer at this step when introducing the unit, and review the information in these sections at unit closure.

Second, discuss and complete information in the Unit Map in order to help students identify and see the structure of main ideas or parts of the unit. If a major part of the unit includes a textbook chapter, ask students to survey the chapter for major headings, discuss probable main ideas, and then write them on the Unit Map in Section 5 of the Unit Organizer. For younger students and for the benefit of those with poor motor skills, help students by showing them how to map out (i.e., draw) the total number of ovals or shapes that correspond to the number of main ideas that will be present on the completed Unit Map. Do so before discussing and writing the names of the main ideas in the ovals. Also, don't forget to include the lines and line labels! Throughout daily lessons in the unit, connect critical details and information to the

Cue It! Do It! Review It!

A Cue-Do-Review sequence is a simple formula for making the most of the Unit Organizer Routine (or any instructional strategy). You can use it to focus students' attention on the Unit Organizer device, implement the device, and check student understanding. Mark Twain might have referred to this as "You tell 'em what you're gonna tell 'em. You tell 'em. And you tell 'em what you told 'em." Here's how it works:

1. **Provide a "Cue."** As with any instructional device (e.g., globe, video, role play activity, graphic organizer), you will enhance students' understanding by (a) directing their attention to the device and explaining what it is (if it is not already obvious), (b) explaining your expectations, and (c) showing how using the device will help students succeed.

2. **In the "Do" step,** use a set of Linking Steps for (a) introducing, (b) using and expanding, and (c) gaining closure on a unit with the Unit Organizer.

3. **In the "Review" step,** use a simple review to check and clarify student understanding of information discussed, as well as the process for using the Unit Organizer.

---

main ideas on the Expanded Unit Map in Section 9. Review the information in both sections at unit closure.

Within the unit map, you should draw lines between the geometric shapes and the unit paraphrase and include "line labels" on each line to indicate the relationships between the parts and the main idea of the unit.

Third, after students see how the critical parts of the unit are structured, ask them to discuss and identify possible relationships or kinds of thinking required to understand the information in the main parts of the unit. Prompt students to analyze the Unit Map, the main ideas contained in it, and the relationships among the main ideas, and their relation to the Unit Paraphrase. Using the completed example in Figure 3, ask questions such as "We have one main

idea regarding the sections of the country. On a test, what might you be asked to do? How might you be asked to think about that information?" Write these unit relationships in Section 6 of the Unit Organizer when the unit is introduced, and be sure to review them at the end of the unit.

Fourth, prompt students to create some good questions that correspond to the different parts of the unit map and unit context. For a moment, students can pretend that they are the teacher and select test questions. Work with students to make sure that critical questions related to mastery of the content are included and recorded in Section 7 of the device. The Unit Relationships also may be clarified at this step as students recognize the kinds of thinking that are required (e.g., listing, explaining, comparing, predicting) to address the questions that they write.

As an alternative, some teachers have found it beneficial to write the Unit Self-Test Questions in Section 7 before analyzing the Unit Relationships in Section 6 because the latter step is less difficult for many students if the self-test questions can be identified first. For example, after writing the questions, some teachers prompt students to identify whether certain questions would require students to compare, explain, name, or problem-solve, or use other thinking skills, and then write students' responses into the Unit Relationships section.

As the unit progresses, record new questions in Section 10. Review the questions from Section 7 of the Unit Organizer and, later, from Section 10 of the Expanded Unit Organizer throughout the unit and at the end of the unit, before any test.

Finally, describe and create the list of assignments and due dates to assist stu-

dents in planning for, managing, and completing tasks and assignments related to the current unit. Prompt students to write these assignments in Section 8 of the Unit Organizer when the unit is introduced. Be sure to review the list throughout the unit.

Using the Unit Organizer, teachers ask students to discuss and identify possible relationships or kinds of thinking required to understand the information in the main parts of the unit.

When co-constructing the first page of the Unit Organizer device at the beginning of a new unit, the "Do" step may take an entire class period (i.e., 45–55 minutes) or more depending on student discussion and content difficulty.

Review

After introducing the unit, after adding daily information in the Expanded Unit

Organizer, and at the closure of a unit, it is important to check student understanding. After co-constructing the Unit Organizer at the beginning of a unit, take a few minutes to review the information contained in all eight parts of the device. Ask questions like these:

- What's the name of the new unit?
- What's another way of writing the name of the unit?
- How many main parts are there in the unit?
- What questions should we be able to answer by the time we finish the unit?
- What process did we go through to really understand this unit?
- When is your test?

Also, ask students to describe how the Unit Organizer helped them to learn.

The Unit Organizer Routine can provide a powerful and effective way for teachers to plan for and teach students with and without disabilities, in content area classes.

Tips, Suggestions, and Modifications

Planning Tips

First, when you are ready to use The Unit Organizer Routine, begin by selecting one class in which to try it out—perhaps your least demanding class in terms of diversity or classroom management. Also consider beginning with a unit that is fairly uncomplicated or one that includes more concrete information rather than more abstract information. For instance, a unit on mammals might be a better place to start than a unit on photosynthesis.

Second, collect the materials you plan to use in your unit, such as slides and textbooks.

Third, always construct a draft of the Unit Organizer device before introducing it to the class. The Unit Organizer truly does work well as a planning routine as well as a teaching routine. In fact, the first time you plan while using the Unit Organizer, you may find that it takes some extra time because you might realize ways to better organize unit information that you may have presented many times before.

Logistical Suggestions

When you are ready to introduce a new unit with the Unit Organizer, consider these suggestions:

- Copy and distribute to students two-sided copies of the Unit Organizer device with the main Unit Organizer on one side and the Expanded Unit Organizer on the second side.
- Cue students to take notes on the Unit Organizer.
- Use fine- or extra-fine-tip overhead transparency pens to add information to the Unit Organizer during presentations.
- Construct the Expanded Unit Map using different geometric shapes (e.g., ovals for main ideas, squares for first level details, and triangles for less important details).
- Vary the colors in construction of the Expanded Unit Map to reflect different levels of information of detail.
- When co-constructing the Expanded Unit Map with students, use "Inspiration" software, from Inspiration Software, Inc., to quickly and neatly lay out the critical and connected details with the use of technology.

Ideas for Modifications

In addition, consider these modifications for students with disabilities and others who are low achieving:

- Rather than constructing a Unit Organizer on an overhead projector, enlarge the device and create a laminated copy to post on the wall and construct it there.
- Create a blank Unit Organizer on a bulletin board, cut out geometric shapes from construction paper, and tack them up on the bulletin board to display unit information.
- Draw empty geometric shapes on a Unit Organizer or partially complete

the Unit Organizer before copying for students.
- Enlarge the Unit Organizer onto legal size (8"x14") paper for students to complete.
- As a review activity before a test, hand out 3"x5" index cards or colored Post-Its or "sticky notes" to small groups of students and prompt them to reconstruct the organization of unit main ideas and details on poster paper, as well as draw in the lines and line labels.

Students can pretend that they are the teacher for a moment and select test questions.

Assessment Considerations

When you are ready to assess student learning at the end of a unit, be sure that your test reflects the emphasis of your Unit Organizer and its sections. In other words, if you have previously used a particular unit test with the same unit in previous school years, evaluate the test to see whether the big ideas are emphasized over the smaller ones. Construct and weight test items that assess understanding of big ideas rather than rote recall of details. More specifically, consider including questions that relate to explaining the unit map and the relationships among critical pieces of information.

Final Thoughts

Research on the Unit Organizer Routine (Lenz, Schumaker, et al., 1993) has shown that teacher planning was enhanced and the performance of low-achieving students, students with learning disabilities, and average-achieving students improved substantially in regard to understanding and retaining information. In fact, the students of teachers who use the routine regularly and consistently scored an average of 15 percentage points higher on unit tests than did students of teachers who used it only irregularly (see box, "Research Supporting the Unit Organizer Routine").

Research Supporting the Unit Organizer Routine

Researchers conducted a study of the Unit Organizer Routine (Lenz, Schumaker, et al., 1993) in the U.S. Midwest across three high school and three middle school general education classrooms identified as being inclusive by the school district. The researchers collected data intensively through the use of single-subject, multiple-baseline designs on two high-achieving, two average-achieving, two low-achieving, and two students classified as having a learning disability. The researchers collected student performance data over a 7-month period.

Research has shown that use of the Unit Organizer Routine enhanced teacher planning and the performance of low-achieving students, students with learning disabilities, and average-achieving students. These students substantially improved their understanding and retention of information. In fact, among these groups, the students of teachers who used the routine *regularly* and consistently scored an average of 15 percentage points higher on unit tests than did students of teachers who used it only *irregularly*.

Teachers also reported that the Unit Organizer Routine helped those students with language problems and whose first language was not English acquire secondary content. Although the overall performance of high-achieving students did not substantially increase in these studies, the researchers observed increases in performance when the content became more difficult and abstract for individual students. Since the original study was conducted, teachers in many culturally and geographically diverse communities throughout the United States have replicated the results.

Teachers and students who achieve these kinds of results are truly winners. This winning attitude was expressed by one teacher who said, "Focusing on the 'big idea' questions enables me to think more clearly about what are the tools or things I can give students to have them see the patterns" (V. Arndt Helgesen, personal communication, 1993). Thus, the Unit Organizer Routine can provide a powerful and effective way for teachers to plan for and teach students with and without disabilities in content area classes because it focuses on quality rather than simply on quantity. Together, teachers and students can more successfully navigate each unit journey from beginning to end without watering down the learning outcomes.

References

Bulgren, J. A., Schumaker, J. B., & Deschler, D. D. (1993). *The concept mastery routine*. Lawrence, KS: Edge Enterprises.

Lenz, B. K., Marrs, R. W., Schumaker, J. B., & Deshler, D. D. (1993). *The lesson organizer routine*. Lawrence, KS: Edge Enterprises.

Lenz, B. K., Schumaker, J. B., Deshler, D. D., Boudah, D. J., Vance, M., Kissam, B., Bulgren, J. A., & Roth, J. (1993). *The unit planning routine: A guide for inclusive planning* (Research Report). Lawrence, KS: University of Kansas Center for Research on Learning.

Novak, J. D., & Gowin, D. B. (1984). *Learning how to learn*. New York: Cambridge University Press.

Daniel J. Boudah (*CEC Texas Federation*), *Assistant Professor, Department of Educational Psychology, Special Education Programs, Texas A&M University, College Station.* **B. Keith Lenz** (*CEC Chapter #665*), *Senior Research Scientist;* **Janis A. Bulgren** (*CEC Chapter #665*), *Senior Research Scientist;* **Jean B. Schumaker** (*CEC Chapter #665*), *Associate Director; and* **Donald D. Deshler** (*CEC Chapter #436*), *Director, Center for Research on Learning, University of Kansas, Lawrence.*

Address correspondence to Daniel J. Boudah, Department of Educational Psychology, Special Education Programs, Texas A&M University, 704 Harrington Education Center, College Station, TX 77843-4225 (e-mail: boudah@acs.tamu.edu).

Additional Resources

Lenz, B. K., Bulgren, J. A., Schumaker, J. B., Deshler, D. D., & Boudah, D. J. (1994). *The unit organizer routine*. Lawrence, KS: Edge Enterprises.

This teacher manual, as well as others in the Content Enhancement Series, are available with training. For more information, contact Janet Roth at The University of Kansas, Center for Research on Learning, 3061 Dole Building, Lawrence, KS 66045. Phone: 785-864-4790; e-mail: JRoth@quest.sped.ukans.edu

UNIT 4

Speech and Language Impairments

Unit Selections

12. **For the Love of Language**, Geoffrey Cowley
13. **Language Differences or Learning Difficulties**, Spencer J. Salend and AltaGracia Salinas
14. **Young African American Children With Disabilities and Augmentative and Alternative Communication Issues**, Phil Parette, Mary Blake Huer, and Toya A. Wyatt

Key Points to Consider

- What is specific language impairment (SLI)? How can a teacher assist in language acquisition?

- How can a multidisciplinary team help prevent the overassignment of linguistically diverse children to communication disordered placements? How can assessment tools be selected and adapted for sensitivity to cross-cultural perspectives?

- Why is cultural sensitivity important to speech/language clinicians who work with clients from diverse backgrounds? What is the importance of family involvement to the success of augmentative and alternative communication?

 Links: www.dushkin.com/online/
These sites are annotated in the World Wide Web pages.

Issues in Emergent Literacy for Children With Language Impairments
http://www.ciera.org/library/reports/inquiry-2/2-002/2-002.html

Speech and Language Disorders Fact Sheet
http://www.nichcy.org/pubs/factshe/fs11txt.htm

Speech Disorders WWW Sites
http://www.socialnet.lu/handitel/wwwlinks/dumb.html

Speech and language impairments, although grouped together as a category of disability by the IDEA (Individuals with Disabilities Education Act), are not synonymous. Language refers to multiple ways to communicate (by writing, signing, body, or voice), whereas speech refers to vocal articulation.

Many children have difficulty learning to read because of speech and/or language impairments. If they cannot receive language and/or express speech sounds correctly, the total lexicon makes less sense. Likewise, some children assessed as dyslexic (difficulty with the lexicon) are reading disabled primarily because of their disorders with speech and/or language. Teas-

ing these disorders apart can be challenging. Learning to communicate may also be difficult for children with hearing impairments, developmental disorders, some physical disorders (e.g., cerebral palsy) and some emotional disorders (e.g., elective mutism).

Speech is the vocal utterance of language. It is considered disordered in three underlying ways: voice, articulation, and fluency. Voice involves coordinated efforts by the lungs, larynx, vocal cords, and nasal passages to produce recognizable sounds. Voice can be considered disordered if it is incorrectly phonated (breathy, strained, husky, hoarse) or if it is incorrectly resonated through the nose (hyper-nasality, hypo-nasality). Articulation involves the use of the tongue, lips, teeth, and mouth to produce recognizable sounds. Articulation can be considered disordered if sounds are mispronounced, or if sounds are added, omitted, or substituted for other sounds, such as using the z sound for the s sound or w for l.

Fluency involves appropriate pauses and hesitations to keep speech sounds recognizable. Fluency can be considered disordered if sounds are very rapid with extra sounds (cluttered) or if sounds are blocked or repeated, especially at the beginning of words. Stuttering is an example of a fluency disorder of speech.

Language is the rule-based use of voice sounds, symbols, gestures, or signs to communicate. Language problems refer to the use of such devices in combinations and patterns that fail to communicate, fail to follow the arbitrary rules for that language, or lead to a delay in the use of communication devices relative to normal development in other areas (physical, cognitive, social).

The prevalence rates of speech and language disorders are higher than the rates for any other condition of disability in primary school. The exact extent of the problem, however, has been questioned because assessment of communication takes a variety of forms. Shy children may be diagnosed with delayed language. Bilingual or multilingual children are often mislabeled as having a language disorder because they come from linguistically and culturally diverse backgrounds. Many bilingual children do not need the special services provided by speech/language clinicians but do benefit from instruction in English as a second language.

All children with language or speech disorders are entitled to assessment and remediation as early in life as the problem is realized. Because children's speech is not well developed between birth and age 3, most disorders are not assessed until preschool. Students with speech/language disorders are entitled to a free and appropriate education in the least restrictive environment possible and to transitional help into the world of work, if needed, after their education is completed.

Disordered language is usually more difficult to remedy than delayed language. Disordered language may be due to a receptive problem (difficulty understanding voice sounds), an expressive problem (difficulty producing the voice sounds that follow the arbitrary rules for that language), or both. Language disorders include aphasia (no language) and dysphasia (difficulty producing language). Many language disorders are the result of a difficulty in understanding the syntactical rules and structural principles of the language (form), or of a difficulty in perceiving the semantic meanings of the words of the language (content).

Many language disorders are also due to a difficulty in using the language pragmatically, in a practical context (function).

Most speech and language impairments are remediated between elementary school and high school. An exception to this is speech problems that persist due to physical impairments such as damage or dysfunction of lungs, larynx, vocal cords, or nasal passages. Another exception is language problems that persist due to concurrent disabilities such as deafness, autism, compromised mentation, traumatic brain injuries, or some emotional and behavioral disorders.

Speech-language clinicians usually provide special services to children with speech and language impairments in pull-out sessions in resource rooms. Computer technology is also frequently used to assist these children in both their regular education classes and in pull-out therapy sessions.

The first article provides a conceptual framework for the development of language in early childhood. Geoffrey Cowley reviews how infants and toddlers acquire language. He also enumerates many of the things that can undermine the process of learning to talk (autism, hearing defects, brain lesions, or social isolation). The problem of specific language impairments (SLIs) is presented as a fairly common problem that occurs in children with normal hearing and normal intelligence. The two possible explanations for it, auditory-processing or grammatical deficit, are discussed. A list of abnormalities in language at 3, 6, and 12 months old and at 2, 3, and 4 years old, developed by the American Speech-Language-Hearing Association (ASLHA), is included to warn parents, teachers, and others of red flags for possible speech problems. Recommendations for how to foster good language are also given.

The second article addresses the confusion that exists over whether a child has a cultural/linguistic difference in speech/language or whether the child is, in fact, disabled in the area of communication. Students with limited English proficiency should not be labeled communication disordered unless they are significantly disabled in their mother tongue as well.

The third article discusses the use of augmentative and alternate communication (AAC) systems. Many users of AAC are children from culturally/linguistically diverse backgrounds. It is important for speech/language clinicians to heed alternate assessment procedures. If a minority child has a significant communication disorder, the clinician must be especially attentive to family and community social values, cultural mistrust, and communication needs. Family involvement is crucial to the success of AAC systems.

For the Love of Language

Learning to speak seems nothing short of a miracle. Scientists are discovering how social and biological forces let children master their native tongue.

By Geoffrey Cowley

AGE IS AN ADVANTAGE IF YOU'RE trying to learn geometry or swing dancing. But language is different. Consider Paige Arbeiter. She was a 2-pound 7-ounce preemie when she earned the nickname "Little Houdini" six years ago. A day and a half after delivery, she pulled the tube off her face to breathe on her own. And she dazzled her intensive-care nurses by inching across her incubator to hang a tiny foot out the door. When Paige went home after six weeks, her parents noticed that loud noises didn't faze her. Their pediatrician told them repeatedly not to worry, but when Paige was 10 months old they took her to New York's Long Island Jewish Speech and Hearing Center for tests. The verdict: she was nearly deaf in both ears. "Most people we told said, 'Oh, you caught it so early, she'll be just fine'," her mom recalls. "But we learned we'd missed a very important period in her speech and language development." Thanks to a cochlear implant and speech therapy, the spunky 6-year-old now proudly counts to 10. But her overall language proficiency remains that of a toddler.

Babies tackle grammar before they learn to wield a fork

Language is one of the most awesome tasks the human mind performs, and babies are uniquely poised to master it. They map meanings onto words while still sporting diapers, and they tackle grammatical analysis before learning to wield a fork. By the age of 3, most kids are generating sentences they've never heard spoken—and using them to alter the contents of other people's minds. Unfortunately, language doesn't always emerge without a hitch. As experts learn more about how kids learn to talk, they're also learning to spot disorders that can undermine the process. Impaired hearing is just one of them.

The journey to language begins in the womb. During the third trimester of pregnancy, many mothers notice that their babies kick and wiggle in response to music or loud noises. The sound of speech may draw a less spirited reaction, but there is little question that fetuses hear it. Researchers at New York's Columbia Presbyterian Medical Center have found that fetuses' heart rates drop predictably when their mothers speak a simple phrase ("Hello, baby"). And French scientists have gone a step further, showing that a fetus who's been hearing the same sound repeated ("babi, babi") will react to a sudden reversal of its elements ("biba, biba"). Within 96 hours of birth, babies distinguish their mother tongue from a foreign language, sucking more vigorously when they hear it spoken.

How does a child start to parse this river of sound into meaningful units? Simple conditioning is part of the story. Anyone bombarded by a particular language hears certain sound combinations more often than others, and babies are quick to home in on the most probable combinations. In one revealing study, a team led by University of Wisconsin psychologist Jenny Saffran familiarized 8-month-old infants with three-syllable nonsense words such as "bidaku" and "padoti" by playing them in random order on a voice synthesizer. Then the researchers reshuffled the syllables and tested the kids again. The babies easily distinguished bidaku and padoti not only from other nonwords like "dadobi" but also from hybrids like "kupado," a sequence they would have heard on the training tape whenever "bida-KU" bumped up against "PADO-ti." Long before they could attach meanings to words, these kids were processing them as discrete units—saying, in effect, "Call me 'pretty' or call me 'baby'. Just don't call me 'ty-ba'."

Conversing with a child of this age, you'd never guess she harbored such thoughts. Most kids are content to coo and scream for the first six months, but during the second half of the first year, they take up speaking in tongues. They'll go on endlessly about "ma-ma-da-da" without the slightest indication that they know what they're talking about. But as psychologists Roberta Michnick Golinkoff and Kathy Hirsh-Pasek observe in their new book, "How Babies Talk," such blather is a step on the road to articulate speech. "Babbling is analogous to putting a puzzle together over and over," they write. "Just as children learn a good deal about how puzzle pieces differ in small but significant ways, so do babies learn how to manipulate the pieces of sound that make up the puzzle of language." It's not just the syllables that make babbling so speechlike. It's the dead-on rhythms and the patterns of intonation. In one French study, laymen listening to recorded statements by babblers from various countries picked out the future Francophones with near-perfect accuracy.

Within months of their 1st birthday, most kids start attaching names to things. And whether they're learning Swahili or Swedish, they go about it in much the same way. Instead of proceeding by trial and error—unsure whether "doggie" refers to a part of a dog, to one dog in particular or to anything with four legs—children start with a set of innate biases. They assume that labels refer to wholes instead of parts (the creature, not the tail) and to classes instead of items (all dogs, not one dog). They also

Red Flags for Speech Problems

Sometimes a child's failure to put two words together by the time he is 24 months old means nothing. Sometimes it means there is a problem. According to the American Speech-Language-Hearing Association, there are some abnormalities that might reflect hearing loss, head injury or other conditions, and so call for a doctor's evaluation:

0–3 months: Does not listen to speech or does not make sounds repeatedly by cooing or gooing

4–6 months: Does not notice noisy toys, look for the source of sounds like the vacuum cleaner, or attend to parents' 'no'

7–12 months: Does not babble either long or short groups of sounds such as 'tata upup bibibibi' and does not say a word or two, even unclearly. Does not respond to her name.

1–2 years: Does not use one- or two-word questions ('Where kitty?'), put two words together ('mommy book') or listen to simple stories, songs and rhymes

2–3 years: Does not have a word for almost everything or use two- to three-word 'sentences' to talk about and ask for things. Can't understand differences in meaning ('go' and 'stop') or follow two requests ('Get the book and put it on the table'). Doesn't notice environmental sounds such as a doorbell.

3–4 years: Does not hear when you call from another room, or understand simple 'who?' 'what?' and 'where?' questions. Cannot be understood by people outside the family. If delays persist until kindergarten, most pediatricians recommend speech therapy.

TESSA NAMUTH

figure that one name is enough for any class of object (if it's a dog, it's not a cow). These assumptions are not always valid—there's only one Lassie, after all, and any dog qualifies as a mammal—but they enable kids to catalog new words with breathtaking efficiency. A typical child is socking away a dozen words a day by 18 months, and may command 2,000 of them by the age of 2.

This is when things get interesting. A chimp with a signboard can learn to asso-

ciate symbols with particular objects and actions, but toddlers do much more than that. Having acquired their words through mimicry, they start combining them—according to abstract rules that no one has taught them—to express their thoughts and feelings. Their first sentences may be crude utterances such as "Gonna cry!" or "Uppy me!" But between 24 and 30 months, kids who have never heard of syntax usually start marrying noun phrases to verb phrases to explain who did what to whom. If they happen to speak English, they know that "man bites dog" and "dog bites man" tell different stories, despite their identical words.

Some scholars have argued that kids learn to form sentences just as they learn to perceive word boundaries—by listening for statistical regularities in other people's speech. Grammatical analysis doesn't require specialized cognitive software, they say; it boils down to operant conditioning. According to this argument, a baby who encounters the sentences "the boy likes apples" and "the boy likes oranges" 50 times each will learn that the words "the," "boy" and "likes" are tightly correlated in certain circumstances, whereas apples and oranges show up only 50 percent of the time. As the baby encounters more sentences, the web of associations expands, providing more templates for original utterances.

But recent studies suggest there is much more to the story—that children actively seek out abstract grammatical rules. In one clever experiment, researchers led by New York University psychologist Gary Marcus presented 7-month-old infants with a language problem that couldn't be solved by operant conditioning alone. First the children spent two minutes listening to a series of three-word "sentences" such as "ga-ti-ga" and "li-na-li." The "words" varied from one sentence to the next, but the syntax didn't: any word appearing in the first position also appeared in the third. After familiarizing the children with these samples, the researchers played a different set of sentences—some obeying the A-B-A rule ("wo-fe-wo"), and some violating it ("wo-fe-fe"). The babies had never heard any of these new utterances, yet their attention patterns suggested that "wo-fe-wo" sounded familiar while the "nongrammatical" A-B-B sequences surprised them. The implication is that the kids weren't merely seeking out associations among "words" they'd already heard. They were spontaneously extracting the principles governing word order in general.

PARENTESE Giving Children the Gift of Gab

Speaking to kids slowly and clearly aids language development

WHEN IT COMES TO VISION, newborns prefer simple sights like circles. But for sounds, they prefer complex stimuli like the highly intonated speech called parentese. The high pitch, slow pace and musicality of parentese may help children forge the brain circuits that let them identify the phonemes—distinct sounds—of their native language, a crucial step in understanding and producing speech. Parentese may also strengthen the neuronal circuits that tie together sounds and meanings in a child's brain. Some of its features:

Speaking **slowly** and with clear **enunciation** gives children a clean template on which to model their speech. More important, it literally trains neurons to specialize in hearing a particular phoneme, an ability crucial for learning to read. Emphasizing one word in a sentence ("Do you see that *bird?*") rivets the child's attention.

Repetition reinforces the neural pathways underlying language. Scientists have a mantra for this: "Cells that fire together, wire together."

In other words, the more a child hears "bed" and sees you point to it, the faster she'll get the connection. But don't turn it into a dreary drill. Children acquire language not by sitting passively while you talk and point but by taking turns in a **conversation.**

Four-month-olds are figuring out which mouth shapes go with which sounds, so chat with them **face to face.** And imitate what they say—babies love the **feedback.** Responding to "bot bot bot" with "yes,

here's your bottle" reinforces her halting attempts at words.

Don't dumb things down for toddlers. Those whose parents use many dependent clauses ("because…" and "which…") progress beyond simple sentences earlier than children of parents who do not. The more you **talk to your child,** the larger the vocabulary he will likely acquire. **Talking** *to* is the crucial part: merely hearing conversations, let alone TV, seems to have little positive influence on language development.

The language instinct runs so deep that even severely retarded children usually learn to talk. But this unique human propensity isn't foolproof. Any number of congenital or early-life problems—autism, hearing defects, brain lesions, social isolation—can derail language development. And an estimated 3 percent to 7 percent of children suffer from a selective, unexplained difficulty known as specific language impairment, or SLI. These kids exhibit normal hearing and intelligence, and have no other known handicaps. Yet they're late to talk, and even after they start, their facility and comprehension lag. They may say things like "I eating ice," even in grade school, and many go on to experience reading difficulties. Studies suggest the problem runs in families, but no one has identified culpable genes.

Unfortunately, there is no widely accepted treatment for SLI. Experts are even divided on the nature of the problem. Some suspect it's an auditory-processing disorder, in which the brain fails to distinguish properly among the brief blasts of sounds that encode language. In separate studies, neuroscientist Paula Tallal of Rutgers University and communication specialist Bev-

erly Wright of Northwestern University have found that SLI children are less adept than their peers at picking out brief tones amid other sounds of similar frequency. Both of these researchers believe that auditory-training programs, in which children hear exaggerated versions of the problematic sounds over and over, can ease SLI by heightening phonological awareness.

Other experts believe SLI is at root a grammatical disorder, and their findings are equally compelling. Working with MIT cognitive scientist Kenneth Wexler, Mabel Rice of the University of Kansas has shown repeatedly that affected children, though aware of grammatical categories, share problems with certain verb forms. Most English speakers learn by the age of 3 to mark regular verbs with "s" in the third person ("he walks"). SLI kids tend to stick with the infinitive, saying "he walk" and "she play." And auditory-processing problems are an unlikely explanation, because the same children effortlessly add "s" to nouns to form plurals. It's possible that SLI is a varied syndrome and that different researchers are charting different manifestations. But in assessing both auditory and grammatical deficits in SLI kids,

researchers led by Oxford University psychologist Dorothy Bishop have found the grammatical ones far more pervasive. "It seems as if we need to look beyond auditory processing," they conclude in a preliminary report.

SLI may never be preventable. By contrast, the more serious language problems facing little Paige Arbeiter can often be prevented today. If a newborn's hearing impairment is diagnosed and treated within six months, says Dr. Lynn Spivak of Long Island Jewish Medical Center, the child usually develops normal speech and language on schedule. But because the critical period for language development is so brief, any delay can have major consequences. Though Paige now thrills her parents by saying words like "butterfly," she may never have an intuitive feel for syntax. When she strings words together, the results tend toward "Go outside, Paige Mommy!" Thanks in part to the 1999 Newborn and Infant Hearing Screening and Intervention Act, 34 states now offer the $25 test for all babies before they leave the hospital. It's a small price to pay for so vast a wonder as language.

With TESSA NAMUTH

Language Differences or Learning Difficulties

The Work of the Multidisciplinary Team

Spencer J. Salend and AltaGracia Salinas

Maria moved to the United States from Mexico and was placed in Ms. Shannon's fourth-grade class where she sat quietly at her desk and kept to herself. Whenever directions were given, she seemed lost and later had difficulty completing tasks and participating in class discussions. During teacher-directed activities, Maria often either looked around to see what her classmates were doing and then mimicked them, or played with materials at her desk.

Ms. Shannon was concerned about Maria's lack of progress in developing English proficiency and her inability to pay attention and complete her work. Ms. Shannon thought Maria might have a learning disability and referred her to the multidisciplinary team to determine if she needed special education. The team organized the assessment process for Maria by considering the following questions:

- Who can assist the team in making decisions about Maria's educational program?
- What factors should the team consider in determining Maria's educational strengths and needs?
- What strategies should the team employ to assess Maria's educational strengths and needs?
- Should the team recommend a special education placement for Maria?

Educators often refer students like Maria for placement in special education (Ortiz, 1997). As Ortiz indicated, students learning a second language and students with learning disabilities often exhibit similar difficulties with learning, attention, social skills, and behavioral and emotional balance. As a result, multidisciplinary teams are increasingly working with educators like Ms. Shan-non to conduct meaningful assessments and determine appropriate educational programs for a growing number of students whose primary language is not English.

Recommendations for Multidisciplinary Teams

Using the experiences of Maria and her teachers, this article provides recommendations for helping multidisciplinary teams accurately and fairly assess second-language learners and differentiate language differences from learning difficulties. The article includes six recommendations, as follows:

- Diversify the composition of the multidisciplinary teams and offer training.
- Compare student performance in both the native and secondary languages.
- Consider the processes and factors associated with second-language acquisition.
- Employ alternatives to traditional standardized testing.
- Identify diverse life experiences that may affect learning.
- Analyze the data and develop an appropriate educational plan.

These recommendations also can assist multidisciplinary teams in developing educational programs for second-language learners and in complying with the Individuals with Disabilities Education Act (IDEA), which states that students should not be identified as having a disability if their eligibility and school related difficulties are based on their proficiency in English, or their lack of opportunity to receive instruction in reading or mathematics.

Diversify the Composition of the Multidisciplinary Teams and Offer Training

IDEA requires that a multidisciplinary team of professionals and family members, with the student when appropriate, make important decisions concerning the education of students referred for special education. Initially, the team determines if students are in need of and eligible for special education services. When teachers refer second-language learners to the multidisciplinary team, the team frequently faces many challenges, such as differentiating linguistic and cultural differences from learning difficulties, and developing an appropriate educational program that addresses students' linguistic, cultural, and experiential backgrounds.

The composition and training of the multidisciplinary team are critical factors in determining the educational needs of second-language learners (Ochoa, Robles-Pina, Garcia, & Breunig 1999). Therefore, the team should include family and community members, as well as professionals who are fluent in the student's native language, understand the student and the family's culture, and can help collect and interpret the data in culturally and linguistically appropriate ways. The inclusion of these people allows the team to learn about the family's and the student's cultural perspective and experiential and linguistic background, and to assist in the determination of the origins of the student's learning difficulties. Team members can help determine what students' learning difficulties can be explained by sociocultural perspectives, experiential factors, and sociolinguistic variables.

The composition of multidisciplinary teams for second-language learners should include educators who are trained in assessing second-language learners and designing educational programs to meet their varied needs. Such membership may include English as a Second Language (ESL) teachers, bilingual educators, and migrant educators. Whereas ESL teachers offer instruction in English to help students build on their existing English language skills, bilingual educators teach students in both their native language and in English. Because bilingual educators are fluent in the family's native language, they can be instrumental in involving family and community members in the team process and in assessing students' skills in their native language. In the case of migrant students like Maria, the team also can benefit from the input of migrant educators, who provide individualized instruction to migrant students and serve as a liaison between the family, the school and the community (Salend, 2001).

For example, the multidisciplinary team assembled for Maria was expanded to include Ms. Garcia, a bilingual migrant educator who worked with Maria and her family in their home and had training and experience with the second language acquisition process, as well as in working with students from culturally and linguistically diverse backgrounds. Ms. Garcia worked with other members of the team to gather information about Maria's school, home-life and experiential background, to interact with and collect information from Maria, her mother, and other family members, to assess Maria's skills in Spanish, and to identify strategies to support Maria's learning.

The multidisciplinary team can foster the success of the process by working as a collaborative and interactive team (Chase Thomas, Correa, & Morsink, 2001; Salend, 2001). The collaborative and interactive nature of the team can be enhanced by agreeing upon goals, learning about each other's beliefs, experiences and expertise, understanding and coordinating each other's roles, being sensitive to cross-cultural perspectives and communication styles, establishing equal status relationships, and addressing differences directly and immediately. Successful teams adopt a problem solving approach and employ effective interpersonal and communication skills so that all team members feel comfortable identifying issues to be considered by the team, collecting and sharing information, seeking clarification from others, participating in discussions, and making decisions via consensus.

Multidisciplinary teams work with educators to conduct meaningful assessments and determine appropriate educational programs for a growing number of students whose primary language is not English.

Teams can enhance the effectiveness of the process for second-language learners by offering training to team members. Teams should provide this training to all school personnel, and it can help the team members be aware of the effect of sociocultural perspectives, experiential backgrounds, and linguistic variables on students' behavior and school performance. Team members also will benefit from training in employing culturally responsive instructional, behavior management and mental health interventions, understanding the second language acquisition process and the problems associated with the assessment of students from culturally and linguistically diverse backgrounds, and selecting and adapting assessment instruments (Salend, Dorney, & Mazo, 1997).

Teams often face mismatches between members of the team and second-language learners in terms of their different cultural, linguistic, and socioeconomic backgrounds (Gay, 2002).

- What is my definition of diversity?

- What are my perceptions of students from different racial and ethnic groups? With language or dialects different from mine?
- What are the sources of these perceptions?
- How do I respond to my students based on these perceptions?
- What kinds of information, skills, and resources do I need to acquire to effectively teach from a multicultural perspective?
- In what ways do I collaborate with other educators, family members and community groups to address the needs of all my students? (p. 4).

Thus, team members may find it helpful to engage in activities to examine their own cultural perspectives and consider how their cultural beliefs affect their expectations, beliefs, and behaviors and may differ from those held by students and their families (Cartledge, Kea, & Ida, 2000; Hyun & Fowler, 1995; Obiakor, 1999). Montgomery (2001) offered a self-assessment tool that team members can use to reflect upon their understanding of diversity. The tool includes the following questions:

Compare Student Performance in Both the Native and Secondary Languages

After multidisciplinary team members meet, they need to make a plan for assessment. The assessment plan for second-language learners should collect data to compare student performance in both the native and secondary languages. Team members can collect data relating to students' performance in both languages through the use of informal and standardized tests, language samples, observations, questionnaires, and interviews. These methods can be employed to examine students' language proficiency, language dominance, language preference, and code switching. Language proficiency relates to the degree of skill in speaking the language(s) and includes receptive and expressive language skills. Although proficiency in one language does not necessarily mean lack of proficiency in another language, language dominance refers to the language in which the student is most fluent and implies a comparison of the student's abilities in two or more languages. Language preference identifies the language in which the student prefers to communicate, which can vary depending on the setting. Code switching relates to using words, phrases, expressions and sentences from one language while speaking another language.

Collect data relating to students' performance in both languages through the use of informal and standardized tests, language samples, observations, questionnaires, and interviews.

Through observations, informal assessment, and interviews with Maria and her family members, the multidisciplinary team found out that Maria was proficient in Spanish but lacked proficiency in English. It was observed that when Maria spoke Spanish, she was expressive, used the correct tense and age-appropriate vocabulary, and understood all the communications directed to her. Whereas Maria used Spanish to initiate and maintain interactions with others in an organized and coherent manner, her English was characterized by the use of gestures and short, basic sentences to communicate. In addition, observations and interviews revealed that Maria preferred to speak Spanish in all settings, and that Spanish was the dominant language spoken at home, since Maria's mother did not speak English.

Consider the Processes and Factors Associated with Second Language Acquisition

The assessment process for second-language learners like Maria should recognize that learning a second language is a long-term, complex, and dynamic process that involves different types of language skills and various stages of development (Collier, 1995). Therefore, when assessing second-language learners, the multidisciplinary team needs to consider the factors that affect second-language acquisition and understand the stages students go through in learning a second language.

Because proficiency in a second language involves the acquisition of two distinct types of language skills, the team needs to assess students' basic interpersonal communication skills and cognitive/academic language proficiency. The former, the interpersonal skills are the social language skills that guide the development of social relationships (e.g., "Good morning. How are you?"). Even though they are relatively repetitive, occur within a specific and clearly defined context, and are not cognitively demanding, research indicates that they typically take up to 2 years to develop in a second language (Cummins, 1984).

Cognitive proficiency, on the other hand, refers to the language skills that relate to literacy, cognitive development, and academic development in the classroom. It includes understanding such complex academic terms as photosynthesis, onomatopoeia, and least common denominator. Because this proficiency does not have an easily understood context, and tends to be cognitively demanding, it often takes up to 7 years for children to develop and use these language skills. Since cognitive skills developed in one's first language foster the development of cognitive proficiency in one's second language, we must gather information on students' proficiency and educational training in their native language.

An analysis of Maria's English language skills indicated that she was starting to develop a mastery of interpersonal language skills and struggling in terms of her cognitive language proficiency. For example, Ms. Shannon reported that when Maria was given directions to perform a classroom activity in English, she had difficulty completing it. However, when the directions were explained in Spanish, she was able to complete the task.

In learning a second language, students go through developmental stages that team members should consider when evaluating students' learning.

In learning a second language, students also go through developmental stages (see Figure 1) that team members should consider when evaluating students' learning (Maldonado-Colon, 1995). Initially, second-language learners' understanding of the new language is usually greater than their production. Many second-language learners go through a silent period in which they process what they hear but refrain from verbalizing. This is often misinterpreted as indicating a lack of cognitive abilities, disinterest in school, or shyness. Once students are ready to speak their new language, their verbalizations gradually increase in terms of their semantic and syntactic complexity.

Observations of Maria in her class indicated that she was focusing on understanding via mimicking others and using visual and context clues, and that she communicated via pointing, physical gestures and the occasional use of one to three-word phrases. Therefore, the multidisciplinary team felt that she was functioning at the preproduction and early production stages of learning English.

The team should also be aware of other factors that may affect students and their developmental progress in maintaining their native language and learning their new language such as age, educational background, and language exposure. Students who have been educated in their native language often progress faster in learning a new language that those who have not had a formal education (Thomas & Collier, 1997). In addition, students may attempt to apply the rules of their first language to their second language, which can affect their pronunciation, syntax, and spelling (Tiedt & Tiedt, 2001). And as some students learn a second language, they may experience language loss in their native language. Similarly, children who simultaneously learn two languages from

birth may initially experience some temporary language delays in achieving developmental language milestones and some language mixing. These tend to disappear over time (Fierro-Cobas & Chan, 2001).

Figure 1. Stages of Second-Language Learning

1. **Preproduction or Silent period.** Students focus on processing and comprehending what they hear but avoid verbal responses. They often rely on modeling, visual stimuli, context clues, key words and use listening strategies to understand meaning, and often communicate through pointing and physical gestures. They may benefit from classroom activities that allow them to respond by imitating, drawing, pointing, and matching.
2. **Telegraphic or Early Production period.** Students begin to use two- or three-word sentences, and show limited comprehension. They have a receptive vocabulary level of approximately 1,000 words and an expressive level that typically includes approximately 100 words. They may benefit from classroom activities that employ language they can understand, require them to name and group objects, and call for responses to simple questions.
3. **Interlanguage and Intermediate Fluency period.** Students speak in longer phrases and start to use complete sentences. They often mix basic phrases and sentences in both languages. They may benefit from classroom activities that encourage them to experiment with language and develop and expand their vocabulary.
4. **Extension and Expansion period.** Students expand on their basic sentences and extend their language abilities to employ synonyms and synonymous expressions. They are developing good comprehension skills, employing more complex sentence structures, and making fewer errors when speaking. They may benefit from classroom literacy activities and instruction in vocabulary and grammar.
5. **Enrichment period.** Students are taught learning strategies to assist them in making the transition to the new language.
6. **Independent Learning period.** Students begin to work on activities at various levels of difficulty with heterogeneous groups.

SOURCE: *Creating Inclusive Classrooms: Effective and Reflective Practices* (4th ed., p. 91) by S. J. Salend, 2001, Columbus, OH: Merrill/Prentice Hall. Reprinted by permission of Pearson Education, Inc.

Employ Alternatives to Traditional Standardized Testing

As mandated by the latest reauthorization of IDEA, rather than relying solely on potentially biased, standardized tests, the multidisciplinary team should employ a variety of student-centered, alternative assessment procedures to assess the educational needs of students from culturally and linguistically diverse backgrounds accurately. Such assessment alternatives include performance-based and portfolio assessment, curriculum-based measurements, instructional rubrics, dynamic assessment, student journals and learning logs, and self-evaluation techniques (Salend, 2001). These assessment alternatives can provide the Multidisciplinary Team with more complete profiles of students like Maria including their academic strengths and needs, learning styles and the impact of the school environment on their learning.

In the case of Maria, the multidisciplinary team worked with Maria and Ms. Shannon to create a portfolio that showed that Maria's decoding and reading comprehension skills in Spanish were age appropriate. It also revealed that she reads phonetically, engages in self-correction, and uses context and semantic cues. These results were also confirmed by Maria's performance on a standardized Spanish reading test.

Identify Diverse Life Experiences That May Affect Learning

Many second-language learners have diverse life experiences that can have a significant effect on their learning. These experiences may include being separated from family members for extended periods of time (Abrams, Ferguson, & Laud, 2001). Identifying these experiences can help the team determine if students' learning difficulties are related to the existence of a disability or other experiential factors. Therefore, the team can use the guidelines in Figure 2 to collect information to determine if a student's difficulties in learning result from language, cultural, and experiential factors, acculturation, psychological and family traumas, economic hardships, racism, or lack of exposure to effective instruction.

Learning a second language is a long-term, complex, and dynamic process that involves different types of language skills and various stages of development.

Ms. Garcia was able to obtain information about Maria by speaking with Maria and her mother. Ms. Garcia reported that Maria had not had an easy life. She lived in a rural village in Mexico and sporadically attended a school that had limited resources. Maria traveled to the United States with her mother and her three siblings a year ago to join her father and two older brothers who had been working in the United States. Two other siblings remained in Mexico with the hope of joining the family when enough money could be saved to bring them to the United States. Two other siblings remained in Mexico with the hope of joining the family when enough money could be saved to bring them to the United States. However, within 6 months of living in the United States, Maria's parents separated; and her father returned to Mexico. Maria reported that she misses her life in Mexico and her siblings who are still living there.

Upon arriving in the United States, Maria's mother found a job working as a migrant farmworker. Because she doesn't speak English, did not attend school, and works long hours to make ends meet, Maria's mother finds it difficult to help Maria with her schoolwork and relies on Maria to help take care of the younger children, and to cook and clean. Maria's mother also said that although her children watch cartoons in English, the interactions in the home are in Spanish. Interactions with the family also revealed that the family has few links to and interactions with the community, and that their lifestyle parallels the traditions of Mexico.

Code switching relates to using words, phrases, expressions and sentences from one language while speaking another language.

This information was helpful to the multidisciplinary team in providing information regarding Maria's learning abilities. First, it revealed that Maria's learning ability may be related to the fact that she has not regularly attended school and that the school she attended in Mexico is very different form her current school. Second, Maria's mother relies on her to help around the house; and Maria has quickly learned to perform these roles, which shows that she learns by active participation and is viewed by her mother as responsible and independent. Third, Maria has had limited exposure to English, which affects her progress in learning English and performing in school.

Analyze the Data and Develop an Appropriate Educational Plan

After the team has collected the data, team members meet to analyze the data and make decisions about students' educational programs. For second-language learners, the analysis should focus on examining the factors that affect learning and language development, determining if learning and language difficulties occur in both languages, and developing an educational plan to promote learning and language acquisition. Damico (1991) offered questions that can guide the team in examining the data to assess the extent to which students' diverse life experiences and cultural and linguistic backgrounds serve as

Figure 2. Life Experience Factors and Questions

Length of Residence in the United States

- How long and for what periods of time has the student resided in the United States?
- What were the conditions and events associated with the student's migration?
- If the student was born in the United States, what has been the student's exposure to English?

Students may have limited or interrupted exposure to English and the U.S. culture, resulting in poor vocabulary and slow naming speed, and affecting their cultural adjustment. Trauma experienced during migration or family separations as a result of migration can be psychological barriers that affect learning. Being born and raised in the United States does not guarantee that students have developed English skills and have had significant exposure to English and the U.S. culture.

School Attendance Patterns

- How long has the student been in school?
- What is the student's attendance pattern? Have there been any disruptions in school?

Students may fail to acquire language skills because of failure to attend school on a regular basis.

School Instructional History

- How many years of schooling did the student complete in the native country?
- What language(s) were used to guide instruction in the native country?
- What types of classrooms has the student attended (bilingual education, English as a second language, general education, speech/language therapy services, special education)?
- What has been the language of instruction in these classes?
- What is the student's level of proficiency in reading, writing, and speaking in the native language?
- What strategies and instructional materials have been successful?
- What were the outcomes of these educational placements?
- What language does the student prefer to use in informal situations with adults? In formal situations with adults?

Students may not have had access to appropriate instruction and curricula, resulting in problems in language acquisition, reading, and mathematics.

Cultural Background

- How does the student's cultural background affect second language acquisition?
- Has the student had sufficient time to adjust to the new culture?
- What is the student's acculturation level?
- What is the student's attitude toward school?

Since culture and language are inextricably linked, lack of progress in learning a second language can be due to cultural and communication differences and/or lack of exposure to the new culture. For example, some culturesrely on the use of body language in communication as a substitute for verbal communication. Various cultures also have different perspectives on color, time, gender, distance, and space that affect language.

Performance in Comparison to Peers

- Does the student's language skill, learning rate, and learning style differ from those of other students from similar experiential, cultural, and linguistic backgrounds?
- Does the student interact with peers in the primary language and/or English?
- Does the student experience difficulty following directions, understanding language, and expressing thoughts in the primary language? In the second language?

The student's performance can be compared to that of students who have similar traits rather than to that of students whose experiences in learning a second language are very different.

Home Life

- What language(s) or dialect(s) are spoken at home by each of the family members?
- When did the student start to speak?
- Is the student's performance at home different from that of siblings?
- What language(s) or dialect(s) are spoken in the family's community?
- Is a distinction made among the uses of the primary language or dialect and English? If so, how is that distinction made? (For example, the non-English language is used at home, but children speak English when playing with peers.)
- What are the attitudes of the family and the community toward English and bilingual education?
- In what language(s) does the family watch television, listen to the radio, and read newspapers, books, and magazines?
- What is the student's language preference in the home and community?
- To what extent does the family interact with the dominant culture and in what ways?

Important information concerning the student's language proficiency, dominance, and preference can be obtained by soliciting information from family members. Similarly, the student's acquisition of language can be enhanced by involving family members.

Health and Developmental History

- What health, medical, sensory, and developmental factors have affected the student's learning and language development?

A student's difficulty in learning and acquiring language may be related to various health and developmental variables.

Source: Creating Inclusive Classrooms: Effective and Reflective Practices (4th ed.; p. 94–95) by S. J. Salend, 2001, Columbus, OH: Merrill/Prentice Hall. Reprinted by permission of Pearson Education, Inc.

Figure 3. Differentiating Instruction for Second-Language Learners

- Establish a relaxed learning environment that encourages students to use both languages.
- Label objects in the classroom in several languages.
- Encourage and show students how to use bilingual dictionaries and Pictionaries.
- Use repetition to help students acquire the rhythm, pitch, volume, and tone of the new language.
- Use simple vocabulary and shorter sentences, and limit the use of idiomatic expressions, slang, and pronouns.
- Highlight key words through reiteration, increased volume and slight exaggeration, and writing them on the chalkboard.
- Use gestures, facial expressions, voice changes, pantomimes, demonstrations, rephrasing, visuals, props, manipulatives, and other cues to communicate and convey the meaning of new terms and concepts.

- Preview and teach new vocabulary, phrases, idioms, structures and concepts through use of modeling, and hands-on experiences.
- Supplement oral instruction and descriptions with visuals such as pictures, charts, maps, graphs, and graphic organizers.
- Offer regular summaries of important concepts and check students' understanding frequently.
- Emphasize communication rather than form.
- Correct students indirectly by restating their incorrect comments in correct form.

Sources: Choice of Languages in Instruction: One Language or Two?, by A. Brice and C. Roseberry-MeKibbin, 2001, *TEACHING Exceptional Children, 33*(4), pp. 10–16.
The Changing Face of Bilingual Education, by R. Gersten, 1999, *Educational Leadership, 56*(7), pp. 41–45.
Below the Tip of the Iceberg: Teaching Language Minority Students, by V. Fueyo, 1997, *TEACHING Exceptional Children, 30*(1), pp. 61–65.

explanations for the difficulties they may be experiencing in schools. These questions include the following:

- What factors and conditions may explain the student's learning and/or language difficulties (e.g., stressful life events, lack of opportunity to learn, racism, acculturation, and experiential background)?
- To what extent does the student demonstrate the same learning and/or language difficulties in community settings as in school and/or in the primary language?
- To what extent are the student's learning and/or language difficulties due to normal second language acquisition, dialectical differences, or cultural factors?
- Did bias occur prior to, during, and after assessment such as in the reliability, validity, and standardization of the test as well as with the skills and learning styles assessed?
- To what extent were the student's cultural, linguistic, dialectic and experiential backgrounds considered in collecting and analyzing the assessment data (e.g., selection, administration, and interpretation of the test's results, prereferral strategies, learning styles, family involvement)?

These questions also can guide the team in differentiating between two types of second-language learners (Rice & Ortiz, 1994), and planning appropriate educational programs for these students. One type of second-language learner demonstrates some proficiency in the native language but experiences difficulties in learning a new language that are consistent with the typical difficulties individuals encounter in learning a second language. Although these kinds of behavior are similar to those

shown by students with learning difficulties, these students' educational needs can best be addressed through participation in a bilingual education or an English as a Second Language (ESL) program.

The other type of second-language learner exhibits language, academic, and social behavior in the first and second languages that are significantly below those of peers who have similar linguistic, cultural, and experiential backgrounds (Ortiz, 1997). These students may benefit from a special education program and individualized educational programs (IEPs) that address their own linguistic, cultural, and experiential needs (Garcia & Malkin, 1993; Ortiz, 1997). Both types of second-language learners would benefit from the use of strategies for differentiating instruction presented in Figure 3.

Team members will benefit from training in employing culturally responsive instructional, behavior management and mental health interventions.

In the case of Maria, the multidisciplinary team determined that she did not have a disability. The assessment data led the team to conclude that Maria had age-appropriate decoding, reading comprehension, and speaking skills in Spanish and that her difficulties in learning English appeared to be related to the normal process of second-language acquisition and cultural and experiential factors. They also decided that Maria didn't qualify for special education services under the IDEA because her school-related difficulties were based on her lack of proficiency in English and the limited opportunities she has had to receive instruction.

The multidisciplinary team determined that Maria would benefit from the services of a bilingual educator because she needed to strengthen her native language skills to learn academic content and to provide a better foundation for learning English. They also recommended strategies for establishing home-school partnerships and communications, and encouraged her teachers to use cooperative learning strategies and the strategies in Figure 3. The team also developed a plan to collect data to examine the effectiveness of these intervention strategies on Maria's learning, language development, socialization, and her success in school.

Final Thoughts

The ability to acquire and use language has a great effect on students' learning behavior and educational performance. As a result, many second-language learners like Maria exhibit types of behavior that resemble students with learning difficulties and are referred to the multidisciplinary team. Because the team process may vary across school districts, educators need to consider how the recommendations can be incorporated into their assessment process to differentiate between language differences from learning difficulties, and to provide second-language learners with appropriate educational programs.

References

Abrams, J., Ferguson, J., & Laud, L. (2001). Assessing ESOL students. *Educational Leadership, 59*(3), 62–65.

Brice, A., & Roseberry-MeKibbin, C. (2001). Choice of languages in instruction: One language or two? *TEACHING Exceptional Children, 33*(4), 10–16.

Cartledge, G., Kea, C. D., & Ida, D. J. (2000). Anticipating differences—Celebrating strengths: Providing culturally competent services for students with serious emotional disturbance. *TEACHING Exceptional Children, 32*(3), 30–37.

Chase Thomas, C., Correa, V., & Morsink, C. (2001). *Interactive teaming: Enhancing programs for students with special needs* (3rd ed.). Columbus, OH: Merrill/Prentice-Hall.[*]

Collier, V. (1995). Acquiring a second language for school. *Directions in Language and Education, 1*(4), 1–12.

Cummins, J. (1984). *Bilingualism and special education: Issues in assessment and pedagogy*. San Diego, CA: College-Hill.

Damico, J. S. (1991). Descriptive assessment of communicative ability in Limited English Proficient students. In E. Hamayan & J. S. Damico (Eds.), *Limiting bias in the assessment of bilingual students* (pp. 157–218). Austin, TX: PRO-ED.[*]

Fierro-Cobas, V., & Chan, E. (2001). Language development in bilingual children: A primer for pediatricians. *Contemporary Pediatrics, 18*(7), 79–98.

Fueyo, V. (1997). Below the tip of the iceberg: Teaching language minority students. *TEACHING Exceptional Children, 30*(1), 61–65.

Gay, G. (2002). Preparing for culturally responsive teaching. *Journal of Teacher Education, 53*(2), 106–116.

Gersten, R. (1999). The changing face of bilingual education. *Educational Leadership, 56*(7), 41–45.

Langdon, H. W. (1989). Language disorder or difference? Assessing the language skills of Hispanic students. *Exceptional Children, 56*, 160–167.

Maldonado-Colon, E. (1995, April). *Second language learners in special education: Language framework for inclusive classrooms*. Paper presented at the international meeting of the Council for Exceptional Children, Indianapolis.

Montgomery, W. (2001). Creating culturally responsive, inclusive classrooms. *TEACHING Exceptional Children, 33*(4), 4–9.

Obiakor, F. E. (1999). Teacher expectations of minority exceptional learners: Impact on accuracy of self-concepts. *Exceptional Children, 66*, 39–53.

Ochoa, S. H., Robles-Pina, R., Garcia, S. B., & Breunig, N. (1999). School psychologists' perspectives on referrals of language minority students. *Multiple Voices, 3*(1), 1–13.

Ortiz, A. A. (1997). Learning disabilities occurring concomitantly with linguistic differences. *Journal of Learning Disabilities, 30*, 321–332.

Rice, L. S., & Ortiz, A. A. (1994). Second language difference or learning disability? *LD Forum, 19*(2), 11–13.

Salend, S. J. (2001). *Creating inclusive classrooms: Effective and reflective practices* (4th ed.). Columbus, OH: Merrill/Prentice-Hall.[*]

Salend, S. J., Dorney, J. A., & Mazo, M. (1997). The roles of bilingual special educators in creating inclusive classrooms. *Remedial and Special Education, 18*, 54–64.

Thomas, W. P., & Collier, V. P. (1997). *School effectiveness for language minority students*. Washington, DC: National Clearinghouse for Bilingual Education.

Tiedt, P. L., & Tiedt, I. (2001). *Multicultural teaching: A handbook of activities, information, and resources* (6th ed.). Boston: Allyn & Bacon.[*]

Spencer J. Salend (CEC Chapter #615), Professor, Department of Educational Studies, State University of New York at New Paltz.
AltaGracia Salinas, Special Education Teacher, Alexandria City Public Schools, Virginia.

Address correspondence to Spencer J. Salend, Department of Educational Studies, OMB 112, SUNY New Paltz, 75 South Manheim Blvd., New Paltz, NY 12561 (e-mail: salends@ newpaltz.edu).

From *Teaching Exceptional Children*, March/April 2003, pp. 36–43. © 2003 by The Council for Exceptional Children. Reprinted by permission.

Early Childhood Special Education

Young African American Children with Disabilities and Augmentative and Alternative Communication Issues

Phil Parette, Mary Blake Huer, and Toya A. Wyatt

INTRODUCTION

Increasing emphasis has been placed on providing augmentative and alternative communication (AAC) systems to young children with disabilities to assist them in receiving a free and appropriate public education (see e.g., Huer, 1994; Soto, Huer, & Taylor, 1997). As defined by the American Speech-Language-Hearing Association (1991), an AAC system is an "integrated group of components, including the symbols, aids, strategies, and techniques used by individuals to enhance communication" (p. 10). AAC devices that are frequently used by young children include low-tech (e.g., communication boards and notebooks) and high-tech (electronic) devices.

A growing population of potential users of AAC devices in early childhood settings are from African American backgrounds. Although such students comprise about 16% of the school-age population (Meese, 2001), they make up a disproportionate number of students among the special education enrollment (van Keulen, Weddington, & DeBose, 1998). By the year 2020, African Americans are expected to be the third largest non-European American population of AAC consumers in the United States (Soto et al., 1997). This represents a 46.7% increase in growth in two decades. Earlier projections reported by Cole (1989) suggested that one-third of the caseload of speech/language pathologists after the run of the century would be children from culturally/linguistically diverse backgrounds, supporting the position taken by the Council for Educational Diagnostic Services (1995) that cultural sensitivity will be a key issue.

The remainder of this article focuses on AAC issues relevant to young African American children with disabilities and their families. Specific areas addressed include family issues and assessment.

ROLE OF THE AFRICAN AMERICAN FAMILY IN AAC SERVICE DELIVERY

Any decision making pertaining to the selection and provision of appropriate AAC devices for young African American children with disabilities should involve families to the greatest extent possible. Numerous professionals have noted the importance of the family in AAC service delivery (see e.g., Angelo, 1996; Beukelman & Mirenda, 1998; Light & McNaughton, 1993; Parette, Brotherson, & Huer, 2000). When family members are not involved in AAC decision-making, important family issues may not be addressed, resulting in the prescription of inappropriate devices (Parette & Angelo, 1996). For example, if family routines and stressors are not considered, abandonment of the AAC device may result (Batavia, Dillard, & Phillips, n.d.; Dillard, 1989).

More recently, Huer, Parette, and Saenz (2001) have discussed the importance of multicultural family issues in the AAC profession, noting that perceptions of AAC service delivery held by children with disabilities and their families from various cultural/linguistic groups perceive the roles of professionals and families in AAC decision making differently (see, e.g., Angelo, 1996; Parette, VanBiervliet, Reyna, & Heisserer, 1999). Ultimately, as noted by Huer et al. (2000), the success of any AAC system will be influenced by family perceptions and understanding of (a) education systems and the professionals serving their children with disabilities, (b) the nature of disabilities, and (c) communication barriers encountered prior to and subsequent to AAC intervention.

Professionals who typically specialize in AAC service delivery for young children and their families are individuals from the mainstream, or Euro American culture (Blackstone, 1993;

Hetzroni & Harris, 1996). As a result, misunderstandings regarding family values, needs, priorities, and resources may sometimes occur during AAC decision making (Kemp & Parette, 2000). Such misunderstandings may affect the efficiency of the decision-making process and resulting appropriateness of AAC recommendations made for a particular child and family who are from African American backgrounds. Specific family issues are described in the following sections.

Stress

Introducing an AAC system into a family setting may often by a stressful event (Parette, Stuart, Huer, Hostetler, & Wommack, 1996), given that such systems require additional caregiving responsibilities beyond daily routines (Angelo, Jones, & Kokoska, 1995; Angelo, Kokoska, & Jones, 1996). Professionals should clearly communicate the expectations and demands that will be placed on family members to learn to use the AAC system and maintain it over time. Once such information is provided to families, alternative AAC systems may be explored to minimize stress.

Communication Partners

When working with families to identify a child's AAC needs, attention must always be given to *communication partners* (e.g., parent[s], grandparent[s], aunts/uncles, siblings, cousins, friends, teachers, therapists, neighbors; Beukelman & Mirenda, 1998; Huer & Wyatt, 1999). For African American children, extended family networks are likely to play a significant role in defining key communication partners and providing sources of support. Willis (1998) noted that in traditional African American communities, there is an emphasis on (a) extended *family networks;* (b) group effort for the common good of all; and (c) family as the primary source of strength, resilience, and survival. In many African American communities, the responsibility for child rearing may be shared by multiple adult members (who may or may not be "kin") as well as older siblings (Harrison & Alvy, 1982; Huer & Wyatt, 1999). The increased likelihood of multiple caregivers becomes an important consideration in designing appropriate AAC intervention systems. As with any young child, it is important for team decision-makers to identify at least two or three communication partners who can provide information about the communication skills of the child. However, early childhood practitioners must recognize that these partners may not always be members of the traditional nuclear family unit and may often be members of the community at large or churches. Within African American communities, churches have historically fulfilled the function of teaching social values and leadership skills, and providing educational and community outreach programs to those in need (Harrison & Alvy, 1982; Willis, 1998). Churches also provide a range of social services to support families and "promote childhood and youth development" (Willis, 1998, p. 188). Given the important supportive role of churches, practitioners should consider how church members and programs may support training

and other AAC services being considered by the team (Huer & Wyatt, 1999).

Another issue relevant to communication partners is the tendency of many African Americans to speak simultaneously with one another (Huer, 1999). This may be an important consideration for some families, as AAC systems may not allow such simultaneous conversation. For example, some AAC systems may require the communication partner to listen and watch the young child with a disability during his or her communication efforts, versus engaging in multiple conversation simultaneously.

Cultural Mistrust

When working with families to obtain information relevant to the AAC decision-making process, early childhood practitioners must consider that numerous factors may negatively impact the type and amount of information disclosed by African American family members. Terrell, Battle, and Grantham (1998) documented the historical experience of African American individuals with institutional racism and discrimination, contributing to a high level of cultural mistrust toward non-African American individuals. As noted by Harris (1996), personal disclosure may be viewed as an open invitation to trouble. It can also affect the overall formation of rapport, acceptance of final recommendations, and/or decisions to seek continued services (Huer & Wyatt, 1999). When working with families, practitioners should provide (a) a rationale for certain questions being asked (e.g., those that are most likely to be viewed with suspicion or as prying and private), and (b) explanations regarding how information will be used during and following the course of intervention (Wyatt, 1998).

Communication Needs and Values

Communication need varies within and between families (Beukelman & Mirenda, 1998). As noted by Huer and Wyatt (1999), the role of the early childhood practitioner is to facilitate improved communication *wherever there is a communication need.* This is achieved by examining the range of alternative forms of communication that augment the student's residual communication skills. With regard to African American young children, the alternative forms of communication chosen should reflect the preferred communication forms and styles used by the family and the community in which the student and family reside. Presented in Table I are communication style issues that may potentially influence AAC decision making.

Language Use Patterns and Communication Style

Much has been written about the linguistic system used by African American individuals (see e.g., Dillard, 1972; Terrell et al., 1998; van Keulen et al., 1998; Wyatt, 1998). Descriptors have been prevalent in the professional literature when discussing characteristics of African American language patterns, including *Black English* (Covington, 1976) and *Ebonics* (Sey-

Table I. Implications for Providing Information and Meeting with Families During AAC Decision-Making

Communication Style Issue Area	Implications
Providing Information	• Eye contact with a conversation partner may be viewed as a sign of disrespect
	• Family members may prefer to observe a person and read their nonverbal cues during a conversation to understand intent
	• Family members may tend to be forthright or direct in stating their opinions, and do not restrict emotions
	• Active participation in discussions may be encouraged, and turn-taking may be viewed as being too restrictive
	• Extended family system may serve as a supportive and therapeutic base
Meetings	• Factors which may contribute to lack of participation in assessment processes include problems with scheduling, transportation, and knowledge of the service plan development process
	• Families may be more oriented to situations than to time

Source: Adapted from "Family, vendor, and related service personnel perceptions of culturally sensitive augmentative and alternative communication service delivery," by H. P. Parette, paper presented to the Symposium on Culturally and Linguistically Diverse Exceptional Learners, New Orleans, LA. © Howard P. Parette, 1997. Adapted with permission.

mour, Champion, & Jackson, 1995). While viewed by non-Euro Americans as being different, to typical African Americans their language is simply considered English (van Keulen et al., 1998). Many young children who have needs for AAC systems will have grown up in communities where African American English is used consistently and is a preferred linguistic style. Even for the nonspeaking African American child, this may be an important factor to consider when designing an AAC system and training program. As much as possible, practitioners should attempt to design systems and training programs that take these potential language differences into account. Such differences are likely to have some impact on decisions about symbols used in the AAC system, vocabulary selected, speech output (in the case of electronic devices), and the use of augmentative nonverbal communication strategies (e.g., eye gaze, gestures) within the communication process (Huer & Wyatt, 1999).

Of particular importance to many families when considering electronic AAC devices is the issue of dialect (Huer, 1999). African American children and their families may want the speech generated by AAC devices to reflect their cultural settings and not sound like Euro American voices—a characteristic of many current electronic speech devices.

Family and Community Social Values

Central to many African American communities is an emphasis on family, community, and group effort (Parette et al., 1999; Roseberry-McKibbin, 1995; Willis, 1998). Children and families may prefer to blend into social and community settings and not be viewed as being different from others. When AAC devices are selected for families, there is often an expectation by the child care facility and school that the family use the device in community settings. Families have reported reluctance to use AAC systems if the device draws unnecessary attention to the child and family in social settings (see e.g., Huer, 1999; Smith-Lewis, 1992). The device may also exacerbate the stigma associated with the child's racial background (i.e., not only does the child have a disability, but he or she is African American; Huer, 1999).

However, there is also strong value placed on *independence*, or "the ability to stand on one's own feet" (Willis, 1998, p. 183). As Huer and Wyatt (1999) have noted, the family is seen as key to the attainment of this goal. Consequently many families will express particular interest in the degree to which an AAC system will promote the young child's independence in the community.

Many families will also value strongly the importance of *interdependence* and *cooperation* (King, 1993; van Keulen et al., 1998). Hence, early childhood practitioners must clearly communicate to the family and child how the AAC device will be used in cooperative settings; similarly, family members and other communication partners may have to be taught cooperative strategies that enable the child who uses to AAC system to most effectively participate in social and other communication settings.

Willis (1998) reported the perceived importance of a *good education* as an important value in the African American community because "it is something that no one can take away" (p. 185). This value is particularly important in light of the historical struggles endured by African Americans in attaining certain educational rights (Billingsley, 1974; van Keulen et al., 1998; Willis, 1998). For practitioners, this emphasis on educational attainment and independence are important considerations when trying to select the most appropriate AAC device, that is, one that provides a young child with the best opportunity to become an independent communicator and to gain access to a quality education (Huer & Wyatt, 1999).

ASSESSMENT MODELS AND AFRICAN AMERICANS

Numerous individuals have described approaches for determining the AAC needs of children with disabilities (Beukelman & Mirenda, 1992; Beukelman, Yorkston, & Dowden, 1985; Blackstone, 1986; Huer, 1987; Huer, 1988; Huer, 1997; Light, 1989). Presented in Table II is an overview of each of these models. Unfortunately, with the early exception of Light's Communication Competence model, which emphasized the im-

Table II. AAC Assessment Models

Model	Key Components
Candidacy Models	• Targets individuals with chronic expressive communication disorders, and strong cognitive/ linguistic capabilities • Individuals with potential to develop speech and lower cognitive functioning were excluded
Competence Model Light (1989)	• Targets the assessment of adequacy of communication based on sufficient knowledge, judgment and skills needed to communicate within one's culture • Emphasizes four areas of communicative competence: linguistic (both disability and indigenous cultures); operational (technical skills to operate AAC system); social (for communication within and outside the person's cultural group); and strategic (communication strategies that may vary from traditional means within the cultural group)
Communication Needs Model Beukelman, Yorkston, & Dowden (1985)	• Targets literate and nonliterate individuals • Documents the communication needs of individuals • Determines how many needs are met using current communication strategies • Reduces the number of unmet communication needs using AAC interventions
Participation Model Beukelman & Mirenda (1988)	• Based on the functional participation requirements of peers without disabilities of same chronological age as potential AAC user • Identifies participation patterns and communication needs • Assesses opportunity barriers • Assesses access barriers • Plans and implements interventions for present and future • Evaluates intervention effectiveness
Communicative Competence and Culture Model (Hetzroni & Harris, 1996)	• Emphasizes assessment of potential AAC user within context of six interrelated domains: extended family, nuclear family, school, community, clinicians and other professionals, and other cultural influences • Evaluators must develop greater awareness of their own microcultures • Uses an inventory based on Competence Model (linguistic, social, operational, strategic)
Cultural Family-Centered Model (Parette, 1998)	• Views family as backdrop against which six interrelated influences are examined: ethnicity; acculturation, culture, service system issues, technology features, child characteristics • External influences (social, life experiences, developmental expectations, dominant/mainstream culture) are evaluated within content of potential impact on family
Culturally Inclusive Assessment of AAC (Huer, 1997)	• Inclusive protocol, emphasizing the need to address cultural features directly *Includes a practitioner self-assessment before engaging in delivery of services to children within cultural communities which may differ from their own • Examines child's communication partners, needs, and capabilities

portance of examining competence within one's culture, many of these approaches advocated in the 1970s and 1980s have typically failed to address cultural factors. More recently, efforts have been described to include cultural issues in AAC decision-making models. For example, Parette (1998) provided a model for decision making that included six issue areas (i.e., acculturation, culture, service system concerns, technology features, child characteristics, and ethnicity) that must be viewed against the backdrop of the family. The family, in turn, is viewed as being affected by a variety of external factors including the dominant/mainstream culture, developmental expectations, social influences, and life experiences.

Hetzroni and Harris (1996) described a model in which a "thin layer" (p. 54) representing the first interactions with the potential AAC user provides the early childhood practitioner with an understanding of (a) the culture learned to a particular point in time, (b) the values and rules learned, and (c) the behaviors resulting from the knowledge. This understanding cuts across six interrelated spheres of influence: (a) community, (b) extended family, (c) nuclear family, (d) school setting, (e) clinicians and other professionals and (f) other cultural influences (Hetroni & Harris, 1996).

One particularly promising culturally sensitive approach— the Culturally Inclusive Assessment of AAC Model—has been described by Huer (1997) and interpreted with regard to African American individuals (Huer & Wyatt, 1999). Generally, this model includes a protocol outlining strategies for self-assessment by practitioners and information-gathering strategies related to a young child's communication partners, needs, and capabilities. This model offered direction for practitioners providing services to African American children with disabilities who do not share similar life experiences with the clinician performing the assessment. As noted by Huer and Wyatt, the model integrates specific and appropriate questions into the evaluation process to ensure the collection of the most accurate and representative information in light of possible culturally based differences.

Asking Appropriate Questions

Using the model proposed by Huer (1997), three basic questions must be asked by early childhood practitioners working with young African American children with disabilities and their families:

1. With whom does the African American child using AAC communicate on a regular basis?
2. What are the needs of the African American child for communication during everyday activities?
3. What specific capabilities, knowledge, and skills, does the African American child demonstrate?

Additional questions that may be useful to ask when working with these individuals include:

4. What are some of the potential barriers to meeting the communication needs of the African American child?
5. What are some of the strategies useful for practitioners when working around potential barriers and enhancing the African American child's current communication abilities?

Huer and Wyatt (1999) noted that to answer these questions, early childhood practitioners should consider the various cultural issues that may influence (a) the type of responses received from the child, as well as (b) the actual information-gathering process. Differing cultural views, beliefs, and attitudes of African American individuals can influence the frequency and nature of communication interactions with others (Huer & Wyatt, 1999). The structural makeup of the child's family and demographic makeup of his/her community can also affect social practices, attitudes, and values as they pertain to communication use patterns. The cultural orientation and language use patterns within the family and community can also lead to culturally based communication style differences.

Each of the above factors is likely to affect the communication assessment and service delivery process when working with young African American children with disabilities and their families. Specifically, they can influence the nature of information gathered and observations made. They can also influence the manner in which information is obtained and observations are made. Differing cultural views toward communication and other disabilities can impact whether final practitioner suggestions and recommendations are accepted. Language code and style preferences can impact on decisions about the type of vocabulary, symbols and AAC systems selected. Family and community resources can also either limit or enhance the delivery of quality services.

CONCLUSIONS

Descriptions of African American culture, lifestyles, family values, and communication styles and patterns are readily available to professionals (see e.g., Roseberry-McKibbin, 1995; Willis, 1998). However, information regarding the practice of AAC within African American communities has only recently begun to emerge, with efforts being made to more effectively educate professionals about the cultural systems of these individuals and their influence on AAC decision making (VanBiervliet & Parette, 1999). It seems reasonable to suggest that if practitioners learn about the lifestyles of persons from various cultures (Barrera, 1993; Hanson, Lynch, & Wayman, 1990;

Harry et al., 1995; Roseberry-McKibbin, 1995) they will plan more appropriate services for young children from various ethnic and cultural backgrounds (Hetzroni & Harris, 1996; Huer, 1997b). Issues explored in this article may potentially assist early childhood professionals to more effectively work with African American families and their children with disabilities during the process of making decisions about AAC devices.

ACKNOWLEDGMENTS

This manuscript is supported in part by Grant No. H029K50072 from the U.S. Department of Education to the first author. Opinions expressed herein are those of the authors alone and should not be interpreted to have agency endorsement.

REFERENCES

American Speech-Language-Hearing Association. (1991). Report: Augmentative and alternative communication. *Asha, 33* (Suppl. 5), 9–12.

Angelo, D. H. (1996). AAC in the family and home. In S. L. Glennen & D. C. Decoste (Eds.), *Handbook of augmentative and alternative communication* (pp. 523–541). San Diego, CA: Singular.

Angelo, D. H., Jones, S. D., & Kokoska, S. M. (1995). Family perspective on augmentative and alternative communication: Families of young children. *Augmentative and Alternative Communication, 11*, 193–201.

Angelo, D. H., Kokoska, S. M., & Jones S. D. (1996). Family perspective on augmentative and alternative communications: Families of adolescents and young adults. *Augmentative and Alternative Communication, 12*, 13–20.

Barrera, I. (1993). Effective and appropriate instruction for all children: The challenge of cultural/linguistic diversity and young children with special needs. *Topics in Early Childhood Special Education, 13*, 461–487.

Batavia, A. I., Dillard, D., & Phillips, B. (n.d.) *How to avoid technology abandonment.* Washington, DC: Request Rehabilitation Engineering Center, National Rehabilitation Hospital.

Beukelman, D., & Mirenda, P. (1992). *Augmentative and alternative communication: Management of severe communication disorders in children and adults.* Baltimore: Brookes.

Beukelman, D. R., & Mirenda, P. (1998). *Augmentative and alternative communication. Management of severe communication disorders in children and adults.* (2nd ed.). Baltimore: Brookes.

Beukelman, D., Yorkston, K., & Dowden, P. (1985). *Communication augmentation: A casebook of clinical management.* Austin, TX: Pro-ed.

Billingsley, A. (1974). *Black families and the struggle for survival: Teaching our children to walk tall.* New York: Friendship Press.

Blackstone, S. W. (Ed.). (1986). *Augmentative communication: an introduction.* Rockville, MD: American Speech-Language-Hearing Association.

Blackstone, S. W. (1993). For consumers. Cultures in the community. *Augmentative Communication News, 6*(2), 1–10.

Cole, L. (1989, September). E pluribus pluribus: Multicultural imperatives for the 1990s and beyond. *American Speech, Language, Hearing Association Newsletter,* 65–70.

Council for Educational Diagnostic Services. (1995, Summer). Assessment issues: A mini-interview with Don Hammill. *CECS Communique, 22*(4), 4.

Covington, A. (1976). Black people and Black English: Attitudes and deeducation in a biased macroculture. In D. S. Harrison & T. Trabasso (Eds.), *Black English: A seminar* (pp. 255–264). Hillsdale, NJ: Erlbaum.

Dillard, D. (1989). *National study on abandonment of technology. 1989 Annual Report on the National Rehabilitation Hospital's Rehabilitation Engineering Center's Evaluation of Assistive Technology* (Cooperative Agreement No. H133E0016). Washington, DC: National Institute on Disability and Rehabilitation Research.

Dillard, J. L. (1972). *Black English: Its history and usage in the United States.* New York: Random House.

Hanson, M. J., Lynch, E. W., & Wayman, K. I. (1990). Honoring the cultural diversity of families when gathering data. *Topics in Early Childhood Special Education, 10,* 112–131.

Harris, J. L. (1996). Issues in recruiting African American participants for research. In A. G. Kamhi, K. E. Pollock, & J. L. Harris (Eds.), *Communication development and disorders in African American children* (pp. 19–34). Baltimore: Brookes.

Harrison, D. S., & Alvy, K. T. (1982). *The context of black parenting.* Studio City, CA: Center for the Improvement of Child Caring.

Harry, B., Grenot-Scheyer, M., Smith-Lewis, M., Park, Hyun-Sook, Xin, F., & Schwartz, I. (1995). Developing culturally inclusive services for individuals with severe disabilities. *Journal of the Association for Persons with Severe Handicaps, 20,* 99–109.

Hetzroni, O. E., & Harris, O. L. (1996). Cultural aspects in the development of AAC users. *Augmentative and Alternative Communication, 12,* 52–58.

Huer, M. B. (1987). 1986 ISAAC Round Table Discussion—Formal assessment tools: What we have, what we need. *The ISAAC Bulletin, 10,* 14–17.

Huer, M. B. (1988). *The nonspeech test for receptive and expressive language.* Wauconda, IL: Don Johnston.

Huer, M. B. (1994, November). *Diversity now: Multicultural issues in AAC.* A miniseminar presented at the National Annual Meeting for the American Speech-Language-Hearing Association, New Orleans, LA.

Huer, M. B. (1997). Culturally inclusive assessments for children using augmentative and alternative communication (AAC). *Journal of Children's Communication Development, 19* (1), 23–34.

Huer, M. B. (1999). Focus group with parents with AAC devices. In H. P. Parette & A. VanBiervliet (Eds.), *Families, cultures, and AAC* (CD-ROM; pp. 194–228). Little Rock, AR: Southeast Missouri State University and University of Arkansas for Medical Sciences.

Huer, M. B., Parette, H. P., & Saenz, T. I. (2001). Conversations with Mexican-Americans regarding children with disabilities and augmentative and alternative communication. *Communication Disorders Quarterly, 22,* 197–206.

Huer, M. B., & Wyatt, T. (1999). Cultural factors in the delivery of AAC services to the African American community. *ASHA Special Division 14 Newsletter, 5* (1), 5–9.

Kemp, C., & Parette, H. P. (2000). Barriers to minority parent involvement in assistive technology (AT) decision-making processes. *Education and Training in Mental Retardation and Developmental Disabilities, 35* (4), 385–393.

King, S. H. (1993). The limited presence of African American teachers. *Review of Educational Research, 63,* 115–149.

Light, J. (1989). Toward a definition of communication competence for individuals using augmentative and alternative communication systems. *Augmentative and Alternative Communication, 5,* 137–144.

Light, J., & McNaughton, D. (1993). Literacy and augmentative and alternative communication (AAC): The expectations and priorities of parents and teachers. *Topics in Language Disorders, 13* (2), 33–46.

Meese, R. L. (2001). *Teaching students with mild disabilities* (2nd ed.). Belmont, CA: Wadsworth Thomson Learning.

Parette, H. P. (1998). Cultural issues and family-centered assistive technology decision-making. In S. L. Judge, & H. P. Parette (Eds.), *Assistive technology for young children with disabilities: A guide to providing family-centered services* (pp. 184–210). Cambridge, MA: Brookline.

Parette, H. P., & Angelo, D. H. (1996). Augmentative and alternative communication impact on families: Trends and future directions. *The Journal of Special Education, 30,* 77–98.

Parette, H. P., Brotherson, M. J., & Huer, M. B. (2000). Giving families a voice in augmentative and alternative communication decision-making. *Education and Training in Mental Retardation and Developmental Disabilities, 35,* 177–190.

Parette, H. P., Stuart, S., Huer, M. B., Hostetler, S., & Wommack, J. D. (1996, November). *Qualitative methodology and AAC decision-making with families across cultures.* Paper presented to the American Speech-Language-Hearing Association 1996 Annual Convention, Seattle, WA.

Parette, P., VanBiervliet, A., Reyna, J. W., & Heisserer, D. (Eds.). (1999). *Families, culture, and augmentative and alternative communication (AAC). A multimedia instructional program for related service personnel and family members.* [On-line]. Source: http://cstl.semo.edu/parette/homepage/database.pdf

Roseberry-McKibbin, C. (1995). *Multicultural students with special language needs.* Oceanside, CA: Academic Communication Associates.

Seymour, H. N., Champion, T., & Jackson, J. (1995). The language of African American learners: Effective assessment and instructional programming for children with special needs. In B. A. Ford, F. E. Obiakor, & J. M. Patton (Eds.), *Effective education of African American exceptional learners. New perspectives* (pp. 89–121). Austin, TX: Pro-ed.

Smith-Lewis, M. (1992). *What is mental retardation? Perceptions from the African American community.* Unpublished manuscript. Hunter College, New York.

Soto, G., Huer, M. B., & Taylor, O. (1997). Multicultural issues. In L. L. Lloyd, D, H. Fuller, & H. H. Arvidson (Eds.), *Augmentative and alternative communication* (pp. 406–413). Boston: Allyn and Bacon.

Terrell, S. L., Battle, D. E., & Grantham, R. B. (1998). African American cultures. In D. E. Battle (Ed.), *Communication disorders in multicultural populations* (2nd ed., pp. 31–71). Boston: Butterworth-Heinemann.

van Keulen, J. E., Weddington, G. T., & DeBose, C. E. (1998). *Speech, language, and the African American child.* Boston: Allyn and Bacon.

VanBiervliet, A., & Parette, H. P. (1999). *Families, cultures, and AAC* [CD-ROM]. Little Rock, AR: Southeast Missouri State University and University of Arkansas for Medical Sciences.

Willis, W. (1998). Families with African American roots. In E. W. Lynch & M. J. Hanson (Eds.), *Developing cross-cultural competence. A guide for working with young children and their families* (2nd ed. pp. 165–207). Baltimore: Brookes.

Wyatt, T. A. (1998). Assessment issues with multicultural populations. In D. E. Battle (Ed.), *Communication disorders in multicultural populations* (2nd ed., pp. 379–425). Boston: Butterworth-Heinemann.

Phil Parette, Southeast Missouri University.

Mary Blake Huer, California State University–Fullerton.

Toya A. Wyatt, California State University–Fullerton.

Correspondence should be directed to Phil Parette, e-mail: pparette @semovm.semo.edu.

From *Early Childhood Education Journal,* Spring 2002, pp. 201-207. © 2002 by Kluwer Academic/Plenum Publishers. Reprinted by permission.

UNIT 5
Developmental Disabilities

Unit Selections

15. **The Secrets of Autism**, J. Madeleine Nash
16. **Citizenship and Disability**, Michael Bérubé
17. **Inscrutable or Meaningful? Understanding and Supporting Your Inarticulate Students**, Robin M. Smith

Key Points to Consider

- How would you explain the surge in autistic disorders? What are social scientists discovering through brain imaging techniques?

- What do we lose as a society if we revoke and/or reinterpret the moral and legal rights of our citizens with developmental disabilities? Do they, in fact, enrich our lives?

- Students with developmental disabilities may have atypical facial expressions and speech. Are these inscrutable or meaningful? How can teachers and others interpret and use these messages?

 Links: www.dushkin.com/online/
These sites are annotated in the World Wide Web pages.

Arc of the United States
http://www.thearc.org
Disability-Related Sources on the Web
http://www.arcarizona.org/dislnkin.html
Gentle Teaching
http://www.gentleteaching.nl

In our efforts to be more "politically correct" and to not inflict pain, we now avoid labels such as "mentally retarded." We always put the individual first and add the condition of disability second (when and if it is necessary). Students and adults who have cognitive skills falling two standard deviations below the norm for their age are now considered cognitively developmentally disabled. Children who have sustained brain damage through traumatic brain injury, even if they score two standard deviations below the intellectual norm for age, are traumatically brain injured, not developmentally disabled. Children and adults with autism or variants of autism (such as Asperger's syndrome) are subsumed under a separate disability category by the U.S. Individuals with Disabilities Education Act (IDEA) as well. Three out of four individuals with classic autism do score two standard deviations below the IQ mean. Nevertheless, cognitive developmental disorders, traumatic brain injuries, and autism are each recognized as separate disability categories by IDEA.

Children with significantly subnormal intelligence were once classified as "educable," "trainable," or "custodial" for purposes of placement. These terms are strongly discouraged today. Even severely developmentally disabled children are educable and can benefit from some schooling. They must leave where they are to be where we hope they can be. The current preferred categorical terms for children who are developmentally challenged are "intermittent," "limited," "extensive," and "pervasive." These terms refer to how much support the individuals need to function and to succeed as much as possible.

IDEA mandates free and appropriate public school education for every child, regardless of mentation. While the legal windows on education are from ages 6 to 16 in the United States, individuals with developmental disabilities are entitled to a free and appropriate education from age of assessment (birth, early childhood) to age 21. This encompasses parent-child education programs and preschool programs early in life and transitional services into the community and world of work after the public school education is completed.

The inclusion of children with disabilities in regular education classes has been controversial (see Unit 1) since 1975. Some school systems have succeeded brilliantly in integrating students with cognitive developmental disabilities into their regular classes. Other schools have fought the law every step of the way. Their histories are full of lawsuits brought by parents to try to obtain the services to which the law entitles them. The less-than-stellar school systems, and some U.S. states that have been notorious laggards, complain that the law is too cumbersome. There have been few negative consequences for school systems or whole state education departments that have resisted placing cognitively disabled students in regular classrooms. Therefore some parents still invoke formal complaint procedures against schools to get their children out of full-time special classes or special schools.

A child with cognitive developmental disabilities who is in the mildest "intermittent" classification needs support at school at times when special needs arise and at times of life transitions. This terminology is generally used for children whose disabilities do not create an obvious and continual problem. These children have slower mentation but also have many abilities.

The next level of support, classified as "limited," is usually used for children who experience daily limitations on their abilities but who can achieve a degree of self-sufficiency after an appropriate education in the least restrictive environment. Limited refers to the period of time from diagnosis until adulthood (age 21). The "extensive" support classification extends the support throughout the lifespan for individuals whose developmental disabilities prohibit them from living independently. The "pervasive" support classification is used infrequently. It is only for those individuals whose disabilities prevent them from most activities of self-help. Pervasive support is intensive and life-sustaining in nature.

The majority of children with developmental disabilities can be placed in the intermittent support classification. To casual observers, they often do not appear to have any disabilities. However, their ability to process, store, and retrieve information is limited. In the past, this group of children was given IQ measurements between two and three standard deviations below the mean (usually an IQ below 70 but above 55). Intelligence testing is an inexact science with problems of both validity and reliability. The current definition of developmental disability endorsed by the American Association on Mental Deficiency (AAMD) does not include any IQ scoring results other than to use the phrase "subaverage intellectual functioning." It emphasizes the problems that individuals with developmental disabilities have with adaptive skills such as communication, self-care, home living, social skills, community use, self-direction, health and safety, functional academics, leisure, and work.

The causes of developmental disabilities (DD) are unclear. About one-half of all individuals with DD are suspected of having sustained some brain damage prenatally, neonatally, or in childhood. Among the better-known factors that damage brain tissue are early birth or low birth weight, anoxia, malnutrition, drugs, viruses, radiation, trauma, and tumors.

The first article in this unit depicts a boy with Asperger's syndrome, a developmental disability that is related to autism. More than a million people in the United States suffer from one of the autistic disorders, five times more than have Down syndrome. The surge in autistic disorders is not well understood. J. Madeleine Nash reviews some of the new research on autism and its related conditions. Advanced brain imaging techniques are revealing neurological factors. Social scientists are exploring the role of the environment.

The second article, "Citizenship and Disability" addresses the question of disability rights. Legal rights granted by IDEA and the Americans With Disability Act (ADA) can be reinterpreted and/or revoked. The author gives cogent reasons for not allowing this to happen, whatever our political and economic straits. Persons with developmental disabilities, nondisabled peers, and democracy (all of us) benefit from moral equality.

The third article, "Inscrutable or Meaningful? Understanding and Supporting Your Inarticulate Students" discusses the importance of deciphering the emotions, behaviors, and atypical processes of students with developmental disabilities.

SCIENCE

THE SECRETS OF AUTISM

THE NUMBER OF CHILDREN DIAGNOSED WITH AUTISM AND ASPERGER'S IN THE U.S. IS EXPLODING. WHY?

By J. MADELEINE NASH

Tommy Barrett is a dreamy-eyed fifth-grader who lives with his parents, twin brothers, two cats and a turtle in San Jose, Calif., the heart of Silicon Valley. He's an honor-roll student who likes math and science and video games. He's also a world-class expert on Animorph and Transformer toys. "They're like cars and trains and animals that transform into robots or humans—I love them!" he shouts exuberantly.

And that is sometimes a problem. For a time, in fact, Tommy's fascination with his toys was so strong that when they weren't around he would pretend to *be* the toys, transforming from a truck into a robot or morphing into a kitten. He would do this in the mall, in the school playground and even in the classroom. His teachers found this repetitive pantomime delightful but disturbing, as did his mother Pam. *more boys than girls*

Autistic disorders may afflict nearly 300,000 kids in the U.S. alone

By that point, there were other worrisome signs. Pam Barrett recalls that as a 3-year-old, Tommy was a fluent, even voluble talker, yet he could not seem to grasp that conversation had reciprocal rules, and, curiously, he avoided looking into other people's eyes. And although Tommy was obviously smart—he had learned to read by the time he was 4—he was so fidgety and unfocused that he was unable to participate in his kindergarten reading group.

When Tommy turned 8, his parents finally learned what was wrong. Their bright little boy, a psychiatrist informed them, had a mild form of autism known as Asperger syndrome. Despite the fact that children with

Asperger's often respond well to therapy, the Barretts, at that moment, found the news almost unbearable.

That's because just two years earlier Pam and her husband Chris, operations manager of a software-design company, had learned that Tommy's twin brothers Jason and Danny were profoundly autistic. Seemingly normal at birth, the twins learned to say a few words before they spiraled into their secret world, quickly losing the abilities they had just started to gain. Instead of playing with toys, they broke them; instead of speaking, they emitted an eerie, high-pitched keening.

Up to 20 genes may be involved in autism, but they're not the only factors

First Jason and Danny, now Tommy. Pam and Chris started to wonder about their children's possible exposure to toxic substances. They started scanning a lengthening roster of relatives, wondering how long autism had shadowed their family.

The anguish endured by Pam and Chris Barrett is all too familiar to tens of thousands of families across North America and other parts of the world. With a seeming suddenness, cases of autism and closely related disorders like Asperger's are exploding in number, and no one has a good explanation for it. While many experts believe the increase is a by-product of a recent broadening of diagnostic criteria, others are convinced that the surge is at least in part real and thereby cause for grave concern.

In the Barretts' home state of California, for instance, the number of autistic children seeking social services has more than quadrupled in the past 15 years, from fewer than 4,000 in 1987 to nearly 18,000 today. So common are

The Geek Syndrome

At Michelle Winner's social-skills clinic in San Jose, Calif., business is booming. Every week dozens of youngsters with Asperger syndrome file in and out of therapy sessions while their anxious mothers run errands or chat quietly in the waiting room. In one session, a rosy-cheeked 12-year-old struggles to describe the emotional reactions of a cartoon character in a video clip; in another, four little boys (like most forms of autism, Asperger's overwhelmingly affects boys) grapple with the elusive concept of teamwork while playing a game of 20 Questions. Unless prompted to do so, they seldom look at one another, directing their eyes to the wall or ceiling or simply staring off into space.

Yet outside the sessions the same children become chatty and animated, displaying an astonishing grasp of the most arcane subjects. Transformer toys, video games, airplane schedules, star charts, dinosaurs. It sounds charming, and indeed would be, except that their interest is all consuming. After about five minutes, children with Asperger's, a.k.a. the "little professor" or "geek" syndrome, tend to sound like CDs on autoplay. "Did you ask her if she's interested in astrophysics?" a mother gently chides her son, who has launched into an excruciatingly detailed description of what goes on when a star explodes into a supernova.

Although Hans Asperger described the condition in 1944, it wasn't until 1994 that the American Psychiatric Association officially recognized Asperger syndrome as a form of autism with its own diagnostic criteria. It is this recognition, expanding the definition of autism to include everything from the severely retarded to the mildest cases, that is partly responsible for the recent explosion in autism diagnoses.

There are differences between Asperger's and high-functioning autism. Among other things, Asperger's appears to be even more strongly genetic than classic autism, says Dr. Fred Volkmar, a child psychiatrist at Yale. About a third of the fathers or brothers of children with Asperger's show signs of the disorder. There appear to be maternal roots as well. The wife of one Silicon Valley software engineer believes that her Asperger's son represents the fourth generation in just such a lineage.

It was the Silicon Valley connection that led *Wired* magazine to run its geek-syndrome feature last December. The story was basically a bit of armchair theorizing about a social phenomenon known as assortative mating. In university towns and R.-and-D. corridors, it is argued, smart but not particularly well-socialized men today are meeting and marrying women very like themselves, leading to an overload of genes that predispose their children to autism, Asperger's and related disorders.

Is there anything to this idea? Perhaps. There is no question that many successful people—not just scientists and engineers but writers and lawyers as well—possess a suite of traits that seem to be, for lack of a better word, Aspergery. The ability to focus intensely and screen out other distractions, for example, is a geeky trait that can be extremely useful to computer programmers. On the other hand, concentration that is too intense—focusing on cracks in the pavement while a taxi is bearing down on you—is clearly, in Darwinian terms, maladaptive.

But it may be a mistake to dwell exclusively on the genetics of Asperger's; there must be other factors involved. Experts suspect that such variables as prenatal positioning in the womb, trauma experienced at birth or random variation in the process of brain development may also play a role.

Even if you could identify the genes involved in Asperger's, it's not clear what you would do about them. It's not as if they are lethal genetic defects, like the ones that cause Huntington's disease or cystic fibrosis. "Let's say that a decade from now we know all the genes for autism," suggests Bryna Siegel, a psychologist at the University of California, San Francisco. "And let's say your unborn child has four of these genes. We may be able to tell you that 80% of the people with those four genes will be fully autistic but that the other 20% will perform in the gifted mathematical range."

Filtering the geeky genes out of the high-tech breeding grounds like Silicon Valley, in other words, might remove the very DNA that made these places what they are today.

—By J. Madeleine Nash.
With reporting by Amy Bonesteel/Atlanta

cases of Asperger's in Silicon Valley, in fact, that *Wired* magazine coined a cyber-age term for the disorder, referring to its striking combination of intellectual ability and social cluelessness as the "geek syndrome." *Wired* went on to make a provocative if anecdotal case that autism and Asperger's were rising in Silicon Valley at a particularly alarming rate—and asked whether "math-and-tech genes" might be to blame (*see box*).

Yet the rise in autism and Asperger's is hardly confined to high-tech enclaves or to the children of computer programmers and software engineers. It occurs in every job category and socioeconomic class and in every state. "We're getting calls from school systems in rural Georgia," observes Sheila Wagner, director of the Autism Resource Center at Atlanta's Emory University. "People are saying, 'We never had any kids with autism before, and now we have 10! What's going on?'"

It's a good question. Not long ago, autism was assumed to be comparatively rare, affecting as few as 1 in 10,000 people. The latest studies, however, suggest that as many as 1 in 150 kids age 10 and younger may be affected by autism or a related disorder—a total of nearly 300,000 children in the U.S. alone. If you include adults, according to the Autism Society of America, more than a million people in the U.S. suffer from one of the autistic disorders (also known as pervasive developmental disorders or PDDs). The problem is five times as common as Down syndrome and three times as common as juvenile diabetes.

No wonder parents are besieging the offices of psychologists and psychiatrists in their search for remedies. No wonder school systems are adding special aides to help teachers cope. And no wonder public and private research institutions have launched collaborative initiatives aimed at deciphering the complex biology that produces such a dazzling range of disability.

In their urgent quest for answers, parents like the Barretts are provoking what promises to be a scientific revolution. In response to the concerns they are raising, money is finally flowing into autism research, a field that five years ago appeared to be stuck in the stagnant backwaters of neuroscience. Today dozens of scientists are racing to identify the genes linked to autism. Just last month, in a series of articles published by *Molecular Psychiatry*, scientists from the U.S., Britain, Italy and France reported that they are beginning to make significant progress.

Meanwhile, research teams are scrambling to create animal models for autism in the form of mutant mice. They are beginning to examine environmental factors that might contribute to the development of autism and using advanced brain-imaging technology to probe the deep interior of autistic minds. In the process, scientists are gaining rich new insights into this baffling spectrum of disorders and are beginning to float intriguing new hypotheses about why people affected by it develop minds that are strangely different from our own and yet, in some important respects, hauntingly similar.

AUTISM'S GENETIC ROOTS

AUTISM WAS FIRST DESCRIBED IN 1943 BY JOHNS HOPKINS psychiatrist Leo Kanner, and again in 1944 by Austrian pediatrician Hans Asperger. Kanner applied the term to children who were socially withdrawn and preoccupied with routine, who struggled to acquire spoken language

GUIDE FOR PARENTS

How do you tell if your child is autistic? And what should you do if he or she is?

WHAT TO LOOK FOR

SIGNS OF AUTISM

(Usually apparent in toddlers; watch for cluster of symptoms)

- No pointing by 1 year
- No babbling by 1 year; no single words by 16 months; no two-word phrases by 24 months
- Any loss of language skills at any time
- No pretend playing
- Little interest in making friends
- Extremely short attention span
- No response when called by name; indifference to others
- Little or no eye contact
- Repetitive body movements, such as hand flapping, rocking
- Intense tantrums
- Fixations on a single object, such as a spinning fan
- Unusually strong resistance to changes in routines
- Oversensitivity to certain sounds, textures or smells

SIGNS OF ASPERGER'S

(Usually diagnosed at 6 or older)

- Difficulty making friends
- Difficulty reading or communicating through nonverbal social cues, such as facial expressions
- No understanding that others may have thoughts or feelings different from his or her own
- Obsessive focus on a narrow interest, such as reciting train schedules
- Awkward motor skills
- Inflexibility about routines, especially when changes occur spontaneously
- Mechanical, almost robotic patterns of speech

(Even "normal" children exhibit some of these behaviors from time to time. The symptoms of autism and Asperger's, by contrast, are persistent and debilitating.)

—*By Amy Lennard Goehner*

yet often possessed intellectual gifts that ruled out a diagnosis of mental retardation. Asperger applied the term to children who were socially maladroit, developed bizarre obsessions and yet were highly verbal and seemingly

GUIDE FOR PARENTS *continued*

Snapshots from the Autistic Brain

REACTING TO FACES OF STRANGERS ...

... AND FACES OF LOVED ONES

Neuroimaging studies confirm what scientists long suspected: autistic brains don't react to facial cues the way normal brains do. But in one regard the conventional wisdom was wrong. In a breakthrough study, Karen Pierce at the University of California at San Diego has shown that when faces of strangers are replaced by faces of loved ones, the autistic brain lights up like an explosion of Roman candles.

WHERE TO START

GET AN EVALUATION: Take your child to a developmental pediatrician with expertise in autism or Asperger syndrome. The pediatrician will evaluate your child with a team of specialists (speech therapists, occupational therapists, behavior therapists) to determine the areas in which your child needs help.

EARLY INTERVENTION: Every state is mandated to provide a free evaluation and early-intervention services for children. To find out whom to contact in your state, consult the National Information Center for Children and Youth with Disabilities (funded by the Department of Education) at 800-695-0285 or *nichcy.org/ index.html*. Ask about support groups in your area.

HOW TO TREAT IT

There is no cure for autism, but there are many treatments that can make a difference:
SPEECH THERAPY: Can help overcome communication and language barriers
OCCUPATIONAL THERAPY: Helps with sensory integration and motor skills
BEHAVIORAL THERAPY: Improves cognitive skills and reduces inappropriate behavior
EDUCATIONAL THERAPY: A highly structured approach works best
MEDICATION: Can reduce some symptoms
SPECIAL DIETS: Eliminating certain food groups, such as dairy, helps some children

HELPFUL WEBSITES

ONLINE ASPERGER SYNDROME INFORMATION AND SUPPORT *www.aspergersyndrome.org*
AUTISM SOCIETY OF AMERICA *autism-society.org*
FAMILIES FOR EARLY AUTISM TREATMENT *www.feat.org*
AUTISM RESOURCES *autism-info.com*
YALE CHILD STUDY CENTER *info.med.yale.edu/ chldstdy/autism*

Network: Other parents can be great sources in finding the right treatments.

quite bright. There was a striking tendency, Asperger noted, for the disorder to run in families, sometimes passing directly from father to son. Clues that genes might be central to autism appeared in Kanner's work as well.

VACCINES
Are the Shots Safe?

Ask the parents of autistic children whether they believe childhood vaccines can cause autism, and the answer will probably be yes. They have heard of too many cases of babies who were perfectly normal until they got their measles, mumps and rubella (MMR) shot and then, within weeks—if not days—started throwing tantrums, losing language skills and generally tuning out.

Ask doctors the same question, and they are likely to cite the panel of experts convened by the Institute of Medicine last year. They studied the evidence but found no explanation for how vaccines might possibly cause autism. Included in the review were studies that showed no significant difference in the incidence of autism disorders before and after MMR immunization became routine in 1988 in Britain. "We bent over backward to look for the biological mechanisms that would support a link," says the panel's chairwoman, Dr. Marie McCormick of the Harvard School of Public Health.

But failing to prove that something can happen is not the same as proving it doesn't, and the issue is still a matter of furious debate. The only scientific evidence against childhood vaccines comes from Dr. Andrew Wakefield, formerly at the Royal Free Hospital in London. His theory is that autism stems from a severe immune reaction to something in the vaccine. In February he published a paper showing that immunized children with autism and bowel disorders have higher levels of measles particles in their intestinal tissue than normal children do. The evidence is not entirely persuasive, however; measles particles in the tissues do not necessarily mean that the virus—or the vaccine—causes autism.

What about all the children whose symptoms appeared shortly after their MMR? The association may be purely coincidental. The shots are given at 15 months, which is when behavior and speech patterns in babies usually become sufficiently pronounced for parents to start noticing that something is wrong. Most of the evidence suggests that autism is primarily a genetic disorder. It may be that some symptoms appear immediately after birth but are too subtle to be spotted in the first year or so of life.

To get more definitive answers, the National Institutes of Health and the Centers for Disease control have each launched their own investigations. Karyn Seroussi of Poughkeepsie, N.Y., for one, supports this research. "If it's the shots, I want to know," says Seroussi, an autism advocate and parent of an autistic son. "If it's not, I want to know what the heck it is that's causing autism." On that, both parents and doctors can agree.

—By Alice Park

But then autism research took a badly wrong turn. Asperger's keen insights languished in Europe's postwar turmoil, and Kanner's were overrun by the Freudian juggernaut. Children were not born autistic, experts insisted, but became that way because their parents, especially mothers, were cold and unnurturing.

In 1981, however, British psychiatrist Dr. Lorna Wing published an influential paper that revived interest in Asperger's work. The disorder Asperger identified, Wing observed, appeared in many ways to be a variant of Kanner's autism, so that the commonalities seemed as important as the differences. As a result, researchers now believe that Asperger and Kanner were describing two faces of a highly complicated and variable disorder, one that has its source in the kaleidoscope of traits encoded in the human genome. Researchers also recognize that severe autism is not always accompanied by compensatory intellectual gifts and is, in fact, far likelier to be characterized by heartbreaking deficits and mental retardation.

Perhaps the most provocative finding scientists have made to date is that the components of autism, far more than autism itself, tend to run in families. Thus even though profoundly autistic people rarely have children, researchers often find that a close relative is affected by some aspect of the disorder. A sister may engage in odd repetitive behavior or be excessively shy; a brother may have difficulties with language or be socially inept to a noticeable degree. In similar fashion, if one identical twin has autism, there is a 60% chance that the other will too and a better than 75% chance that the twin without autism will exhibit one or more autistic traits.

How many genes contribute to susceptibility to autism? Present estimates run from as few as three to more than 20. Coming under intensifying scrutiny, as the papers published by *Molecular Psychiatry* indicate, are genes that regulate the action of three powerful neurotransmitters: glutamate, which is intimately involved in learning and memory, and serotonin and gamma-aminobutiric acid (GABA), which have been implicated in obsessive-compulsive behavior, anxiety and depression.

Those genes hardly exhaust the list of possibilities. Among the suspects are virtually all the genes that control brain development and perhaps cholesterol and immune-system function as well. Christopher Stodgell, a developmental toxicologist at New York's University of Rochester, observes that the process that sets up the brain resembles an amazingly intricate musical score, and there are tens of thousands of genes in the orchestra. If these genes do what they're supposed to do, says Stodgell, "then you have a Mozart's *Concerto for Clarinet*. If not, you have cacophony."

A DIFFERENCE OF MIND

AUTISTIC PEOPLE OFTEN SUFFER FROM A BEWILDERING ARRAY of problems—sensory disturbances, food allergies, gas-

FIRST PERSON

My Brother

KARL TARO GREENFELD

My autistic brother Noah and I once played together. He was two, and I was a year older. We wrestled, and I tickled him. He responded in a high-pitched giggle, halfway between a baby's gurgle and a child's laughter. I can't remember ever playing with him again. Noah stayed forever a baby, profoundly retarded, always dependent, never very communicative. And my role changed, much too early, from playmate to steward. There was barely any sibling rivalry. There were no battles to be fought. He would always be the center of attention.

I was treated as a sort of supporting player. Because my father had written a trilogy of books about our family with Noah as the title character (starting with *A Child Called Noah*; 1972), I would often be asked what it was like having an autistic brother. I never figured out how to respond. The answer I always gave—that I had never known any other life or any other brother—seemed cryptic and somehow unsatisfactory.

But that remains the only answer I can give. Noah, who can't speak, dress or go to the bathroom completely unassisted, will always be the center of our family. He never earned that role; his needs dictated it. I wasn't consciously resentful of this as a child. There was no more reason to be angry about this than there was about the rigid laws of basic arithmetic.

I accepted the fact that Noah and his problems could fill a battleship of parental duty and obligation, leaving my mother and father too spent to worry about the more banal problems of their normal son. But at some point in my early teens, in the confusing years of adolescence, I stopped having friends over. Noah's condition dictated what we ate and when we slept and to a great degree how we lived. We never had fancy furniture because he chewed on the couch cushions and spit on the carpets. He would pull apart anything more complicated than a pencil. I was ashamed of our home and family. Already marked as different by virtue of being Asian American in a predominantly white community, I came to see Noah as an additional stigmatizing mark.

My father used to say every family has a skeleton in its closet. Only ours was out in the open. I don't even remember if I talked about Noah in school. My friends knew about him, but after the first few questions, there wasn't much to say. Noah didn't change. Autism is a condition, I knew from close up, for which there are no miraculous cures. So he always stayed Noah. This kid who shared the same black hair and brown eyes as I had but couldn't talk and wanted to be left alone. So what was there to say about Noah? He was my brother who was never going to grow up.

Noah is 35 now and has been living in institutions since he was 18. My parents visit him every weekend at the state-run Fairview Developmental Center in Costa Mesa, Calif. I go whenever I am in town. (Currently I live in Hong Kong.) We bring Noah his favorite foods: sushi, fresh fruit and Japanese crackers and take him for a walk or a ride. Sometimes he lashes out at me. Spitting. Scratching. Pulling hair. but he knows me; I can tell by the wary squint he gives me. We're brothers, after all.

My parents are now in their 70s. My father underwent open-heart surgery a few years ago. Eventually, the responsibility for Noah will fall solely upon me. I imagine I may have to move my own family back to California to visit him every weekend, so that those caring for him will know that despite Noah's temper tantrums and violent outbursts, he is loved; he is a brother and part of a family. He is still the center of my life. My travels, from Los Angeles to New York City to Paris to Tokyo to Hong Kong, will always bring me back to him. I don't know any other life. I have no other brother.

Greenfeld is the editor of TIME ASIA.

---

trointestinal problems, depression, obsessive compulsiveness, subclinical epilepsy, attention-deficit hyperactivity disorder. But there is, researchers believe, a central defect, and that is the difficulty people across the autistic spectrum have in developing a theory of mind. That's psychologese for the realization, which most children come to by the age of 4, that other people have thoughts, wishes and desires that are not mirror images of their own. As University of Washington child psychologist Andrew Meltzoff sees it, the developmental stage known as the terrible twos occurs because children—normal children, anyway—make the hypothesis that their parents have independent minds and then, like proper scientists, set out to test it.

Children on the autistic spectrum, however, are "mind blind"; they appear to think that what is in their mind is identical to what is in everyone else's mind and that how they feel is how everyone else feels. The notion that other people—parents, playmates, teachers—may take a different view of things, that they may harbor concealed motives or duplicitous thoughts, does not readily occur. "It took the longest time for Tommy to tell a lie," recalls Pam Barrett, and when he finally did, she inwardly cheered.

FIRST PERSON

My Son

AMY LENNARD GOEHNER

I didn't know the world that my friends with normal—or, as we call them, typically developing—kids live in until recently. Two and a half years ago, my husband and I adopted our second child, Joey. And as he has grown to be a toddler, every milestone he has reached has been bittersweet—a celebration but also a painful reminder of all the milestones our 8-year-old son Nate has never reached.

Before Joey could talk, he pointed—as if to say, "Hey, Mom, look at that dog over there"—the way kids do to engage you. I flashed back to the evaluation forms we filled out for Nate when we were taking him to specialists. One question that appeared on every form was "Does your child point?" It's a major developmental step, a gesture that communicates a child's desire to share something outside himself. Nate never pointed.

When Nate was 2 and not talking, we took him to a big New York City hospital to get him evaluated. The neurologist gave us his diagnosis almost apologetically, in a very quiet voice. I remember just two words: "Maybe autistic."

When I stopped crying, I went to my office and called everyone I had ever met who was in any way connected to the world of special-needs kids. We made a lot of mistakes before finding the perfect match for Nate (and us)—a wonderful speech therapist whom we later dubbed our captain. When she met Nate, he was nonverbal and running around her office like a self-propelled buzz saw. She looked at us calmly and said, "Let's get busy. We've got work to do."

We've been working ever since. In addition to continual speech, behavior and occupational therapy, we have dabbled in what one of our doctors called "the flavor of the week"—vitamins and supplements and other "can't miss" cures. We shelled out a small fortune for every must-have tool that Lori, Nate's occupational therapist, mentioned even casually, including weighted vests (to help "ground" Nate) and special CDs (to help desensitize him to loud sounds). "Every time Lori opens her mouth, it costs me a hundred bucks," my husband once said.

Recently I read Joey a picture book that contained illustrations of fruit. Joey pretended to pick the fruit off the page and eat it, offering me a bit. Again I flashed back to those evaluation forms: "Does your child engage in pretend/imaginative play?" Nate's idea of play is to drop sticks and small stones into a drain at the playground. He could do this for hours if we let him. Last week Joey took a long noodle from his bowl of soup, dragged it across the table and said, "Look, it's a train. There's the freight car." Then Nate took a noodle from his soup. He tossed it onto the ceiling.

Yet maybe because I entered motherhood through the special-needs world, I somehow feel more a part of it than I do the "normal" one. The challenges in this world are greater, but the accomplishments—those firsts—are that much sweeter.

The other day I heard Joey singing a song about trains, and I realized that I couldn't remember the first time I heard my second son sing. I just took it for granted. With Nate, I never take anything for granted.

When Nate was 6, I was invited to hear his class put on a concert. I had no idea what to expect, as Nate doesn't sing. What he does do is make loud, repetitive noises, occasionally while rocking back and forth. But I went anyway. And when the music teacher approached Nate and began to sing a song Nate loved to listen to, Nate looked down, stared at his hands and very quietly chimed in, "A ram sam sam, a ram sam, gooly, gooly, gooly… " The other moms rushed to hand me tissues as tears streamed town my face. I was listening to Nate sing. For the first time.

Goehner is head arts reporter at TIME

Meltzoff believes that this lack can be traced to the problem that autistic children have in imitating the adults in their lives. If an adult sits down with a normal 18-month-old and engages in some interesting behavior—pounding a pair of blocks on the floor, perhaps, or making faces—the child usually responds by doing the same. Young children with autism, however, do not, as Meltzoff and his colleague Geraldine Dawson have shown in a series of playroom experiments.

The consequences of this failure can be serious. In the early years of life, imitation is one of a child's most powerful tools for learning. It is through imitation that children learn to mouth their first words and master the rich nonverbal language of body posture and facial expression. In this way, Meltzoff says, children learn that drooping shoulders equal sadness or physical exhaustion and that twinkling eyes mean happiness or perhaps mischievousness.

For autistic people—even high-functioning autistic people—the ability to read the internal state of another person comes only after long struggle, and even then most of them fail to detect the subtle signals that normal individuals unconsciously broadcast. "I had no idea that other

FIRST PERSON

Myself

TEMPLE GRANDIN

I was 2 ½ years old when I began to show symptoms of autism: not talking, repetitive behavior and tantrums. Not being able to communicate in words was a great frustration, so I screamed. Loud, high-pitched noises hurt my ears like a dentist's drill hitting a nerve. I would shut out the hurtful stimuli by rocking or staring at sand dribbling through my fingers.

As a child, I was like an animal with no instincts to guide me. I was always observing, trying to work out the best ways to behave, yet I never fit in. When other students swooned over the Beatles, I called their reaction an ISP—interesting social phenomenon. I wanted to participate but did not know how. I had a few friends who were interested in the same things I was, such as skiing and riding horses. But friendship always revolved around what I did rather than who I was.

Even today personal relationships are something I don't really understand. I still consider sex to be the biggest, most important "sin of the system," to use my old high school term. From reading books and talking to people at conventions, I have learned that autistic people who adapt most successfully in personal relationships either choose celibacy or marry someone with similar disabilities.

Early education and speech therapy pulled me out of the autistic world: Like many autistics, I think in pictures. My artistic abilities became evident when I was in first and second grade, and they were encouraged. I had a good eye for color and painted watercolors of the beach.

But words are like a foreign language to me. I translate them into full-color movies, complete with sound, which run like a videotape in my head. When I was a child, I believed that everybody thought in pictures. Not until I went to college did I realize that some people are completely verbal and think only in words. On one of my earliest jobs I thought the other engineer was stupid because he could not "see" his mistakes on his drawings. Now I understand his problem was a lack of visual thinking and not stupidity.

Autistics have trouble learning things that cannot be thought about in pictures. The easiest words for an autistic child to learn are nouns because they relate directly to pictures. Spatial words such as *over* and *under* had no meaning for me until I had a visual image to fix them in my memory. Even now, when I hear the word under by itself, I automatically picture myself getting under the cafeteria tables at school during an air-raid drill, a common occurrence on the East Coast in the early 1950s.

Teachers who work with autistic children need to understand associative thought patterns. But visual thinking is more than just associations. Concepts can also be formed visually. When I was little, I had to figure out that small dogs were not cats. After looking at both large and small dogs, I realized that they all had the same nose. This was a common visual feature of all the dogs but none of the cats.

I credit my visualization abilities with helping me understand the animals I work with. One of my early livestock design projects was to create a dip-vat and cattle-handling facility for a feed yard in Arizona. A dip vat is a long, narrow, 7-ft.-deep swimming pool through which cattle move in single file. It is filled with pesticide to rid the animals of ticks, lice and other external parasites. In 1978 dip-vat designs were very poor. The animals often panicked because they were forced into the vat down a steep, slick decline. They would refuse to jump into the vat and would sometimes flip over backward and drown.

The first thing I did when I arrived at the feedlot was put myself inside a cow's head and see with its eyes. Because their eyes are on the sides of their head, cattle have wide-angle vision. Those cattle must have felt as if they were being forced to jump down an airplane escape slide into the ocean.

One of the first steps was to convert the ramp from steel to concrete. If I had a calf's body and hooves, I would be very scared to step on a slippery metal ramp. The final design had a concrete ramp at a 25° downward angle. Deep grooves in the concrete provided secure footing. The ramp appeared to enter the water gradually, but in reality it abruptly dropped away below the water's surface. The animals could not see the drop-off because the dip chemicals colored the water. When they stepped out over the water, they quietly fell in because their center of gravity had passed the point of no return.

Owners and managers of feedlots sometimes have a hard time comprehending that if devices such as dip vats and restraint chutes are properly designed, cattle will voluntarily enter them. Because I think in pictures, I assume cattle do too. I can imagine the sensations the animals feel. Today half the cattle in the U.S. are handled in equipment I have designed.

Grandin is an assistant professor of animal sciences at Colorado State University.

people communicated through subtle eye movements," says autistic engineer Temple Grandin, "until I read it in a magazine five years ago" (*see box*).

At the same time, it is incorrect to say autistic people are cold and indifferent to those around them or, as conventional wisdom once had it, lack the high-level trait known as empathy. Last December, when Pam Barrett felt overwhelmed and dissolved into tears, it was Danny, the most deeply autistic of her children, who rushed to her side and rocked her back and forth in his arms.

Another misperception about people with autism, says Karen Pierce, a neuroscientist at the University of California at San Diego, is the notion that they do not register faces of loved ones as special—that, in the words of a prominent brain expert, they view their own mother's face as the equivalent of a paper cup. Quite the contrary, says Pierce, who has results from a neuroimaging study to back up her contention. Moreover, the center of activity in the autistic mind, she reported at a conference held in San Diego last November, turns out to be the fusiform gyrus, an area of the brain that in normal people specializes in the recognition of human faces.

In a neuroimaging study, Pierce observed, the fusiform gyrus in autistic people did not react when they were presented with photographs of strangers, but when photographs of parents were substituted, the area lit up like an explosion of Roman candles. Furthermore, this burst of activity was not confined to the fusiform gyrus but, as in normal subjects, extended into areas of the brain that respond to emotionally loaded events. To Pierce, this suggests that as babies, autistic people are able to form strong emotional attachments, so their social aloofness later on appears to be the consequence of a brain disorganization that worsens as development continues.

In so many ways, study after study has found, autistic people do not parse information as others do. University of Illinois psychologist John Sweeney, for example, has found that activity in the prefrontal and parietal cortex is far below normal in autistic adults asked to perform a simple task involving spatial memory. These areas of the brain, he notes, are essential to planning and problem solving, and among their jobs is keeping a dynamically changing spatial map in a cache of working memory. As Sweeney sees it, the poor performance of his autistic subjects of the task he set for them—keeping tabs on the location of a blinking light—suggests that they may have trouble updating that cache or accessing it in real time.

To Sweeney's collaborator, University of Pittsburgh neurologist Dr. Nancy Minshew, the images Sweeney has produced of autistic minds in action are endlessly evocative. They suggest that essential connections between key areas of the brain either were never made or do not function at an optimal level. "When you look at these images, you can see what's not there," she says, conjuring up an experience eerily akin to looking at side-by-side photographs of Manhattan with and without the Twin Towers.

A MATTER OF MISCONNECTIONS

DOES AUTISM START AS A GLITCH IN ONE AREA OF THE brain—the brainstem, perhaps—and then radiate out to affect others? Or is it a widespread problem that becomes more pronounced as the brain is called upon to set up and utilize increasingly complex circuitry? Either scenario is plausible, and experts disagree as to which is more probable. But one thing is clear: very early on, children with autism have brains that are anatomically different on both microscopic and macroscopic scales.

For example, Dr. Margaret Bauman, a pediatric neurologist at Harvard Medical School, has examined postmortem tissue from the brains of nearly 30 autistic individuals who died between the ages of 5 and 74. Among other things, she has found striking abnormalities in the limbic system, an area that includes the amygdala (the brain's primitive emotional center) and the hippocampus (a seahorse-shaped structure critical to memory). The cells in the limbic system of autistic individuals, Bauman's work shows, are atypically small and tightly packed together, compared with the cells in the limbic system of their normal counterparts. They look unusually immature, comments University of Chicago psychiatrist Dr. Edwin Cook, "as if waiting for a signal to grow up."

An intriguing abnormality has also been found in the cerebellum of both autistic children and adults. An important class of cells known as Purkinje cells (after the Czech physiologist who discovered them) is far smaller in number. And this, believes neuroscientist Eric Courchesne, of the University of California at San Diego, offers a critical clue to what goes so badly awry in autism. The cerebellum, he notes, is one of the brain's busiest computational centers, and the Purkinje cells are critical elements in its data-integration system. Without these cells, the cerebellum is unable to do its job, which is to receive torrents of information about the outside world, compute their meaning and prepare other areas of the brain to respond appropriately.

Several months ago, Courchesne unveiled results from a brain-imaging study that led him to propose a provocative new hypothesis. At birth, he notes, the brain of an autistic child is normal in size. But by the time these children reach 2 to 3 years of age, their brains are much larger than normal. This abnormal growth is not uniformly distributed. Using MRI-imaging technology, Courchesne and his colleagues were able to identify two types of tissue where this mushrooming in size is most pronounced.

These are the neuron-packed gray matter of the cerebral cortex and white matter, which contains the fibrous connections projecting to and from the cerebral cortex and other areas of the brain, including the cerebellum. Perhaps, Courchesne speculates, it is the signal overload caused by this proliferation of connections that injures the Purkinje cells and ultimately kills them. "So now," says Courchesne, "a very interesting question is, What's driving this abnormal brain growth? If we could understand that, then we might be able to slow or stop it."

A proliferation of connections between billions of neurons occurs in all children, of course. A child's brain, unlike a computer, does not come into the world with its circuitry hard-wired. It must set up its circuits in response to a sequence of experiences and then solder them together through repeated neurological activity. So if Courchesne is right, what leads to autism may be an otherwise normal process that switches on too early or too strongly and shuts off too late—and that process would be controlled by genes.

Currently Courchesne and his colleagues are looking very closely at specific genes that might be involved. Of particular interest are the genes encoding four brain-growth regulators that have been found in newborns who go on to develop mental retardation or autism. Among these compounds, as National Institutes of Health researcher Dr. Karin Nelson and her colleagues reported last year, is a potent molecule known as vasoactive intestinal peptide. VIP plays a role not only in brain development but in the immune system and gastrointestinal tract as well, a hint that other disorders that so frequently accompany autism may not be coincidental.

The idea that there might be early biomarkers for autism has intrigued many researchers, and the reason is simple. If one could identify infants at high risk, then it might become possible to monitor the neurological changes that presage the onset of behavioral symptoms, and someday perhaps even intervene in the process. "Right now," notes Michael Merzenich, a neuroscientist at the University of California, San Francisco, "we study autism after the catastrophe occurs, and then we see this bewildering array of things that these kids can't do. What we need to know is how it all happened."

The genes that set the stage for autistic disorders could derail developing brains in a number of ways. They could encode harmful mutations like those responsible for single-gene disorders—cystic fibrosis, for instance, or Huntington's disease. They could equally well be garden-variety variants of normal genes that cause problems only when they combine with certain other genes. Or they could be genes that set up vulnerabilities to any number of stresses encountered by a child.

A popular but still unsubstantiated theory blames autism on the MMR (measles, mumps and rubella) vaccine, which is typically given to children at around 15 months (*see box*). But there are many other conceivable culprits. Researchers at the University of California at Davis have just launched a major epidemiological study that will test the tissues of both autistic and nonautistic children for residues of not only mercury but also PCBs, benzene and other heavy metals. The premise is that some children

may be genetically more susceptible than others to damage by these agents, and so the study will also measure a number of other genetic variables, like how well these children metabolize cholesterol and other lipids.

Drugs taken by some pregnant women are also coming under scrutiny. At the University of Rochester, embryologist Patricia Rodier and her colleagues are exploring how certain teratogens (substances that cause birth defects) could lead to autism. They are focusing on the teratogens' impact on a gene called HOXA1, which is supposed to flick on very briefly in the first trimester of pregnancy and remain silent ever after. Embryonic mice in which the rodent equivalent of this gene has been knocked out go on to develop brainstems that are missing an entire layer of cells.

In the end, it is not merely possible but likely that scientists will discover multiple routes—some rare, some common; some purely genetic, some not—that lead to similar end points. And when they do, new ideas for how to prevent or correct autism may quickly materialize. A decade from now, there will almost certainly be more effective forms of therapeutic intervention, perhaps even antiautism drugs. "Genes," as the University of Chicago's Cook observes, "give you targets, and we're pretty good at designing drugs if we know the targets."

Paradoxically, the very thing that is so terrible about autistic disorders—that they affect the very young—also suggests reason for hope. Since the neural connections of a child's brain are established through experience, well-targeted mental exercises have the potential to make a difference. One of the big unanswered questions, in fact, is why 25% of children with seemingly full-blown autism benefit enormously from intensive speech- and social-skills therapy—and why the other 75% do not. Is it because the brains of the latter are irreversibly damaged, wonders Geraldine Dawson, director of the University of Washington's autism center, or is it because the fundamental problem is not being adequately addressed?

The more scientists ponder such questions, the more it seems they are holding pieces of a puzzle that resemble the interlocking segments of Tommy Barrett's Transformer toys. Put the pieces together one way, and you end up with a normal child. Put them together another way, and you end up with a child with autism. And as one watches Tommy's fingers rhythmically turning a train into a robot, a robot into a train, an unbidden thought occurs. Could it be that some dexterous sleight of hand could coax even profoundly autistic brains back on track? Could it be that some kid who's mesmerized by the process of transformation will mature into a scientist who figures out the trick?

—*With reporting by Amy Bonesteel/Atlanta*

Citizenship and Disability

Michael Bérubé

IN THE SIX YEARS since I published a book about my son Jamie, *Life As We Know It*, a great deal has changed in Jamie's life—starting with his realization that there is a book about him. When I completed the book Jamie was only four, and had not yet entered the public K–12 system. But I did not stop serving as Jamie's recorder and public representative when I finished that book: I still represent him all the time, to school officials, camp counselors, babysitters and friends, to academic audiences, and to Down Syndrome Associations. I take it as one of my tasks to watch for important things he's never done before, as a way of charting and understanding the irreplaceable and irreducible little person he is, especially as he gets less and less little, and more and more capable of representing himself.

Jamie is now in his sixth year of school, having entered kindergarten in 1997–1998. In the intervening years he has not continued to perform at grade level (he is repeating fourth grade, at age eleven), and he has occasionally presented his schoolmates with some eccentric behavior. On the other hand, he has learned to read, to do two- and three-digit addition and subtraction, to multiply two-digit numbers, and most recently to do division by single numbers, with and without remainders. My wife, Janet, and I did not teach him these things, but the minute it became clear that he could do them in school, we picked up the ball and ran with it. We've tried to make every available use of his startlingly prodigious memory, and we've learned that when he tells us that such and such bird is not a parrot but is instead a scarlet macaw, he's usually right. He has some idiosyncrasies that do not serve him well in school or in testing situations: at one point he memorized the numbers on the wrong side of his flash cards, the serial numbers that indicate each card's place in the deck. He likes to pretend that he does not know left from right, referring instead (with perverse delight) to his "left foot" and his "other foot." He is a stubborn ignatz, as people find whenever they try to get him to do something he has no interest in, or whenever his teachers or aides try to make him move from one task to another. For a while he tried to put off unpleasant tasks by telling his teachers or therapists, "Let's do that tomorrow"; before long he realized that this didn't work, and began

saying instead, "We did that yesterday"—a ruse with which he has had some success.

His conversational skills are steadily improving, but unless you're talking to him about one of the movies he's seen or one of the routines he's developed at school or at home, you'll find that his sense of the world is sometimes unintelligible, sometimes merely a bit awry. He recently received an invitation to a classmate's birthday party (his third such invitation since we moved to central Pennsylvania sixteen months ago: we count and cherish each one), and Janet asked him what the birthday boy looked like: "he's a small boy," said Jamie, holding his hand around his shoulder level.

"What color is his hair?" she asked.

"Black," Jamie replied.

"What color are his eyes?"

"Blue."

"Does he wear glasses?" (Jamie has worn glasses for about five years.)

"No," Jamie said, "just eyes."

But then, Janet and I did not expect him to be able to describe his classmates at all. Nor did we expect him to be so talented a mimic; he can imitate both of us, just as he can imitate break dancers and gymnasts and snakes and lemurs. We did not expect him to be able to do multiplication or division; we did not expect him to open books and ask us to "read and tell all the things"; we did not expect him to be able to ask us "why" questions, as when he asked me why I could not leave him alone in a hotel room while I went to park the car. We did not expect him to win a spelling award in second grade for maintaining an average above 90 on his spelling tests for the year. We did not expect him to be designated by his classmates in third grade as the kid with the best sense of humor.

Over eleven years, then, we've come to expect that Jamie will defeat or exceed our expectations when we least expect him to. And from this I draw two points. One, he's a child. Two, and this is a somewhat more elaborate conclusion, although it can be derived from point one: it might be a good idea for all of us to treat other humans as if we do not know their potential, as if they just might in fact surprise us, as if they might defeat or exceed our expectations. It might be a good idea for us to check the history of the past two centuries whenever we think we know what "normal"

human standards of behavior and achievement might be. And it might be a very good idea for us to expand the possibilities of democracy precisely because democracy offers us unfinished and infinitely revisable forms of political organization that stand the best chance, in the long run, of responding adequately to the human rights of the unpredictable creatures we humans are. That might be one way of recognizing and respecting something you might want to call our human dignity.

JAMIE IS, of course, one reason why I am drawn to the question of disability rights and their relation to democracy: every morning I take him to school, I know how very fortunate he is to be living under a social dispensation that entitles him to a public education alongside his nondisabled peers. But beyond my immediate interest in forwarding Jamie's interests, I want to argue that disability issues are—or should be—central to theories of social justice in a much broader sense. Nancy Fraser's account of the "politics of recognition" and the "politics of redistribution" (*Adding Insult to Injury: Social Justice and the Politics of Recognition*), for example, offers a theory that tries to accommodate what were the two major strands of American progressive-left thought in the 1990s, multiculturalism and democratic socialism (in all their varieties)—or what Richard Rorty, in *Achieving Our Country*, termed the "cultural left" and the "reformist left," the former concerned primarily with combating social stigma and the latter concerned primarily with combating greed. Fraser has shown convincingly that the politics of recognition and redistribution offer a productive way to think about feminism: cultural politics with regard to body images or sexual harassment, for example, are not to be understood as distractions from "real" politics that address comparative worth or the minimum wage. Rather, recognition politics have consequences for the redistribution of social goods and resources even though they cannot be reduced to their redistributive effects. And since many left intellectuals in the 1990s were all too willing to think of politics as a zero-sum game in which any attention paid to multiculturalism had to come at the expense of democratic socialism and vice versa, Fraser's work seems to offer a way for the left to champion a progressive tax code and an end to racial profiling at the same time.

It is striking, nonetheless, that so few leftists have understood disability in these terms. Disability is not the only area of social life in which the politics of recognition are inseparable from the politics of redistribution; other matters central to citizenship, such as immigration, reproductive rights, and criminal justice, are every bit as complex. Nonetheless, our society's representations of disability are intricately tied to, and sometimes the very basis for, our public policies for "administering" disability. And when we contemplate, in these terms, the history of people with cognitive and developmental disabilities, we find a history in which "representation" takes on a double valence: first, in that people who were deemed incapable of representing themselves were therefore represented by a socio-medical apparatus that defined—or, in a social-constructionist sense, created-the category of "feeblemindedness"; and second, in the sense that the visual and rhetorical representations of "feebleminded" persons then set the terms for public policy. One cannot plausibly narrate a comprehensive history of ideas and practices of national citizenship in the post–Civil War United States without examining public policy regarding disability, especially mental disability, all the more especially when mental disability was then mapped onto certain immigrant populations who scored poorly on intelligence tests and were thereby pseudo-scientifically linked to criminality. And what of reproductive rights? By 1927, the spurious but powerful linkages among disability, immigration, poverty, and criminality provided the Supreme Court with sufficient justification for declaring involuntary sterilization legal under the Constitution.

T HERE IS AN obvious reason why disability rights are so rarely thought of in terms of civil rights: disability was not covered in the Civil Rights Act of 1964. And as Anita Silvers points out, over the next twenty-five years, groups covered by civil rights law sometimes saw disability rights as a dilution of civil rights, on the grounds that people with disabilities were constitutively incompetent, whereas women and minorities faced discrimination merely on the basis of social prejudice. Silvers writes, "[t]o make disability a category that activates a heightened legal shield against exclusion, it was objected, would alter the purpose of legal protection for civil rights by transforming the goal from protecting opportunity for socially exploited people to providing assistance for naturally unfit people." The passage of the Americans with Disabilities Act (ADA) in 1990 did add disability to the list of stigmatized identities covered by antidiscrimination law,

but thus far the ADA has been interpreted so narrowly, and by such a business-friendly judiciary, that employers have won over 95 percent of the suits brought under the act.

Perhaps if plaintiffs with disabilities had won a greater number of cases over the past thirteen years, the conservative backlash against the ADA—currently confined to a few cranks complaining about handicapped parking spaces and a wheelchair ramp at a Florida nude beach—would be sufficiently strong as to spark a movement to repeal the law altogether. But then again, perhaps if the law were read more broadly, more Americans would realize their potential stake in it. In 1999, for instance, the Supreme Court ruled on three lower-court cases in which people with "easily correctable" disabilities—high blood pressure, nearsightedness—were denied employment. In three identical 7–2 decisions, the Court found that the plaintiffs had no basis for a suit under the ADA precisely *because* their disabilities were easily correctable. As disability activists and legal analysts quickly pointed out, this decision left these plaintiffs in the ridiculous situation of being too disabled to be hired but somehow not disabled enough to be covered by the ADA; or, to put this another way, plaintiffs' "easily correctable" disabilities were not so easily correctable as to allow them access to employment. One case involved twin sisters who were denied the opportunity to test as pilots for United Airlines on the grounds that their eyesight did not meet United's minimum vision requirement (uncorrected visual acuity of 20/100 or better without glasses or contacts) even though each sister had 20/20 vision with corrective lenses (*Sutton v. United Airlines, Inc.*); another involved a driver/mechanic with high blood pressure (*Murphy v. United Parcel Service*); the third involved a truck driver with monocular vision (20/200 in one eye) who in 1992 had received a Department of Transportation waiver of the requirement that truck drivers have distant visual acuity of 20/40 in each eye as well as distant binocular acuity of 20/40 (*Albertson's, Inc. v. Kirkingburg*). Because, as Silvers argues, "litigation under the ADA commonly turns on questions of classification rather than access," all three plaintiffs were determined to have no standing under the law. The question of whether any of them was justly denied employment was simply not addressed by the Court. Indeed, in writing her opinion for the majority, Justice Sandra Day O'Connor explicitly refused to consider the wider question of "access," noting that 160 million Americans would be covered by the ADA if it were construed to include people with "easily correctible" disabilities (under a "health conditions approach"), and since Congress had cited the number 43 million in enacting the law, Congress clearly

could not have intended the law to be applied more widely. "Had Congress intended to include all persons with corrected physical limitations among those covered by the Act, it undoubtedly would have cited a much higher number of disabled persons in the findings," wrote O'Connor. "That it did not is evidence that the ADA's coverage is restricted to only those whose impairments are not mitigated by corrective measures."

It is possible to object that O'Connor's decision was excessively literalist, and that the potential number of Americans covered by the ADA is, in any case, quite irrelevant to the question of whether a woman can fly a plane when she's got her glasses on. But I've since come to believe that the literalism of the decision is an indirect acknowledgment of how broad the issues at stake here really are. If the ADA were understood as a broad civil rights law, and if it were understood as a law that potentially pertains to the entire population of the country, then maybe disability law would be understood not as a fringe addition to civil rights law but as its very fulfillment.

R IGHTS CAN BE created, reinterpreted, extended, and revoked. The passage of the ADA should therefore be seen as an extension of the promise of democracy, but only as a promise: any realization of the potential of the law depends on its continual reinterpretation. For the meaning of the word, just as Wittgenstein wanted us to believe (in order that we might be undeceived about how our words work), lies in its use in the language. Similarly, the Individuals with Disabilities Education Act of 1975 (originally the Education for All Handicapped Children Act) was not some kind of breakthrough discovery whereby children with disabilities were found to be rights-bearing citizens of the United States after all, and who knew that we'd had it all wrong for 199 years? On the contrary, the IDEA *invented* a new right for children with disabilities, the right to a "free and appropriate public education in the least restrictive environment." And yet the IDEA did not wish that right into being overnight; the key terms "appropriate" and "least restrictive" had to be interpreted time and again, over the course of fifteen years, before they were understood to authorize "full inclusion" of children with disabilities in "regular" classrooms. Nothing about the law is set in stone. The only philosophical "foundation" underlying the IDEA and its various realizations is our own collective political will, a will that is tested and tested again every time the Act comes up for reauthorization. Jamie Bérubé currently has a right to an inclusive public education, but that right is neither intrinsic nor innate. Rather, Jamie's rights were invented, and implemented slowly and with great difficulty.

The recognition of his human dignity, enshrined in those rights, was invented. And by the same token, those rights, and that recognition, can be taken away. While I live, I promise myself that I will not let that happen, but I live with the knowledge that it may: to live any other way, to live as if Jamie's rights were somehow intrinsic, would be irresponsible.

Of course, many of us would prefer to believe that our children have intrinsic human rights and human dignity no matter what; irrespective of any form of human social organization; regardless of whether they were born in twentieth-century Illinois or second-century Rome or seventh-century central Asia. But this is just a parent's—or a philosophical foundationalist's—wishful thinking. For what would it mean for Jamie to "possess" rights that no one on earth recognized? A fat lot of good it would do him. My argument may sound either monstrous or all too obvious: if, in fact, no one on earth recognized Jamie's human dignity, then there would in fact be no human perspective from which he would be understood to possess "intrinsic" human dignity. And then he wouldn't have it, and so much the worse for the human race.

In one respect, the promise of the IDEA, like the promise of the ADA, is clear: greater inclusion of people with disabilities in the social worlds of school and work. But in another sense the promise is unspecifiable; its content is something we actually cannot know in advance. For the IDEA does not merely guarantee all children with disabilities a free appropriate public education in the least restrictive environment. Even more than this, it grants the right to education in order that persons with disabilities might make the greatest possible use of their other rights—the ones having to do with voting, or employment discrimination, or with life, liberty, and the pursuit of happiness.

IDEA is thus designed to enhance the capabilities of all American children with disabilities regardless of their actual abilities—and this is why it is so profound a democratic idea. Here again I'm drawing on Nancy Fraser, whose theory of democracy involves the idea of "participatory parity," and the imperative that a democratic state should actively foster the abilities of its citizens to participate in the life of the polity as equals. Fraser's work to date has not addressed disability, but as I noted above, it should be easy to see how disability is relevant to Fraser's account of the politics of recognition and the politics of redistribution. This time, however, I want to press the point a bit harder. Fraser writes as if the promise of democracy entails the promise to enhance participatory parity among citizens, which it does, and she writes as if we knew what "participatory parity" itself means, which we don't. (This is why the promise of disability rights is unspecifiable.)

LET ME EXPLAIN. First, the idea of participatory parity does double duty in Fraser's work, in the sense that it names both the state we would like to achieve and the device by which we can gauge whether we're getting there. For in order to maintain a meaningful democracy in which all citizens participate as legal and moral equals, the state needs to judge whether its policies enhance equal participation in democratic processes. Yet at the same time, the state needs to enhance equal participation among its citizens simply in order to determine what its democratic processes will be. This is not a metatheoretical quibble. On the contrary, the point is central to the practical workings of any democratic polity. One of the tasks required of democrats is precisely this: to extend the promise of democracy to previously excluded individuals and groups some of whom might have a substantially different understanding of "participatory parity" than that held by previously dominant groups and individuals.

Could anything make this clearer than the politics of disability? Imagine a building in which political philosophers are debating, in the wake of the attacks of September 11, 2001, the value and the purpose of participatory parity over against forms of authoritarianism or theocracy. Now imagine that this building has no access ramps, no Braille or large-print publications, no American Sign Language interpreters, no elevators, no special-needs paraprofessionals, no in-class aides. Contradictory as such a state of affairs may sound, it's a reasonably accurate picture of what contemporary debate over the meaning of democracy actually looks like. How can we remedy this? Only when we have fostered equal participation in debates over the ends and means of democracy can we have a truly participatory debate over what "participatory parity" itself means. That debate will be interminable in principle, since our understandings of democracy and parity are infinitely revisable, but lest we think of deliberative democracy as a forensic society dedicated to empyreal reaches of abstraction, we should remember that debates over the meaning of participatory parity set the terms for more specific debates about the varieties of human embodiment. These include debates about prenatal screening, genetic discrimination, stem-cell research, euthanasia, and, with regard to physical access, ramps, curb cuts, kneeling buses, and buildings employing what is now known as universal design.

Leftists and liberals, particularly those associated with university humanities departments, are commonly charged with being moral relativists, unable or unwilling to say (even after September 11) why one society might be "better" than another. So let me be especially clear on this final point. I think there's a very good reason to extend the franchise, to widen the conversation, to democratize our debates, and to make disability central to our theories of egalitarian social justice. The reason is this: a capacious and supple sense of what it is to be human is better than a narrow and partial sense of what it is to be human, and the more participants we as a society can incorporate into the deliberation of what it means to be human, the greater the chances that that deliberation will in fact be transformative in such a way as to enhance our collective capacities to recognize each other as humans entitled to human dignity. As Jamie reminds me daily, both deliberately and unwittingly, most Americans had no idea what people with Down syndrome could achieve until we'd passed and implemented and interpreted and reinterpreted a law entitling them all to a free appropriate public education in the least restrictive environment. I can say all this without appealing to any innate justification for human dignity and human rights, and I can also say this: Without a sufficient theoretical and practical account of disability, we can have no account of democracy worthy of the name.

Perhaps some of our fellow citizens with developmental disabilities would not put the argument quite this way; even though Jamie has led me to think this way, he doesn't talk the way I do. But those of us who do participate in political debates, whether about school funding in a specific district or about the theory and practice of democracy at its most abstract, have the obligation to enhance the abilities of our children and our fellow citizens with disabilities to participate in the life of the United States as political and moral equals with their nondisabled peers—both for their own good, and for the good of democracy, which is to say, for the good of all of us.

MICHAEL BÉRUBÉ is the Paterno Family Professor in Literature at Pennsylvania State University. This article is adapted from a talk given at the 2002 convention of the Arc of the United States (formerly the Association of Retarded Citizens of the United States).

From *Dissent*, Spring 2003. © 2003 by Dissent Magazine.

Inscrutable or Meaningful?

Understanding and Supporting Your Inarticulate Students

Robin M. Smith

Interpreting movement.
Time.
Assistive technology.
Choice.
Audiotapes.
Sticky notes.

What do these dissimilar items or concepts have in common? Teachers can use them all in adapting lessons for students who have difficulties in communicating with others.

This article explores ways teachers can build competence in such students, rather than focus on their deficits. Along the way, you can learn how to observe your students to discover their strengths and weaknesses, translate body language, unravel the ways they process language, appreciate indications of humor, and interpret different kinds of behavior and its intent. Tips include ways to encourage group membership and participation, ways to influence student behavior, and ways to encourage communication and independent decision making by students.

Understanding Teaching Approaches

All three students described in this article (see box, "What Does It Mean to be Nonverbal?") studied with two kinds of teachers—which we will refer to as deficit-oriented and competence-oriented (Smith, 2000). How these teachers perceive their students affected how they taught and evaluated them. Their students often responded according to how they were treated and perceived in class (Smith, Ryan, & Salend, 2001). How teachers perceive their students will influence how they instruct, evaluate, and affect their students (Biklen & Duchan, 1994; Rosenthal, 1997; Smith, 1999).

Focusing on Deficits

Deficit-oriented teachers often perceive their students with developmental disabilities as inscrutable—that is, because the students are difficult to understand, they think the students must therefore be lacking basic understanding of the things going on around them. Those students who also have cognitive disabilities may not have typical speech or facial expression; and the students may also experience language-processing disabilities, such as problems with word retrieval, delayed understanding of complex speech, or need for a longer response time in conversation.

Deficit-oriented teachers tend to teach to a medial model of repairing the (often) irreparable individual. Their descriptions of students foster ranking, sorting, and diagnosing. Such medical-model descriptions obscure the individual abilities of students who may have unusual approaches to communicating their understanding, wants, and needs. For example, teachers may consider a nonverbal student who is labeled with severe mental retardation to be unable to participate in class discussions, and therefore may have the student doing something different elsewhere in the classroom or even in another room.

Deficit-oriented teachers who think their students are inscrutable and uncomprehending may miss student communications and key skills and strengths or fail to see their relevance. In the example of Tyrone (see box), his deficit-oriented teacher had no idea Tyrone understood the class discussion and therefore made few requests that he respond. Tyrone's teacher accepted his homework assignments but did not ask about missing assignments.

Focusing on Competence

Competence-oriented teachers, on the other hand, perceive students as whole persons and teach with the students' strengths in mind. Instead of questioning if students can participate in a class activity, these teachers think about *how* students can be involved in the activity. Such teachers acquire the skill of "reading" students who communicate in ways that greatly differ from their peers. They learn how students show engagement, boredom, contentment, and dissatisfaction. They are aware of their students' strengths and how these strengths might be used to support learning and achievement.

Competence-oriented teachers' descriptions of students tend to foster understanding and communication with students. For example, in Teresa's case (see box), whereas her competence-oriented teacher assisted her with exams, essays, and had meaningful typed conversations with her, her deficit-oriented teacher frequently encountered passive and active resistance from Teresa and experienced little or no meaningful communication with her.

Understanding Student Communication

You might compare students like Teresa, Tyrone, or Gerard—who differ from peers in the way they move, process information, and communicate—to a foreign visitor who does not speak your language very well but is likely to understand it. As the "native speaker," you as teacher can take on the role of interpreter as you learn the student's own language.

The following guidelines, summarized in Table 1, are designed to help you

What Does It Mean to be Nonverbal? Three Students

Many of us tend to focus on the student's disability, not the person, and thus see students who are nonverbal or inarticulate as simply "difficult to understand." Students who are labeled mentally retarded or who have impaired communication, especially, are the victims of such first impressions (Goode, 1989).

The three students described here have studied with two kinds of teachers, which will become evident as you read. The first type of teachers regarded their students as inscrutable or incompetent, rather than as sources of meaningful activity and communication. They had difficulty seeing intelligence and using the strengths of their students. The second category of teachers not only saw the students' intelligence and competencies, but also helped them engage academically.

Gerard was a high school student labeled mentally retarded who spoke in short phrases. When asked a direct question, he often responded, "I don't know." Several of his teachers, both general and special education, said that he understood little of what was going on in class. A paraprofessional who did feel Gerard understood his schoolwork was working with him on some questions in a textbook about managing money. She asked him what he should do with his paycheck. Gerard shook his head and said, "I don't know." She said,

"Let me put this another way. When you work at [your job], what do you do with your check? Does your mom put it in the bank or do you spend it?" He said, "Bank."

Tyrone, a student with autism, spoke in short phrases and often repeated favorite expressions and topics in his conversation. Two teachers described him as "a mystery" and had no idea if he understood what was happening in class. One day, one of these teachers was questioning the students about a history worksheet they had done on the early 1900s, asking them about historic people and events. "John Jacob Astor?" A student replied, "American Fur Company." The teacher mentioned the Broadway musical about the Astor family, asking for the title. Tyrone called out, "Scrooge." The teacher laughed, "Good guess."

Teresa was nonverbal and communicated inconsistently by pointing and making sounds. Teachers supported her pointing to answer choices written on Post-It notes. With gentle physical support, she could sustain pointing to letters in a large keyboard for a short time. She took quizzes and typed short conversations with a teacher assigned to help her with communication skills. Her other teacher assigned for the same purpose, however, was unable to engage Teresa in typed conversations and said, in her presence, "I don't think she knows her letters."

learn about your students and become an effective interpreter.

Get to Know Your Students' Communication Strengths and Needs

Your ability to engage students depends on your knowledge of their communication strengths and needs. If you spend some time getting to know your students, you can identify these strengths and needs by doing the following:

- Sharing with the students that you are trying to get to know them, their communication styles and patterns, and their interests, and thus explaining why you are asking some questions that might seem obvious to them. Let them know you want to learn about what they have invented as strategies to communicate.

- Drawing on the knowledge of others who know the student—for example, paraprofessionals, family members, and friends.

- Observing students and asking yourself questions like these:
  —How does this student typically show interest?
  —How does this student show understanding?

—Are there atypical or meaningful body movements that are special to this student?

—Is this student following the conversation even when looking around or pacing? How do I know?

Understand Movement Differences

Some students have movement differences associated with their disability. We must not misinterpret movement differences as discipline problems, resistance, boredom, or incomprehension. For example, although Tyrone often walks around the room during a discussion, he is a full participant, understanding others' communication and making relevant contributions on request.

When Tyrone is seated in class, however, he has a different way of being in motion. Although he often writes a list of five names over and over, apparently engrossed in his notebook, he will answer a question when asked. Though some teachers may consider him disengaged, his repetitive writing helps him concentrate by blocking out other distractions. You can learn about and examine your students' movement differences by observing them and asking yourself:

- Does this student have trouble starting, executing, stopping, combining, continuing, or switching activities? These are some common movement differences identified by Donnellan and Leary (1995, p. 80) in people with autism and mental retardation. These behaviors reflect neither intention nor intelligence. They reflect the need for understanding and accommodation.

- Do the movements have particular meaning? Sometimes the movements have no meaning. Students with Tourette's syndrome, for example, cannot control certain words, shouts, or twitches.

Understand Language-Processing Differences

Some students can speak, but are inarticulate. Whereas students may be capable of one- or two-word sentences or short phrases, their teachers may think they are intellectually limited or lazy.

Some common indications that students have difficulty with processing language are as follows:

- Difficulty with word retrieval when answering a direct question. Gerard (see box) was inarticulate and also had difficulty finding the words he

---

Table 1. Understanding Students' Communication

Get to know communication strengths/needs	Let them know you want to learn about their communication strategies. Draw on the knowledge of others: family, friends, paraprofessionals. Observe how students show interest and understanding. Learn how unique body movements can be interpreted as meaningful.
Understand movement differences	Identify problems with starting, executing, stopping, combining, continuing, or switching activities. Identify meanings of recurring movements or intensity of movements.
Understand processing differences such as:	Difficulty with word retrieval Limited response repertoire Longer wait time to respond Difficulty responding to someone else's initiated conversation
Look for signs of sophisticated thinking	Humor Insight
Understand refusal or resistance relating to:	Personal considerations or preferences Academic considerations such as needs for modifications; appropriateness of the task; need for coaching; ability to physically carry out the task.
Understand unintentional behaviors	Abrupt behaviors may not be related to noncompliance, nonunderstanding, or lack of interest. Student may be "stuck" in a repetitive thought or feeling. Less participation may be fatigue rather than disinterest.

---

needed to communicate with others. Sometimes, when he replied, "I don't know," his conversation partner repeated the question in a different way that also gave him extra time to come up with an answer. Sometimes Gerard could immediately answer a question if his attention were already on the topic, such as during a class discussion. In the previous example, Gerard selected the correct answer from choices presented to him.

- Some students may have a limited response repertoire. As a result, they rely on consistent alternative responses. When asked a direct question, Gerard responded "Yes," "No," or "I don't know." In health class, he responded appropriately to every question the teacher asked, including rhetorical ones. ("Would you get on a plane if the pilot were high?" "No.")
- Some students need a longer wait time to prepare and articulate their responses. Therefore, teachers need to provide students with a sufficient amount of time in which to respond.
- Some students have difficulty responding in conversations that someone else has initiated. Regarding Gerard's social conversation skills, his special education teacher said he was lazy because he answered, "I don't know" so often.

Yet, he initiated a conversation with a teacher about plans for the weekend; and when asked what he was going to do, said that his parents were taking him to a concert.

You can change the way you communicate with students once you realize they process language differently. You can speak slower or with longer wait time in between thoughts. You also can ask more "yes/no" questions or phrase questions to include the words students need to respond appropriately. When students appear to be restless, you can ask them if they are bored or need a break.

Look for Signs of Sophisticated Thinking, Such as Humor or Insight

Students who are nonverbal or inarticulate may show sophistication with a few choice words, a joke, a comeback, or the timing of a behavior.

For example, Tyrone's naming the Astor play, "Scrooge," was an obvious sign of sophistication. Tyrone's jokes and his correct one-word answers in other classes were also a sign of sophisticated thinking. One time his paraprofessional yawned when helping with a worksheet and said, "Excuse me." Tyrone responded, "You need a blanket."

Understand Refusal and Resistance

Although teachers generally consider refusal and resistance unproductive and inappropriate, for some students these strategies may be their most effective method of communication. This is particularly true of students who lack the motor coordination to write or type and who do not speak.

For example, one day a teacher was absent; and the students had a period of reading, resting, and chatting. Gerard's paraprofessional tried in vain to get him to work on yesterday's assignment. Gerard looked around and leafed through a magazine.

After a few minutes, the paraprofessional asked, "Are you being this way because all the other kids don't have to work today and you don't want to, either?"

He responded, "Yes."

Like Gerard's paraprofessional, you can attempt to understand your students' refusal and resistance by examining the following:

- Are there personal considerations and preferences? Ask students questions to find out if they are tired, sick, thirsty, bored, dislike this topic, or want to do the same thing as other students.
- Are there academic considerations? Does the task need to be modified in any way? Does the expected task

Table 2. Competence-Oriented Supports	
Plan ahead for student participation	Pre-arrange a time to call on students Call on students for yes/no or choice answers Assign a task the student can do to contribute to the whole class Prepare choices students can point to during group discussions Prepare prerecorded choices and answers the student can activate with a switching device
Maximize student decision making	Support decisions at each step of a project Use sticky notes to write exam choices Use augmentative communication systems: communication, picture/symbol/word books; pointing, recording devices, keyboard devices, etc. Use alternative forms of written communication (e.g., arranging sentence cards for essays) Ask student to confirm answers or meaning of their communication.
Minimize effect of unintentional behaviors	Study consistency of certain behaviors Discover appropriate prompts to help students through problematic movements

make sense to the student? Does the student need coaching to stay focused and on task? Can the student physically carry out the task?

Understand When Students' Behaviors Are Unintentional

Sometimes students have unusual verbal responses and utterances, as well as nonverbal actions they cannot control. Understanding such behavior will help you to carefully interpret unusual and unexpected verbal responses and nonverbal behavior.

Because students' processing delays and unintentional verbal and physical types of behavior may be misinterpreted, based on the responses of typical students, you can inquire into such differences by considering the following:

- Is unintentional behavior misinterpreted as noncompliance, nonunderstanding, or lack of interest? Some students with developmental disabilities have unintentional types of behavior, appearing as abrupt behavior changes. Students may have tics, use inappropriate language, call out irrelevant phrases, pace, strike or challenge others, or walk out of the room or building. An event, a feeling, or a physical response to the environment, such as the sound of fluorescent lights or computer hard drives, may trigger some of this behavior.
- Are repetitive words or phrases signs that student is "stuck" in an emotion? A student may be involuntarily involved in a repetitive thought or feeling, particularly when nervous. Some coaching or prompting may help a student move

on. It may help to ask the student if he or she is "stuck."

- Is less-than-usual participation or speech misinterpreted as lack of interest? For some students, this lack of participation may be a sign of the effort it takes to suppress an involuntary behavior, such as a movement, sound, or tic.

Competence-Oriented Supports to Involve Inarticulate or Nonspeaking Students

As you get to know your students, you do not have to wait until you are expert in "their language." The use of competence-oriented strategies, summarized in Table 2, can cause you to see how your students demonstrate engagement and understanding.

In addition, you will be providing more opportunity for participation. Eugene Marcus (personal communication, 1994), a man with autism who communicates by typing said, "Treat every individual who you meet as a dignitary from another country who does not speak your language very well." The following are some suggestions for implementing Marcus's mandate in your classes.

Plan Ahead for Participation During Group Discussions

Pre-arrange a time to call on students. For example, Teresa's special education teacher met with the health teacher and arranged with him to call on Teresa for a particular question from the homework assignment. Then, she prerecorded the answer into Teresa's speaking device. Teresa pushed a button on her speaking

device when called on in class to answer the question.

Call on students for yes/no or choice answers. For example, a student named Nick could not speak but nodded his head when the teacher asked him if he agreed with what another student said.

Assign a task students can do to contribute to a small group or the whole class. For example, Gerard's social studies teacher asked him to find a picture of the Great Wall in the school library. With the help of his paraprofessional, he found the picture while the class was doing a written assignment; and then he showed the photo to his social studies class during a discussion about China.

Arrange choices for students to point to when answering questions during whole-group and small-group lessons and during exams. Teachers, paraeducators, or peers can prepare these choices in advance or spontaneously use Post-it notes or an erasable white board.

Use recording devices with switches students can operate. For example, with the help of teachers and peers, students can answer questions with prerecorded responses, give reports, turn on background sounds for others' reports, and even prepare small-talk conversations in advance using a cassette recorder.

Maximize Students' Decision Making

Support students to decide during each step of a project they cannot physically do alone. For example, Tyrone did not have the fine-motor coordination to cut and paste pictures for a collage in his health class. His paraeducator asked him to decide on a topic for a collage. Tyrone chose the materials, the color scheme, which pictures to cut out, and where to glue them.

Use Post-it notes to record possible choices during exams or spontaneous conversations and ask students to select their responses. For example, during an exam, the teacher wrote the choices for fill-in-the-blank questions on Post-it notes; and Teresa then pointed to her choice. Because Teresa was not always consistent in her movements, the teacher then confirmed the choice by changing the order of the three choices—and Teresa would point to the same one.

Use communication books (pictures with words, phrases, or sentences on laminated cards) for the common conversations. Communication books work well in role-plays, pairs, and small groups, as peers or teachers support students to participate and contribute.

Use alternative forms of written communication. Teachers can help students write drafts using Post-it notes or cards, and then make sure the students approve of the order. For an essay on health careers, Teresa chose sentences from texts that her paraprofessional wrote on cards. She later put them in order, along with transitional sentences suggested by her paraeducator.

Use augmentative communication systems, such as typing, pointing to letters or pictures, or facilitated communication to facilitate independent choice making. Nick, who did not speak and lacked fine-motor coordination, was looking at menu choices that were in small type and close together. When the paraeducator wrote the prices larger and farther part, Nick was able to point to the correct choice through a type of facilitated communication: Paraeducator provided only slight resistance by pulling back on his sleeve (Biklen & Cardinal, 1997).

Seek confirmation when students are too concise, inconsistent, or are engaging in automatic and repetitive phrases. You can encourage detail by saying, "I don't understand what you meant; please type/ say it again," or "Please say more." If a student is inconsistent when pointing and is taking an exam, you might ask after each choice, "Is that your answer?"

Minimize the Effect of Unintentional Behavior

Learn if there is consistency for particular unintentional behaviors. For example, teachers can learn if behaviors such as pacing or walking out of the room are related to anxiety and try to discover ways to ease students' anxiety.

Discover appropriate prompts and indirect means to overcome unintentional and problematic differences in movement. Some students have trouble initiating and need pre-arranged cues to begin a task, whereas others have problems completing several steps of a task and need a series of cues to complete the task. Still others will have difficulty stopping. Necessary accommodations will be different for each student, and these supports will help with such problems as difficulty in starting, continuing, and stopping an activity (see Donnellan & Leary, 1995).

For example, touching Teresa's elbow enabled her to begin pointing to her answers on a test. A picture schedule helped another student, Sally, go through the steps of a classroom activity that included getting out her supplies, using them correctly, and putting them away without prompting.

Both teachers and peers can incorporate all these suggestions. Peers can learn to draw out responses from each other and may even provide the educators with creative, fresh approaches.

Final Thoughts

We need to think of our roles not only as developers of social, academic, and functional skills in students, but also as interpreters and communication allies of inarticulate students. These are the same sensitivities we automatically use with students without disabilities in general education settings, with our peers, and often with young children—when we remember how much they really do understand.

References

Biklen, D., & Cardinal, D. (1997). *Contested words, contested science: Unraveling the FC controversy.* New York: Teachers College Press.

Biklen, D., & Duchan, J. (1994). I am intelligent: The social construction of mental retardation. *Journal of the Association for Persons with Severe Handicaps, 19*(3), 173–184.

Donnellan, A. M., & Leary, M. R. (1995). *Movement differences and diversity in autism/mental retardation: Appreciating and accommodating people with communication and behavior challenges* (4th ed.). Madison, WI: DRI Press.

Goode, D. A. (1989). Who's Bobby? Ideology and method in the discovery of a Down syndrome person's competence. In P. M. Ferguson, D. L. Ferguson, & S. J. Taylor (Eds.), *Interpreting disability: A qualitative reader* (pp. 197–212). New York: Teachers College Press.

Rosenthal, R. (1997). *Interpersonal expectancy effects: A forty-year perspective.* Paper presented at the American Psychological Association Convention, Chicago. (ERIC Document Reproduction Service No. ED 415 460)

Smith, R., Ryan, S., & Salend, S. (2001). Watch your language: Closing or opening the special education curtain. *TEACHING Exceptional Children, 33*(4), 18–23.

Smith, R. M. (1999). Academic engagement of students with significant disabilities and educators' perceptions of competence. *The Professional Educator, 22*(1), 17–31.

Smith, R. M. (2000). View from the ivory tower: How academics construct disability. In B. B. Swadner & L. Rogers (Eds.), *Semiotics and disability: Interrogating the categories of difference* (pp. 55–733). New York: State University of New York (SUNY) Press.

Robin M. Smith *(CEC Chapter #615), Assistant Professor of Special Education, Educational Studies, State University of New York at New Paltz, New York.*

Address correspondence to the author at Educational Studies Department, State University of New York–New Paltz, 75 S. Manheim Blvd., New Paltz, NY 12561 (e-mail: smithrm@newpaltz.edu)

UNIT 6

Emotional and Behavioral Disorders

Unit Selections

Key Points to Consider

- How does the wraparound system work? What are some tips for teachers using this system?

- How have choice-making opportunities for students with emotional and behavioral problems helped break the cycle of negative responses that hinders their progression through the educational system?

- After reading the article by Jacqueline Smollar, what would you suggest as measures to reduce the number of homeless adolescents?

- How can chronic and intense behavioral difficulties be ameliorated in the classroom to allow learning to take place?

 Links: www.dushkin.com/online/
These sites are annotated in the World Wide Web pages.

Educating Students With Emotional/Behavioral Disorders
http://www.nichcy.org/pubs/bibliog/bib10txt.htm
Pacer Center: Emotional Behavioral Disorders
http://www.pacer.org/ebd/
Resources in Emotional or Behavioral Disorders (EBD)
http://www.gwu.edu/~ebdweb/

The definition of a student with emotional behavioral disorder (EBD) usually conjures up visions of the violence perpetrated by a few students who have vented their frustrations by taking guns to school. One of the hot topics in special education today is whether students with emotional and behavioral disorders are too dangerous to be included in regular education classes. The statistics show that students with EBDs are as likely to be the victims of violence or bullying by nondisabled classmates as to be the troublemakers. The definition of EBDs broadly includes all emotionally disordered students with subjective feelings such as sadness, fear, anger, guilt, or anxiety that give rise to altered behaviors that are outside the range of normal.

Should children with chronic and severe anger, already convicted of problem behaviors such as violent acts or threats of violence, be reenrolled in inclusive regular education classes with individualized education plans (IEPs)? Although teachers, other pupils, and school staff may be greatly inconvenienced by the presence of one or more behaviorally disordered students in every classroom, the law is clear. The school must "show cause" if a child with EBD is to be permanently moved from the regular classroom to a more restrictive environment.

The 1994 Gun-Free Schools Act in the United States requires a one-year expulsion of a student who brings a firearm to school. The Individuals with Disabilities Education Act (IDEA) in its 1997 reauthorization made a compromise for students with EBDs or other conditions of disability. If bringing a gun to school is related to their disability (for example, as the result of being teased or bullied), they are exempt from the Gun-Free Schools Act legislation. They can be expelled, but only for 10 days while the school determines their degree of danger to others. If they are judged to really be dangerous, they can temporarily be given an alternate educational placement for 45 days, subject to reassessment. Their IEPs should not be rewritten to place them in a permanent restrictive setting unless their acts were clearly unrelated to their disabilities (hard to prove). This double standard is very controversial. Students without disabilities are expelled with no educational provisions for one full year.

For educational purposes, children with behavior disorders are usually divided into two main behavioral classifications: (1) withdrawn, shy, or anxious behaviors and (2) aggressive, acting-out behaviors. The debate about what constitutes a behavior disorder, or an emotional disorder, is not fully resolved. The *Diagnostic and Statistical Manual of Mental Disorders* (4th edition) *(DSM-IV)* sees serious behavioral disorders as a category first diagnosed in infancy, childhood, or adolescence. Among the *DSM-IV* disorders of childhood are eating disorders, tic disorders, elimination disorders, separation anxiety disorders, reactive attachment disorders, oppositional defiant disorder, and conduct disorder.

An alliance of educators and psychologists proposed that IDEA should remove the term "serious emotional disturbances" and instead focus on behaviors that adversely affect educational performance. Conduct usually considered a sign of emotional disorder, such as anxiety, depression, or failure of attachment, can be seen as behaviorally disordered if it interferes with academic, social, vocational, and personal accomplishment. So, also, can eating, elimination, or tic disorders and any other responses outside the range of "acceptable" for school or other settings. Such a focus on behavior can link the individualized educational plan curriculum activities to children's behavioral response styles.

Inclusive education does not translate into acceptance of disordered behaviors in the regular education classroom. Two rules of thumb for the behavior of all children, however capable or incapable, are that they conform to minimum standards of acceptable conduct and that disruptive behaviors be subject to fair and consistent disciplinary action. In order to ensure more orderly, well-regulated classroom environments, many schools are instituting conflict management courses.

What causes students to act out with hostile, aggressive behaviors directed against school personnel or other students? An easy, often-cited reason is that they are barraged with images of violence on the news, in music, on videos, on television programs, and in movies. It is too facile: Media barrage is aimed at everyone, yet only a few decide that they want to become violent and harm others. Aggressive, bullying children commonly come from homes where they see real violence, anger, and insults. They often feel disconnected, rejected, and afraid. They do not know how to communicate their distress. They may appear to be narcissistic, even as they seek attention in negative, hurtful ways. They usually have fairly easy access to weapons, alcohol, and other substances of abuse. They usually do not know any techniques of conflict management other than acting out.

The first article addresses the need to identify children with EBDs as early as possible and do primary prevention using Uri Bronfenbrenner's ecological model. The authors suggest support services involving many team members and many components of intervention. Parents, children, and other team members work together at conflict management and social skills development in wraparound ways.

The second and third articles describe characteristics of students with EBDs. The authors of "Making Choices—Improving Behavior—Engaging in Learning" suggest that allowing students to make choices and engage in their own education can help break the cycle of negative responses. Jacqueline Smollar then describes homeless youth. She suggests that helping students to develop a sense of connectedness to adults with whom they can engage in loving, positive, productive behaviors is essential.

The fourth article, "Classroom Problems That Don't Go Away" gives suggestions for ameliorating and/or preventing conflicts and antisocial acts within the regularized education curriculum by teaching alternative behaviors.

Wraparound Services for Young Schoolchildren with Emotional and Behavioral Disorders

Susanna Duckworth • Sue Smith-Rex • Suzanne Okey • Mary Ann Brookshire • David Rawlinson
Regenia Rawlinson • Sara Castillo • Jessie Little

#2
- **Suspension cut in half.**
- **Almost one-half fewer absences.**
- **Referrals to the office reduced by two-thirds.**
- **Parent conferences increased four-fold.**

Would you like to see results like these for your students with emotional and behavioral disorders? This article shows how.

In communities across the United States, educators, mental health practitioners, parents, and students have come face to face with the fact that even young elementary schoolchildren can become a threat to society and to themselves. The reauthorization of the Individuals with Disabilities Education Act (Public Law 105-17, IDEA Amendments of 1997, P.L. 105-17, 300.520, 64 Stat. 12412 [199]) makes it less difficult to expel dangerous or violent students with special needs from general and special education classrooms. In addition, IDEA provides suggestions regarding alternative settings as a means for delivering appropriate educational interventions. Being removed from school, however, should be a last resort; and educators should explore every avenue before a child is either expelled or placed in an alternative setting.

This article describes a project we conducted in a suburban location in the southeastern United States and suggests ways other educators might develop such supports for children and their families.

A dynamic process involves establishing trust, relationship building, and continuous assessment.

Meeting the Needs of Children and Their Families

We designed this project to meet the needs of young elementary schoolchildren with severe and complex emotional and behavioral disorders (EBD). These were children who were often angry, violent, and vulnerable to abuse. The intervention project for this self-contained class of children with EBD began in January 1999 and continued until May 2000. At the beginning of the project, the class contained 8 male students, who had been identified as early as kindergarten or first grade. During the project, class enrollment ranged from 8 to 12 students, 11 males and 1 female, whose ages ranged from 6 to 9 years. A behavioral support team determined that the children should remain in school.

To increase the chances for these children to be included in a general education setting, we implemented a family-centered system using "wraparound" services for the children and their parents (see Clark & Clarke, 1996; Eber, Nelson, & Miles, 1997; Eber, Osuch, & Redditt, 1996; VanDenBerg & Grealish, 1996). A wraparound system is "a needs-driven process for creating and providing services for individual children and their families" (Eber et al., 1997). We used this definition to direct our project. To better understand how to use a wraparound system, we studied the application of systems theory (see box, "Systems Theory").

Our review of the literature led us to develop the following guiding questions, which then provided the impetus for our project:

- What are the features of a hands-on wraparound system of services to serve young children with EBD?

- How can we increase parents' participation in their child's educational program?

- What can we learn from parental needs and concerns that will help us to better serve children with EBD?

- How can we better prepare our future teachers to meet the behavioral challenges of the 21st century?

We then created a behavioral support team to plan and address the guiding questions. Figure 1 shows our conceptualization of a wraparound system. Note the integration of school, team, and community services "wrapping around" the group of children and parents involved in our 18-month intervention project.

Systems Theory and a Wraparound System

The most common framework for understanding family assets, needs, resources, and perceptions is systems theory. This theory spotlights family values, priorities, and needs within a responsive, hierarchical, and methodical environment (von Bertalanffy, 1968). As early as 1970, Hobbs applied systems theory concepts to "ecological strategies" in his program for children with emotional disturbance, Project Re-Ed. Bronfenbrenner's (1977; Bronfenbrenner & Nevill, 1994) systems theory model focuses on human development and renewing support for children and families.

Systems theory, using Bronfenbrenner's research, has been put into practice by Bailey, who has written extensively about preschool children with special needs (Bailey & Wolery, 1992). It is from Bailey's interpretation of Bronfenbrenner's work, as well as Brooks-Gunn (1995), that we took our ideas and developed a wraparound system of services for helping children with EBD and their parents.

Role of the Behavioral Support Team

Members of the behavioral support team were people who expressed an interest in working with one another to support young children with EBD and their parents. The team, which consisted of professionals from a local university, a public school district, and a mental health agency (see Figure 2), met monthly to plan, problem-solve, and determine answers to the guiding questions. Parents were considered members of the behavioral support team because of their knowledge of their own needs, as well as the needs of their children. Parents were also recipients of wraparound services.

We developed several components to achieve the goal of implementing successful interventions for young children with EBD:

- *Data-based behavioral instruction* was directed by data collected in an observation booth by university students, teachers, and other professionals. The observation booth was available to parents, who were invited to observe their children at any time during the school day.

Figure 2. Behavioral Support Team Members

- University Special Education Professors (2)
- University Education Majors Serving as Mentors (12)
- Special Education Teacher
- Teaching Assistant
- Guidance Counselor
- Principal
- Clinical Child Psychologist from Local Mental Health Agency
- Director of the Local Alternative School Program
- Parents of the Children with Emotional and Behavioral Disorders

- *An innovative suspension program,* provided by the school's principal, was called "The Therapeutic Day" (see box). This program reduced full-day suspensions.

- *Cost-free, direct services* in the classroom provided by a clinical child psychologist from the local mental health agency. In addition, free individual family counseling was available at the agency site.

- *A mentoring program* conducted by university education majors. Each mentor was assigned a student from the class. Mentoring options included having lunch, tutoring, and participating in outdoor activities such as touch football, basketball, and miniature golf.

- *The use of the research-based social skills curriculum, Second Step* (Committee for Children, 1999).

Figure 1. A Wraparound System

- *Monthly evening parent meetings,* scheduled with parental input, were held in the school library, with transportation provided as needed by the members of the behavioral support team. These meetings turned out to be the most important component of the program.

TO INCREASE THE CHANCES FOR THESE CHILDREN TO BE INCLUDED IN A GENERAL EDUCATION SETTING, WE IMPLEMENTED A FAMILY-CENTERED SYSTEM USING "WRAPAROUND" SERVICES

In addition, we visited consenting families in their homes so that the team could further clarify questions about the purposes of the project and of wraparound services.

We were enthusiastic with the process from the beginning, but we had to continuously remind ourselves to review and revise what we were doing with the children and their parents. We felt that if the project were to be successful, parents must be able to enhance their child-rearing skills and must be able to establish levels of trust with all members of the behavioral support team.

"The Therapeutic Day" # 1

The purpose of "The Therapeutic Day" was to *increase* the amount of time a child would stay in school rather than to *increase* referrals to the principal and out-of-school suspensions. To these ends, the teacher used a cell phone programmed with the phone numbers of each child's parents so that phone calls could be immediate and, through conferencing and problem-solving, could increase parental participation for taking responsibility to help their children stay in school. The principal was a positive support, rather than symbolizing punishment.

Also, the principal coordinated with the university special education professors in providing opportunities for the education majors to serve as mentors—tutoring students, having lunch with them, and sponsoring a monthly "Fabulous Friday" event. Students earned points from a classroom behavior plan to participate in special events. As noted in Table 1, the discipline actions taken brought results.

The Participating Children and Their Parents

As the behavioral support team attempted to address our original guiding questions, which focused on parental needs and concerns about children with EBD and parental participation in educational programs, we reviewed some statistical data: 92% of the parents were single, and 92% of the students qualified for participation in the federal free lunch program. These data gave insight into parents' financial needs and their family structures. We asked ourselves how we could address the needs of parents who were single-handedly juggling employment issues and parental responsibilities while they were confronting pressures brought about by raising children with EBD.

We decided to have monthly parent meetings during which various behavioral support team members would present topics, such as effective discipline (Rawlinson, 1997), character building, behavior modification, mental health issues, and medications. We hoped that the topics would provide parents with an array of options to use at home that would support the educational program offered at school. We knew we could not conduct the parent meetings, however, without input from the parents themselves.

THE WRAPAROUND SYSTEM HELPED ANSWER THE PERENNIAL QUESTION, HOW CAN WE INCREASE PARENTS' PARTICIPATION IN THEIR CHILD'S EDUCATIONAL PROGRAM?

To that end, the first monthly meeting session began with a parental needs assessment. Outcomes from the assessment determined the topics selected for the subsequent meetings (see box, "Who Says My Child Has Behavior Problems in School?"). All participating members of the behavioral support team reviewed the needs-assessment findings, which demonstrated to all how parental requests for help were being honored. The following monthly discussion topics came out of the parental needs assessment:
- Feelings and attitudes.
- Who says my child has behavior problems in school?
- Family issues.
- How to handle stress.
- Losing a job.
- Finances.
- How to handle failure.
- Transportation problems.
- Dealing with unacceptable behavior.
- Trust-building and communication.
- Available community resources.
- How values are learned in life.
- How to communicate encouragement to your child.

During the sessions that followed, we began talking about feelings, attitudes, and character building. We also discussed situations arising at home, which cause children to behave inappropriately. We presented strategies to help parents with their children's problem behaviors; one source of strategies was *Second Step,* which uses a simple step-by-step method to modify behavior.

Behavioral support team members learned that parental needs, just as the students', were concrete. Issues of transportation, jobs, recreation, mental health, and childhood psychotropic medications were stresses in parents' lives. They had real survival needs that had to be addressed. Over 6 months, the parents listened to community representatives, as well as members of the behavioral support team, who could answer questions and facilitate meetings.

Who Says My Child Has Behavior Problems in School?

Steps that take place:

1. The *teacher* is usually the first to notice that a behavior problem interferes with a child's progress in the classroom. Some examples of behavior problems:

hitting	**showing signs of depression**
having tantrums	**refusing to obey**
being too quiet or withdrawn	**using bad language**
yelling	**demonstrating uncontrolled anger**

2. The *teacher* tells the *principal* or *school psychologist* about the child and the problem. This is called "referral."

3. The *school psychologist* observes the child in the classroom for several days.

4. The *school psychologist* gives the child several tests. Some examples of tests are behavior checklists, social/interaction tests, intelligence tests.

5. The *school psychologist* uses test results to see if the child's behavior fits the label "emotional disturbance," a category determined by the state education agency and used by the local school district.

6. If the child's behavior fits the label, the *school psychologist* sets up an individualized education program (IEP) meeting with the *parent, general education teacher, special education teacher, principal,* and others.

7. If all parties agree, *special education* services are provided for the child.

All behavioral support team members—including the parents—began to see one another as people with similar problems, hopes, and dreams. Trust was established. Many parents admitted that they, themselves, had experienced adjustment problems in school and that they continued to have little control over their own anger. They also admitted that there were serious problems at home with their children. The parents began to ask for help from people they now trusted. It became apparent that parents, as well as children, would not be open to learning unless it was relevant to their lives, presented in a meaningful way, and facilitated by someone who has taken the time to form a relationship of trust with them.

CELL PHONES AND AN OBSERVATION BOOTH WERE ESSENTIAL PARTS OF THE WRAPAROUND SERVICE

The Principal as a Major Key to Success

The school principal was a member of our behavioral support team. He was pivotal in getting the program off the ground. He had an in-depth knowledge of the students, their families, and the school's and communities' needs. Because of his associations and good communication with the school district office, he was able to obtain funds for the construction of the observation booth that helped us answer some of the wraparound systems' guiding questions dealing with parental participation and teacher preparation. The observation booth provided

- Opportunities for parents and professionals to observe children in their daily school setting.
- A specific milieu for university education majors to use observational recording techniques and to reflect on effective teaching practices.

10 Tips for Teachers

1. Use frequent positive reinforcement. Research says five positive reinforcements for *each* negative, (Beck & Williamston, 1993).

2. Ignore negative behavior that does not interfere with others' learning or influence others' behavior.

3. Tell children specifically what you want them *to do,* rather than what you want them *to stop doing.* For example, if a child is swinging his arms around and bothering another child, tell him to put his hands in his pockets or fold his arms instead of telling him to stop swinging his arms.

4. Use lots of humor.

5. Once you have stated that a certain consequence will follow a specific action, you *must* follow through with the consequence.

6. Give students the choice of two options, *both* of which are acceptable to you.

7. Change the physical environment, that is, rearrange the desks, and so forth.

8. Elicit support from parents in the form of "pep talks" before behavior is out of control.

9. Use masking tape on the floor to delineate personal space.

10. Spend plenty of time teaching procedures, and review them frequently during the year.

The principal provided essential leadership in finding alternative methods of support for the classroom teacher when the students' behaviors were violent and unacceptable. As the project progressed, he no longer viewed full-day suspension as the preferred option. Through the use of "The Therapeutic Day" (see box), students were able to remain in school or the classroom for at least a half-day and often for the entire day, instead of being suspended (see Table 1).

Table 1. Discipline Report from the Osiris Database

Discipline Actions Taken	1998–1999	1999–2000	% Decrease or Increase
Referrals to the office	128	46	- 64
Absences—partial day	78	18	- 230
Absences—full day	182	102	- 44
Suspensions	84	41	- 49
Parent Conferences	19	79	+ 415

As noted in Table 1, there was a significant decrease in referrals to the office, school absences, and suspensions. "The Therapeutic Day" technique was used in building cultural competence. For students to be culturally competent, they must have appropriate adaptive behavior and academic skills.

The Teacher as the Creator of Cultural Competence

Another member of the behavioral support team was the special education teacher in the self-contained class. Her role was to provide daily academic and behavioral instruction that would build *cultural competence* in the students (see box, "10 Tips for Teachers").

Academic Instruction

Academic instruction was based on each student's IEP. The teacher individualized all work and used a variety of instructional formats, including direct instruction. The students closely followed the general education curriculum, with allowances for their strengths and weaknesses. As well, the teacher used state curricular standards and a variety of instructional materials.

Behavior Management and Social Skills Development

Use of behavior management strategies, such as those found in "10 Tips for Teachers," and the administration of the *Second Step* program allowed the teacher to devote more class time to academic instruction, thereby enhancing the development of cultural competence. The teacher obtained documentation of student adaptive and academic behavior outcomes by means of a point-based behavior plan. Students and parents were able to monitor performance by reviewing total daily points that students earned for appropriate behaviors demonstrated in school.

The *Second Step* curriculum is a research-based program that teaches strategies for behavior management and appropriate social interaction. Mastery of the *Second Step* strategies leads children toward cultural competence. Topics in the curriculum include
- Developing empathy.
- Controlling impulses.
- Managing anger.

Instruction is teacher directed, based on posters, activities, and scripts provided by the publisher. Students with EBD are encouraged to generalize and transfer strategies learned in the *Second Step* program to other situations. For example, in our project, the teacher encouraged students to use *Second Step* role-playing activities to demonstrate empathy after reading a story about a student who had lost her home in a fire. Students who displayed appropriate social skills were allowed to participate in art, music, and physical education classes with their general education peers. To be effective with children with EBD, the teacher was committed to addressing academic, social, and behavioral needs.

What We Learned

In search of answers to the wraparound system's guiding questions, we gained insight and drew the following conclusions:
- The features of an ideal wraparound system of services for young children with EBD should include
  –A systems theory framework.
  –A continuing pledge by a behavioral support team to improve the lives of children and their parents.
  –A data-based program design that includes planning, problem-solving, and implementing interventions.
  –Creative and positive administrative leadership
  –Use of preferred practice based on research ("*OSEP Provides Solutions*," 2000).

OUR BEHAVIORAL SUPPORT TEAM CONSISTED OF PROFESSIONALS FROM A LOCAL UNIVERSITY, A PUBLIC SCHOOL DISTRICT, AND A MENTAL HEALTH AGENCY—AND PARENTS OF THE CHILDREN IN THE CLASS.

- To increase parent participation in a child's educational program,
  –Trust must be established.

–Parent meetings must be perceived as meaningful and enjoyable.

–The school must project a supportive tone for children and their families.

- We can learn from parents that they have as many needs as their children do, and that parents must trust the school before change can occur.

- To better prepare teachers to address the challenging behaviors of children in the 21st century, teacher education programs must include

  –Access to data-collection opportunities.

  –Preferred practices that are research based.

  –Instruction in trust-building skills.

  –A long-term commitment to intervention programs.

We must overcome other obstacles if we are going to educate children with EBD in their least restrictive environment. Students' success will be significantly increased if schools consider using a wraparound system of services, attempt to build programs that increase parental trust and support, and identify alternatives to the expulsion of students with severe and complex emotional and behavioral disorders. As school districts continue to examine means of helping children with EBD and their parents, we must create systems of services that are supportive, are family-centered, and address the needs of educators.

References

Bailey, D. B., & Wolery, M. (1992). *Teaching infants and preschoolers with disabilities* (2nd ed., p. 66). Englewood Cliffs, NJ: Prentice-Hall.

Beck, R., & Williamston, R. (1993). *Project Ride for preschoolers: Responding to individual differences in education.* Longmont, CA: Sopris West.

Bronfenbrenner, U. (1977). Toward an experimental ecology of human development. *American Psychologist, 32,* 513–531.

Bronfenbrenner, U., & Nevill, P. R. (1994). America's children and families: An international perspective. In S. L. Kagan & B. Weissbourd (Eds), *Putting families first: America's family support movement and the challenge of change* (pp. 3–27). San Francisco: Jossey-Bass.

Brooks-Gunn, J. (1995). Children in families in communities: Risk and intervention in the Bronfenbrenner tradition. In P. Moen, G. H. Elder, Jr., K. Luscher, & H. E. Quick (Eds.), *Examining lives in context: Perspectives on the ecology of human development* (pp. 467–519). Washington, DC: American Psychological Association.

Clark, H. B., & Clarke, R. T. (1996). Research on the wraparound process and individualized services for children with multiple-system needs. *Journal of Child and Family Studies, 5*(1), 1–5.

Committee for Children. (1999). *Second Step Program,* Seattle, WA: Author.

Eber, L., Nelson, C. M., & Miles, P. (1997). School-based wraparound for students with emotional and behavioral challenges. *Exceptional Children, 63,* 539–555.

Eber, L., Osuch, R., & Redditt, C. A. (1996). School-based applications of the wraparound process: Early results on service provision and student outcomes. *Journal of Child and Family Studies, 5*(1), 83–99.

Hobbs, N. (1970). Project Re-Ed: New ways of helping emotionally disturbed children. In Joint Commission on Mental Health of Children (Ed.), *Crisis in child mental health: Challenge for the 1970s.* New York: Harper & Row.

IDEA Amendments of 1997, Public Law 105-17, 300.520, 64 Stat. 12412 (199). [ERIC document Reproduction Service]

OSEP provides solutions to improve student behavior. (2000, March). *CEC Today, 6*(6), 1–15.

Rawlinson, R. M. (1997). *From discipline to responsibility: Principles for raising children today.* Minneapolis, MN: Educational Media Corporation.

VanDenBerg, J. E., & Grealish, E. M. (1996). Individualized services and support through the wraparound process: Philosophy and procedures. *Journal of Child and Family Studies, 5*(1), 7–21.

von Bertanlanffy, L. V. (1968). *General systems theory.* New York: George Brazilles.

Making Choices— Improving Behavior— Engaging in Learning

Kristine Jolivette, Janine Peck Stichter, and Katherine M. McCormick

Do you have students who display inappropriate types of behavior, or who seem depressed, or who lack friends? Perhaps these are students with emotional and behavioral disorders (EBD; see box), and maybe the students present challenges that you find difficult to deal with and that interfere with their educational progress.

This article highlights one strategy, providing opportunities to make choices, that is effective in increasing appropriate behaviors for students with EBD (Munk & Repp, 1994), most notably when used by classroom teachers during ongoing classroom routines (Jolivette, Wehby, Canale, & Massey, 2001b; see also the box, "What Does the Literature Say?" for a link between the research literature on choice and related behavioral characteristics of students with EBD.)

We present a hypothetical case example to show how a teacher might incorporate choice-making opportunities for a student with EBD who is failing math in school. In the course of this article, we suggest practical strategies that both special and general education teachers may use in their academic curricula to encourage students to make appropriate choices. These opportunities may have benefits that long outlast the particular task or situation, to enhance relationships within the classroom, engage stu-

dents in learning, and promote a positive classroom environment.

Opportunities to Make Choices

Choice-making opportunities provide students the opportunity to make decisions that may affect their daily routines (e.g., choice of academic task). For example, a student may choose

- From a list of explorers which explorer to write a report on.
- To begin another game with a different peer during free time.
- To use colored markers while illustrating a picture as part of a book report.
- The type of medium (poster, costume, movie) to use for a presentation on a country in social studies.

These varied choice-making opportunities occur frequently in most classrooms. They may seem trivial at first glance, but such choices can have significant implications for the type and level of student participation (Jolivette, Stichter, Sibilsky, Scott, & Ridgely, 2001a).

Several recent classroom investigations into the use of "choice" for students with EBD have shown that this strategy is effective in increasing (or decreasing) specific behaviors in school (Cosden, Gannon, & Haring, 1995; Dunlap et al., 1994; Jolivette et al., 2001b). These results suggest that providing students with EBD the opportunity to make

What Are Characteristics of Students with Emotional and Behavioral Disorder?

Students with EBD often have these characteristics:

- An inability to learn that cannot be explained by intellectual, sensory, or health factors.
- An inability to build or maintain satisfactory interpersonal relationships with peers and teachers.
- Inappropriate types of behavior or feelings under normal circumstances.
- A general pervasive mood of unhappiness or depression.
- A tendency to develop physical symptoms or fears associated with personal or school problems (Individuals with Disabilities Education Act, IDEA, 1997, CFR 300.7 (a) 9).

In addition, students with EBD may display these characteristics during academic situations when teacher demands are consistently high and if they have a history of school failure (e.g., performing below grade level).

choices during academic situations can promote increased levels of functional and prosocial student behavior. Here are some findings:

- Cosden et al. (1995) found that student accuracy and completion of academic tasks increased when the students were provided with opportunities to choose the task or reinforcer.
- Dunlap et al. (1994) found that the levels of task engagement increased while levels of disruptive behavior decreased when students were provided with opportunities to choose the academic task to complete.
- Jolivette et al. (2001b) found that student task engagement increased, as did the number and accuracy of attempted problems, when students were provided with opportunities to choose the order in which to complete three tasks (same concept but variable formats).

Case Study: Isaac

Isaac is a 7-year-old first-grader with EBD who attends a combined first/second-grade special education class for students with EBD. He had a full-scale IQ of 79 (verbal = 85 and performance = 74), according to the WISC-III. Isaac's teacher reports that he performs below grade level in mathematics and that he is noncompliant and off task during independent math seatwork activities.

Isaac performs at the grade equivalence of beginning kindergarten (K.0) on the Woodcock-Johnson Calculation, Applied Problems, and General Math subtests (Woodcock & Johnson, 1989). In addition, Isaac is rated in the clinical range for the areas of hyperactivity, aggression, conduct problems, and somatization on the Behavior Assessment System for Children (BASC).

Isaac commonly displays the following behaviors during 15-minute regularly scheduled independent math activities:

- Ripping up or throwing the math worksheet to the floor when prompted to begin to work.
- Verbally disrupting the peer next to him.
- Making black pencil marks over the surface of the worksheet instead of solving the problems.
- Asking a peer for assistance on the first few problems.

- Asking the teacher for access to various manipulative items for use with the worksheet and if given a negative verbal response, verbally threatening the teacher.
- Walking around the classroom when the expectation was for him to be at his desk.
- Questioning the teacher as to what he was going to do after math.

The teacher also reports that because of Isaac's inappropriate behaviors during math, Isaac was experiencing academic failure in math and was not meeting his individualized education program (IEP) math objectives.

To address Isaac's inappropriate behavior, the teacher removed privileges (e.g., free time), moved Isaac's desk away from the other desk pods, and retaught basic math skills on a one-to-one basis during his free time. The teacher states, however, that Isaac's inappropriate behaviors have only escalated; and he continues to make little progress in math.

Strategies for Infusing Opportunities to Make Choices into Math

Given Isaac's behavior and lack of success in math, we suggest providing Isaac with opportunities to make choices during his regularly scheduled, independent math periods to increase his appropriate social and academic behaviors. Because the punitive consequences (loss of privileges and isolation) were ineffective, perhaps the teacher can try another approach: providing opportunities to make choices. This may be a more proactive plan in addressing Isaac's inappropriate behaviors and math failure, and perhaps it will encourage Isaac to display appropriate behavior and achieve success during math activities and tasks.

For this particular student, the focus for choice-making opportunities will be on academic activities related to math instruction and related IEP objectives. There are several ways to implement these opportunities into the existing curricula for Isaac, either before or during tasks, to provide environmental predictability and a sense of control for him. Note that the provision of choice does not alter the curricular objective for Isaac: accurately completing math worksheets.

Choices Before the Task Demand

To provide Isaac with predictability in his independent math seatwork period, Isaac's teacher may provide him with the opportunity to decide *when he will begin* his math worksheet. For example, many students are expected to perform a variety of tasks in the classroom that can be completed throughout the day. Such tasks may include watering the plants, returning library books, and picking up and returning lunch tickets. In Isaac's case, he was expected to straighten the workbook shelf and sharpen the pencils each day. His teacher could then state those two tasks along with the math task demand and provide Isaac with the choice of when to start his math: before he completes those two tasks or after completion of the two tasks. The choice of when to begin his worksheet may provide Isaac with a sense of predictability and a sense of control over his math routine and thus decrease his displays of inappropriate behaviors.

If Isaac were observed to request information regarding what events were scheduled for him after completing his math worksheets, it may indicate that the teacher was not following a consistent classroom routine or that Isaac's daily schedule was more complicated than he could effectively follow on his own. Providing Isaac with this information before or while giving him his task demand may influence his behavior based on whether the event is preferred (e.g., free time) or nonpreferred (e.g., spelling test).

Students may engage in inappropriate behavior to obtain a predictable response from the teacher.

To promote appropriate behavior, his teacher may provide an opportunity for Isaac to *choose the event that will occur immediately following* completion of his math task, even if it is just for a few minutes, before another regularly scheduled class activity. For example, Isaac may select between a computer-simulated math game, a math card game with a peer, or a math board game. Thus, Isaac is rewarded for task completion with a selected event.

If the observation data suggested that Isaac's inappropriate behavior (e.g., out of seat behavior, disruption) increased because of his frustration with the math task, it may be helpful for his teacher to provide Isaac with *the choice of terminating the task* for brief periods of time (e.g., 30 seconds) so as to provide him with a "cooling off" period. Teaching Isaac to better regulate his own behavior within the context of a choice-making opportunity provides a functional and lifelong skill that most people could use.

> *Having opportunities to make choices in academic tasks can provide the environmental predictability needed to minimiize inappropriate behaviors of students, while strengthening appropriate responses and increased levels of engagement.*

As the task is presented to Isaac, his teacher may remind Isaac that he has the option to take "mini-breaks" while working on the worksheet. For example, his teacher may ask Isaac how many problems he will attempt before choosing to take a break. Isaac may select three problems. The teacher then would remind Isaac: "After you work out three problems, you may choose to take a 30-second break before starting on your worksheet again." These mini-breaks are controlled by Isaac and provide him with the ability to self-regulate his behavior while still working on the task and may decrease his subsequent inappropriate behaviors.

The teacher can also allow Isaac to *select items* he feels he will need to complete his math task successfully. For example, the teacher may present Isaac with the math task and prompt him to prepare his work area. In this case, the teacher may ask him what type of writing utensil (e.g., pencil, pen, colored pencil), what kind of eraser (e.g., stuck on the pencil, hand-held eraser), and what color of scrap paper for his work (e.g., white, yellow, blue) he will need to complete his math task. By preparing his work area through choice-making opportunities, the teacher is minimizing Isaac's out-of-seat behavior—his selected supplies are at hand.

Choices During the Task Demand

To provide Isaac with predictability and consistency, as well as to give him perceived control *during* the task, his teacher may give him a variety of choice-making opportunities. For example, if Isaac is expected to complete more than one worksheet during the independent math period, his teacher may allow him to *select the order* in which to complete the worksheets. After presenting Isaac with all the worksheets he needs to complete, his teacher may ask him which worksheet he wants to complete first, second, and so on. Then the teacher (or Isaac) can write the numbers 1 and 2 on top of the worksheets to indicate his order preference.

To reinforce the order Isaac has chosen, the teacher may give Isaac one worksheet at a time and, on completion, give him the second or third worksheet while saying, "Good job! You are ready for the worksheet you chose to complete second."

Isaac may also have been observed to seek out assistance from his peers during independent math periods, thus affecting his peers' ability to complete their math tasks. No matter if Isaac is displaying these behaviors as a means to gain peer attention or to escape the math task–his teacher can manipulate the environment so that Isaac is appropriately interacting with his peers during this time. For instance, when the task is given to Isaac, he may be permitted to *select a peer with whom to work* on the task. Isaac may complete the even-numbered problems while his peer completes the odd-numbered problems, and then each can "check" the answers of the other. In this case, the task demand has not been changed; Isaac still needs to complete all the math problems (solving and check-

ing). Or Isaac may be permitted to *select the communication mode* with which to gain teacher attention (e.g., assistance). When the teacher gives Isaac a math task to work on at his desk, the teacher may prompt Isaac to select either raising his hand, holding up a red note card (provided by the teacher), or making a thumbs-up gesture to solicit assistance with the task. Such a choice provides Isaac with a means to appropriately gain teacher attention without disrupting his peers or leaving his seat.

In addition, Isaac may have been observed to wander around the room during seatwork periods, disrupting his peers who remain in their seats. While presenting Isaac with his math task, his teacher may provide him with an opportunity to *select where in the room* he wants to complete his math work-sheet(s). In many classrooms, empty desks or portions of large tables may be available as choices. If Isaac has a history of displaying increased levels of inappropriate behaviors when in close proximity to certain peers, then empty desks in that area would not be part of his choice. In that case, the teacher may limit the possible areas in the room that Isaac can select from.

When multiple math worksheets are not part of the task, nor are other choices involving peer partners or different locations feasible, Isaac's teacher may permit him to *choose the methods* in which he will complete the task. For example, Isaac could start at the bottom of the page and work to the top of the page, work from right to left, or randomly select the order of the problems from the worksheet. The teacher may also remind Isaac to be careful not to skip problems. Again, the task does not change, but how Isaac can complete the task has been manipulated.

In addition, Isaac may have occasionally asked his teacher for access to math manipulatives to use while he worked on his task. When appropriate, Isaac's teacher may provide him with opportunities to select the *type of manipulatives (materials)* he wants to use to complete the task. For example, he may select base-ten blocks, blocks, or beans. Or he may select a one-hundred chart, counting strip, or counting bracelet.

Benefits of Infusing Choice-Making Opportunities into the Classroom

Initial research in classrooms on the use of choice-making opportunities for students with EBD indicates that providing opportunities to make choices during ongoing academic activities is an effective, efficient classroom strategy (Cosden et al., 1995; Dunlap et al., 1994; Jolivette et al., 2001b). The following benefits may result:

- Providing a student with EBD an opportunity to choose among *already existing materials* may be a cost-effective-method to minimize some of the inappropriate behaviors typically displayed by these students during academic situations. Teachers can manipulate existing environmental conditions, materials, and natural consequences without using scarce time and money to create "new" instructional materials (e.g., where to sit in the room to complete a task, order of completion for existing tasks, methods to use to complete a given task).

- Providing choices may *promote more positive relations among all students, better teacher-student interactions, and a more focused classroom environment* (Shores et al., 1993). Providing opportunities to make choices can help teachers assign tasks in a more positive way, while providing predictability for the student in the current task situation.

For example, when a student selects to raise his or her hand to communicate "I need help," then the teacher reinforces the student's choice and comes over and offers assistance. And when the student completes the task with accuracy, the teacher provides the student a choice of what to do next (e.g., put a puzzle together, work on any home-work assignments, check out a book from the library).

- By providing the student with opportunities to make choices, *the teacher is relinquishing some of the decision-making power in the classroom*. Being able to make choices during academic tasks may provide students with skills needed in other academically focused programs.

For example, a small group of students may have the task of creating a bulletin board as part of their report on the human body. Instead of the teacher telling the students that they will create a bulletin board on the digestive system and will highlight it with an interactive component, the teacher may allow the group to select the specific content for the bulletin board but provide parameters for their choice. These parameters may include (a) select one of the following body systems-nervous, digestive, circulatory; (b) provide a detailed visual with supporting information on the selected system; (c) incorporate an interactive activity; and (d) double check all information for accuracy and organization. Thus, the teacher has provided the small group with multiple opportunities to make choices while completing an academic task. This example would be appropriate for older students, but can be adapted for younger students like Isaac.

- The provision of choice-making opportunities may *simultaneously affect social and task-related behaviors of students with EBD*. Students with EBD seek opportunities to influence (control) their classroom environments; unfortunately they may do so by displaying inappropriate behaviors. Guess, Benson, and Siegel-Causey (1985) suggested that choice-making opportunities not only provide a student with the power to manipulate variables but the ability to exert control over environmental events through appropriate means. For students with EBD, this is significant given their use of inappropriate behavior as a means to create more preferred contexts. By adding the predictability to the tasks, as well as providing the student with "power" to manipulate those tasks through choices, the teacher may encourage students to display higher rates of appropriate social behavior while making academic improvement.

In Isaac's case, he was provided with opportunities to make choices within the context of his math tasks, which provided predictability in the math routine and the ability to manipulate events within it.

Implications for Practice

When considering opportunities to infuse increased choice-making within the curriculum, consider the following issues:

1. Start small and think "manageable" in terms of successive steps. Instead of offering students with EBD opportunities to make choices throughout the entire school day, begin with one or two curricular areas or periods of time. A convenient place to start is during student free time or when students are finishing tasks on a varied schedule. For example, during free time, provide a student with EBD with three options from the classroom environment, such as access to the computer, a book from the teacher's bookshelf, or a puzzle with which to play. Once the student demonstrates the ability to make choices, combine choice-making opportunities. For instance, provide the student with choice options and, once an option is selected, allow the student a choice of where in the room to use the free-time option.

For students with EBD, predictability and control may be critical concepts and skills that are necessary for appropriately coping with the environment.

2. Begin infusing opportunities to make choices within the curricular area in which the student will gain the most. With Isaac, we suggested starting in math because he was experiencing high rates of both academic and social difficulties in that area, contributing to his school failure. When selecting the specific area, review existing student data (e.g., anecdotal records, grade summaries) to guide area selection.

3. View opportunities to make choices along a continuum. For example,

What Does the Literature Say About Choice-Making and Environmental Predictability and Control?

What are Choice-Making Opportunities? Providing students with EBD opportunities to make choices means that the student is provided with two or more options, is allowed to independently select an option, and is provided with the selected option. For example, before distributing a test, the teacher states that each student will complete 25 multiple-choice questions but may choose to either write two essay responses or five short-answer responses as the second part of the test. Each student is called to the teacher's desk to make a selection and is then provided with the selection and told to sit at his or her desk and complete the test. Once all students are at their desks, the teacher says, "When you finish the test, turn it in, take an enrichment folder, and follow the directions inside." This example highlights the provision of choice-making opportunities within naturally occurring classroom events and the connection between choice and environmental predictability.

What is Predictability? Predictability may be defined as a person's ability to accurately judge and interpret what environmental events precede or follow other specific environmental events. That is, the students are provided with an opportunity to make a choice, the choice option is honored, and the events after the test are known. Positive effects of choice-making opportunities may be due, in part, to this predictability once a choice is made (Brown, Belz, Corsi, & Wenig, 1993).

The ability to predict environmental relationships through choice-making opportunities provides the student with an opportunity to act in a manner that helps assure the occurrence of expected environmental events, such as positive interactions with others, cessation of tasks, or reinforcement for a behavior. In the test-taking *with choices*, the students knew what they were expected to do (make a choice and complete the test) and what event was going to occur after the test (work on tasks in enrichment folder). It is common, however, for students with EBD to have difficulty regulating their behaviors when environmental events are perceived to be unpredictable.

In the test-taking example, if the student selected the five short-answer responses but the teacher gave him or her the two essay questions instead, that would create unpredictability. In the student's search for a known or predictable environmental event, the student may consequently display high rates of inappropriate behaviors because he or she knows what the consequences of these behaviors will be. Although potentially undesirable, the consequences are, nevertheless, predictable. For example, a student may act out to gain teacher attention during independent seatwork if teacher attention does not occur when the student displays appropriate behavior and is consistently provided for inappropriate behavior during seatwork times. A student with EBD, however, with the skill to predict potential consequences of his or her own behavior, may display higher rates of appropriate behavior to help ensure the desired teacher attention.

The need for predictability may influence students' behavior even when the ability to exert control over the environment is unavailable (Gunter, Shores, Jack, Denny, & DePaepe, 1994). Given this need for predictability, it is important to assess and modify environments proactively to assist students in making positive choices that will result in both predictable and desirable outcomes (Brown et al., 1993).

How are Predictability and Inappropriate Behavior Linked? Current research in classrooms for students with behavior problems suggests that, unfortunately, predictability most often comes as the result of inappropriate behavior. For example, Van Acker, Grant, and Henry (1996) investigated the interactions that occurred between teachers and students at risk for EBD by conducting a study of 25 teachers and 206 students with mild levels of behavioral problems or higher levels of behavioral problems. These researchers found that most predictable teacher and student interaction patterns were that of teacher demand (academic or social)-to-student noncompliance behavior-to-teacher reprimand-to-student noncompliance behavior. When students engaged in appropriate behavior, however, there was less consistency in teacher responses to the student. Therefore, not surprisingly, if predictability in interactions were important, *students might engage in inappropriate behavior to obtain a predictable response from the teacher.*

The simultaneous effects of choice-making opportunities on both academic and social behaviors is an area that has been underexplored (Powell & Nelson, 1997) and will be an important area for future research and application of choice in the classroom for students with EBD.

How Do We Break the Cycle of Negative Responses? Providing opportunities for students with EBD to make choices related to academic tasks may disrupt the negative cycle of teacher-student interactions described by Van Acker et al. (1996), as well as provide consistency and predictability to academic contexts. For students with EBD, predictability and control may be critical concepts and skills that are necessary and required for appropriately interpreting and coping with the environment, as well as practicing new prosocial skills. When students with EBD perceive their environments to be less threatening and perceive themselves as able to predict and control events, they may increase appropriate kinds of behavior.

For example, in the test-taking scenario *with choices*, the test became more predictable through teacher direction and known events after completion of the test, and the students were able to control the type of written responses required—short answer or essay. Thus, the use of choice-making opportunities can provide the environmental predictability needed to minimize the characteristically inappropriate behaviors exhibited by students with EBD during task situations, while strengthening appropriate responses and increased levels of engagement.

the choices provided to Isaac were basic and concrete. That is, those choices were not significant to decisions he will need to make in the future (e.g., such as what job to train for) but still provided practice in choice-making critical to his proficiency and success in making more important choices.

4. Be consistent in both the presentation and follow-through with choice-making opportunities. For example, offer the same number of choice-making opportunities for the targeted area; and when a student makes a choice, reinforce the selection by providing him or her with the selected item.

By considering these four issues before infusing opportunities to make choices into the curricula for students with EBD, you may provide the appropriate environmental context for both student and teacher success.

Final Thoughts

Overall, research on classroom environments for students with EBD has suggested that punishing students (e.g., withholding rewards, denying choices) for inappropriate behavior only promotes negative and inconsistent interactions between teachers and students (Steinberg & Knitzer, 1992; Van Acker et al., 1996). These findings support the classroom components cited by Reitz (1994) as necessary for students with EBD to experience school success (e.g., high rates of social reinforcement and student academic involvement and achievement).

The provision of choice-making opportunities for students with EBD is a viable curricular modification that links student involvement with student decision making for social and academic suc-cess (Mathur, Nelson, & Rutherford, 1998).

References

Brown, F., Belz, P., Corsi, L., & Wenig, B. (1993). Choice diversity for people with severe disabilities. *Education and Training in Mental Retardation, 28,* 318–326.

Cosden, M., Gannon, C., & Haring, T. G. (1995). Teacher-control versus student-control over choice of task and reinforcement for students with severe behavior problems. *Journal of Behavioral Education, 5,* 11–27.

Dunlap, G., DePerczel, M., Clarke, S., Wilson, D., Wright, S., White, R., & Gomez, A. (1994). Choice making to promote adaptive behavior for students with emotional and behavioral challenges. *Journal of Applied Behavior Analysis, 27,* 505–518.

Guess, D., Benson, H. A., & Siegel-Causey, E. (1985). Concepts and issues related to choice making and autonomy among persons with severe disabilities. *Journal of the Association of Persons with Severe Handicaps, 10,* 79–86.

Gunter, P. L., Shores, R. E., Jack, S. L., Denny, R. K., & DePaepe, P. (1994). A case study of the effects of altering instructional interactions on the disruptive behavior of a child identified with severe behavior disorders. *Education and Treatment of Children, 17,* 435–444.

Individuals with Disabilities Education Act Amendments of 1997, P. L. 105–17. 105th Congress, 1st Session.

Jolivette, K., Stichter, J., Sibilsky, S., Scott, T. M., & Ridgely, R. (2001a). *Naturally occurring opportunities for preschool children with and at-risk for disabilities to make choices.* Submitted for publication.

Jolivette, K., Wehby, J. H., Canale, J., & Massey, N. G. (2001b). Effects of choice making opportunities on the behavior of students with emotional and behavioral disorders. *Behavioral Disorders, 26,* 131–145.

Mathur, S. R., Nelson, J. R., & Rutherford, R. B. (1998). Translating the IEP into practice: Curricular and instructional accommodations. In L. M. Bullock & R. A. Gable (Eds.), *Implementing the 1997 IDEA: New challenges and opportunities for serving students with emotional/be-havioral disorders.* Reston, VA: Council for Exceptional Children.*

Munk, D. D., & Repp, A. C. (1994). The relationship between instructional variables and problem behavior: A review. *Exceptional Children, 60,* 390–401.

Powell, S., & Nelson, B. (1997). Effects of choosing academic assignments on a student with attention deficit hyperactivity disorder. Journal of *Applied Behavior Analysis, 30,* 181–183.

Reitz, A. L. (1994). Implementing comprehensive classroom-based programs for students with emotional and behavioral problems. *Education and Treatment of Children, 17,* 312–331.

Shores, R. E., Jack, S. L., Gunter, P. L., Ellis, D. N., DeBriere, T. J., & Wehby, J. H. (1993). Classroom interactions of children with behavior disorders. *Journal of Emotional and Behavioral Disorders, 1,* 27–39.

Steinberg, Z., & Knitzer, J. (1992). Classrooms for emotionally and behaviorally disturbed students: Facing the challenge. *Behavioral Disorders, 17,* 145–156.

Van Acker, R., Grant, S. H., & Henry, D. (1996). Teacher and student behavior as a function of risk for aggression. *Education and Treatment for Children, 19,* 316–334.

Woodcock, R. W., & Johnson, M. B. (1989). *Woodcock-Johnson Psycho-Educational Battery-Revised.* Allen, TX: DLM.

Kristine Jolivette, *Assistant Professor, Department of Special Education and Rehabilitation Counseling, University of Kentucky, Lexington.* **Janine Peck Stichter** (*CEC Chapter #27*), *Associate Professor, Department of Special Education, Central Michigan University, Mt. Pleasant.* **Katherine M. McCormick** (*CEC Chapter #180*), *Assistant Professor, Department of Special Education and Rehabilitation Counseling, University of Kentucky, Lexington.*

Address correspondence to Kristine Jolivette, Department of Special Education and Rehabilitation Counseling, University of Kentucky, 119 Taylor Education Building, Lexington, KY 40506-0001 (e-mail: kjolive@uky.edu).

Homeless Youth in the United States

By Jacqueline Smollar, Ph.D.

Homeless youth in the United States are defined as individuals age twenty-one or younger who meet at least one of the following criteria:

- They have run away from their homes or from their alternative care placements and remained away for a long period of time with little or no connection with their families or caretakers.
- They have been pushed out of their homes or foster care placements, have been abandoned by their parents, or have left home for the streets with their parents' knowledge and consent.
- They have no stable place of residence; lack adult supervision, guidance, and care; and have little likelihood of reunification with parents.

The current number of homeless youth in the United States is not known and estimates are dated. In 1991 the National Network for Youth estimated the number of homeless youth ranged from 100,000 to 500,000. Although estimates of one to two million have appeared in the literature, these larger estimates include youth who run away from home and return fairly quickly, usually within a few days.

History of Homeless Youth

Homeless youth have been a part of U.S. society since its early history. During the settlement of the thirteen colonies and the ensuing westward expansion, many adolescents left home to seek adventure and economic opportunity. Homeless youth were also prevalent in the 1800s, but they were perceived as criminals constituting a significant social problem. In the early 1900s, many youth became homeless during the Great Depression. However, because large segments of the population were homeless during the era, the specific problem of youth homelessness was generally ignored.

In the 1960s, a new group of homeless youth, referred to as "runaways," began to be perceived as a significant social problem. Unlike earlier homeless youth, these adolescents left middle- and upper-class homes and forfeited the educational advantages and future professional prospects available to them as part of their families' socio-economic status. Congress enacted the Runaway Youth Act of 1974, which provided funds for establishing shelters to temporarily house the youth and reunite them with their parents. Shelter staff were required to inform parents or legal guardians of a youth's presence within forty-eight hours of arrival.

The Runaway Youth Act was revised in 1977 and renamed the Runaway and Homeless Youth Act. This revision was in response to reports from youth shelter personnel that they were seeing many youth who had not run away from home but had been pushed out of their homes, been abandoned by parents, or left home for life on the street with their parents' knowledge and consent. Although the 1977 act continued to stress family reunification, it acknowledged that both youth and their families needed extensive services for reunifications to be successfully accomplished.

Many youth had not run away from home but had been pushed out of their homes, been abandoned by parents, or left home for life on the street with their parents' knowledge and consent.

The number of teens seen by the shelter system who had not run away from home but had been pushed out, abandoned, or remained away with parental consent continued to increase during the 1980s. Shelter personnel reported that these youth exhibited multiple psychological and behavioral problems and came from families characterized by parental substance abuse, family violence, child maltreatment, long-term family conflict, and dysfunctional parents (many of whom had severe psychological and behavioral problems of their own).

In the 1990s, family dysfunction continued to be a primary cause of youth homelessness, although poverty once again emerged as a potential contributing factor. The 1990s also saw an increase in the numbers of youth who were homeless as a result of their families' homelessness.

Today's Homeless Youth

Accurate knowledge about homeless adolescents is limited by the fact that most studies focus on young people who are seen by the shelter system, which is only a small percentage of the total number of homeless youth. A report by the Office of the Inspector General estimated that only one in twelve homeless youth ever comes into contact with the shelter system. Despite the limitations, there is sufficient research to draw some general conclusions about the causes of youth homelessness, the characteristics of homeless youth, and the nature of life on the streets.

The primary cause of youth homelessness is family dysfunction, specifically parental neglect, physical or sexual abuse, family substance abuse, and family violence. Furthermore, these family problems have been found to be long-standing ones, rather than single episodes occurring shortly before youth leave home.

Homeless youth lead unstable and hazardous lives. They rarely reside in one location for long, and many have been found to live in four or more places over a six-month period. Homeless youth are at high risk for health problems, particularly hepatitis, respiratory problems (asthma and pneumonia), scabies, and trauma. They exhibit high levels of depression, suicidal tendencies, and suicide attempts, although one study reported that the incidence of suicide attempts was higher prior to leaving home than after leaving. Homeless youth also exhibit poor mental health, high use of alcohol and other drugs, and high risk factors for contracting HIV.

Accurate knowledge about homeless adolescents is limited by the fact that most studies focus on young people who are seen by the shelter system.

Lesbian and gay homeless youth have been found to have a greater and more severe incidence of problems such as depression and suicide than other homeless youth. In one study of homeless street youth, 53% of lesbian and gay adolescents had attempted suicide, compared to 32% of a cohort that did not differentiate individuals by sexual orientation.

Although the developmental implications of youth homelessness in the United States have not been examined directly, the research on developmental processes during adolescence may be used to understand the consequences of youth homelessness. The results of this research and their implications for developmental outcomes among homeless youth may serve to guide future program, research, and policy initiatives directed toward this population.

Adolescent Development

Development is a process that occurs through reciprocal and dynamic interactions that take place between individuals and various aspects of their environment, with the person and the environment simultaneously influencing one another. Through examining the individual and environmental characteristics that foster positive development among adolescents, it is possible to draw inferences about the developmental prospects for homeless youth.

Four specific characteristics that foster positive developmental pathways from childhood to adulthood have been identified:

- A sense of industry and competency,
- A feeling of connectedness to others and to society,
- A sense of control over one's fate in life, and
- A stable sense of identity.

A Sense of Industry and Competency. Individuals who are confident in their own abilities develop a sense of industry and competency. Being involved in productive activities in school, at home, or in the community, and winning recognition for their productivity, nurtures this sense of industry and competency in children. This in turn fosters the development of a stable identity during adolescence and the perception of oneself as a potentially productive member of society.

Youth who become homeless do not appear to have the opportunity to engage in interactions and activities that foster the development of a sense of industry or competency in their school environments. Homeless youth have been found to have a history of school failure that often dates back to their early school years. One study found that only 44% of homeless youth had attended school regularly before leaving home, 43% had failed or repeated a grade in school, and 11% had failed more than once.

The home environments of homeless youth also do not appear to provide many opportunities for developing a sense of industry or competency. While living at home these youth reported that their parents or caretakers constantly denigrated them, frequently expressed dissatisfaction with them, and spent very little time with them. Once they are homeless, many youth have the opportunity to experience a sense of industry and competency, often for the first time in their lives. Youth who develop the survival skills necessary for life on the streets are able to win recognition from other homeless individuals in the street culture who value those skills. However, because these skills often include shoplifting, stealing, swindling, pickpocketing,

CASE STUDY—NINA

Eighteen, pale, petite and dressed in black, Nina's ears, nose and fingers are studded with rings and her black hair is teased into a new-wave frizz. She is an alternative kid in a non-alternative town, and she knows how very different she is. A lesbian, she left for California when she was only 16. Though she was seeking greater acceptance, what she found was life on the streets. After a few months she hitched her way back to Maine. She found an apartment with a bunch of other kids, but recognizes now that none of them knew what they were doing. Life there was chaos. She worked nights, and often couldn't rouse herself in the morning to go to school. "I wanted to stay in school," she says now, looking back. "I wanted to get my diploma, even go to college. But things change when life becomes more real. When you're living on your own, you work the third shift, you got to get up at six in the morning and walk to school? It's like, it's way too much of an inconvenience to worry about, so you end up not going." When she did go, she found that she was so far behind that she was chalking up F's instead of her usual A's. "Nobody ever asked me why," she says. She ended up dropping out and going for a GED instead.

From M. Wilson & A. Houghton (1999). *A Different Kind of Smart: A Study of the Educational Obstacles Confronting Homeless Youth in New England.* New England Network for Child, Youth & Family Services. Reprinted with permission.

prostitution, and begging, they are not consistent with skills valued by mainstream society. Consequently, the sense of competency developed in the context of the street culture may further impede the potential of these youth for becoming integrated into mainstream society. In fact, youth services professionals have reported that the most difficult youth to reach are often those who have achieved the greatest success in adapting to street life.

A Feeling of Connectedness to Others. Interactions that promote development of a sense of connectedness to other people are those in which adults provide social and emotional support to adolescents while permitting them psychological and emotional independence. Interactions in which adults attempt to control adolescents' behaviors by monitoring their activities and applying sanctions in a consistent and caring manner also promote the development of a sense of connectedness because they signal to adolescents that adults care about them and are willing to become involved in their lives.

Research on the family lives of homeless youth prior to leaving home suggests that they have few opportunities to develop a sense of connectedness to parents. Most homeless teens are leaving homes in which they were abused or neglected rather than supported or encouraged. In one study, it was found that 60% of youth in shelters nationwide were physically or sex-

ually abused by parents. Furthermore, the parents of homeless youth, rather than monitoring them in a caring and consistent manner, were found to be excessively strict, use excessive punishment, or be highly neglectful.

The lack of connectedness between homeless youth and their families is evident in the fact that parents often knew that their children were leaving home and informed shelter personnel that they did not want their children to return.

Some researchers have suggested that one of the reasons many of these children leave home is to find the connectedness that is missing in their lives—the love and support they did not get at home. In fact, many homeless youth report that they were able to find adults who cared about them while living on the streets. Unfortunately, these adults often exploited them and involved them in criminal activities.

Homeless youth lead unstable and hazardous lives.

While on the streets, homeless youth also appear to develop a strong sense of connectedness to one another, which offers them a semblance of security and comfort. Street companions often provide the friendship, acceptance, and understanding previously lacking at home or in foster care placements. As difficult as life is on the streets, many homeless youth prefer it to the homes they left.

Although homeless youth may be able to develop a sense of connectedness to other persons, they are not developing a sense of connectedness to society. As a result of years of victimization by parents or other caretakers, homeless youth are mistrustful and fearful of society's institutions and do not believe that these institutions are concerned about their welfare. For that reason, homeless youth typically have not made use of traditional services and community resources. Shelter personnel frequently report that the most difficult task in working with street youth is gaining their trust.

Sense of Control Over One's Fate in Life. Adolescents who have a sense of control over their fate believe that they have some influence over what happens to them. When adults consistently respond to prosocial behaviors with positive sanctions and to misbehaviors with negative sanctions, children learn that their behaviors are related to particular responses. The dysfunctional families of many homeless youth do not provide these kind of responses. Parental substance abuse and family violence often result in parent-child interactions characterized by random responses to children's behaviors. Consequently, children in these families are likely to develop a sense of helplessness rather than control. For many of these youth, leaving home may be a means of trying to gain some control over their fate in life. However, life on the streets does not appear to provide these youth with many opportunities to engage in interactions that foster the development of a sense of control over their lives.

Youth services professionals have reported that the most difficult youth to reach are often those who have achieved the greatest success in adapting to street life.

Sense of Identity. Development of a stable identity has been found to be associated with positive interpersonal relationships, psychological and behavioral stability, and productive adulthood. The development of a stable identity is derived from an adolescent's sense of competency, connectedness to others and to the larger society, and control. Homeless youth are unlikely to have opportunities to engage in interactions that foster the development of these characteristics prior to leaving their homes. Consequently, they are unlikely to have formed the basis for a stable identity before becoming homeless.

The fact that some homeless youth are able to develop a sense of competency with respect to survival skills on the streets and connectedness to others in their street communities may provide a basis for identity development. However, the identity that develops out of this process is likely to reflect alienation from society and identification with the street culture.

Implications for Social Policies and Services

Because homeless youth in the United States tend to come from severely dysfunctional families, they are already at risk for negative development outcomes prior to running away. Although leaving home may be an adaptive response to a threatening situation, those who leave to escape serious family problems often face equally threatening problems on the street.

The prospects for homeless youth making a successful transition from childhood to adulthood are not positive. These youth do not have families that offer guidance, structure, and encouragement; they are isolated from the institutions of society; and although they often develop a sense of connectedness to the street community, that community generally does not provide the assistance and support necessary to foster positive developmental pathways.

One implication for social policies and services is that homeless youth need not only safe places to live, access to education and job training, and physical and mental health services, but also environments in which they can engage in interactions with adults and peers that are productive of positive developmental pathways. Although the youth shelter system offers these kinds of environmental opportunities, the efforts of this system are often impeded by the short time period in which youth can remain in the shelter and by the scarcity of long-term care options for youth. The focus on reunification with families needs to be rethought in the light of the evidence that many of these youth do not have families to which they can turn, and many of the families they could return to are likely to be highly dysfunctional.

Altering the developmental pathways or outcomes of homeless youth is not an easy task. A major challenge is that only a small percentage of homeless youth seek assistance from the community agencies that have been established to help them. This suggests that more outreach is needed to contact these youth and provide the services that they need.

Another challenge to helping homeless youth develop along more positive pathways is the absence of advocacy efforts for youth among professional organizations. Developmentalists, long active in advocating services for young children, have not made the same effort on behalf of adolescents. Increased advocacy, as well as increased research efforts by professionals and their organizations, would foster services to help homeless youth develop along more positive pathways.

This article is condensed from J. Smollar (1999). Homeless Youth in the United States: Description and Developmental Issues. *New Directions for Child and Adolescent Development*, 85, 47–58. Copyright 1999 by Jossey-Bass Publishers. Used with permission. References are available on the web site (www.TPRonline.org) or in the original article.

Jacqueline Smollar, Ph.D. is a Senior Research Associate with James Bell Associates in Arlington, Virginia.

From *The Prevention Researcher*, Vol. 8, Iss. 2, 2001, pp. 1-5. © 2001 by Integrated Research Services, Inc. The original article appears in *New Directions for Child and Adolescent Development*, 85, 1999, pp. 47-58, Jossey-Bass Publishers. This material is used by permission of Integrated Research Services, Inc. and John Wiley & Sons, Inc.

Classroom Problems That Don't Go Away

Laverne Warner and Sharon Lynch

Wade runs "combat-style" beneath the windows of his school as he makes his getaway from his 1st-grade classroom. It is still early in the school year, but this is the third time Wade has tried to escape. Previously, his teacher has managed to catch him before he left the building. Today, however, his escape is easier, because Mrs. Archie is participating with the children in a game of "Squirrel and Trees" and Wade is behind her when he leaves the playground area. She sees him round the corner of the school, and speedily gives chase. When she reaches the front parking lot of their building, however, she cannot find him. Wade is gone!

Experienced and inexperienced teachers alike, in all grade levels, express concern about difficult classroom problems—those problems that don't ever seem to go away, no matter what management techniques are used. Wade's story and similar ones are echoed time and again in classrooms around the world as adults struggle to find a balance between correcting children's behavior and instructing them about self-management strategies.

Educators emphasize an understanding of appropriate guidance strategies, and teachers learn about acceptable center and school district policies. An abundance of books, videotapes, and other teacher resources are available to classroom practitioners to enhance their understanding of appropriate guidance strategies. Professional organizations such as the Association for Childhood Education International define standards of good practice. Textbooks for childhood educators define well-managed classrooms and appropriate management techniques (e.g., Marion, 2003; Morrison, 2001; Reynolds, 2003; Seefeldt & Barbour, 1998; Wolfgang, 2001).

Despite this preparation, educators daily face problems with guiding or disciplining children in their classrooms. Understanding the developmental needs of children and meeting their physical needs are two ingredients to happy classroom management. It is also important to look at the larger problems involved when children's misbehaviors are chronic to the point that youngsters are labeled as "difficult." Are these children receiving enough attention from the teacher? Are they developing social skills that will help them through interactions and negotiations with other children in the classroom?

Mrs. Archie's guidance philosophy is founded on principles that she believes are effective for young children. Taking time at the end of the day to reflect on Wade's disappearance, Mrs. Archie concluded that she had done what she could, as always, to develop a healthy classroom climate.

She strives to build a classroom community of learners and act with understanding in response to antisocial behavior in the classroom, and she knows that the vast majority of children will respond positively. Mrs. Archie's classroom layout promotes orderly activity throughout the day and is well-stocked with enough materials and supplies to keep children interested and actively engaged in their learning activities. Although the activities she provides are challenging, many simple experiences also are available to prevent children from being overwhelmed by classroom choices.

Furthermore, Mrs. Archie's attitude is positive about children, like Wade, who come from families that use punitive discipline techniques at home. Her discussions with Wade's mother prior to his escape had been instructive, and she thought that progress was being made with the family. Indeed, when Wade arrived at home the day he ran off, his mother returned him to school immediately.

So what is the teacher to do about children, like Wade, with chronic and intense behavioral difficulties? If serious behavior problems are not addressed before age 8, the child is likely to have long-lasting conduct problems throughout school, often leading to suspension, or dropping out (Katz & McClellan, 1997; Walker et al., 1996). Since the window of opportunity to intervene with behavior problems is narrow, childhood educators must understand the nature of the behavior problem and design an educative plan to teach the child alternative approaches.

The ABC's of the Problem

The first step in analyzing the behavior problem is to determine the "pay-off" for the child. Challenging behaviors usually fall into one of the following categories: 1) behavior that gets the child attention, either positive or negative; 2) behavior that removes the child from something unpleasant, like work or a task; 3) behavior that results in the child getting something she or he wants, like candy or a toy; and 4) behavior that provides some type of sensory stimulation, such as spinning around until the child feels dizzy and euphoric.

To understand the pay-off for the child, it is important to examine the ABC's of the behavior: the antecedents, behaviors, and consequences associated with the problem. The *antecedent* requires a record, which describes what was happening just prior to the incident. The actual *behavior* then can be described in observable, measurable terms: instead of saying that the misbehaving child had a tantrum, detail that he threw himself to the floor, screamed, and pounded his fists on the floor for four minutes. Finally, we examine the pay-off (*consequences*) for the behavior.

Did the behavior result in close physical contact as the child was carried into the adjoining room and the caregiver attempted to soothe him? Did the behavior result in his being given juice so that he could calm down? Did the behavior result in scolding by the teacher, providing the kind of intense individual attention that some youngsters crave because it is the only demonstration of love and caring they have experienced? When teachers and caregivers examine the ABC's of the behavior, they are better able to understand the child's motivation, establish preventive strategies, and teach alternative social skills the child can use to meet his or her needs.

Prevention Strategies

Mrs. Archie knows that she needs to learn specific strategies that will help her work with "difficult" behaviors, like those of Wade, because these problems certainly don't seem to go away on their own. The following intervention methods are designed to preempt anti-social behaviors and often are referred to as prevention strategies. It is always better to prevent the behavior as much as possible.

Accentuate the Positive For the child who demonstrates inappropriate behavior to gain attention, the teacher should find every opportunity to give the child positive attention when he or she is behaving appropriately. Often, these opportunities to "catch the child being good" occur relatively early in the day. When children receive plenty of positive attention early in the day and the teacher continues to find opportunities for praise and attention as the day goes on, the child is not as likely to misbehave for attention as his need is already being met (Hanley, Piazza, & Fisher, 1997). This intervention is based on the principle of deprivation states. If the child is deprived of attention and is "hungry" for adult interaction, he will do anything to gain the attention of others, even negative attention.

Player's Choice When educators see a negative pattern of behavior, they can anticipate that the child is likely to refuse adult requests. This is often referred to as "oppositional behavior." A teacher may remark, "It doesn't matter what I ask her to do, she is going to refuse to do it." One successful strategy for dealing with this type of oppositional behavior is to provide the child with choices (Knowlton, 1995). This approach not only gives the child power and control, but also affords the child valuable opportunities for decision making. Example of choices include, "Do you want to carry out the trash basket or erase the chalkboard?," "Do you want to sit in the red chair or the blue chair?," or "Do you want to pick up the yellow blocks or the green blocks?"

The teacher must be cautious about the number of choices provided, however. Many children have difficulty making up their minds if too many choices are presented—often, two choices are plenty. Also, adults need to monitor their own attitude as they present choices. If choices are presented using a drill sergeant tone of voice, the oppositional child is going to resist the suggestions.

On a Roll When adults anticipate that a child is going to refuse a request, teachers can embed this request within a series of other simple requests. This intervention is based on the research-based principles of high-probability request sequences (Ardoin, Martens, & Wolfe, 1999). The first step in this procedure is to observe the child to determine which requests she consistently performs. Before asking the child to perform the non-preferred request, ask her to do several other things that she does consistently. For example, 8-year-old Morgan consistently resists cleaning up the dollhouse area. While she is playing with the dollhouse, her teacher could ask her to "Give the dolls a kiss," "Show me the doll's furniture," and "Put the dolls in their bedrooms." After she has complied with these three requests, she is much more likely to comply with the request to "Put the dolls away now" or "Give them to me."

Grandma's Rule This strategy often is referred to as the Premack Principle (Premack, 1959). When asking a child to perform an action, specifying what he or she will receive after completing it more often ensures its completion. Examples here include: "When you have finished your math problems, then we will go outside," "When you have eaten your peas, you can have some pudding," and "After you have rested awhile, we will go to the library."

A Spoonful of Sugar Helps the Medicine Go Down This principle involves pairing preferred and non-preferred activities. One particular task that is difficult for preschoolers, and many adults, is waiting. Most of us do not wait well. When asking a child to complete a non-preferred activity such as waiting in line, pairing a preferred activity with the waiting will make it more tolerable.

Businesses and amusement parks use the principle of pairing when they provide music or exhibits for customers as they wait in line. Similarly, with young children, teachers can provide enjoyable activities as children wait. Suggested activities that can be used during waiting periods include singing, looking at books, reading a story, or holding something special such as a banner, sign, or toy.

Another difficult activity for many young children is remaining seated. If the child is given a small object to hold during the time she must remain seated, she may be willing to continue sitting for a longer period. The principle of pairing preferred and non-preferred activities also gives the child increasing responsibility for her own behavior, instead of relying on teacher discipline.

Just One More This particular intervention is most effective when a child behaves inappropriately in order to escape a low-preference task. The purpose of the intervention is to improve work habits and increase time on task. The first step is to identify how long a particular child will work at a specific task before exhibiting inappropriate behavior. Once the teacher has determined how long a child will work on a task, the teacher can give the child a delay cue to head off misbehavior. Examples of delay cues are "Just one more and then you're finished," "Just two minutes and then you're finished," or "Do this and then you're finished."

In this intervention, a teacher sets aside preconceived ideas about how long children *should* work on a task and instead focuses on improving the child's ability to complete tasks in reference to his current abilities. As the children's challenging behaviors decrease, the adult gradually can increase the time on task, and the amount of work completed, before giving them the delay cue and releasing them from the task.

The More We Get Together Another way to improve task completion is by making the job a collaborative effort. If a child finds it difficult to complete non-preferred activities, then the instructor can complete part of the task with the student. For example, when organizing the bookshelf, the adult completes a portion of the task, such as picking up the big books as the student picks up the little books. She prefaces that activity by stating, "I'll pick up the big books, and you pick up the little books." As the child becomes more willing to complete her part of the task, the caregiver gradually increases the work expectations for the child while decreasing the amount of assistance.

Communication Development

In addition to preventing inappropriate behavior, another tactic is replacing the problem behavior by teaching the child alternative behaviors. The key to this process is "functional equivalence." Teachers must determine the *function* or pay-off for the inappropriate behavior and then teach an alternative *equivalent* action that will service the same purpose as the negative behavior. This often is referred to as the "fair pair" rule (White & Haring, 1976). Rather than punishing the behavior, teaching children a better way to behave assists in meeting their needs.

Bids for Attention The first step in addressing attention-seeking negative behaviors is to reduce their occurrence by providing plenty of attention for the child's appropriate behaviors. The next step is to teach the child appropriate ways to gain attention from others. Most children learn appropriate social skills incidentally from their family and teachers; some children, however, have learned negative ways to gain social attention. Some of the social skills that may need to be taught include calling others by name, tapping friends on the shoulder for attention, knowing how to join others in play, and raising one's

hand to gain the teacher's attention. Numerous other social skills may require direct instruction. Any time a behavior is considered inappropriate, adults need to teach the child a better way to have his needs met.

When teaching social skills to chldren, break the skill into a maximum of three steps. Then model the steps and have the child demonstrate the skill. Provide positive and negative examples of the step and have the children label the demonstration as correct or incorrect. Use class discussion time to role-play and talk about when this particular social skill is appropriate. Throughout the day, set up situations that allow practice of the social skill and encourage the child to use the new skill. Finally, promote carry-over of the skill by communicating with the family about the social skills instruction in order for the child to practice the social skills outside of the classroom—on the playground, in the lunch room, and at home.

Ask for Something Else If we know that the child has disruptive behaviors when presented with tasks that are disliked, then the teacher can present the child with an alternative task or materials, something she likes, *before* the problem behavior occurs. Then the child can be taught to ask for the alternative activity or object. When the child requests the alternative, provide it and preempt the negative behavior. In this way, children can learn to communicate their needs and prevent the challenging behavior from occurring.

Ask for Help Many children behave disruptively because they are frustrated with a task. Teachers usually can determine when the child is becoming frustrated by observing and reading non-verbal communication signals. Possible signs of frustration might be sighing, fidgeting, reddening of the face, or negative facial expressions. Noticing these signs helps the teacher know that it is time to intervene. Rather than offering help when the child needs it, the teacher says, "It looks like you need some help. When you need help, you need to tell me. Now you say, 'I need help.'" After the child has responded by saying, "I need help," the teacher provides assistance. This strategy is much more effective if the group already has role-played "asking for help."

Ask for a Break This strategy is similar to the two listed above; in this case, educators teach the child to ask for a break during a difficult and frustrating task. Prior to presenting the task, the teacher can explain that she knows that the activity can be difficult, but that the child can have a break after spending some time working hard at it. Then, the child can be taught to request a break while other students are engaged in various tasks.

Although teachers would like to think that instruction and activities are always fun for children and that learning should be child-directed, certain important activities must be mastered if children are to become successful in school. Especially as children progress into the primary grades, teachers expect them to work independently on pencil-and-paper tasks. Teaching youngsters communication skills that will help them handle frustration and low-preference activities will improve their outcomes as learners in school and in life.

Reviewing Options

Mrs. Archie, in reviewing her options for working with Wade, is gaining confidence in her ability to work more carefully with the family and with Wade to ensure his successful re-entry to her classroom. Her resolve is to continue developing a "community of learners" (Bredekamp & Copple, 1997) by helping Wade become a functioning member of her group. She intends to teach him how to enter a play setting, negotiate for what he wants in the classroom, and learn how to make compromises, while nurturing him as she would any child. These are goals that she believes will help turn around Wade's negative behavior.

Mrs. Archie also knows that her administrator is a caring woman, and, if necessary, Wade could be placed in another classroom so that he could have a "fresh start" with his entry into school. Her hope is that this will be a last-resort strategy, because she understands how much Wade needs a caring adult who understands him and his needs. Her phone call to Wade's mother at the end of the day will be friendly and supportive, with many recommendations for how the school can assist the family.

A Long-Term Plan

Most children with chronic difficult behaviors did not learn them overnight. Many of these children experience serious ongoing problems in their families. As teachers, we cannot change home dynamics or family problems. Sometimes a parent conference or parent education groups can be helpful, as the family learns to support a difficult child at home. With others, we do well to teach the child socially appropriate behavior in the classroom. As a child learns socially appropriate behavior in school, she learns that the behavior is useful in other settings. Often, the school is the only place where the child has the opportunity to learn prosocial behaviors. Children's negative behaviors may have, in a sense, "worked" for them in numerous situations for a substantial period of time. When we work to teach the child a better way to get his or her needs met, we must recognize that this process takes time and effort. When we as educators invest this time and effort with children during childhood, we are pro-viding them with the tools that can make the difference in their school careers and in their lives.

References

Ardoin, S. P., Martens, B. K., & Wolfe, L. A. (1999). Using high-probability instruction sequences with fading to increase student compliance during transitions. *Journal of Applied Behavior Analysis, 32*(3), 339–351.

Bredekamp, S., & Copple, C. (Eds.). (1997). *Developmentally appropriate practice in early childhood programs* (Rev. ed.). Washington, DC: National Association for the Education of Young Children.

Hanley, G. P., Piazza, C. C., & Fisher, W. W. (1997). Noncontingent presentation of attention and alternative stimuli in the treatment of attention-maintained destructive behavior. *Journal of Applied Behavior Analysis, 30*(2), 229–237.

Katz, L., & McClellan, D. (1997). *Fostering children's social competence: The teacher's role.* Washington, DC: National Association for the Education of Young Children.

Knowlton, D. (1995). Managing children with oppositional defiant behavior. *Beyond Behavior, 6*(3), 5–10.

Marion, M. (2003). *Guidance of young children* (3rd ed.). Englewood Cliffs, NJ: Prentice Hall.

Morrison, G. (2001). *Early childhood education today* (8th ed.). Englewood Cliffs, NJ: Prentice Hall.

Premack, D. (1959). Toward empirical behavior laws: I. Positive reinforcement. *Psychological Review, 66,* 219–233.

Reynolds, E. (2003). *Guiding young children* (2nd ed.). Mountain View, CA: Mayfield.

Seefeldt, C., & Barbour, N. (1998). *Early childhood education: An introduction* (4th ed.). Columbus, OH: Merrill.

Walker, H. M., Horner, R. H., Sugai, G., Bullis, M., Sprague, J. R., Bricker, D., & Kaufman, M. J. (1996). Integrated approaches to preventing anti-social behavior among school-age children and youth. *Journal of Emotional and Behavioral Disorders, 4*(4), 194–209.

White, O. R., & Haring, N. G. (1976). *Exceptional teaching.* Upper Saddle River, NJ: Merrill/Prentice Hall.

Wolfgang, C. H. (2001). *Solving discipline and classroom management problems* (5th ed.). New York: John Wiley and Sons.

Laverne Warner is Professor, Early Childhood Education, and Sharon Lynch is Associate Professor of Special Education, Department of Language, Literacy, and Special Populations, Sam Houston State University, Huntsville, Texas.

From *Childhood Education*, Winter 2002/2003, pp. 97-100. © 2002 by the Association for Childhood Education International.

UNIT 7

Vision and Hearing Impairments

Unit Selections

Key Points to Consider

- Looking back, what are the major accomplishments of a half-century of educating children with hearing impairments? Looking forward, what can we hope to accomplish in the next half-century?

- What important lessons can teachers and students with good vision learn from a student who is blind and participating in an inclusive classroom?

 Links: www.dushkin.com/online/
These sites are annotated in the World Wide Web pages.

Info to Go: Laurent Clerc National Deaf Education Center
http://clerccenter.gallaudet.edu/InfoToGo/index.html

The New York Institute for Special Education
http://www.nyise.org/index.html

Earlier, more adequate prenatal care, preventive medicine, health maintenance, and medical technology have reduced the number of children born either blind or deaf. In the future, with knowledge of the human genome and with the possibility of genetic manipulation, all genetic causes of blindness and deafness may be eliminated. Now and in the future, however, environmental factors will probably still leave many children with vision and hearing impairments.

Children with visual disabilities that cannot be corrected are the smallest group of children who qualify for special educational services through the Individuals with Disabilities Education Act (IDEA). Legally, a child is considered to have low vision if acuity in the best eye, after correction, is between 20/70 and 20/180 and if the visual field extends from 20 to 180 degrees. Legally, a child is considered blind if visual acuity in the best eye, after correction, is 20/200 or less or if the field of vision is restricted to an area of less than 20 degrees (tunnel vision). These terms do not accurately reflect a child's ability to see or read print.

The educational definition of visual impairment focuses on what experiences a child needs in order to be able to learn. One must consider the amount of visual acuity in the worst eye, the perception of light and movement, the field of vision (a person "blinded" by tunnel vision may have good visual acuity in only a

very small field of vision), and the efficiency with which a person uses any residual vision.

Public Law 99-457, fully enacted by 1991, mandated early education for children with disabilities between ages 3 and 5 in the least restrictive environment. This has been reauthorized as PL102-119. It requires individualized family service plans outlining what services will be provided for parents and children, by whom, and where. These family service plans (IFSPs) are updated every 6 months. This early childhood extension of IDEA has been especially important for babies born with low vision or blindness.

In infancy and early childhood, many children with low vision or blindness are given instruction in using the long cane as soon as they become mobile. Although controversial for many years, the long cane is increasingly being accepted. A long cane improves orientation and mobility and alerts persons with visual acuity that the user has a visual disability. This warning is very important for the protection of persons with blindness/low vision.

Children with visual impairments that prevent them from reading print are usually taught to read braille. Braille is a form of writing using raised dots that are "read" with the fingers. In addition to braille, children who are blind are usually taught with Optacon scanners, talking books, talking handheld calculators, closed-circuit televisions, typewriters, and special computer software.

Hearing impairments are rare, and the extreme form, legal deafness, is rarer still. A child is assessed as hard-of-hearing for purposes of receiving special educational services if he or she needs some form of sound amplification to comprehend oral language. A child is assessed as deaf if he or she cannot benefit from amplification. Children who are deaf are dependent on vision for language and communication.

When children are born with impaired auditory sensations, they are put into a classification of children with congenital (at or dating from birth) hearing impairments. When children acquire problems with their hearing after birth, they are put into a classification of children with adventitious hearing impairments. If the loss of hearing occurs before the child has learned speech and language, it is called a prelinguistic hearing impairment. If the loss occurs after the child has learned language, it is called a postlinguistic hearing impairment.

Children whose hearing losses involve the outer or middle ear structures are said to have conductive hearing losses. Conductive losses involve defects or impairments of the external auditory canal, the tympanic membrane, or the ossicles. Children whose hearing losses involve the inner ear are said to have sensorineural hearing impairments.

In 1999 The Newborn and Infant Hearing Screening and Intervention Act in the United States provided incentives for states to test the hearing of newborns before hospital discharge. Thirty-four states now offer this test for a small fee. When an infant is diagnosed with deafness or hearing loss, an appropriate early education can begin immediately under the auspices of IDEA.

Students with vision or hearing impairments whose disabilities can be ameliorated with assistive devices can usually have their individualized needs met appropriately in inclusive classrooms. Students with visual or hearing disorders whose problems cannot be resolved with technological aids, however, need the procedural protections afforded by law. They should receive special services from age of diagnosis through age 21, in the least restrictive environment, free of charge, with semiannually updated individualized family service plans (IFSPs) until age 3 and annually updated individualized education plans (IEPs) and eventually individualized transition plans (ITPs) through age 21. The numbers of children and youth who qualify for these intensive specialized educational programs are small.

Many professionals working with individuals who are deaf feel that a community of others who are deaf and who use sign language is less restrictive than a community of people who hear and who use oral speech. The debate about what has come to be known as the deaf culture has not been resolved.

The first article in this unit deals with the progress that has been made in the last 50 years in the education of children with hearing impairments or deafness. Six areas are reviewed: use of American Sign Language (ASL), audiology, medicine, mental health, vocation and career preparation, and legislation that has facilitated the first five areas. Despite the improved quality of life for individuals with hearing impairments, the author argues that there is still a long way to go.

The second article is the story of a girl, blind from infancy, who was warmly welcomed in an inclusive classroom. She gave lessons on hope and wonder as she received lessons in academics. Two support staff aides helped her classroom teacher, and some modifications of the classroom were necessary, but the efforts were small compared to the enormous benefits experienced by all.

A Half-Century of *Progress* for Deaf Individuals

By McCay Vernon

Merv Garretson, a highly respected leader in the deaf community (who is deaf himself) recently commented, "The past 50 years saw an amazing increase in the quality of life for people who are deaf."

This article will look at those 50 years of progress from the viewpoint of a person who is deaf. Six major areas will be considered: vocational rehabilitation and careers, American Sign Language, education, audiology, medicine, mental health and legislation.

Vocational Rehabilitation and Careers

What follows is a personal example of what vocational rehabilitation was like in the 1950s.

My late wife, Edith, was deaf. Early in the 1950s, she went to vocational rehabilitation in order to get help for a job or for education. The counselor she was sent to could not sign, declined to write to her and provided no interpreter. Instead, he chased her around his office and tried to seduce her. When she broke down crying, he gave her 25 cents and told her to leave.

This is an extreme example, but until the 1960s, there were no specialized counselors who could sign in the Division of Vocational Rehabilitation nor were vocational rehabilitation counselors trained to serve deaf clients. This was critical, because most deaf people had to depend upon vocational rehabilitation if they wanted to go to college or get vocational training after leaving

school. Subsequent legislation has greatly improved this situation. Most states now have specially trained counselors who sign and can serve deaf clients. If not, there are funds for interpreters. Today, many rehab counselors are deaf themselves.

In terms of careers, a half-century ago, residential schools for the deaf had strong vocational departments. They taught trades such as printing, barbering, shoe repair, cabinet making, upholstering, body and fender work, etc. Many graduates of these schools learned one of these trades while in school and applied what they had learned to earn decent livelihoods for the rest of their working days.

For example, the printing trade used to be one of the highest paid of all crafts. It was unionized, and there was a constant demand for printers—especially linotype operators. Once a deaf person became a printer and got a union card, he could go anywhere in the United States or Canada and find work. Assured of a job, many drifted all over, seeing the country. Because schools for the deaf—and industry in general—were resistant to hiring deaf college graduates into decent professional jobs, many of the deaf men graduating from Gallaudet worked as linotype operators as late as the 1950s.

Technology has changed all of this. Today for a bright, educated deaf person there are many career options available with good pay and excellent working conditions. For the lower 60 to 70 percent of deaf people who lack good edu-

cation, jobs that pay much more than minimum wage are hard to come by. Many of these individuals have turned to SSI and SSDI, which is unfortunate.

American Sign Language

By far, the major contribution made by linguists was that of the late William Stokoe. Until his book proving American Sign Language (ASL) was a bona fide language, it was thought to be only a gross, primitive set of unattractive gestures, mime, and ugly facial expressions. Educators, audiologists and other professionals in deafness, as well as some deaf professionals, perceived it in this way. Stokoe was reviled for his book on ASL by his colleagues at Gallaudet, where he was a professor. Initially, his work was rejected by his peers in deafness. However, other linguists—scholars such as Norm Chomsky—and a nucleus of Stokoe's deaf and hearing students recognized the tremendous significance of his contribution. Gradually and begrudgingly, as Stokoe continued his work and disciples—such as Ursula Bellugi and others—followed in his path, sign language gained in stature.

Today, ASL plays a major role in deaf education and deaf theater. Books on sign language are by far the best selling publications in the field of deafness. Thousands of hearing people study American Sign Language in colleges, universities and through non-credit courses. In theater, it has become almost a form of choreography. An entire profession—that of sign language interpreters—has grown, in part as a result of the pioneering work of Stokoe and his students.

Deaf people have been given access to hundreds more educational opportunities than ever before because of Stokoe's contributions and their implications relative to interpreting services. Today, sign language has a status that makes deaf people proud instead of ashamed, as was the case 50 years ago.

> The use of sign language in education… has improved educational achievement, but not to the levels that are needed for success in today's world.

Two examples illustrate the situation: In the 1950s, Gallaudet was the only college in the U.S. teaching signs. Even there, the only course offered related to sign language was called "dactology," in order to conceal the fact that Gallaudet was teaching sign language. At that time, such a stigma was attached to ASL that no academic institution wished to be associated with it. In the dactology class, fingerspelling was taught, as were signs, but not sign language (ASL). Students were taught to fingerspell and to sign a vocabulary of 150 to 200 words. No instruction was offered in the syntax of ASL—which, at that time, was still not thought to be a language.

Education

Unfortunately, when one looks at the bottom line, education has not made the progress that has been achieved in other areas. Today, 30 percent of deaf adults are still functionally illiterate. Average reading levels remain around fourth to fifth grade for most deaf school students.

However, there are pluses. Fifty years ago, the overwhelming majority of deaf youth attended classes in which sign language was forbidden. Few teachers even knew how to sign. Many schools forbid the use of sign language in classes, on playgrounds and in dormitories. However, starting in the late 50's and early 60's, research on the dismal educational results of oralism was being made

public. Coupled with the findings of linguists regarding sign language, educational methodology started to change. First, it went to simultaneous communication, known as "Total Communication." More recently, the bilingual-bicultural method is becoming widespread.

The use of sign language in the education of deaf students has improved educational achievement, but not to the levels that are needed for success in today's world.

At Gallaudet University in the 50's, deaf people wanting to teach were not permitted in the graduate program for teachers. Only hearing applicants were accepted. Whereas hearing students could practice teach at the Kendall Demonstration School on Gallaudet's campus, deaf would-be teachers were not allowed to practice teach at all, but could only do individual tutoring.

From the 1950's almost until the "Deaf President Now" movement at Gallaudet in 1988, deaf teachers were a relatively small minority in residential schools and only beginning to be accepted in mainstream programs. Those deaf teachers who were hired were usually given classes of very slow, difficult students and assigned additional time consuming activities, such as Boy Scout leader, coach, dormitory counselor, etc. There were no deaf school superintendents and only a few deaf lower level administrators. For many years, Tom Dillon in the New Mexico School was the only deaf educator to reach the level of principal.

This treatment of deaf educators, coupled with the stigma placed on sign language, bears considerable responsibility for the limited gains made in education over the last 50 years.

Currently, two trends in education are of concern: First is the lack of any national standards for mainstream programs. These programs are expanding rapidly, but in ways that are not always in the best interest of deaf youth. For example, most small mainstream programs are administered by school principals with no preparation or experience in deafness and often lacking interest in the field. This means that key decisions—such as those involving money, class size, psychological services, teacher

qualifications, educational curricula, interpreter standards, etc.—are often made by people who know little or nothing about deaf children. In large day schools, the situation is much better, but there are still no national standards, and key decisions are made by people who lack training and experience in deafness.

The other trend of concern is decreasing enrollments in residential schools. In the past, these schools educated the majority of deaf youth and have always hired the most deaf teachers and administrators. They are now in a fight for survival. There is a great need for national leadership on the part of the administrators of these schools if their schools are to survive as schools and not merely custodial facilities for severely multiply handicapped deaf youth.

On the positive side, educational opportunities are far better than ever before for bright, motivated deaf people. They can attend any college or university in the U.S. for which they are qualified and be provided an interpreter or CART service. Gallaudet continues to offer a fine liberal parts program. The National Technical Institute for the Deaf (NTID) provides excellent opportunities in technology and science. California State University at Northridge offers the same wide range of courses available in most large state universities, plus excellent support services for deaf students. There are also junior college programs in most states. These programs have both vocational and academic courses. Many also offer strong deaf support services.

This broad range of educational options was unheard of 50 years ago. At that time, it was essentially Gallaudet or nothing for a deaf person wanting to attend college.

Today, deaf individuals desiring to go into education have the opportunity to become teachers, principals, superintendents and state-level officials.

Audiology

For the last half century, audiology has been a bastion of oralism, and to some extent, still is. Through its influence in the powerful American Speech and Hearing Association (ASHA), it controlled many teacher preparation programs, all of which were oral and none of which hired deaf faculty or accepted deaf students.

In recent years, ASHA's position has modified some, but audiologists and speech therapists still have an influence on how deaf children are taught that far exceeds their knowledge of what deafness is all about.

On the plus side, audiologists have improved hearing aids dramatically. Fifty years ago, they were cumbersome instruments requiring the user to wear a box-like container in front with a wire attached to the ear mold. These devices were crude and tended to amplify as much noise as they did speech.

Today, hearing aids are so sophisticated that about 30 percent of the people who functioned as deaf 50 years ago are now "hard of hearing," meaning that with amplification they can converse orally, both expressively and receptively. For this, hearing impaired people owe audiologists a lot.

Medicine

The major contributions of medicine have been twofold; by discovering and perfecting antibiotics and vaccines, many major etiologies of deafness—such as scarlet fever, rubella, meningitis, whooping cough, mumps, etc.—have either been eliminated or greatly reduced as a cause of hearing loss.

Until the mid to late 1960s, complications of Rh factor caused a significant amount of childhood deafness. Half of these children were both deaf and had cerebral palsy. Through transfusion techniques and a vaccine, Rh factor is no longer a significant cause of deafness.

Currently, the major medical contributions have come from the invention and perfection of the cochlear implant and advances in genetics. Implants have proved a blessing to many individuals who were deafened adventitiously. Some have gone from being deaf to being able to understand speech. However, the procedure has also produced many failures. These tend to be covered up.

The use of cochlear implants with prelingually deaf children is far more controversial and has a lower rate of success. However, there is no question some

children born deaf have been helped by implants. Whether implants are significantly more effective than hearing aids for those born deaf remains a debatable issue.

Unfortunately, most of the published research on cochlear implants is being done by the surgeons, audiologists and speech therapists who are doing the surgery and rehabilitation—and making a fortune in the process. As a consequence, it is almost impossible to get any research published in audiological or medical journals that addresses the failures of cochlear implants. Many infants born with significant residual hearing are being implanted, despite laws to the contrary.

As indicated above, another new area of medical progress is genetics. About half of deafness is due to genetics. The locations of many of the genes causing different forms of deafness are being discovered; this offers the possibility for the future eradication of these particular causes of hearing loss.

Mental Health

Fifty years ago, there were about five psychologists in the United States and one psychiatrist who devoted as much as 20 percent of their time to the field of deafness. If a deaf person had a mental health problem, there were no outpatient clinical services that provided signing therapists or sign language interpreters. This meant there were no outpatient facilities that could offer meaningful help to patients who were deaf. Those who needed hospitalization were placed in mental hospitals where there were no staff who could sign, no interpreters, nor any other deaf patients. This was, in essence, anti-therapeutic custodial isolation, designed more for the convenience of society than for treatment of patients who were deaf. Consequently, deaf patients stayed in the hospital much longer than hearing patients.

Often they were misdiagnosed as mentally retarded by psychologists who used the wrong tests or by psychiatrists who confused their jumbled written syntax as being indicative of schizophrenia.

In the 1960s, a few pioneering psychiatrists—such as Rainer, Grinker, Alt-

shuler, Kallmann, and Robinson—took an interest in mentally ill deaf patients. They set up units for them in hospitals in New York, Chicago and Washington, D.C. Their research and publications led to other states establishing inpatient units for deaf patients and eventually to outpatient clinics. Gallaudet started programs to prepare school psychologists, school counselors and clinical psychologists. Both NTID and Gallaudet also established departments to train social workers. Many of the graduates of these programs are deaf.

As a consequence, today most deaf people have reasonable access to mental health services, except in rural areas. Most residential schools now have school psychologists and social workers, and some have school counselors and consulting psychiatrists. However, in the majority of mainstream programs, many of the psychologists responsible for working with deaf students have little or no experience with or preparation for evaluating youth who are deaf. This has led to a situation where misdiagnoses are common and the recommendations of these psychologists are often inappropriate and do damage to the deaf student.

Despite the "amazing increase in quality of life... there is still a long way to go."

In recent years, through the efforts of psychologists, such as Pollard and Marschark, and psychiatrists, such as Steinberg, work in mental health with deaf people has moved more into the mainstream of psychology and psychiatry. This is a very positive change from previous times, when deafness was of little interest to either the American Psychological Association or the American Psychiatric Association.

Legislation and Advocacy

Federal legislation—some facilitated by the Center for Law and Deafness—has been the basis for much of the progress made by deaf people over the last half century.

For several reasons, laws passed during the last 30 years have made possible what Merv Garretson referred to as "the amazing increase in the quality of life for people who are deaf." First, they guaranteed every deaf child an education up until 21 years of age. Second, they mandated affirmative action policies be implemented in all business, government and private agencies which receive any government funding. The Telecommunications Act is responsible for captioned TV and TDDs in essential places such as police stations, airports, fire stations, hospitals, etc.

The most sweeping law, the Americans with Disabilities Act of 1990, is intended to prevent discrimination in every aspect of society, including employment.

For example, it requires all state and local agencies, hotels, theaters, restaurants, etc. be accessible to those who are deaf.

The greatest progress made by people who are deaf has come from the political activism that has resulted in these revolutionary laws affecting deaf and hard of hearing people. Once this legislation started to be passed, the National Association of the Deaf—with the help of Gallaudet—set up the Law Center for the Deaf, and other advocacy law agencies came into being. These agencies brought test cases that established exactly what rights these laws provided for deaf people. More importantly, these test cases

facilitated the enforcement of these critically important laws.

Despite the "amazing increase in the quality of life for people who are deaf" referred to by Merv Garretson, there is still a long way to go, especially in the area of education. We also need to do much more for the 30–50 percent of deaf adults with educational levels at fourth to fifth grade or below.

McCay Vernon's career in deafness spans the 50 years he has written about in this article. He has worked as a psychologist, teacher, coach, professor and is an author of six books.

From *CSD Spectrum*, Summer 2002, pp. 12-15. © 2002 by CSD Spectrum, a publication of CSD, www.c-s-d.org.

Seeking the Light:
Welcoming a Visually Impaired Student

Anita Meyer Meinbach

Every once in a while, if you are lucky, you will have a student in your classroom who reaches into your heart, touches your soul, and stays with you a lifetime. Once in a while, if you are lucky, you will have a student whose wisdom and *joie de vivre* are a constant reminder of the choices we have to make every day, the perspectives we choose to take, and how we choose to see the proverbial glass. I was one of the lucky ones—a teacher with a very special student whose determination, outlook, and indomitable spirit provided special lessons in living. Gathary sees the beauty in what is invisible to the eye. She takes delight in everything around her and celebrates life. Her mind is filled with images; her heart is filled with joy. Those of us fortunate enough to know Gathary have gained in countless ways. She has forced us to reassess what we perceive to be our own limitations and has made us aware that each of us is responsible for determining what limits we reach. Gathary is blind, and has been from infancy; but, in a sense, Gathary has opened our eyes by sharing her visions of hope and wonder.

Gathary joined our sixth grade class, a language arts and geography block, in January 1997. For most of us, it was our first opportunity to interact with someone who is blind. While every day did not go smoothly, the journey was worth every bump; and in the end, we all gained in kindness, understanding, and empathy. What follows is based on a conversation that took place at the end of the school year. Gathary, her mother Leslie (an art teacher at our school), Beth Gordon (the visual itinerant teacher), three friends, and I met to discuss many issues that affected Gathary, her classmates, and teachers and to evaluate the ways in which the classroom atmosphere and curriculum met the needs of the visually impaired. As the classroom teacher, I was especially anxious to know what changes and adaptation were most worthwhile and what I might have done differently to contribute to an even more successful experience.

With the growing popularity of inclusion, more and more teachers will be concerned with mainstreaming and its ramifications. Teaching middle school adds to the challenge simply because of the very nature of middle school students who are experiencing dramatic physical, social, and emotional changes. It is sometimes difficult for middle school students, who are coping with their own lives, to empathize and reach out to others. Often, their own lack of confidence and lowered self-esteem cause them to appear heartless and unfeeling. Their need for peer-acceptance makes inclusion not only difficult for the special needs students who so desperately want to fit in, but also for the regular classroom students who desire conformity and wish to find their own place in which to fit.

Since the conversation shed light on many important issues affecting the visually impaired in the mainstreamed setting of a middle school, a synthesis of the responses to specific questions pertinent to teachers are being shared in the hope that it will provide ideas and inspiration for those working with middle school students who face special challenges.

Gathary has made wonderful friends this year; and, according to Gathary, these are the first strong friendships she has made with peers who are sighted.

Issue: Mainstreaming

Question: What considerations were most important in determining whether or not to fully mainstream Gathary into Southwood Middle School?

A close working relationship among the teachers in a school is critical for a blind student. Since Southwood Middle has an extremely close knit faculty, both Gathary's parents and the support staff, provided by Dade County schools, who have worked with Gathary over the years, believed this would be the best setting to allow Gathary to "spread her wings." Gathary was first mainstreamed in the second grade, but it was a more sheltered atmosphere, which was appropriate at the time. For part of the day she was in a class with eight other visually impaired students (K–4), all functioning at different levels. She was only mainstreamed for a short time each day (45 minutes, two times a day). This was not enough time to develop friendships. It also made it hard for her to gain a perspective on peers. This year, except for math class, Gathary has been completely mainstreamed. She has learned how to cope and deal with situations she probably would not confront in a more protective environment. She also has been more challenged academically and has risen to this challenge. Gathary has made wonderful friends this year; and, according to Gathary, these are the first strong friendships she has made with peers who are sighted.

Question: What qualities are most important for teachers with students who have special needs?

Perhaps the most important quality for teachers working with special needs students is attitude. There needs to be a willingness to work with the itinerant vision teacher and other members of the support staff. Teachers working with special students must realize that they are part of a team. While the support staff tries not to pull Gathary out of content area classes, there have been times when this was necessary, and it was important that the classroom teacher make allowances. While every teacher tends to believe that his or her subject is the most important and can not be missed, in reality there are other important skills such as assistive technology and life skills instruction that students like Gathary must master. Therefore, there are times that the training for this must take precedence over subject matter curriculum. The support of mainstream teachers is imperative.

Additionally, because there is a need for special equipment and materials, teachers have to be quite flexible and adapt these materials into lessons. The flip side is also true; sometimes there may not be materials in braille, for example, to support the lesson. The teacher must then attempt to find ways in which the material can best be taught. In science lab, for example, much of the learning is empirical. In Gathary's case, the teacher found ways for Gathary to become involved through the use of senses other than sight.

Finally, teachers of students with special needs must be especially organized and able to plan well in advance. Supplementary materials and resources need to be gathered and there needs to be sufficient time for worksheets, notes, and tests to be transcribed in braille and available in time for the lessons.

Issue: Use of paraprofessionals

Question: Often students with physical disabilities are provided with a paraprofessional. Did Gathary have this option?

In some situations, the use of a paraprofessional is advisable to aid the visually impaired with mobility and assist with classroom adaptations. However, in Gathary's case, her itinerant vision teacher felt it was not necessary. She seems to be functioning well under the guidance of two support staff members who work directly with Gathary and indirectly with the classroom teacher. The two support staff members include Beth, the itinerant vision teacher, and an orientation and mobility (O&M) instructor. Acting as a liaison with her classroom teachers, Beth sees Gathary on a daily basis to provide instruction in the use of her assistive technology compensatory academic skills including Nemeth code (mathematical braille code), social interaction skills, and other life skills. This curriculum is provided to facilitate her full integration into the mainstream classroom environment.

> **At the beginning of each school year, a team meeting is set up with all of Gathary's teachers. The support staff is introduced and suggestions are offered to help the classroom teachers fully integrate her into their class routines.**

Another factor in deciding against the use of a paraprofessional was the fact that Gathary needed to be more independent. Knowing how middle school students are beginning to assert their independence from adults, we were confident that she would have more of an opportunity to make friends without a paraprofessional by her side. Additionally, as Leslie explained, "If there were a paraprofessional, I was concerned that there might not be the direct relationship between student and teacher, but rather between the teacher and paraprofessional." As it was, there were many opportunities to discuss Gathary's progress with support staff and to ask questions and get advice on materials and techniques to help Gathary become successful in learning specific subject matter. Sometimes, we met during a planning period, other times during lunch, or sometimes in the few minutes between classes.

Question: How was Gathary able to maneuver about the school; what special training did she receive?

Before Gathary goes to a new school, she is usually given extensive mobility training. In addition, the O&M

instructor works with Gathary for thirty minutes, two times a week. This instruction is ongoing, throughout the school year, and will be maintained each year she is in mainstreamed situations.

Figure 1

Organizations

American Foundation for the Blind
15 W. 16th St. NY, NY 10011
(212)620-2000 (800)232-5463

American Printing House for the Blind
1839 Frankfort Ave., Louisville, KY 40206
(502)895-2405

Association for Education and Rehabilitation of the Blind and Visually Impaired (AER)
206 N. Washington St., Suite 320
Alexandria, VA 22314-2528 (703)548-1884

Council for Exceptional Children, Division for the Visually Handicapped
1920 Association Dr., Reston, VA 22091 (703)620-3660

Howe Press of the Perkins Schools for the Blind
175 North Beacon St., Watertown, MA 02171
(617)924-3400

Library of Congress National Library Service for the Blind and Physically Handicapped/Talking Book Library
1291 Taylor St., NW, Washington, DC 20542
(202)707-5100 (800)424-9100
www.loc.gov/nls/nls.html

National Braille Press
88 St. Stephen Street, Boston, MA 02115 (800)548-7323

National Federation of the Blind
1800 Johnson St., Baltimore, MD 21230 (410)659-9314
http://www.nfb.org

Recording for the Blind and Dyslexic
20 Roszel Road, Princeton, NJ 08540 (609)452-0606
http://www.rfbd.org/

Seedlings Braille Books for Children
P.O. Box 51924, Livonia, MI 48151-5924 (800)777-8552

Before Gathary would attempt to maneuver the halls of Southwood Middle, the O&M instructor first created a three dimensional layout of the school for Gathary to study. This layout is like a raised map that allowed Gathary to mentally conceptualize the space. The second part

of the instruction involved mobility skills so that Gathary could move about the space safely.

Gathary also learned about sighted guide techniques (how to safely use a sighted person as a guide), how to use auditory clues to maneuver and find her way, and how to use her cane. I selected several students to assist Gathary when she needed help. These students walked to class with Gathary to make sure she arrived safely and Gathary taught them the correct way for guiding her. While this was successful the majority of the time, Gathary often felt the need for more independence. Her guides, however, were afraid to let go, afraid Gathary would fall. Gathary, however, anticipated the falls, knowing they were necessary if she were to become more self-sufficient.

Question: What special training is usually given to teachers?

Generally, at the beginning of each school year, a team meeting is set up with all of Gathary's teachers. At this time, the support staff is introduced and suggestions are offered to help the classroom teachers fully integrate her into their class routines. Additionally, a full day, county-wide inservice is provided in the fall for classroom teachers and administrators to provide more comprehensive curriculum and background information on mainstreaming our visually impaired students.

While it is important that teachers be prepared and trained to work with special needs students, teachers must also be prepared to deal with the attitudes of a classroom of students—each with their own problems who do not always empathize or even attempt to understand the specific needs, problems, or concerns of those around them. If mainstreaming is to be successful, students and teachers must work together as a team.

Gathary came to our school in the middle of the school year, and unfortunately, none of her teachers were given the chance to take advantage of this special training opportunity. However, teachers working with special needs students should be well versed in the exceptionality and explore the different classroom dynamics that may occur as the result of mainstreaming.

Issue: Classroom curriculum and classroom modifications

Questions: What modifications needed to be made in the classroom to accommodate Gathary?

Gathary needed to be seated in a desk that facilitated her entering and leaving the classroom easily. Her work area also needed to be situated close to the shelves in which the braille books were stored so that she could reach them independently.

Because it is important that the visually impaired be able to safely move around the room and feel comfortable doing so, students in the class had to be very aware of where they put their own materials such as bookbags and lunch boxes so that Gathary would not trip over anything. Care was given to ensure that cabinet doors were closed. Special procedures for fire drills and other emergencies had to be established to ensure Gathary's safety and specific students were selected to guide Gathary in the event of an emergency. However, regarding emergencies, some authorities suggest that the blind child "be instructed to take hold of the nearest moving child or adult and quickly and quietly follow others" (Torres & Corn, 1990, p. 25).

The other students resented her going to lunch early and felt that Gathary got special treatment.

Another area of concern is in the use of the restroom. It is extremely important that blind students have someone of the same sex accompany them to the restroom so stalls can be checked to make sure that they are reasonably sanitary and to ensure that no one is hiding in one. Additionally, several students were selected to take turns being Gathary's sighted guide on the way to lunch and other classes. Southwood Middle is two stories high and even for a sighted person the stairways are not always easily maneuvered. Consequently, we allowed Gathary and one other student to leave class five minutes before the bell so that she could get to her next class without having to "fight" the crowds. We also allowed her to leave for lunch a few minutes earlier so that she could get through the line more easily. The other students, however, resented this and felt that Gathary got special treatment. To them, Gathary is lucky—she gets to go to lunch early. "Why should she get special privileges?" they asked. This problem reflects the importance of involving students, especially at the middle school level, in sensitivity training which is paramount to a successful mainstreaming effort.

During a biography unit, we read about Louis Braille. This gave Gathary the springboard for talking about her experiences learning braille.

Another area of modification is in the realm of discipline. Children with special needs must be held accountable to the same code of conduct as the other students in the classroom. I sometimes bent the rules for Gathary and this actually was a tremendous disservice to her. It angered the other students who tended to see issues only in

black and white, not shades of gray. This characteristic of the middle school students leads to their strong sense of justice and they were incapable of understanding why I would allow Gathary to do something they were not allowed to do.

Finally, as with all students, special students need positive feedback and acknowledgment that they have done a good job. It is important that the teacher remember that non-verbal communication—a smile, body language, etc. needs to be transformed for the visually impaired into a pat on the back or a quiet, "Good job."

Question: What modifications needed to be made in the curriculum to accommodate Gathary?

Opportunities for tactual and auditory learning need to be considered. In some cases, for example, Gathary was "walked" through an activity area to get a feeling for the environment before the class participated in a specific activity. It is also important to provide concrete experiences and suggest ways that parents can supplement these at home.

Curriculum should include issues that related to the visually handicapped. For example, during a biography unit, we read about Louis Braille. This gave Gathary the springboard for talking about her experiences learning braille. It is, however, important to remember that these modifications to the curriculum be subtle.

During class, I involve students in a great deal of oral reading, writing, discussion, and cooperative learning. Gathary was not only able to take part in these, but students were consistently amazed at her fluency in reading braille. I did find that I minimized my use of the chalkboard and overhead transparencies, although there were times I needed to use these to illustrate a point or to model writing. If teachers find, however, that the modifications for a specific activity are so great that they significantly change the focus or objective of the activity, than perhaps a parallel activity designed for the special needs student should be considered. While the goal of mainstreaming is to make adaptations so that all students can be involved, this may occasionally prove difficult. In some content areas, for some lessons, alternative teaching methods should be considered.

Specific materials for the visually impaired can help advance the lessons. Special measurement tools are available to teach math skills such as braille clocks and rulers. Special maps with raised borders can be ordered to augment geography lessons. A variety of trade books and text books are available on audio tape as well as in braille (see Figure 1). When our class read specific literary works, Gathary not only had a copy of the book in braille, but also listened to the words read aloud on auditory tapes. The best lessons, I discovered, included the use of both braille text and audio tapes. The braille allows the student to better understand the structure of language and revisit certain sections.

According to Beth, "The most successful of the blind are those who have been readers of braille." Many textbooks are available in braille but usually have to be ordered well in advance, in June if possible. We are able to get most of our textbooks on loan from the Florida Instructional Materials Center.

The key, as with working with any student, is to find and encourage the strengths and talents that will allow the student to "shine" in any type of learning environment.

In order to make communication between the classroom teachers and the support staff more efficient, a special mailbox in the teacher's workroom was set aside. Any worksheets, class notes, tests, or other instructional materials that needed to be written in braille were placed in this box. Beth then either transcribed the material herself, or if time allowed, sent the material to a transcriber in the county office. The transcribed braille worksheets were placed in another specially labeled box and a note was placed in our mailbox to advise us that the material was ready. The mailbox also afforded us an opportunity to ask questions, present concerns, and make special requests for help.

Question: How was Gathary provided with specific information that could not be put into braille?

This question was at the heart of my biggest concern when I learned Gathary was joining our class. It is not uncommon for me, as I am sure it is for most teachers, to change my lesson plans at the last minute. When it was impossible to have the material I needed for a revised lesson transcribed into braille, Gathary worked with another student who read the material aloud. Often, Gathary took a copy of the material home so that she could "reread" it with her family. Each week, for example, our class received a copy of a special current events magazine. Students took turns describing different pictures and features in the magazine and others read articles aloud. When videos were shown, a student was selected to sit next to Gathary and quietly describe what Gathary could not see. I realized that not only was this helpful to Gathary, but it was also extremely beneficial to the other students because they became aware of the power of words to bring pictures to life and create mental images. In their own way, they enabled Gathary to "see." Descriptive videos are available in which a narrator describes much of the action. Companies such as Descriptive Video Service (DVS) provide narration for certain shows that air on public television as well as commercially produced vid-

eos. The videos are excellent and rich in language and vocabulary. They are also the perfect tool for training students in this type of narration.

Question: What group configurations worked best?

While Gathary worked well independently, she seemed to truly enjoy working in a cooperative group. Gathary brought many talents to group settings. Her group project on the pyramids of Egypt resulted in the creation of a video in which Gathary used her ear for languages and accents to play the part of an English archaeologist. On a mythology project, she and her team created a mythological crossword puzzle using special tiles with raised letters that could be felt. Having her work with others in her group not only helped them create unique products but also allowed other members of the group to know Gathary in a new context. This, in turn, led to tremendous social growth and friendships.

The key, as with working with any student, is to find and encourage the strengths and talents that will allow the student to "shine" in any type of learning environment. As students such as Gathary become acknowledged for their abilities, they become more confident, more secure of their place in the classroom, more accepted, and more accepting.

Issue: Technology equipment

Question: What special equipment is needed to help the visually impaired progress successfully?

One of the biggest concerns facing a parent of a special needs student in the mainstreamed environment is that their child be able to compete academically in the classroom. In addition, Gathary's parents were especially determined that Gathary "not be a burden to the classroom teacher." As a consequence, Gathary's parents made every effort to equip Gathary with special equipment that would enable her to function more independently and more efficiently in the classroom. Some of the equipment was provided by the county but certain other devices were purchased by her parents. Gathary uses a Braille Lite which is a computerized braille note taker. It is quite small and easy to manipulate. Her Braille Lite fits into her book bag and takes up little room on her desk. It has many of the features of a computer which allow her to edit her work and then print it on a printer or emboss it for her own use. Additionally, it has a raised braille display so that Gathary can tactually read what she has typed in. Before she received her Braille Lite, everything Gathary brailled had to be transcribed. Now, she can plug the Braille Lite into a regular printer and a printed copy is generated for the sighted teacher. As a result, she is much less dependent on a sighted transcriber to complete assignments. This equipment enabled Gathary to take almost the same exams and tests as did her classmates, typing the answers into her Braille Lite and then printing them so they could be graded. Once in a while, certain questions were eliminated from a test when it was not possible to create an appropriate tactual equivalent. For example, some questions used maps and graphs which could not easily be transcribed into braille.

Question: Did the special equipment needed ever present a problem?

The students in the class were naturally very curious about the equipment and wanted to experiment with it. Since Gathary's equipment allows her to function more self-sufficiently and experience added success and independence, she is extremely protective of her things. During the year, she was quite apprehensive that something would be broken and, in a sense, cut her connection to the visual world—a very frightening and real possibility. As a result, it is vital that students be taught to understand the importance of these devices and how they assist Gathary. When Gathary first entered Southwood, Beth Gordon came to the classroom and, with Gathary's assistance, demonstrated the use of each piece of equipment. Students were especially impressed with the fluency with which Gathary read braille when they could not even "feel" the raised dots. However, while a majority of students understood the need to respect Gathary's equipment, there was still a handful of students, who despite the repeated demonstrations and explanations, continued to "tease" Gathary by touching her equipment—another reminder of the importance of sensitivity training. Others continued to touch the equipment out of curiosity. "The challenge," as Leslie aptly put it, "is to make the equipment interesting to others but, at the same time, make sure they understand its importance to Gathary and learn to respect it."

Question: What equipment is most important for the visually impaired to have in the classroom?

There were two different perspectives in regard to this question. According to Gathary," As far as academics are concerned, the computer (Braille Lite) is most important to me. As far as mobility, my cane is the most important." Beth, however says that, "Actually, it's not the equipment but rather the braille proficiency and listening skills that our visually impaired students have learned that allow them to be successful in the classroom. However, the braille note takers have certainly enhanced our students' abilities to be competitive with their mainstream peers."

Issue: Socialization

Question: In terms of friendships, what has Gathary experienced at Southwood?

When asked this question, Gathary's face lights up—and so does her mom's! "I've made great friends—for the first time!" Gathary explained. Her mom added, "This is the first time Gathary has fostered strong friendships with sighted peers. It's the first time she's been to 'sleepovers' at someone's home other than a relative." On Mondays, Gathary would come to class regaling us with all the new and wonderful experiences she had had over the weekend with her friends.

Question: From the first time you met Gathary, how has your impression changed?

It did not take any of us long to change any preconceptions we might have had about the blind. We soon realized that Gathary is much more like the other students than she is different. We began to see her simply as someone who must do some things a bit differently. Her friends both responded similarly, saying," We see her as a person, just like us. She just doesn't have the ability to see. She uses her hands to read."

However, while mainstreaming has taken away the veil of mystery surrounding the blind, it has changed Gathary's perception of herself. Leslie explained, "For the first time in her life, Gathary is beginning to realize that she doesn't have something others have." Yet, she is dealing with this and makes the most of the gifts she does have—a lesson all of us need to learn.

Question: While Gathary made many friends at Southwood, she also seemed to have difficulty with some students. What problems occurred and what do you think could be done to improve the situation?

"Sometimes students poked me and screamed in my ear. They frightened me," Gathary explained. One of her friends responded to this, "being blind is hard. I wish they could understand what it's like. I get frustrated seeing others tease her. It almost makes me cry inside."

I am terribly troubled when I reflect on the way in which some of my students treated Gathary. While so many were kind, caring, and went out of their way to help Gathary whenever possible, there were others who went out of their way to inflict added pain. I found that just talking to students about this issue was not always sufficient. Many could not see beyond their own problems and did not have the capacity to empathize. "Most who tease Gathary," Leslie acknowledged, "never gave much thought to what it would be like to suddenly approach a person who is in darkness."

Leslie, however, expressed optimism in terms of our ability to affect the way in which students react to one another, "I think sensitivity can be developed—maybe not to the same level in each person, however. People need to become sensitive not only to the challenges a blind person must face, but also sensitive to the issue of how hard a blind person must work to make accomplishments appear effortless." Again, the need for sensitivity training is evident.

Figure 2

Print Resources for Teachers

Hazekamp, J. and Huebner, K.M. (Eds.). (1989). *Program planning and evaluation for the blind and visually impaired students: National guidelines for educational excellence.* New York: American Foundation for the Blind.

Mangold, S.S. (Ed.). (1982). *A teacher's guide to the special educational needs of blind and visually handicapped children.* New York: American Foundation for the Blind.

Torres, I. and Corn, A.L. (1990). *When you have a visually handicapped child in your classroom: Suggestions for teachers.* New York: American Foundation for the Blind.

Unfortunately, as mentioned earlier, because Gathary entered our school in the middle of the year, our students did not receive any type of sensitivity training. "In the past though," Beth explained, "we had a workshop for teachers and put devices on their eyes to simulate different eye problems. This was very successful and helped teachers gain an appreciation for what visually impaired students experience. I believe this type of simulation could benefit not only teachers but students as well. However, because of the seriousness of this exercise, students should be exposed to the situations in small group counseling situations with a counselor to follow up the simulation with discussion that allows students to freely discuss their experience and how it will determine or affect their behavior.

Question: Why is it important that students with disabilities be in the regular classroom?

We have all seen tremendous growth in Gathary not only academically but socially. As Leslie explained, "I know how much better she's doing and how much more 'normal' she's acting in social situations outside of school. This is critical so that she can function in the world as an adult. The things she's grappling with now are things all of us deal with. Frustrations are part of the growth pattern."

Being in this school and being successful have given Gathary the confidence she needs to deal with new situations. Students with disabilities need to have the opportunities to interact with all kinds of children. This promotes their social and emotional growth and affords the other students an opportunity to see how proficient students with disabilities can be.

However, mainstreaming does not just benefit the special needs student. It benefits us all, as the responses to the final questions suggest. Because of the nature of these questions, I would like the reader to "hear" the answers just as they were spoken—from the heart:

Question: How has knowing Gathary changed you?

Lauren: I think I've become a better person. She helps me know how to treat all people better.

Amanda F: She's taught me that I can help others and she's shown me how. I respect what Gathary does for herself and I have also become more sensitive.

Amanda A: Having her as a friend makes me look at life from a different point of view. I learned what it means to have a true friend, how to treat friends, and what it's like to be blind. Knowing Gathary has made me respect people more, those with other problems, not just the blind.

Question: In 10 years, where do you see Gathary?

Beth: I can't wait to see where Gathary is in years to come. I see her as a journalist, traveling the world. She has a zest for life, an ability with languages, and she has a way with people and with words.

Leslie: I anticipate she'll have a full education and travel. I see opportunities for her to use her love for different cultures, especially the Hispanic culture. She becomes completely absorbed in every culture she is introduced to.

Gathary: I would like to be a translator. I want to speak to people in their language

Question: What is one word that best describes Gathary?

Lauren R and Amanda F: Amazing
Amanda A: *So* amazing there's no word
Anita: Joyful
Beth: A gift

A Final Note

The 1997–98 school year was one of tremendous growth and awareness of the various considerations and adaptations that must be addressed to insure successful mainstreaming of the visually impaired in the middle school. But beyond that, and far more critical, is the way Gathary helped illuminate that which is important. From her we all gained a deeper appreciation for life, and a sense that "nothing is impossible." These were the lessons Gathary taught us—her gifts to those lucky enough to embrace them. As teachers we must remember that all our students are gifts. We must remember to nurture their dreams and encourage their visions for tomorrow. And if we are smart, the lessons we learn from students such as Gathary will become part of us as we consistently seek the light of understanding.

Anita Meyer Meinbach is a teacher at Southwood Middle School, Miami, Florida.

UNIT 8
Multiple Disabilities

Unit Selections

Key Points to Consider

- What types of preplanning and planning are required to develop IEPs for students with multiple disabilities being integrated into general education settings? Why is collaboration essential?

- Can paraeducators make a difference in the education of students with multiple disabilities? How can paraeducators be taught specialized skills quickly?

- Can teachers access state-of-the-art technology to assist in their education of students with multiple disabilities? How?

 Links: www.dushkin.com/online/
These sites are annotated in the World Wide Web pages.

Activity Ideas for Students With Severe, Profound, or Multiple Disabilities
http://www.palaestra.com/featurestory.html
Severe and/or Multiple Disabilities
http://www.nichcy.org/pubs/factshe/fs10txt.htm

For most of the twentieth century, children with multiple disabilities (MD) were kept hidden in their parents' homes or put into institutions. Any father or mother presenting such a child at a public school for admission was ridiculed and turned away. The 1975 Individuals with Disabilities Education Act (IDEA) in the United States has turned this around. Such children may now be enrolled in general education classes if that is appropriate. They are entitled to a free education in the least restrictive environment that serves their needs. IDEA has allowed millions of students, who once would have been written off as "uneducable," to be given some form of schooling.

A child placed in the category of multiple disabilities (MD) has two or more cooccurring areas of exceptionality. Each child with MD is very special and very needy. Consider the physicist, Steven Hawking, who has a brilliant mind but cannot communicate or move without augmentative technology. While many MD students have some cognitive disabilities, many have normal or above normal intellect. Their impairments may be developmental disabilities, speech and language impairments, autism, traumatic brain injuries, emotional and behavioral disorders, visual impairments, hearing impairments, orthopedic impairments, health impairments, or any combination of these.

Schools are attempting to provide students with MD with the best education possible. Often, when schools fail, it is some condition(s) outside the school's control that share the onus of responsibility. Schools, when they fail to be effective, usually provide inadequate services due to lack of professional development. Without adequate teacher preparation and sufficient teaching support, education of all children in inclusive classrooms becomes unfeasible. Professional development must be both improved and expanded to give regularized education a leg to stand on.

Another problem that looms large in the appropriate education for children with MD is lack of acceptance and preparation by the lay public and the macrosystem to accept their inclusion in public schools. Advocates for the rights of disabled individuals have used the term "handicapism" to describe this prejudice and discrimination directed at disabled students. The greater the disability, the greater the prejudice. A disability (not able) is not the same as a handicap (hindrance, not at an advantage). The words should not be used interchangeably. A person who is not able to do something (walk, see, hear) has a disability but does not have to be handicapped. Schools and communities may impose handicaps (hindrances) by preventing the student with the disability from functioning in an alternative way. Thus, if a student who cannot walk can instead locomote in a wheelchair, he or she is not handicapped. If a building or classroom has no ramps, however, and is inaccessible to a wheelchair user, then the school has imposed a handicap by preventing access to that particular property of the environment. If a student cannot use vocal cords to communicate and is provided with an augmentative and alternate communication (AAC) system, he or she is not handicapped. If a building or classroom has no power supply or other provisions for use of the AAC system, then the environment again has imposed a handicap. There are millions of ways in which properties of our environments and characteristics of our behavior prevent children with multiple disabilities from functioning up to their potentialities.

Some public schools have resisted the regular education initiative (REI) that calls for general education classes rather than special education classes to be primarily responsible for the education of students with more severe and multiple disabilities. The inclusive school movement, which supports the REI, would have special education teachers become consultants, resource specialists, collaborative teachers, or itinerant teachers rather than full-time special education teachers. While arguments for and against the REI have not been resolved, most educators agree that an appropriate education for each child with a disability may require a continuum of services. Some children, especially those with multiple disabilities, may require an environment more restrictive than a general education classroom for at least part of the day in order to get the type of assistance they need to function to their potentialities. Teacher education typically does not offer comprehensive preparation for working with children with MD who require extensive special educational services. In addition, children with MD often require related services (as chemotherapy, physical therapy, psychotherapy, transportation) to enable them to learn in a classroom environment. Hopefully, teacher preparation, inservice education, and professional development will address some of these concerns of service delivery in the near future.

Many children and youth with MD suffer from a lack of understanding, a lack of empathy, and handicapist attitudes that are directed at them. They present very special problems for teachers to solve. Often the message they hear is, "Just go away." The challenge of writing an appropriate individualized education plan (IEP) is enormous. Updating the IEP each year and preparing an individualized transition plan (ITP), which will allow the student with MD to function as independently as possible after age 21, is mandated by law. These students must be served. Teachers must be given the time and support needed to do so. Excuses such as no time, no money, and no personnel to provide appropriate services are unacceptable. Teachers can expect progress and good results, even with the most multiply disabled.

The first article in this unit, "Making Inclusion a Reality for Students With Severe Disabilities," emphasizes the how, when, and where of inclusion. Collaborative planning is essential for appropriate integration and education of students with MD. A cascade of integration options makes it possible for students with MD to be included even during content area instruction. The authors give suggestions for designing IEPs with workable instructional objectives.

The second article in this unit suggests that paraeducators can play a very important role in giving one-on-one services to students with MD in inclusive education settings, but it is necessary that inservice training be provided for paraeducators. This selection describes a one-day workshop that gives paraeducators an overview of effective methods of teaching adaptive skills to students with MD. Many highly successful teaching strategies can be learned quite quickly in this program.

The unit's final article discusses the uses of new technology to construct alternate portfolios for students with multiple disabilities. Four students with physical, cognitive, and behavioral characteristics of disability who were unable to learn on a standard computer were taught to use the assistive Intellikeys instead. They had a smorgasbord of other technological aids and customized Intellikeys overlays. All four students showed increased achievement and independence.

Making Inclusion a Reality for Students With Severe Disabilities

Pamela S. Wolfe and Tracey E. Hall

Let's end the debate about *whether* to include students with severe disabilities in the general education classroom (see box, "What Does the Literature Say?"). Let's focus on *how* and *when* and *where*. This article provides helpful perspectives and suggestions for teachers, students, and parents in the struggle to provide an appropriate education for all students.

Here, we provide a cascade of integration options for inclusion. These integration options are based on the work of many researchers (Bradley, King-Sears, & Tessier-Switlick, 1997; Giangreco, Cloninger, & Iverson, 1998; Janney & Snell, 2000; Stainback & Stainback, 2000).

The social integration focus of inclusion negates the opportunity for the student with disabilities to receive instruction in content areas.

In these options, we have applied content area instruction to inclusive settings, using a case example. We have also outlined a system designed to facilitate collaborative planning between general and special education teachers, using a student's individualized education program (IEP) as a foundation for decision making. Use of the IEP ensures that educational programming is both individualized and integrated with the general classroom curriculum.

The Cascade of Integration Options

The Individuals with Disabilities Education Act (IDEA) promotes the concept of placement of students with disabilities into the least restrictive environment (LRE). The concept of LRE is based on the belief that educators must provide a range of placement options (Mastropieri &

Scruggs, 2000; Thomas & Rapport, 1998). A cascade of placement options can range from the home-school and general education class setting to institutional placements. This cascade of services highlights the need to individualize and base decisions for placement on the student's unique needs.

As noted, schools and districts are placing more students with severe disabilities in general education settings. But placement alone is insufficient to guarantee that the student with disabilities will benefit educationally. The optimal integration option is based on two factors:

- The type of activity undertaken in the general education setting.

- The objectives stated on the student's IEP.

Decisions about including a student with severe disabilities are frequently oriented toward fitting the student into the existing general education classroom activities and focus primarily on social integration (Scruggs & Mastropieri, 1996). The social integration focus negates the opportunity for the "included" student to receive instruction in content areas. Although we acknowledge the value of social integration, we advocate that programming should emanate from the student's IEP objectives. Teachers should consider content area coursework as a means by which the student may meet his or her IEP objectives. For example, teachers can address many objectives from the IEP in the general education setting by considering a range of adaptations and accommodations.

The Cascade of Integration Options illustrates a range of accommodations for students with severe disabilities who are included in general education settings (see box, "Cascade of Integration Options"). This cascade includes the following poles:

- The least restrictive inclusion option in which no changes are made (unadapted participation in the general education curriculum).

What Does the Literature Say About Inclusion for Students With Severe Disabilities?

The inclusion of students with severe disabilities into general education classrooms has become increasingly prevalent (Katsiyannis, Conderman, & Franks, 1995; Sailor, Gee, & Karasoff, 2000; U.S. Department of Education, 2000). Although IDEA '97 does not mandate the inclusion of students with disabilities, the legislation strongly encourages consideration of appropriate placement in general education settings.

Definition. The term *inclusion* has many interpretations. We have adopted the definition of inclusion noted by Mastropieri and Scruggs (2000) in which *students with disabilities are served in the general education classroom under the instruction of the general education teacher.* Specifically it involves providing support services to the student in the general education setting versus excluding the student from the setting and their peers. Inclusion requires the provision of adaptations and accommodations to classroom curriculum to ensure that the student will benefit from the placement. The definition, however, does not require that the student with special needs perform at a level comparable to peers without disabilities.

Benefits of Inclusion. Many research studies have shown that the inclusion of students with severe disabilities into general education settings is beneficial for all students (those with and without disabilities) particularly in relation to social acceptance, self-esteem, and social skills (Kennedy, Shukla, & Fryxell, 1997; Mu, Siegel, & Allinder, 2000). Although some research has indicated academic gains, teachers are more challenged to appropriately include students with severe disabilities in the content areas (Heller, 2001). Content domain areas include social studies, sciences, health, and related academic subjects.

Role of IEP. Given that the goal of inclusion is to assure that *all* students benefit from instruction, educators must provide programming that meets the needs of *all* students including those with disabilities. For students with disabilities, the IEP serves as the document to guide program planning and instruction. Educators should use the IEP to determine *what* should be taught, *how* the content should be taught, and *who* can most appropriately provide instruction.

Roles of Professionals. There are many professions involved in providing services for students with severe disabilities in included settings. Two frequent members to this team of professionals are the general education and special education teachers. The collaboration of these teachers is essential to assure that the student with disabilities is successful in the placement both socially and academically (Jackson, Ryndak, & Billingsley, 2000; Salend, 2001; Salisbury, Evans, & Palombaro, 1997; Snell & Janney, 2000). Both teachers need to be aware of the student's IEP objectives and use this document to guide program planning decisions and data collection procedures. To meet the needs of students with disabilities in the general education classroom, changes in the curriculum may be necessary.

- A more restrictive option in which students with severe disabilities are temporarily removed from the setting (functional curriculum outside the general education classroom).

The cascade also includes a series of questions designed to help educators make decisions concerning the most appropriate integration options during content area instruction.

Collaborative Planning for Inclusion

As noted previously, the collaboration of educators involved with the student having severe disabilities is essential to ensure appropriate integration and educational programming. Special and general education teachers must share knowledge about teaching strategies when planning effective instruction. Through collaborative teaming, teachers set the stage for student achievement of goals.

We have identified two stages of planning for special and general education teachers when considering options for content area integration. Table 1 lists these stages as *preplanning* and collaborative *planning* activities.

- *In the preplanning stages,* the general education teacher reflects on the content area unit activities and conducts a task analysis to identify key components of the lessons. Once the general education teacher has identified components of the unit, the special education teacher is asked to reflect upon the individual student's IEP objectives and how those objectives can be addressed in the general education content area unit. This stage is a *thinking* or *reflection activity* before a meeting; or the teachers could hold a face-to-face meeting to think together.

- *In the collaborative planning stage,* the two teachers meet to determine the most appropriate integration options in relation to the IEP, what adaptations or accommodations will be re-

Cascade of Integration Options

Unadapted participation in the general curriculum
Same activities, same objectives, same setting
- Can student complete the activities as written for the general education classroom?
- Do one or more lesson objectives match the student's IEP?

Adaptations to the general curriculum
Same activities, different (related) objectives, same setting
- Can the student meet the lesson objectives with minor modifications (time, response mode)?

Embedded skills within the general curriculum
Similar activity, different (related) objectives, same setting
- Are there components of the activity that can be met by the students, even if not the central objective of the lesson but match an IEP objective?

Functional curriculum in the general education classroom
Different activities, different (related) objectives, same setting
- Are the class activities greatly unrelated to the student's IEP? Are there IEP? Are there IEP objectives that could be met in the same setting?

Functional curriculum outside general education classroom
Different activities, different (unrelated) objectives, different setting
- Are the class activities greatly unrelated to the student's IEP? Are IEP objectives better met in a different setting (require equipment, repetition, etc.)?

quired, what additional supports are needed, and how student progress will be monitored (see Table 1).

Case Study of Collaborative Planning

Table 2 shows a case example of the Cascade of Integration Options in operation, as educators implement accommodations for a student included in content area instruction. The example reflects the plan for a student named Billy, who is included in a sixth-grade classroom.

Billy's IEP contains instructional objectives in a variety of domain areas, including communication, functional academics, socialization, fine and gross motor skills, hygiene, and leisure and recreation. The teachers formed their instructional plan based on Billy's IEP objectives.

The teachers collaboratively determined how they could meet many of Billy's IEP objectives within the content area of social studies.

Critical to the successful application of the Cascade is a well-designed IEP with clearly stated instructional objectives

---

As Table 2 illustrates, the integration option varies across the activities and days of the instructional unit. Further, note that the teachers considered the need for additional support to implement instruction (adaptive equipment, additional personnel, technical support). In this case Billy was able to work on nearly all of his IEP objectives in the content area unit. The one exception is Billy's IEP objective related to hygiene; for programming related to showering and shaving, Billy is temporarily removed from the general education setting (functional curriculum outside the general classroom conducted during an adapted physical education class).

As Table 2 shows, teachers used a variety of integration options. Through the use of integration options, Billy was able to obtain instruction on important IEP objectives even though he did not always work on the general education social studies outcomes. Further, by employing the Cascade of Integration Options, Billy's teachers were able to provide Billy with the following:

- Social skills practice.
- Instruction on social studies information.
- Instruction on IEP objectives that focused on Billy's needs.

Although this article focused on the case of Billy, educators can apply the Cascade of Integration Options with most students and areas of instruction, throughout the school year. Critical to the successful application of the Cascade is a well-designed IEP with clearly stated instructional objectives.

Final Thoughts

Inclusion of students with disabilities requires the provision of curriculum and classroom adaptations. But inclusion does not require that the student with special needs perform at a level comparable to peers without disabilities. Students with disabilities may be included during content area instruction if teachers consider the Cascade of Integration Options.

If teachers collaborate to employ such options through carefully planned instruction, they can include students with severe disabilities in general education settings in meaningful ways—for *all* students.

Table 1. Stages of Planning for Curriculum Adaptations for Student With Disabilities in General Education Settings

Preplanning		Planning
General Education Teacher Unit Plan Analysis	*Special Education Teacher*	*General and Special Education Teacher Planning Meeting*
What are the objectives of my lessons? • What is the purpose of the unit? • What skills do I want students to obtain? What are the steps students must undertake to complete the unit? • What are the component activities within the series of lessons? (list in order) • Do the activities directly relate to the overall objective of the unit? • Are the steps logically sequenced? Will the completion of the unit include individual and/or group activities? • Cooperative Learning Groups • Individual • Group activities • Individual and Group What learner products are expected? • Written report • Oral Report • Tests • Computer Question • Concept maps/graphic displays What is the time frame to complete the activities for this unit? • Single day • Monthly • Weekly • Bimonthly • Longer term What are the required materials for the activities and/or unit? • Resource materials • Class text • Computer internet • Misc. materials (school, home) How will student progress be assessed throughout the unit? • End-of-unit test • Rubric • Performance or subjective evaluation	What are the IEP objectives for the included student(s)? What domain areas from the IEP can be addressed in the instructional unit? Does this student have characteristics that will require adaptations? Have I considered: • Cognitive skills • Motor skills • Communication skills • Social skills What levels of adaptations from the continuum are appropriate for this student for different activities within the unit? What required unit adaptations could be made for this student in terms of the following: • Materials • Time requirements • Product expectations	Based on the unit analysis, what IEP objectives can be worked on during content area instruction? What adaptations or accommodations will be required to work on these objectives? What other supports will the general education teacher need to successfully complete the activity? • Teaching assistant present • Adaptive equipment • Technical support • Materials adaptations • Co-teach with special education teacher Are the student's IEP objectives being addressed in this unit in a meaningful way? How will teachers communicate about student progress throughout the unit? • Informal discussion • Weekly meetings • Report from assistant • Communication journal How will progress toward attainment of IEP goal(s) be assessed?

Table 2. Case Example of Collaborative Planning in Content Area Instruction (Social Studies)

Preplanning					
	Day 1	**Day 2**	**Day 3**	**Day 4**	**Day 5**
Activity	Assign to one of three map groups. • Political map • Geographic map • Natural resources map Start research for map information. Textbook, Encyclopedia. Newspaper, Library books, CD-ROM, Internet. 30-minute library time.	Continue research. Draw the map on 3' x 5' poster board, include scale, legend, major cities, and landmarks. Each student must draw and color a minimum of 10 features for specific map in appropriate location. 1-hour map making.	Continue map making: Draw the map on 3' x 5' poster board, include scale, legend, major cities, and landmarks. Draw or color features for specific map in appropriate location. 1-hour map making.	Final map construction. Preparation for oral presentation. Division of speaking roles. 30-minutes map work. 30-minutes presentation work.	Three groups orally present maps to class. 30-minute presentations for each group.
IEP Objective	**Communication:** Initiate conversation about map with group members using communication device. **Functional Academics Reading:** Identify parts of newspaper for peers to find map information. **Social Skills:** Take turns interacting with peers during research; maintain appropriate personal space. **Gross Motor:** Manipulate wheelchair to and within library.	**Fine Motor:** Cut out three pictures that represent resources on the map with adaptive scissors. **Functional Academics Math:** Count the number of resource features group members made (10 each). **Communication:** Initiative with peers if ready for them to count if number of items is correct using communication device.	**Fine Motor:** Paste the three objects on the map. **Functional Academics Math:** Alert the group when time is up map making. **Communication:** Initiate communication with peers using device.	**Functional Academics Reading:** While students are completing research information for presentation, student uses newspaper to identify leisure activities (movie section, TV guide). **Leisure:** Select preferred leisure activity for the weekend. **Functional Academics Math:** Practice time-telling in preparation for group presentation, day 5.	**Communication:** Introduce members of the working group to the class using communication device. **Functional Academics Math:** Keep time for the group. Notify members when half-hour period is over.
Planning					
Level of Adaptation	Embedded skills within the general curriculum. Similar activities, different objectives, same setting.	Adaptations to the general curriculum. Same activities, different objectives, same setting.	Adaptations to the general curriculum. Same activities, different objectives, same setting.	Functional curriculum in the general education classroom. Different activities, different objectives, same setting.	Unadapted participation in the general curriculum. Same activities, same objective, same setting.
Support from Special Education Teacher	Co-teach presentation of the map assignment to class. Needed technical support.	Provide adapted scissors to general education room. Provide enlarged pictures for student to cut. Needed technical support.	Needed technical support.	Needed technical support.	None.

References

Bradley, D. F., King-Sears, M. E., & Tessier-Switlick, D. M. (1997). *Teaching students in inclusive settings.* Boston: Allyn & Bacon.

Heller, K. W. (2001). Adaptations and instruction in science and social studies. In J. L. Bigge, S. J. Best, & K. W. Heller (Eds.), *Teaching individuals with physical, health, or multiple disabilities* (4th ed., pp). Upper Saddle River, NJ: Merrill.

Giangreco, M. F., Cloninger, C. J., & Iverson, V. S. (1998). *Choosing outcomes and accommodations for children* (2nd ed.). Baltimore: Paul H. Brookes.

Jackson, L., Ryndak, D. L., & Billingsley, F. (2000). Useful practices in inclusive education: A preliminary view of what experts in moderate to severe disabilities are saying. *Journal of The Association for Persons with Severe Handicaps, 25*(3), 129–141.

Janney, R., & Snell, M. E. (2000). *Teachers' guide to inclusive practices: Modifying schoolwork.* Baltimore: Paul H. Brookes.

Katsiyannis, A., Conderman, G., & Franks, D. J. (1995). State practices on inclusion: A national review. *Remedial and Special Education, 16,* 279–287.

Kennedy, C. H., Shukla, S., & Fryxell, D. (1997). Comparing the effects of educational placement on the social relationships of intermediate school students with severe disabilities. *Exceptional Children, 64,* 31–47.

Mastropieri, M. A., & Scruggs, T. E. (2000). *The inclusive classroom. Strategies for effective instruction.* Upper Saddle River, NJ: Merrill.

Mu, K., Siegel, E. B., & Allinder, R. M. (2000). Peer interactions and sociometric status of high school students with moderate or severe disabilities in general education classrooms. *Journal of The Association for Persons with Severe Handicaps, 25*(3), 142–152.

Sailor, W., Gee, K., & Karasoff, P. (2000). Inclusion and school restructuring. In M. E. Snell & F. Brown (Eds.), *Instruction of students with severe disabilities* (5th ed.), *31–66.* Upper Saddle River, NJ: Merrill.

Salend, S. J. (2001). *Creating inclusive classrooms. Effective and reflective practices* (4th ed.). Upper Saddle River, NJ: Merrill.

Salisbury, C. L., Evans, I. M., & Palombaro, M. M. (1997). Collaborative problem-solving to promote the inclusion of young children with significant disabilities in primary grades. *Exceptional Children, 63,* 195–209.

Scruggs, T. E., & Mastropieri, M. A. (1996). Teacher perceptions of mainstreaming/inclusion 1958–1995: A research synthesis. *Exceptional Children, 63,* 59–74.

Snell, M. E., & Janney, R. (2000). *Teachers' guides to inclusive practices: Collaborative teaming.* Baltimore: Paul H. Brookes.

Stainback, S., & Stainback, W. (Eds.). (2000). *Inclusion: A guide for educators.* Baltimore: Paul H. Brookes.

Thomas, S. B., & Rapport, M. J. K. (1998). The least restrictive environment: Understanding the directions of the courts. *The Journal of Special Education, 32*(2), 66–78.

U.S. Department of Education. (2000). *Twenty-second annual report to Congress on the implementation of the Individuals with Disabilities Education Act.* Washington, DC: Author. (ERIC Document Reproduction Service No. ED 444 333)

Pamela S. Wolfe, *Associate Professor, Department of Educational and School Psychology and Special Education, The Pennsylvania State University, University Park.* **Tracey E. Hall** *(CEC Chapter #18), Senior Research Scientist/ Instructional Designer, Center for Applied Special Technology (CAST), Peabody, Massachusetts.*

Address correspondence to Pamela S. Wolfe, 212A CEDAR Building, The Pennsylvania State University, University Park, PA 16802 (e-mail; psw7@psu.edu).

From *Teaching Exceptional Children,* March/April 2003, pp. 56-61. © 2003 by The Council for Exceptional Children. Reprinted by permission.

Training Basic Teaching Skills to Paraeducators of Students with Severe Disabilities

A One-Day Program

Lakeisha beams at the teacher as she demonstrates her new skills at setting the table with plates, cups, forks, an napkins.

The new paraeducator can't wait to report that he successfully taught Jon to put on his coat independently.

Finally conquering the copy machine at her workplace, Susan proudly delivered 30 copies of the newsletter to her co-workers.

Marsha B. Parsons
Dennis H. Reid

Since the early 1970s, a technology for teaching students with severe disabilities has been evolving. Research behind the development of this teaching technology has indicated that the strategies for teaching students with severe disabilities are somewhat different from strategies used with students who have mild or moderate disabilities. Whereas the latter students may benefit substantially from teaching strategies based on verbal instruction, students with severe disabilities often require more individual instruction, using a high degree of physical guidance.

This article shows that when teachers and other staff members proficiently use physical guidance in conjunction with other teaching strategies, such as task analysis, prompting, reinforcement, and error correction, students with severe disabilities can learn useful skills (Parsons, Reid, & Green, 1993). And paraeducators can

quickly learn to assist students with their learning.

The role of paraeducators is becoming even more important as greater numbers of students with severe disabilities receive their education in inclusive settings.

Paraeducators in Inclusive Settings

The valuable role paraeducators can play in teaching students with severe disabilities is currently well recognized and is becoming even more important as greater

numbers of students with severe disabilities receive their education in inclusive settings. Whereas special education teachers often learn appropriate teaching strategies during their preservice training, paraeducators rarely have specific preservice training in how to use the teaching strategies that constitute "best practice" for these students. Hence, a major need in special education is to provide inservice training for paraeducators in effective methods of teaching adaptive skills to students with severe disabilities.

TSTP is efficient because the program can be conducted in one 8-hour workday.

Characteristics of Successful Staff Training Programs

Research has delineated four characteristics of successful staff training programs (Reid, Parsons, & Green, 1989). Each of these characteristics is particularly relevant in selecting a program for training paraeducators to teach students with severe disabilities.

1. Training focuses on *performance-based skills:* The training emphasizes what staff *do* when teaching their students. Although many programs provide interesting and *potentially* useful knowledge regarding teaching processes, such programs rarely train staff specifically how to apply the knowledge in actual teaching situations. How well paraeducators translate knowledge about the teaching process into the action of teaching directly affects the quality of education students receive.

2. Training is conducted *efficiently:* When paraeducators attend training away from the students' classrooms, schools and districts often must hire substitute personnel to assist with instruction, as well as with other essential routines, such as transportation and lunch. For school systems to have the resources to maintain well-trained paraeducators, cost factors must be contained by providing staff training as quickly as possible.

3. Training must be *effective:* In one sense, declaring that staff training should be effective seems to be asserting the obvious. School systems, however, frequently invest large sums of money in a staff training program with little, if any, verification of the program's effectiveness. Educators must examine the effectiveness of a training program from two perspectives:
   - The program should result in staff mastery of the skills taught by the program. Staff should not complete the training until they achieve a criterion of satisfactory, hands-on teaching performance.
   - The program is truly effective only if students learn when staff use their newly acquired teaching skills.

4. For long-term success of staff training programs, the training must be *acceptable* to staff. When staff dislike the training process, they are less willing to be involved in the training. Staff's negative reactions to training also result in unpleasantness for the staff trainer, which can cause the individual charged with staff training duties to become reluctant to conduct the training.

Teaching-Skills Training Program

We developed the Teaching-Skills Training Program (TSTP) to ensure that human service personnel are adequately prepared to teach people with severe disabilities. We conducted research over a 5-year period to meet each of four criteria for successful staff training (see box, "Characteristics of Successful Staff Training Programs"; Jensen, Parsons, & Reid, 1997; Parsons et al., 1993; Parsons, Reid, & Green, 1996; Reid & Parsons, 1996).

In initial research conducted to validate the program's effectiveness, we taught 9 direct-support staff and 4 supervisors in a residential program for people with severe disabilities to apply basic teaching strategies, with at least 80% proficiency (Parsons et al., 1993). In subsequent research, we trained 24 staff members, including group home personnel, paraeducators, and undergraduate teaching interns, to teach with 80% proficiency using TSTP (Parsons et al., 1996). Acceptability research has indicated that staff respond favorably to the training procedures (Parsons et al., 1993; Reid & Parsons, 1996). Finally, TSTP is efficient because the program can be conducted in one 8-hour workday (Parsons et al., 1996).

Since the initial validation research, educators have used TSTP to successfully train more than 300 paraeducators and other support personnel. Equally important, students with severe disabilities have made progress toward acquiring adaptive skills when their paraeducators have used the skills they learned during the program (Parsons et al., 1993).

To illustrate, graduates of TSTP have taught children with severe disabilities in an inclusive preschool program the following skills:
- Wash hands.
- Recognize numbers and letters of the alphabet.
- Operate a cassette player.
- Eat with a spoon.
- Respond to one-step directions.

In a school classroom for students with severe multiple disabilities, other graduates have taught students the following skills:
- Drink from a cup.
- Press a switch to activate a radio or TV.
- Use augmentative communication devices.

Other graduates have used the teaching strategies developed through TSTP to teach job skills to adults with severe disabilities—at the workplace.

Figure 1. Sample Activity Illustrating the Rationale for Using Task Analyses

Why Is a Task Analysis Important When Teaching a New Skill?

1. If you were asked to teach someone to prepare a place setting incorporating a plate, cup, napkin, knife, fork, and spoon, draw the placement of the items on a placemat. Assume that the placemat is already on the table in the appropriate place.

2. Compare what you have drawn to the drawings of others in the group. How many place settings among the group were exactly like yours?

3. Draw a place setting following the task analysis provided by the instructor.

4. Compare what you have drawn by following the task analysis to the drawings of others in the group. How many place settings were exactly like yours?

Task Analysis for Place Setting

1. Place the plate in the center of the placemat.
2. Place the napkin directly beside and to the left of the plate.
3. Place the fork on the napkin.
4. Place the knife directly beside and to the right of the plate.
5. Place the spoon directly beside and to the right of the knife.
6. Place the cup directly above the tip of the knife.

Teaching Skills

TSTP focuses on four basic teaching competencies: task analysis, least-to-most assistive prompting, reinforcement, and error correction.

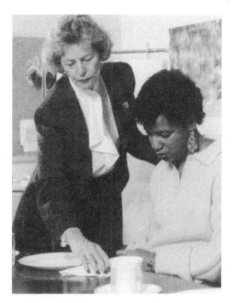

Types of prompts range from mild forms of assistance, such as gesturing to the student, to more directive prompts, such as physically guiding the student through a skill.

Task Analysis

We teach staff that to use task analysis, they should list each specific behavior in performing a targeted skill sequentially, in the order the behavior should occur for the skill to be performed correctly. They teach the kinds of behavior, or steps, in the order specified in the task analysis to facilitate learning so that each step becomes a signal for the performance of each subsequent step in the task analysis. Figure 1 illustrates a task analysis for teaching students how to set a table for lunch or dinner.

Using the Least-to-Most Assistive Prompting Strategy

When teaching a student to put on her coat, the first step of the task analysis is to pick up the coat. If the student does not pick up the coat independently, the paraeducator might begin by saying to the student, "Pick up your coat."

If the verbal prompt does not result in the student's picking up the coat, the paraeducator might tell her to pick up the coat while simultaneously pointing to the coat.

Subsequently, if the combined verbal and gestural prompt as just described does not evoke the student's picking up the coat, the paraeducator might tell the student to pick up the coat while guiding her hand toward the coat (verbal and partial physical prompts).

Least-to-Most Assistive Prompting

Providing assistance on a continuum of least-to-most prompting involves giving a student only the assistance necessary to correctly complete each step of the task analysis. Types of prompts range from mild forms of assistance, such as gesturing to the student, to more directive prompts, such as physically guiding the student through a skill.

We teach staff that if the level of assistance they provide at first does not enable the student to correctly complete a step in the task analysis, they should gradually increase assistance—level of prompting—until the student successfully performs the step (see box, "Using the Least-to-Most Assistive Prompting Strategy").

Reinforcement and Error Correction

The third and fourth teaching competencies work together. *Reinforcement* is the means by which a paraeducator can increase the likelihood across successive teaching sessions that a student will perform the skill that the paraeducator is attempting to teach. We teach staff that a reinforcing consequence is more than a reward or provision of a preferred item. A consequence provided in the context of a teaching program can be regarded as a reinforcer only if student performance of the skill improves over time. Hence, one of the most important skills of paraeducators who teach people with severe disabilities is determining what constitutes reinforcement for a given student, and effectively providing that reinforcement to encourage student learning. Praise and attention are effective reinforcers for many students. Also, engaging in preferred activities following teaching sessions can function as a reinforcer.

TSTP focuses on four basic teaching competencies: task analysis, least-to-most assistive prompting, reinforcement, and error correction

---

When a student incorrectly performs a step within a skill, a staff member must deal with the *error* in a manner that promotes student learning. In essence, errors are opportunities for students to practice the wrong way of completing a skill and should be prevented whenever possible.

We teach paraeducators to prevent errors by increasing the assistance provided on a given step when they see that the student is about to make an error. When the staff member cannot prevent an error, he or she immediately stops the student and has the student repeat the step of the task while providing enough assistance to prevent the error from occurring a second time. For example, when a student who is learning to use a copier loads the paper incorrectly, the paraeducator should stop the student, remove the paper, and provide more assistance so that the student loads the paper a second time with no mistake.

Training Format

For paraeducators in our program, we use a training format consisting of classroom-based instruction, on-the-job monitoring and feedback, and follow-up supervision.

Classroom-Based Component

The primary purpose of the classroom-based training is to familiarize paraeducators with the *rationale* for each teaching competency (task analysis, prompting, and so forth) and the terminology used in describing the teaching process.

For example, using the activity shown in Figure 1, we show the rationale for using a *task analysis* to ensure that staff members teach students a skill in a consistent way. When several staff trainees draw a place setting without the task analysis, almost invariably the placement of cups, plates, and other items will differ across the staff trainees. Thus, if each trainee were teaching a student the task, the task would differ each time it was taught, so that a student with severe disabilities would find it difficult to learn to perform the task. If all trainees follow the task analysis when drawing the place setting, however, the completed drawings should look the same.

A second purpose of the classroom-based training is to begin training staff in the *performance skills* necessary to teach students with severe disabilities by having trainees practice the skills in a role-play situation. We limit the group size of classroom-based training to six trainees. Working with a small group allows the instructor sufficient time for the instruction, observation, and feedback necessary to ensure that each trainee acquires the teaching competencies.

During classroom-based training, we teach prospective paraeducators the skills of task analysis, prompting, reinforcement, and error correction, one at a time. We provide a rationale for using each skill to teach people with severe disabilities, and we demonstrate both correct and incorrect applications of each skill. Trainees practice and receive feedback about their performance from the instructor until each trainee can perform each respective teaching skill proficiently in a role-play situation (see box, "Modeling, Practice, and Feedback").

On-the-Job Monitoring and Feedback

The primary purpose of on-the-job monitoring and feedback is to ensure that trainees can apply the teaching skills learned during the classroom-based component in an actual teaching situation with their students. The instructor observes the trainee's teaching in the classroom and provides feedback regarding the trainee's application of the teaching skills. Through monitoring, the instructor determines the trainee's proficiency in applying each of the teaching competencies.

Modeling, Practice, and Feedback

Instructor demonstration of a teaching skill, followed by trainee practice of the skill with subsequent feedback from the instructor, is the most important aspect of classroom-based training.

Modeling. When training paraeducators how to use a least-to-most assistive prompting strategy, the instructor first demonstrates a prompting sequence in a teaching program with a staff trainee who plays the role of a student.

Practice. Each trainee practices implementing the prompting strategy, with another trainee playing the role of the student.

Feedback. After the trainee practices the prompting strategy, the instructor provides the paraeducator feedback regarding the accuracy of his or her prompting.

Using an Observation Form. To facilitate the instructor's job in this respect, we use the form shown in Figure 2, in conjunction with the criteria listed in Table 1. The form in Figure 2 guides the instructor in focusing on whether or not the trainee performs each of the teaching skills proficiently.

To use the observation form, the observing instructor lists steps of the task analysis (e.g., steps for setting a table) in the appropriate order along the left side of the form. As illustrated in Figure 2, the observer scores each teaching skill under the column labeled for the respective skill on the line corresponding to the designated step of the task analysis. The observer scores each performed skill as being either correct (+) or incorrect (-). Nonapplicable (NA) is scored if there is no opportunity to perform one of the teaching skills for a given step of the task analysis. Table 1 shows the specific criteria for scoring a teaching skill as correct.

In small groups, paraeducators role-play effective teaching strategies.

Providing Feedback. Following observation of the student-teaching session, the instructor provides the trainee with feedback by explaining the teaching skills that were correctly and incorrectly performed. For those teaching skills that the trainee performed incorrectly, the instructor describes or demonstrates how the skill should have been performed.

The trainee's teaching proficiency is calculated by dividing the total number of *correctly* implemented teaching skills across all program steps by the *total* number of all skills taught, and multiplying by 100%. This calculation results in a percentage of correct teaching skill application, as illustrated in Figure 2. We consider a staff trainee *proficient* when he or she scores at least 80% correct during two separate observations of student teaching.

Follow-up Supervision

We designed the final component of TSTP, follow-up supervision, to ensure that paraeducators maintain their teaching skills at the 80% proficiency level. Establishing maintenance procedures is essential for the long-term success of staff training programs (Reid et al., 1989, Chapter 4). This part of the program, of course, lasts longer than 1 day!

Follow-up supervision entails implementing a schedule for continued observation of staff teaching and provision of feedback. The frequency of follow-up sessions is determined by how proficiently a given paraeducator continues to teach—the more proficient the teaching skills, the

less frequently observations with feedback are needed, and vice versa.

Role of Special Education Teachers and Administrators

We have successfully implemented TSTP using two different staff training models: direct training and pyramid training.

Direct Training

A model that works well in settings where fewer than 10 staff require training involves having one instructor directly train all staff. The instructor is responsible for the classroom-based training, on-the-job observations, and follow-up supervision for all staff in a school or agency. The instructor may be a principal, supervising teacher, or educational consultant—essentially, anyone with experience using the teaching strategies, observing staff performance, and providing feedback. The *Teaching-Skills Training Program Instructor's Manual*, available from the authors, serves as a guide in implementing the program (Reid & Parsons, 1994).

Pyramid Training

In school systems where a large number of staff require training, other researchers have successfully used the *pyramid* staff training model (Demchak & Browder, 1990). Using the pyramidal model, one instructor initially trains all *supervising teachers*, who, in turn, directly train the paraeducators whom they supervise. The type of training teachers should receive is twofold:

- Teachers may need to complete TSTP to ensure that the teachers themselves are proficient in the skills they will be training to paraeducators.
- Teachers should be trained in the supervisory skills of systematically observing the teaching skills of others and providing feedback to improve the teaching process. This focused supervisory training for teachers is often essential to the successful training of paraeducators because, although teachers are expected to supervise paraeducators, few teachers have had training in effective strategies for supervision.

Figure 2. Sample of a Completed Form for Observing Teaching Proficiency

Teaching-Skills Observation Form

Trainee __Anna__   Instructor __Mary__   Student __Joe__

Skill __using a table napkin__   Date __5-22-98__

+ correct
- incorrect
NA nonapplicable

TRAINING STEPS	ORDER	PROMPTS	REINFORCES	ERROR CORRECTION
STEP 1 pick up napkin	✗ - NA	✗ - N̶A̶	✗ - NA	+ - N̶A̶
STEP 2 wipe mouth	✗ - NA	+ - N̶A̶	+ - ✗	+ - ✗ NA
STEP 3 replace napkin in lap	✗ - NA	+ - N̶A̶	✗ - NA	+ - N̶A̶
STEP 4	+ - NA	+ - NA	+ - NA	+ - NA
STEP 5	+ - NA	+ - NA	+ - NA	+ - NA
STEP 6	+ - NA	+ - NA	+ - NA	+ - NA
STEP 7	+ - NA	+ - NA	+ - NA	+ - NA
STEP 8	+ - NA	+ - NA	+ - NA	+ - NA
STEP 9	+ - NA	+ - NA	+ - NA	+ - NA
STEP 10	+ - NA	+ - NA	+ - NA	+ - NA

OBSERVATION SUMMARY

$$\frac{\text{\# CORRECT TEACHING SKILLS}}{\text{\# CORRECT AND INCORRECT TEACHING SKILLS}} = \frac{6}{7} \times 100\% = \underline{86}\ \%$$

Feedback __Nice job! Appropriate prompting on step 1; use more assistance during error correction to avoid another error__

Table 1. Definitions for Correct Application of the Basic Teaching Skills

Teaching Skill	Definition for Correct Application
Order	The steps of the task analysis are taught in sequence so that each step taught is preceded by the specific step listed in the task analysis.
Prompt	Each successive prompt (if more than 1 prompt is used) provided for a given step in the task analysis involves more assistance than the previous prompt.
Reinforcement	A positive consequence is provided following the last correct step of the task analysis and is not provided following any incorrectly performed step. Reinforcement could be provided following any correctly performed step but must be provided following the last correctly performed step.
Error Correction	When the student incorrectly performs a step of the task analysis (i.e., a behavior incompatible with the step), the student is required to repeat the step; and a more assistive prompt is provided on the second trial. The prompt on the second trial should provide sufficient assistance so the student completes the step without another error.

Focused supervisory training (in observation and feedback methods) for teachers contributes to the successful training of paraeducators

Supervisory training for teachers should include practice in observing another staff member teach, completing the observation form, and giving feedback in a role-play situation. A protocol for teachers to use as a guide for giving diagnostic feedback is presented in Figure 3. Once a teacher is competent in observing and providing feedback in a role-play situation, the instructor observes the teacher on the job as the teacher observes the paraeducator conduct a teaching session. When the teacher can provide accurate feedback to the paraeducator regarding the latter's teaching skills, then the teacher independently observes and provides feedback to the paraeducator several times each week until the paraeducator can perform the basic teaching skills.

Research has indicated that when teachers complete TSTP, as well as the additional supervisory training, they can train paraeducators to implement the basic teaching skills through observation and feedback in the classroom and *without the paraeducators participating in the classroom-based component* (Jensen et al., 1997). Moreover, these researchers found that the supervisory training improved the teacher's *own teaching skills* when those skills were below the 80% proficiency criterion prior to training. The supervising teacher provides follow-up supervision for paraeducators through intermittent observations and feedback.

Figure 3 shows a checklist that supervising teachers can use to guide their feedback sessions. This form actually constitutes a "task analysis" for providing feedback, beginning with setting a positive

tone and ending with making a positive statement.

Figure 3. Protocol for Giving Diagnostic Feedback to a Staff Member Following the Observation of a Teaching Session

Student and Parent Input

The highly effective teaching strategies espoused by the Teaching-Skills Training Program require brief teaching sessions involving one student at a time. Individual instruction, however, is only one component of a quality educational experience for students with severe disabilities. Students and family members should have significant input into which skills warrant teaching in this manner and how much time should be directed to individual teaching services versus other valuable educational supports.

When individualized teaching, embedded within the daily routine, is deemed necessary, the TSTP provides paraeducators with the requisite teaching skills to improve student achievement.

References

Demchak, M., & Browder, D. M. (1990). An evaluation of the pyramid model of staff training in group homes for adults with severe handicaps. *Education and Training in Mental Retardation, 25*, 150–163.

Jensen, J. E., Parsons, M. B., & Reid, D. H. (1997). *Multiple effects of training teachers to improve the data recording of teacher aides.* Manuscript submitted for publication.

Parsons, M. B., Reid, D. H., & Green, C. W. (1993). Preparing direct service staff to teach people with severe disabilities: A comprehensive evaluation of an effective and acceptable training program. *Behavioral Residential Treatment, 8, 163–185.*

Parsons, M. B., Reid, D. H., & Green, C. W. (1996). Training basic teaching skills to community and institutional support staff for people with severe disabilities: A one-day program. *Research In Developmental Disabilities, 17, 467–485.*

Reid, D. H., & Parsons, M. B. (1994). *Training to teach in a day: The teaching skills training program instructor's manual.* Morganton, NC: Carolina Behavior Analysis and Support Center, Ltd.

Reid, D. H., & Parsons, M. B. (1996). A comparison of staff acceptability of immediate versus delayed verbal feedback in staff training. *Journal of Organizational Behavior Management, 16*(2), 35–48.

Reid, D. H., Parsons, M. B., & Green, C. W. (1989). *Staff management in human services: Behavioral research and application.* Springfield, IL: Charles C Thomas.

Marsha B. Parsons, *Associate Director, Carolina Behavior Analysis and Support Center, Ltd., Morganton, North Carolina.* **Dennis H. Reid,** *Associate Professor, Louisiana State University Medical Center, New Orleans.*

Address correspondence to Marsha B. Parsons, Carolina Behavior Analysis and Support Center, Ltd., P.O. Box 425, Morganton, NC 28680.

Using Technology to Construct Alternate Portfolios of Students with Moderate and Severe Disabilities

Anne Denham

Elizabeth A. Lahm

The 1997 Amendments to the Individuals with Disabilities Education Act (IDEA '97) require that all states include students with disabilities in their measures of account-ability. Such measures may be part of the statewide and districtwide general education assessment programs through appropriate accommodations or through alternate assessments for those who cannot complete the general education assessment (Kleinert & Kearns, 1999).

Inclusion in Statewide Assessments

Since 1992, Kentucky has been including all students in the statewide assessment and going beyond federal regulations by including all students in the accountability system. Students receiving special education services are assessed in one of three ways:
- Through participation in the general education assessment program.
- Through participation in the general assessment program with accommodations.
- Through participation in the alternate portfolio system.

This article shares how the students in one classroom achieved "Distinguished" ratings, the highest of ratings, on their alternate portfolios, using assistive technology (see box, "What Is an Alternate Portfolio?").

Student Profiles

We conducted multiple case studies in one Kentucky classroom for students with moderate to severe cognitive disabilities to explore the process of using the IntelliKeys keyboard as an alternative computer input device for the production of the alternate portfolio. The classroom is located in a small elementary school (430 fourth- and fifth-grade students) in rural Kentucky. The students receive instruction in the general education classroom, the community, and a special class. The teacher has 12 years' experience servicing students in both the general and special education environment, is a recent graduate of an assistive technology educational specialist degree program, and holds an Assistive Technology Practitioner certificate. The students use a selection of assistive technology devices commensurate with their needs, to include single communication aids; a variety of switches to access tape recorders, electric kitchen mixer, and television through an environmental control; and an adaptive keyboard with custom overlays to access the computer.

How do we provide alternate assessments for those who cannot complete the general education assessment?

Four of the seven students in the class were in the age groups of students in the fourth and eighth grades and were thus required to participate in the Kentucky assessment program. Three were 9-year-old females, and one was a 13-year-old male. Two students were classified as having severe cognitive disabilities and two as having multiple disabilities. Table 1 describes these students further, according to physical, cognitive, and behavioral domains. The teacher determined that they qualified to participate in the assessment by completing an alternate portfolio.

What Is an Alternate Portfolio?

The alternate portfolio showcases student work where educators can assess learning across life domain activities in a comprehensive way. It represents performance-based evaluation, using a multidisciplinary approach, and models the use of holistic scoring. As with the general education portfolio scoring system, educators score alternate portfolios on four different levels: novice, apprentice, proficient, and distinguished. To qualify for a distinguished score, the highest level, the student must show the following:

• Progress on specifically targeted skills that are meaningful in current and future environments.

• Planning, monitoring, and evaluating self progress.

• Evaluation used to extend performance.

• Extensive evidence of Kentucky Academic Expectations in all entries.

• Natural supports.

• Use of adaptations, modifications, and/or assistive technology to evidence independence.

• Performance occurring in a variety of integrated settings, within and across all entries.

• Clearly established mutual friendship(s) with peers without disabilities.

• Choice and control in age-appropriate portfolio products within and across all entries.

The alternate portfolio assessment was designed by Kentucky educators specifically for those students whose limitations in cognitive function prevented completion of the standard assessment program (see below "Alternate Portfolios in Kentucky"). Eligibility is determined by the IEP committee, by considering cognitive function, adaptive behavior, cause of limited function, application skill level, use of community-based instruction, and level of performance with supports. Kleinert, Kearns, and Kennedy (1997) stated that between 0.5% and 1.0% of the public school students meet such requirements.

In addition to becoming part of the school's accountability indexes, alternate portfolios serve as "an 'instructional organizer' to give clarity and focus to the student's daily educational program, and as a teaching tool for students to learn higher order self-management, planning, and self-evaluation skills" (Kleinert, Haigh, Kearns, & Kennedy, 2000, p. 24). Such organizers provide teachers with a solid framework from which to work.

Alternate Portfolios in Kentucky

For more information about alternate portfolios, as implemented in Kentucky, visit the following Web sites:
Kentucky Alternate Portfolio Online
http://www.ihdi.uky.edu/projects/KAP/
Kentucky Alternate Portfolio Assessment Teacher's Guide (PDF format)
http://www.ihdi.uky.edu/projects/KAP/downloads/ap%20book99.pdf

Each of the four students was required to produce five entries for their alternate portfolio, in addition to demonstrating their use of a daily schedule and writing a letter to the reviewers. Table 2 shows the activities selected for these students to illustrate Kentucky's academic expectations within four content areas. Statements in black are target skills, and statements in italic are questions they had to respond to in order to demonstrate that skill. For example, Amanda demonstrated her computation skills by responding to the question "Did I count the cans?" on her activity sheet for loading the soda machine. One curricular area entry for each student was the focus of the study and is used to demonstrate the assessment process.

Students used a smorgasbord of assistive technology: single communication aids; a variety of switches to access tape recorders, electric kitchen mixer, and television through an environmental control; and an adaptive keyboard with custom overlays to access the computer.

All four students were unable to use the standard computer keyboard effectively. The teacher determined that the IntelliKeys keyboard was an appropriate adaptation for each. Three of the students used switches plugged into the IntelliKeys, in addition to the IntelliKeys keyboard itself. The switches were used to highlight and read text on the activity sheet with the use of text reading software.

The teacher constructed a custom overlay for each student, using Overlay Maker (IntelliTools, 1996) to support each student's individual needs. The overlay provided response choices to be used in the completion of a data sheet that was displayed on the computer (see Figure 1). By pressing a response choice on the overlay, the student caused the text programmed into that cell to be entered into the data sheet. The amount of text in the response depended on the student's level of functioning. For example, one student was able to record a complete sentence by sequencing three response choices, whereas another had only "yes" or "no" programmed as response choices. Color and location were used on the overlays to provide visual cues as to which response choices should be used for each of the assessment questions. Figure 2 is an example of one student's overlay.

The teacher provided a short training session for each student and one peer buddy on all components of the assessment process. For each student, the IntelliKeys with a custom overlay was used to respond to the assessment

Table 1. Profile of the Students in the Study

Subject	Physical Characteristics	Cognitive Characteristics	Behavioral Characteristics	Disability
Sandra: Age 9	Hearing impaired; hyperactive; impaired speech	Exceedingly low academic ability compared with typical peers	Noncompliant; resists authority	Multiple: hearing impaired and severe cognitive disability
Christine: Age 9	Low to fluctuating tone; nonambulatory; verbal though not clearly understood by anyone other than parent	Exceedingly low academic ability compared with typical peers	Friendly but demanding; persistent presence	Multiple: physical and severe cognitive disability
Amanda: Age 9	Small, ample stamina to function well with peers	Very low academic ability; beginning academics; delayed language skills	Friendly, predominantly smiling; enjoys being the center of attention; loud; silly behaviors	Severe cognitive disability
Brent: Age 13	Very small and thin; exhibits self-stimulatory behaviors; nonverbal; ambulatory but resistant	Nonparticipatory	Self-stimulatory behaviors; little response to peers or adults; very little interaction with others	Severe cognitive disability

questions. The teacher created an activity data sheet using a word processor with table capabilities (Microsoft, 1997). Figure 1 shows one of these activity data sheets. The text-to-speech feature of the software (textHELP! 1999) was used to read each assessment question to the student. The student responded using the custom overlay, and their answer was read back to them so they could confirm the correctness of the answer.

The teacher provided a short training session for each student and one peer buddy on all components of the assessment process.

Each student had content area tasks for which they were responsible. One student was in charge of filling the soda machine; another, shopping for ingredients for a cooking activity. After the activities were completed, they rated and commented on their performance using the activity data sheet. With a peer, they sat at the computer workstation. They responded to the assessment questions that were read aloud by the computer, using the activity-specific IntelliKeys overlay to "type" their response to each question. The peer provided prompts and assistance when needed. On the activity sheet, independent responses were recorded in blue and assisted responses

were recorded in red. Based on that record, each student's level of independence was determined across four trials. Table 3 (page 14) shows the increase in independence across the trials for each student.

Examples of Student Use of Portfolio Entries

Amanda

We used Amanda's math entry for this study with the following activities: (a) filling the soda machine with a peer, (b) taking cans to the recycling center, and (c) purchasing items at the store. Targeting improvement in computation and money skills, Amanda planned, monitored, and evaluated her activities by using the IntelliKeys and the custom overlay to respond to the questions on the activity sheet. The activity sheets and overlays were designed to allow Amanda to read the text with the text-reading software and construct a variety of sentences in response to the questions posed on the activity sheet. The response keys on the custom overlay were grouped according to color and use to facilitate correct choice (Figure 3).

On the first trial activity sheet, 48% of Amanda's responses were made independently. By the fourth trial, Amanda had increased her independence to 88%. Figure 4 illustrates how on one response item, the quality of her responses also improved. Before using the IntelliKeys, Amanda was limited to handwriting her response, which was painstakingly slow. The IntelliKeys system allowed her to write 56 words in 20 minutes, a feat she could not have accomplished without it. Amanda's reaction to the IntelliKeys system was, "This is neat."

Table 2. Student Evidence of Performing Each of the Nine Criteria for a "Distinguished" Rating

Assessment Dimension and Requirements of the Alternate Portfolio	Amanda-Math • Loading soda machine • Recycling cans • Shopping at the store	Christine-Lang.Arts • Cooking • Purchasing items for cooking	Sandra-Soc.Studies • Art activity • Shoping for art supplies	Brent-Science • Pet care • Purchase items at the store
Performance:				
Progress on specifically targeted skills which are meaningful in current and future environments	Increased accuracy by 20% or more in computation and coin values	Increased accuracy by 20% or more in visual scanning ability	Increased frequency of requesting assistance in an appropriate manner by 20% or more	Increased accuracy by 20% or more in selecting the correct object
	Did I count the cans?	Did I scan my pictures?	Did I follow directions?	Did I touch the correct object?
Planning, monitoring, and evaluating self progress	Evaluating performance	Reporting and following a sequence of tasks	Following a sequence of tasks	Following a sequence of tasks
	Did I say I am ready?	What will I do first?	Do I know what to do?	Did I wash my hands when I finished?
Evaluation used to extend performance	Developing a goal for the next session	Making a quality choice using visual scanning	Making a quality choice related to a targeted skill	Making a quality choice related to a targeted skill
	Next time I will try harder with...	Did I try harder with...	Next time I will try harder with...	Did I try harder with...
Extensive evidence of Kentucky Academic Expectations in all entries	E.G. Quantifying, How many cans did we need?	E.g. Reading, Did I use pictures to read the recipe?	E.g. Accessing information, Did I ask for help if I needed it?	E.g. Constancy, Did I follow my schedule? What do I plan to do first?
	Classifying, Did I put the soad in the right space?	Production, What am I making	Democratic principles, Did I have good manners in class?	Speaking, Did I use my switch to ask for food?
Supports:				
Natural support	Peers working on estimation and mental math skills	Peers working on math skills wihtin the cooking activity	Peers exploring a variety of media within the art activity	Peers learning about domestic animals within the pet care activity
	Who worked with me today?	What friend cooked with me today?	Who did I sit with today?	Which friend helped me today?
Use of adaptations, modifications, and/or assistive technology to evidence independence	Big key calculator; IntelliKeys to record performance on the computer	Switch controlled electric mixer; IntelliKeys to record performance on the computer	Modified goals; IntelliKeys to record performance on the computer	Auditory switch device; IntelliKeys to record performance on the computer
Settings:				
Performance occurring in a variety of integrated settings, within and across all entries	Teacher's lounge, office, stockroom, recycle center, store	Classroom, kitchen, store, office, other classrooms	Art room, classroom, cafeteria, store	Classroom, kitchen, restroom, store, recycle center
	Where did I go?	Where did I go?	Where did I go?	Where did I go?
Social Relationships:				
Clearly established mutual friendship(s) with non-disabled peers	Time spent in activities with peers to facilitate friendships	Time spent in activities with peers to facilitate friendships	Time spent in activites with peers to facilitate friendships	Time spent in activities with peers to facilitate friendships
	Who helped me today?	What friend cooked with me today?	Who did I sit with today?	Which friend helped me today?
Context:				
Choice and control in age-appropriate portfolio products within and across all entries	Multiple opportunities for choice and decision making	Multiple opportunities for choice and decision making	Assuming personal responsibility	Multiple opportunities for choice and decision making
	Did I make a choice?	Did I say I was ready?	Did I ask for help correctly?	What do I plan to do first?

Table 3. Level of Independent Performance During Completion of Activity Sheets

		Percentage of Responses Made Independently				
Student	Activity	Trial 1	Trial 2	Trial 3	Trial 4	Overall Gain
Amanda	Soda	48	56	72	88	25%
	Recycle	55	66	82	71	
	Store	62	72	85	82	
Christine	Cooking	25	54	60	75	43%
	Store	35	53	71	--	
Sandra	Art class	4	24	16	35	22%
	Store	18	22	31	30	
Brent	Pet care	7	25	44	56	32%
	Store	40	40	50	56	

Figure 1. Soda Machine Activity Sheet

Prompt	Response			
Date				
Did I use my schedule?				
Did I say I am ready?				
What will I do first?				
Did I use my sheet so I know what to do next?				
Where did I go?	Office Lounge	Office Lounge	Office Lounge	Office Lounge
Did I write what sodas were needed?				
Did I use my list to say what sodas were needed?				
Did I count the cans?				
Did I make a choice?				
How many cans did we need?				
Did I put the can in the right place?				
Did I do a good job?				
Did I try harder?				
Next time I will do better at …				
Who helped me today?				
What did my friend do?				

sheets. That was accomplished with physical assistance from a peer or adult to assist in stamping and reading the questions. The overlay was designed to be simple, with large keys outlined in black. The keys were arranged by color and location to facilitate correct responses. The overlay keys also directly addressed her individualized education program (IEP) objectives—to visually scan pictures or objects from left to right or from top to bottom. Christine also used two color-coded single switches plugged into the IntelliKeys, to highlight activity sheet cells on the computer and to have it read each question.

Sandra's initial trial with the art class activity showed that 4% of her responses were made independently. By the fourth trial she increased her independence to 35%.

As with Amanda, by the fourth trial Christine had increased her performance level substantially, achieving 75% of her responses independently with the cooking activity sheet. Christine attended well to the reporting activity and appeared to enjoy the print output. She asked to take it home with her.

Christine

Christine's alternate portfolio activities targeted her language arts objectives. She engaged in two activities to demonstrate her achievements: cooking and buying items from the store. Before using the IntelliKeys for recording responses. Christine was limited to using a rubber stamp to indicate a yes/no response to questions on the activity

Sandra

Sandra's portfolio demonstrated her achievements in social studies. She participated in two activities: shopping for art supplies, and participating in a general education art class. Sandra's overlays were simple, using color coding and

Figure 2. Amanda's IntelliKeys Overlay

Figure 3. Amanda's Additional IntelliKeys Overlay

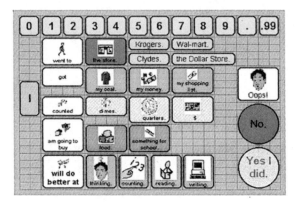

location, to facilitate correct responses. When using the IntelliKeys, Sandra listened to the peer who cued her verbally and with gestures, as necessary. She also used switches to highlight and read the text. Sandra responded well to peer cues, tolerating their guidance, following their directions, and remaining seated during the activity. Sandra's initial trial with the art class activity showed that 4% of her responses were made independently. By the fourth trial she increased her independence to 35%. A similar gain was found in the shopping activity. She apparently enjoyed working on the computer with the IntelliKeys. She grinned and clapped as each entry was keyed into the cell, and read with the text reader as it was typed. She anxiously waited for the printed output so she could take it from the printer's paper tray.

The design of the custom overlay is an important consideration in the success of student use of the IntelliKeys.

Brent

Brent's example is for his science entry. Two custom overlays were used—one overlay was restricted to two cells demonstrating a yes/no response to the activity sheet questions, and the other with five keys giving Brent the opportunity to document a high-quality independent choice over his area of improvement (Figure 5). Two

switches were used to highlight and read the text as with the other students.

Brent averaged a 32% gain in independent performance. Brent's responses were more erratic than the others, but this is typical for Brent. He requires consistent cueing and often hand-over-hand instruction with physical cues. Brent is nonverbal and at present has an inconsistent system of communication. He required physical guidance to be seated and consistent cueing to remain seated. Brent's response to the question regarding improved performance was generated through activation of two out of five keys linked to his IEP goals and targeted skills. He consistently chose either the "choose the right one" or "look" key, both located at the bottom of the overlay toward the left (Figure 6 on page 16). It is not clear if the location of the activated keys on the overlay was a factor.

Figure 4. Example of Amanda's Responses to One Activity Question

Prompt	Student Response			
	Day 1	Day 2	Day 3	Day 4
Did I use my money?	Yes I did.	Yes I did. I $	Yes I did.	Yes I did. I counted $ 1.

External Review

Each alternate portfolio in this study was scored at the regional level by trained teams of scorers using a double-blind method. Table 4 presents the two scores awarded each portfolio. Out of a total of 40 possible scores when including each dimension, the portfolios carried 36 distinguished ratings and 4 proficient ratings. This results in a 90% distinguished rating when considering each dimension separately. The alternate portfolio is scored holistically, however, assigning one score to each complete portfolio. These four students received a rating of "distinguished."

> # The design of the custom overlay is an important consideration in the success of student use of the IntelliKeys.

Figure 5. Brent's IntelliKeys Overlay

Matching.

Following directions.

Choosing the right one.

Looking.

Working with objects.

Overlay Design

The design of the custom overlay is an important consideration in the success of student use of the IntelliKeys. Thorough knowledge of student need and capabilities of the device is essential to use the customizing features and maximize student potential. As a result of this study, we can share several design tips (see box "Design Tips for Customizing IntelliKeys Overlays"). Experimentation based on observation, however, is the most important element.

First, overlay design must be student centered. Motor and cognitive abilities guide the spatial arrangement of the overlay. Range of motion and reach are considerations for the placement of buttons. Items that will be needed more frequently should be easily within reach to avoid fatigue and frustration. Fine motor abilities are factored into button size. For students with cognitive impairments, color and clustering can facilitate use. Buttons in close proximity should be related to a single task and may be highlighted in

a specific color to provide cues to the student for their use. These design considerations are especially useful with more complex overlays.

Cognitive abilities play a role in the number of buttons or response options, and the design of the button depends on the student's cognitive level (for example, contrast Amanda's overlay in Figure 2 with Brent's in Figure 5). Type of graphic representation of a response option is critical. Pairing the written word with the picture will be beneficial for some students, but detrimental to others.

If using different layouts for different tasks, it is important to maintain as much consistency across the layouts as possible. For example, you may always put program commands (e.g., enter, space, delete) in the upper left quadrant and task-specific content keys in the lower right. In doing so, you reduce the cognitive load on the students as they complete each response. Taking both cognitive and motor abilities into account, you facilitate increased accuracy and reduction of time, which both contribute to fatigue.

Table 4. Scores Received from Two Reviewers on the Alternate Portfolio Dimensions

Student	Amanda	Christine	Sandra	Brent
Performance	Distinguished Distinguished	Distinguished Distinguished	Distinguished Distinguished	Distinguished Distinguished
Support	Distinguished Distinguished	Distinguished Distinguished	Proficient Distinguished	Distinguished Distinguished
Settings	Distinguished Distinguished	Distinguished Distinguished	Distinguished Distinguished	Distinguished Distinguished
Social relationships	Proficient Distinguished	Distinguished Distinguished	Distinguished Proficient	Proficient Distinguished
Contexts	Distinguished Distinguished	Distinguished Distinguished	Distinguished Distinguished	Distinguished Distinguished

Figure 6. Example of Brent's Responses to One Science Activity Question

Prompt	Student Response			
	Day 1	Day 2	Day 3	Day 4
Next time I will try harder with …	Choose the right one.	Choose the right one.	Look.	Look.

Design Tips for Customizing IntelliKeys Overlays

• Student needs and functioning level must drive the content and format.

• Use voice output to read the prompt and read the response back to the user.

• Group keys according to color to facilitate correct responses.

• Enable the "nonrepeat" function to ensure only one entry per response.

• Use left-to-right formats to naturally facilitate sentence construction.

• Size the text and the keys to match the visual abilities of the user.

• Program whole words and phrases into the keys to speed responses.

• Match the programmed responses to the student's cognitive ability (e.g., single-word responses limit the construction of complete sentences).

• Outline keys in black to improve contrast.

• Place frequently used keys on the user's dominant side of the keyboard.

• Include graphics on the keys with the text for the nonreader.

• Consider the complexity of training issues when choosing keys (e.g., arrow keys for directional movement are very difficult to teach).

• Place keys that are common across overlays in a consistent location on each.

Sample Peer Responses to Interview Questions

Six general education peers helped the students use the IntelliKeys during recording sessions. The overwhelming consensus was that the peers liked using the IntelliKeys with the students, primarily because it enhanced the student level of performance and increased their independence. The following are some of their responses:

• One peer appeared quite shocked at Amanda's performance within her math entry, and remarked that he did not know "she could do all that."

• Most peers were surprised with work that the students were able to produce with the IntelliKeys, and admitted that it elevated their opinion of the students' ability.

• Observations indicated that the peers enjoyed the process of working with the students, though this was in the form of a peer-tutor relationship.

• Each peer reported that working with a student helped him or her to get to know the student better, since they spent more time together. Spending time with one another provided the opportunity for relationships to develop, an important element within the social relationships dimension of the alternative portfolio.

Sample Student Responses Recorded in Observation Notes

• "Amanda appears to enjoy the technical aspects of the program; perhaps it gives her a sense of independence that she cannot get from other methods of reading and writing."

• "Amanda appears pleased with her work. At no time does she appear hurried or anxious to get finished. The teacher does not have to remind her to remain on task."

• "Christine was compliant in coming to the computer. She appears to enjoy computer tasks since it does give her an avenue for written expression and she likes to take things home."

• "Christine's mother came into the classroom when she was completing the activity sheets and Christine became animated and demanded that her mother watch what she was doing."

• On her first trial with the IntelliKeys, Sandra "grinned and clapped as each entry was keyed into the cell and read with the text-to-speech software as she typed."

• During Brent's first trial completing the science activity sheet, "Brent voiced and resisted being seated in the chair by the computer. He looked upwards at all times and avoided contact with the IntelliKeys and the monitor."

• Brent "does better on the computer than he does with the stamps since he is selecting the key and is the cause of the entered text."

Final Thoughts

In addition to the data showing the achievements of the students with disabilities, observations of the students working with their peers on these tasks confirmed other benefits of the program. Overall, the peers gained a better perspective on the students' abilities, and the students responded positively to their accomplishments and interactions with their peers (see boxes, "Sample Student Responses," for student observations and peer interviews).

This series of case studies denotes a beginning level of research, and is an indication for further definitive research at a critical time when states are looking to include students with moderate and severe disabilities in their accountability indexes. Studies of a more rigorous method of inquiry and more reliable data collection in the area of student support and assistive technology and assessment are essential. Kentucky is the only state fully including the assessment of this population in their school accountability indexes, and thus provides an excellent base for research.

Another area of focus for future research is on overlay design issues, because it is apparent that they influence output. Researchers and practitioners might look at overlay design and attempt guidelines to facilitate increased independence, increase output, and minimize the potential for student error.

References

IntelliTools. (1996). Overlay maker. [Computer software]. Novato, CA: Author.

Kleinert, H., Haigh, J., Kearns, J., & Kennedy, S. (2000). Alternate assessment. Lessons learned and roads not taken. *Exceptional Children, 67*, 51–66.

Kleinert, H., & Kearns, J. (1999). A validation study of the performance indicators and learner outcomes for Kentucky's alternate assessment for students with significant disabilities. *Journal of the Association for Persons with Severe Handicaps, 24*(2), 100–110.

Kleinert, H., Kearns, J., & Kennedy, S. (1997). Accountability for all students: Kentucky's alternate portfolio assessment for students with moderate and severe cognitive disabilities. *Journal of the Association for Persons with Severe Handicaps, 22*(2), 88–101.

Microsoft Corporation. (1997). WORD 97. [Computer software]. Redmond, WA: Author.

textHELP! (1999). Read & write. [Computer software]. Antrim, N. Ireland: Author.

Anne Denham (CEC Chapter #5), Teacher, Mason County Public Schools, Maysville, Kentucky. **Elizabeth A. Lahm** (CEC Chapter #180), Assistant Professor, Department of Special Education and Rehabilitation Counseling, University of Kentucky, Lexington.

Address correspondence to Elizabeth A. Lahm, Department of Special Education and Rehabilitation Counseling, University of Kentucky, 229 Taylor Education Building, Lexington, KY 40506-0001 (e-mail: ealahm1@pop.uky.edu).

UNIT 9

Orthopedic and Health Impairments

Unit Selections

Key Points to Consider

• What is the importance of giving young children with orthopedic disabilities mobility instruction within the context of typical daily activities? Describe the MOVE® program.

• What kinds of accommodations are appropriate for students with health impairments (e.g., cancer, asthma, epilepsy)?

• What are some techniques that teachers can use to help students with ADHD adjust to their regular education classroom?

 Links: www.dushkin.com/online/
These sites are annotated in the World Wide Web pages.

Association to Benefit Children (ABC)
http://www.a-b-c.org

An Idea Whose Time Has Come
http://www.boggscenter.org/mich3899.htm

Resources for VE Teachers
http://www.cpt.fsu.edu/tree//ve/tofc.html

Try using the word "handicapped" on a computer with a spell check. Today's computers are programmed to advise you that this is a derogatory term when applied to any individual. Older dictionaries defined "handicapped" as inferior and in need of an artificial advantage. People were described as handicapped if they were encumbered by physical limitations. Today, handicapped means limited by something in the environment. Handicap is synonymous with hindrance. If a property of the environment prevents a person with an orthopedic or health impairment from functioning to the best of his or her abilities, then the environment has imposed a handicap.

Children and youth with orthopedic and health impairments can be divided into classifications of mild, moderate, and profound. Within most impairments, the same diagnosis may not produce the same degree of disability. For example, children with cerebral palsy may be mildly, moderately, or profoundly impaired.

Orthopedic impairments are usually defined as those that hinder physical mobility or the ability to use one or more parts of the skeletomuscular system of the body. Orthopedic problems may be neurological (brain or spinal cord) or skeletomuscular (muscles or skeletal bones). Regardless of etiology, the child with an orthopedic impairment usually has a problem with mobility. He or she may need crutches or other aids in order to walk or may be in a wheelchair.

Health impairments are usually defined as those that affect stamina and predominantly one or more systems of the body: the cardiovascular, respiratory, gastrointestinal, endocrine, lymphatic, urinary, reproductive, sensory, or nervous systems. Children with health impairments usually have to take medicine or follow a medical regimen in order to attend school. The degree of impairment (mild, moderate, profound) is usually based on limitations to activity, duration of problem, and extent of other problems.

Attention-deficit hyperactive disorder (ADHD) is formally recognized as a health impairment, as well as a learning disability. Often children with ADHD are also assessed as gifted or as emotionally-behaviorally disordered. It is possible for a child with ADHD to have characteristics of all of these categories. ADHD will be covered in this unit.

Orthopedic and health impairments are not always mutually exclusive. Many times a child with an orthopedic impairment also has a concurrent or contributing health impairment, and vice versa. In addition, children with orthopedic and health impairments may also have concurrent conditions of educational exceptionality.

Some children with orthopedic and health impairments have only transitory impairments, some have permanent but nonworsening impairments, and some have progressive impairments that make their education more complicated as the years pass and may even result in death before the end of the developmental/educational period.

Each of the dimensions defined in the preceding paragraphs makes educational planning for children with orthopedic and health impairments very complicated.

The reauthorization of IDEA mandated that schools must pay for all medical services required to allow orthopedically or health impaired students to attend regular education classes. The only exceptions are the actual fees for physician-provided health services. Thus, if children need ambulances to transport them to and from school, the schools must pay the tab. Federal appropriations for special educational services only pay about 10 percent of the bills. Thus high-cost special needs students can quickly drain the funds of state and local education departments.

Teachers may resent the need to spend teacher time giving medications or providing quasi-medical services (suctioning, changing diapers) for students with health impairments in the many U.S. schools that no longer have school nurses. Resentment is common in parents of nondisabled students who feel that the education of high-cost disabled students robs their children of teacher time, curriculum, and supplies to which they should be entitled. More than 95 percent of special needs students attend regular schools today. About 3 percent attend separate schools and about 2 percent are served at home, in hospitals, or in residential facilities.

When orthopedic or health impairments are diagnosed in infancy or early childhood, an interdisciplinary team usually helps plan an individualized family service plan (IFSP) that includes working with parents, medical and/or surgical personnel, and preschool special education providers.

When the orthopedic or health impairment is diagnosed in the school years, the schoolteachers collaborate with outside agencies, but more of the individualized educational planning (IEP) is in their hands. Children who have orthopedic or health impairments need psychological as well as academic support. Teachers need to help them in their peer interactions. Teachers should also work closely with parents to ensure a smooth transition toward a lifestyle that fosters independence and self-reliance. By middle school, individualized transition plans (ITPs) should be developed. They should be implemented throughout high school and until age 21 when the students move to adult living, and they must be updated every year. Schools are held accountable for their success in helping students with orthopedic and health impairments to make smooth transitions to maturity.

The first article emphasizes the importance of giving young children with orthopedic disabilities mobility instruction within the context of typical daily activities. Keith Whinnery and Stacie Barnes recommend the MOVE® curriculum, an integrated therapy with high expectations that supports and motivates children. A case study of 4-year-old Breanna, who has cerebral palsy, illustrates how it works.

The second selection for this unit suggests some of the accommodations that school systems must make to ensure that students with orthopedic and health impairments receive an appropriate education. It explains the 504 plans required under the Americans With Disabilities Act. MaryAnn Byrnes points out that the teaching profession is about allowing students to learn. Removing barriers will do that.

The last selection in this unit addresses the need to help students with attention deficit hyperactive disorder (ADHD) adjust to their regular education classrooms. Despite the use of medication (usually Ritalin) to help them attend better and fidget less, students with ADHD may contribute to chaos during their lessons. The Schlozmans suggest a number of teaching techniques that can reduce confusion and help children with ADHD learn more effectively.

Mobility Training Using the MOVE® Curriculum

A Parent's View

Keith W. Whinnery, Stacie B. Barnes

Breanna is a 4-year-old girl who loves playing outside. Today she and her mom, Trellis, are taking a walk to feed the dogs, chase the chickens, and pick flowers. Though this might seem like a fairly common scenario for a parent and young child, it is quite extraordinary for Breanna and Trellis. Breanna contracted meningitis and encephalitis at 3 1/2 weeks of age, resulting in cerebral palsy with a mixture of high and low muscle tone, limited strength for standing or sitting upright, and difficulty holding her head upright. Since that time, life for Breanna and her family has consisted of numerous doctors' appointments, regular therapy sessions at a child development center, and constant strengthening and stretching exercises at home.

This article presents an interview with Trellis, Breanna's mother, who is using a new mobility curriculum with her daughter. The interview provides a glimpse into Trellis's concerns and expectations for Breanna's future independence, as well as her feelings about the use of the curriculum. The article also provides an overview of the curriculum and discusses Breanna's mobility progress.

A Parent's Search for Help

Despite continuous therapy sessions and Trellis's diligent home therapy program, Breanna still required significant physical assistance and was at risk for eventual hip dislocation. High muscle tone in her legs was causing "scissoring," which was increasing the degree of separation in her hip joints. Recently one of Breanna's doctors had recommended surgery to resolve the problem.

As with many parents of children with disabilities, Trellis was constantly searching for ideas and programs

to help Breanna. After reading about the MOVE program (see section "How MOVE Works") in a Rifton Company catalog (1999), Trellis requested information on the program. She was sent literature and videotapes and was also given the names of two university professors in her area who were involved with training and research on the program.

Mobility instruction should occur within typical daily activities that are functional for the child.

A Find: How to Facilitate Mobility

After an introduction to MOVE, Trellis went through a 2-day training program to better understand the curriculum and how to implement it. As part of the MOVE program at home, Trellis was encouraged to think of activity-based instruction opportunities. It was explained that mobility instruction should occur within typical daily activities that were functional for Breanna. Initially, Trellis selected activities if Breanna enjoyed them, and if mobility skills could be embedded within them. This included daily dressing, eating, bathing, and playing activities. Although Breanna was able to participate only partially in these activities and needed extensive physical support, Trellis continued to be interested and participate because of the motivation of the activity.

The physical supports or prompts used in the MOVE curriculum are designed to *facilitate* the use of mobility skills, not to *replace* them. In this case, prompts to help support weight, provide balance, and guide the legs for reciprocal steps were provided. These prompts were fre-

Figure 1. Breanna's Mobility Progress

First Week--11/8/99 to 11/15/99	Last week*--4/16/00 to 4/23/00 *end of data collection and recording
Mean Number of Steps Taken (with adult assistance)	**Mean Number of Steps Taken** (with adult assistance)
15	509
Mean Number of Steps Taken (with gait trainer)	**Mean Number of Steps Taken** (with gait trainer)
0	125
Mean Time Standing	**Mean Time Standing**
45 seconds	4.02 minutes

quently provided by the mother and sometimes by the use of a gait trainer. The curriculum provides a guide for the use of prompts; however, as soon as prompts are implemented, a systematic plan for their removal is also developed.

In these activity-based learning opportunities, Trellis took every opportunity to let Breanna physically participate to the fullest degree possible.

Some of the activities Trellis selected to teach Breanna walking skills included feeding the dogs, feeding the chickens and checking for eggs, walking across the yard to Grandma's house, and picking flowers in the yard. Activities that required standing included washing hands at the sink, playing at the sink, and standing at the blackboard to play letter and number games. In these activity-based learning opportunities, Trellis took every opportunity to let Breanna physically participate to the fullest degree possible. For example, when learning games were to be played in the bedroom, the activity might start with Trellis helping Breanna to transfer from a sitting position to a standing position in the living room. Breanna would then walk with support to the bedroom and stand at the board while playing the game. Although it would have been easier for Trellis to have picked her up and carried her to the bedroom, the anticipation of playing the games motivated Breanna to participate in the mobility practice.

The MOVE Curriculum is typically used in school settings, where the team can measure and chart the students'

progress. During this home-based implementation of MOVE, we asked Trellis to keep records of the progress that Breanna made while using the MOVE Curriculum. She recorded the number of steps taken during activities that required walking inside and outside. She also recorded the number of seconds of weight-bearing during standing activities throughout the day (see Figure 1). In addition, we conducted an interview with Trellis to present her perspectives on MOVE. A portion of the interview follows.

A Concerned Parent's Words

We know you were doing a lot with Breanna before MOVE. What made you want to try MOVE?

After I watched the tape of *Kids on the MOVE* (Barnes, 1997) and saw how much they were able to do, I was willing to try just about anything. It seemed like those kids were able to do so much after MOVE; and I thought, if they can do it, then so could Breanna.

Was this approach, the MOVE Program, different from what you were doing?

They [the people on the video] were doing things I wasn't doing. After I saw it, I thought, this makes a lot of sense. Before, I was getting Breanna to stand up and sit down from a chair and walk, but it was just a lot of therapy exercises. The kids in the video were doing these things in regular activities. Now I can have Breanna stand up and sit down from the potty chair—she's being potty trained now! I was just moving her, but now we do these things all through the day in our regular routine. It's so much easier now that it is just part of what we do during the day, and we can practice standing and walking while playing.

We know that in the past you were discouraged because you were doing so much for Breanna and you were worried about the future.

I had gotten frustrated because it's like I told my husband: I said that I don't want to sit here and hold Breanna for the rest of her life. I want her to get up and walk; I want her to be independent. I want to have a little time to do something I want to do, and that's the reason I'm pushing her now and doing what I do. I don't want to do this for the next 20 years. I got discouraged and talked to the doctor about it one time, and she told me I needed to just take a little break and find a hobby or do something.

Did you follow the doctor's advice?

I have backed off, and I don't do as much as I did before; and the reason is last year I got really stressed out. I just wore down. We were doing so much on weight-bearing a day and so much of this and so much of that. By night if I didn't do everything I had planned, I would just almost freak out because I didn't do what I wanted to do; and I just thought the more I do, the better she's going to be. I guess that's true to a point, but I've also realized that after speaking with a therapist and a doctor, I've got to let her be a little girl too and let her have some free play time. So now I try to incorporate training when she's having a fun activity; I make her walk to it, I don't push her, and we take our time a little more. I just don't rush her from place to place like I did before, because I had these goals set that by a certain time I would have this done or that done, and I was just wearing myself out.

So maybe now you're accomplishing as much but enjoying it more?

I think so; I don't feel guilty now—I feel better. I used to have my list of exercises and practice to do, and if I didn't do my list, I felt frustrated. I just wanted a break, but now the practice is like playing. It's more enjoyable for the whole family. My husband, Jeff, has always wanted to be involved with this, but he wasn't sure what to do. Now we go outside and play hide and seek. We've found that one thing she likes is our pond. We can go catch fish in the pond, and we'll drive th golf cart down because it's a pretty good ways down the hill. Jeff will drop us off at one point, and he'll go somewhere else. We'll have to walk to where he is to help get the fish off [the hook], and she thinks that's fun. So she's getting in walking while we have fun and play together.

Now that you've been through the MOVE training and after you've been using the MOVE Curriculum, what are your thoughts about the program? Do you think it has helped you accomplish any of your goals?

Oh, I know it has. For instance, like the steps in front of the sink. You know, I never thought about putting steps in front of a sink and making her walk up the steps to wash her hands. Normally, what I would have done is pick her up and hold her over the sink and wash her as best I could. Now if she wants to go somewhere, you know, I'll stand her up, and instead of just picking her up, I'll make her push up with her legs and use her muscles to stand up; and then we'll walk to where she wants. If she wants to go to her room, I make her walk. I don't just pick her up and carry her like I did most of the time, and I think that's why she's developed the strength that she has in her legs because she's using them more.

Can you give us an example of one thing that she wasn't doing before starting the MOVE program that she is doing now?

When we first started her measurements in the hallway, like with me holding her arms, her most steps when we first started was about 20. Then I remember when it got up to 50 and 60, the length of the hallway; and we were running out of space to measure. So now we measure outside, and she has gone 500 steps without stopping for more than 20 seconds.

"I want her to know that I know she's going to do it, and I push her and challenge her to do it."
—Breanna's mother

In the year that we have known you and have worked with you, we have become aware of your expectations for your daughter. In general, do you think adult expectations of a child's success or failure has an effect on the child's overall performance?

I do. I say that I have high hopes for Breanna. She's already successful in moving from where she was to where she is now. She's done nothing but improve. I don't ever see her getting any worse, or I hope I don't. Because I see her improving, I push her. I want her to know that I know she's going to do it, and I push her and challenge her to do it. If I thought she wasn't able to do it, then we wouldn't even attempt it; and then, who would know? She might not ever do it.

Has this project made you change your expectations?

I still have high expectations for Breanna, and I always wanted her to walk independently without any supports. I guess I had too many expectations a year or a year and a half ago, because I thought she would walk by age 5 or 6; but I really don't think now that that is a realistic goal. She has progressed, but more slowly. Now I think it will be later. That's changed, but I don't think it's because of the MOVE program. It's just that I think I was expecting too much. I wanted too much too early.

Do you feel okay with this slower rate of progress?

Yes, I'm fine with that. I want her to be as independent as possible, and if she never walks without supports—I mean if she has to walk with a walker, or crutches, or a cane—that's fine because I don't want her to always have to rely on me to hold her. I want her to get around and be the most that she can. If she's 10, that's fine; I mean, she has many years after 10, I hope, to live and enjoy life.

You've mentioned in past conversations that a few people have tried to discourage you. Can you think of anything specific that anyone has said that has discouraged you or that has made you...

Mad?

Yes.

Yes, one of her orthopedists. He told me this child would never walk; and I said, "No, you're wrong, and one day I'm going to bring her to your door; and you're going to see her walk to the opposite end of the room." I don't take that lightly. No, every child is different, and she may not walk without supports; but if she's able to walk at all independently and in any shape or form, she's walking.

Did he say why he thought that?

He said that from his experience, and he said that he could tell by his experience that she would never walk, comparing her with all the other kids. That was basically what he told me. He said that she would not be able to sit up independently, and he sat her up on his table. Well, for one thing, she was crying and screaming her head off, and she was so upset that she just reared back and she wouldn't even try to do anything for him. And he just said, "Well, I tell you, she's never going to walk."

When we started this process you had switched doctors. The doctor that you were seeing at that time was thinking that surgery might be needed.

Yes, let me tell you, we went back to the doctor, and when she went, she had subluxation on her right hip at 28%. That's what it was calculated at. When we went to the doctor in March, it was down to 23%; and it's actually gone back in a little into her socket.

That's wonderful. Did the doctor comment about that?

He said it was because she was up and mobile and getting weight through her legs and hips. He said that she was improving.

That's great

So he told us that because her hip was doing well, we wouldn't need another visit for 6 to 8 months.

So now he's not considering surgery this time?

No.

Good. So all of that walking that you have been making her do seems to be helping. What was it like trying to get Breanna to walk more when she had been used to being carried?

I think it was hard for her, and she wouldn't try as much; but now because she is so much stronger and her muscles are not as tight, she's got more control. Weight shifting is easier for her, so she's going to do more. Now, she knows she can.

> *"If it's something that she wants to do, like play hide and seek, or go outside and pick something, or chase a ball, or chase a rooster, she'll do it"*
>
> —Breanna's mother

And does she seem to enjoy walking more now?

Oh, yes, she likes to do things she's not supposed to. If it's something that she wants to do, like play hide and seek, or go outside and pick something, or chase a ball, or chase a rooster, she'll do it. One day, when we were walking down the road, she started looking in the direction of my parents' house, so I asked her if she wanted to go; and she gave me a kiss for yes. I said okay, we'll go and walk down there (about 600 feet). So we did. She was very determined, and she got almost all the way—she got to their yard before she gave out. But she wanted to go.

You have found that there are more things that she wants to do now. Do you think motivation plays a role in her accomplishments?

If she doesn't want to do something, there's really no competition. That's why I've got to find things that are fun and motivating. Because if I tell her, let's walk to your room, we're going to get on the bolster and wedge to exercise, she's not going to go. And I know she's not. But if I tell her to go to her room because we're going to paint, she'll go.

You have mentioned that she seems to have better head and trunk control now. Has this made it easier to do other things around the house?

Yes, I can… just hold her. I mean, if we're standing and not walking, I have let her go and not helped her; and she has stood on her own for a couple of seconds. I can just barely have my arms on her, and she's fully supporting herself. I mean she's supporting herself even when I have my arms wrapped around her; but if I just let go and loosely touch her just so she knows I'm there, she'll stand. She's got so much more strength and control and balance.

Now that Breanna is more mobile, do you see changes in her relationships with other people?

I know I've told you before that Breanna is hard to handle physically. I mean, she has her special needs; and other people didn't know how to do her therapy. They would just carry her, but now they can walk with her because she can stand upright more. They can stand her on the ground and hold her arms rather than just carry her.

What would you recommend to other parents who have children with similar disabilities?

I think all parents ought to know that the more they do for their children when they are young, the more independent they're going to be and be able to do. Breanna's improved a lot since you first met her. I want parents to know that if they worked with their children, they can do better, and they will improve.

Trellis, this is wonderful information. Is there anything else that comes to your mind?

Well, you gave me some ideas when we started the [MOVE] program, and I thank you both for helping her and helping us. You gave me a lot to think about. Before, I was more interested in saving time, and that's maybe why I would pick her up and carry her instead of waiting for her to walk. But I found that she got so much more out of it when I helped her to walk from here to there. Instead of trying to save 9 minutes of time, we were better off taking the 10 minutes. Before I started the program, I didn't make her walk as much because I would carry her a lot to quickly get to the place where we would do our exercises. Now I make her go that extra distance and I think that's why she's improving like she is.

The MOVE Curriculum helps to provide the support, the motivation, and the high expectations to facilitate the development of functional motor skills.

Another example of what she is doing now happened just the other day at my sister's house. I had to run to the bathroom before lunch to wash up. My mom and my sister were in the kitchen fixing us some sandwiches. I put Breanna on the couch with Jordan, her cousin, I told Jordan to sit beside Breanna and not to let her fall off. She wouldn't fall off anyway because she can sit on a couch by herself now. So I went to the bathroom, and the next thing I knew my mom and sister were hollering, "Come here, come here, look at Breanna!" She had gotten off the couch and was standing holding the couch and just laughing. And they swore up and down that they did not help her, and Jordan had gotten down and come to the kitchen. When she did, they looked to make sure Breanna was still okay, and she was sitting on the couch. And the next time they looked, she had gotten off by herself. I think she must have seen Jordan getting off, and she did it, too. I put her on the couch and told her to do it again, and she wouldn't do it. But, she's done it once, she's going to do it again.

That's like when she walked from here to my parents'—she can do it again. It may not be today, and it may not be tomorrow. It may take her a few days, but she will do it again.

How MOVE Works

The MOVE Curriculum helps to provide the support, the motivation, and the high expectations to facilitate the development of functional motor skills. Although this can be accomplished in a variety of settings, such as the home, the curriculum is ideally suited for the school environment (see box, "MOVE Foundations").

Team Approach

Adopting the MOVE Curriculum allows the school team to develop a common focus based on the family's goals and dreams. Related services, such as occupational therapy and physical therapy are then embedded into meaningful activities that incorporate the skills needed to achieve the goals. MOVE uses data-based instruction in which repeated measures are taken on both student progress and the level of support required. Physical support from adults or equipment is provided to allow partial participation in the activity; and the support is reduced as skills increase. In this approach, eating lunch may change from a daily routine to a daily instructional opportunity, as follows:

- Transitioning from sitting to standing.
- Bearing weight (to wash hands at sink).
- Taking reciprocal steps (walking to and from table).
- Maintaining balance in a traditional classroom chair (while eating).

Within the structure of meaningful activities, the team can also incorporate functional academic, communication, and socialization goals. This allows educational teams to write integrated goals that focus on the needs of the individual, rather than on the isolated skills of specific disciplines.

Integrated Curriculum

MOVE is a top-down, activity-based curriculum designed to teach people with physical disabilities the basic, functional motor skills needed for greater participation within home, school, and community environments (Kern County Superintendent of Schools, 1999). The curriculum was developed by Linda Bidabe, a teacher in Bakersfield, California, who was frustrated with the lack of progress of many of her students who had severe disabilities. She recognized that small developmental gains in motor skills frequently gave way to growing bodies and that many of these students remained in wheelchairs, or returned to them, before they ever achieved independent mobility.

Bidabe's solution to this situation was to focus on the functional skills of standing, walking, and sitting, as opposed to prerequisite or developmental skills, such as raising head from a prone position, rolling over, and crawling. In this "top-down" approach to program planning, the team selects instructional activities and basic skills, based on functional outcomes, and incorporates events dispersed throughout the day. Assessment, planning, and instruction are accomplished through transdisciplinary teams that include parents, educators, and therapists who work together to achieve the family's goals for the student.

MOVE was developed on the following foundations:

- *Functional Curriculum*—Learning occurs within meaningful activities.

- *Natural Environments*—Skills are practiced where they will be used.

- *Family Centered*—Family priorities are an essential part of MOVE.

- *Integrated Therapy*—Team collaboratively plans, sets goals, and intervenes in students' natural environments.

- *Partial Participation*—Students participate in meaningful activities to the greatest degree possible.

MOVE uses motivating activities to teach functional mobility skills that

- Are age-appropriate.
- Increase independence.
- Increase access to the community.
- Reduce custodial care.
- Promote communication, social, and daily-living skills.

Final Thoughts

When working with individuals with limited mobility, it is important that the adults who are facilitating learning have high expectations and provide multiple opportunities for practice. This task can be challenging.

As an integrated, engaging, and motivating approach to education for students with mobility and other needs, MOVE holds great promise for teams of educators, students, and families. As Breanna and her mother discovered, learning independent skills can be fun and can lead to great strides in learning and improvement.

References

Barnes, S. B. (Producer). (1997). *Kids on the MOVE: Holm elementary* [Video]. (Available from MOVE International, 1300 17th Street, City Centre, Bakersfield, CA 93301-4533.)

Barnes, S. B., & Whinnery, K. W. (1997). Mobility Opportunities Via Education (MOVE): Theoretical foundations. *Physical Disabilities: Education and Related Services, 16*, 33–46.

Barnes, S. B., & Whinnery, K. W. (in press). Effects of functional mobility training for young students with physical disabilities. *Exceptional Children*.

Bidabe, D. L., Barnes, S. B., & Whinnery, K. W. (2001). M.O.V.E.: Raising expectations for individuals with severe disabilities. *Physical Disabilities: Education and Related Services, 19*, 31–48.

Campbell, S. K., Vander Linden, D. W., & Palisano, R. J. (2000). *Physical therapy for children* (2nd ed.). Philadelphia: W. B. Saunders.

Dunn, W. (1991). Integrated related services. In L. H. Meyer, C. A. Peck, & L. Brown (Eds.), *Critical issues in the lives of people with severe disabilities* (pp. 353–377). Baltimore: Paul H. Brookes.

Heriza, C. (1991). Motor development: Traditional and contemporary theories. In M. J. Lister (Ed.), *Contemporary management of motor control problems: Proceedings of the II Step Conference* (pp. 99–126). Alexandria, VA: Foundation for Physical Therapy.

Horak, F. B. (1991). Assumptions underlying motor control for neurologic rehabilitation. In M. J. Lister (Ed.), *Contemporary management of motor control problems: Proceedings of the II Step Conference* (pp. 11–27). Alexandria, VA: Foundation for Physical Therapy.

Kern County Superintendent of Schools. (1999). M.O.V.E.: Mobility Opportunities Via Education. Bakersfield, CA: Author.

Orelove, F. P., & Sobsey D. (1996). *Educating children with multiple disabilities* (3rd ed.). Baltimore: Paul H. Brookes.

Rainforth, B., & York-Barr, J. (1997). *Collaborative teams for students with severe disabilities: Integrating therapy and educational services*. Baltimore: Paul H. Brookes.

Rifton: Community Playthings. (1999). *Rifton equipment* (catalog). Rifton, NY: Community Products LLC.

Snell, M. E., & Brown, F. (2000). *Instruction of students with severe disabilities* (5th ed.). Upper Saddle River, NJ: Prentice-Hall.

Vockell, E. L., & Asher, J. W. (1995). *Educational research* (2nd ed.). Englewood Cliffs, NJ: Merrill.

Keith W. Whinnery (CEC Chapter #770), Associate Professor; and **Stacie B. Barnes**, (CEC Chapter #770), Assistant Professor, Special Education Department, University of West Florida, Pensacola.

Address correspondence to Keith W. Whinnery, Special Education Department, University of West Florida, 11000 University Parkway, Pensacola, FL 32514 (e-mail: kwhinner@at@;uwf.edu).

Accommodations for Students with Disabilities: Removing Barriers to Learning

Secondary school principals frequently encounter questions about educating students with disabilities. Sometimes the questions revolve around seeking a deeper understanding of the disability and the best way to meet student needs. Other times, the questions focus on all the changes that must be made to ensure students receive an appropriate education. What questions do teachers ask about accommodations for students with a disability?

By MaryAnn Byrnes

Think about taking a driver's test without wearing glasses (if you do, that is). Not fair, you say; you need the glasses to see. You have just identified an accommodation that you need. Wearing glasses does not make a bad driver better or make driving easier; rather, wearing glasses makes driving possible. Glasses are so much a part of our lives that we do not even consider that they remove a barrier caused by a disability.

Secondary school teachers encounter students every day on an Individualized Education Plan (IEP) or 504 Plan, both of which address programs for students with disabilities. Most likely, the person charged with monitoring this plan has indicated that particular students need changes in teaching style, assignments, or testing strategies.

It is usually easy to understand the need for glasses or wheelchairs or hearing aids. These sound like changes the student must make. Other adjustments, modifications, or accommodations on these plans, such as extended time, may not be as clear.

What is an accommodation?

An accommodation is an adjustment, to an activity or setting, that removes a barrier presented by a disability so a person can have access equal to that of a person without a disability. An accommodation does not guarantee success or a specific level of performance. It should, however, provide the opportunity for a person with a disability to participate in a situation or activity.

Think of that pair of glasses, or the time you broke your leg and could not drive. Think of how your life was affected by these conditions. Your competence did not change. Your ability to think and work did not change. Your ability to interact with (have access to) the reading material may be very limited without your glasses. Your ability to get to (have access to) work or the grocery store may be very limited without someone to transport you. The support provided by the glasses—or the driver—made it possible for you to use your abilities without the barrier presented by less than perfect vision or limited mobility.

> An accommodation is an adjustment, to an activity or setting, that removes a barrier presented by a disability so a person can have access equal to that of a person without a disability.

The accommodations in IEPs or 504 Plans serve the same purpose. They identify ways to remove the barrier presented by a person's disability.

Why do we need to provide accommodations?

Accommodations are required under Section 504 of the Federal Rehabilitation Act of 1974 as well as the Americans with Disabilities Act. Both these federal laws prohibit discrimination against individuals who have a disability. Situations that limit access have been determined to be discriminatory.

Accommodations must be provided not just by teachers to students, but by employees for workers and governments for citizens. Curbs have been cut to provide access. Doors have been widened and door handles altered to provide access to people for whom the old designs posed a barrier. Employers provide computer adaptations or other adjustments in work schedules and circumstances.

For employers and schools, individuals with disabilities may have a document called a 504 Plan, which details the types of accommodations that are required. Students who have a 504 Plan will not require special education services, just changes to the environment or instructional situation.

Students who have a disability and require special education services in addition to accommodations will have this information contained in an IEP, which also details the types of direct services that need to be provided and the goals of these services. Accommodations will be listed within this IEP.

With the recent changes in IDEA '97, the federal law governing special education, you will be addressing accommodations that must be made so a student with a disability can participate in large-scale districtwide or statewide assessment systems as well as classwork and school life.

Who needs accommodations?

According to Section 504, an individual with a disability is any person who has "a physical or mental impairment that limits one or more major life activities." IDEA '97, the federal special education law, lists the following disabilities: autism, deaf-blindness, deafness, hearing impairment, mental retardation, multiple disabilities, orthopedic impairment, other health impairment, serious emotional disturbance, specific learning disability, speech or language impairment, traumatic brain injury, and visual impairment.

Students who have a 504 Plan will not require special education services, just changes to the environment or instructional situation.

Some conditions are covered by Section 504, but not special education. These can include attention deficit disorder—ADD, (also attention deficit hyperactivity disorder—ADHD); chronic medical conditions (such as cancer, Tourette Syndrome, asthma, or epilepsy); communicable diseases; some temporary medical conditions; physical impairments; and disorders of emotion or behavior. To qualify, there must be a demonstrated and substantial limitation of a major life activity.

Students (or adults) who have disabilities may require accommodations to have equal access to education. Not every student with a disability will require accommodations, and not every student with a disability requires the same accommodation all the time.

Think of Jim, a student who has limited mobility in his hands, affecting his ability to write. This disability will present a barrier in a class that requires the student to take notes quickly or write long essays in class. In a class that does not require either of these activities, no barrier may be present. Equal access is possible without accommodation. The student can learn and demonstrate what he knows and can do unaffected by his disability.

What kind of accommodations are there?

Just as there is no limit to the range of disabilities, there is no limit to the range of accommodations. The point is to understand disability and determine if it presents a barrier to equal access. If so, decide whether an accommodation can be identified to remove the barrier—and make sure the accommodation is implemented.

Not every student with a disability will require accommodations, and not every student with a disability requires the same accommodation all the time.

Think of the student described above. The limited mobility in Jim's hands presents a barrier in a class that requires rapid note taking or the writing of long essays in class. There are several accommodations that can result in equal access. Jim might tape the lesson and take notes later. These notes could be written or dictated into a computer. Essays could be composed verbally at a computer workstation or dictated into a tape recorder or to a scribe. A computer might be adapted so typing becomes an effective way to record information on paper. In yet another type of accommodation, essays could be replaced by oral reports.

Are there some accommodations that should not be used?

Like many difficult questions, the answer depends on the context. An accommodation should not alter the essential purpose of the assignment. If the skill you want to measure is the ability to make multiple rapid hand movements, then there is probably no accommodation that is appropriate. Jim will not do well because of his disability. Alternately, if the purpose of a task is to see if someone has perfect vision without glasses, using those glasses is not an appropriate accommodation. If the purpose is to see if you can read, the glasses become a reasonable accommodation.

Who decides about accommodations?

The team that writes IEPs and 504 Plans reviews the disability and determines what accommodations, if any, are necessary. These are then written into the EIP or 504 Plan.

Once more, return to Jim. As you consider the requirements of your class, think of the most appropriate way to remove the barrier that is presented by the limited mobility Jim has in his hands.

If we use accommodations, how will the student ever be prepared for independent life in college or the world of work?

Some people are concerned that the supports provided in school will result in the student being unable to work productively when he or she leaves school. As a matter of fact, Section 504 applies to colleges and employers as well. Colleges offer support centers and provide accommodations upon documentation that a disability exists. Employers are required to provide reasonable accommodations to any person who is otherwise qualified to fulfill the elements of the job.

If companies remove barriers at the workplace, educators should be willing and able to take barriers out of the school activities that prepare a student for the workplace. Teachers can help a student identify the type of accommodation that will be the least cumbersome for everyone, and those that will permit the student to be most independent.

Don't accommodations just make school easier?

That depends on how you view the world. Does wearing glasses make driving easier? Not really—for a person with limited vision, wearing glasses makes driving *possible*. With or without glasses, you need to be able to drive to pass the test. The same is true of an academic accommodation; whether or not the accommodation is provided, the students still must demonstrate that they know required material.

An accommodation should not alter the essential purpose of the assignment.

Think about the important elements of your class: Is it more important that Jim take notes in class or understand the material? Is it more important that Jim demonstrate good handwriting or the ability to communicate thoughts in print? Often, when you identify the main purpose of your assignments and consider the skills and abilities of a student, you will see that an accommodation lets you determine more clearly what a student knows, understands, and can do.

Does a student need to follow the IEP accommodations in all classes?

The IEP or 504 Plan needs to address any area in which the student's disability affects life in school. Sometimes this means in all classes, but not always. For example, a student who was blind would need to use Braille in all classes dealing with written material. Jim, our student with limited mobility in his hands, might not require accommodations in world languages or physical education.

Can we make accommodations without having students on an IEP?

Many accommodations are just different ways of teaching or testing. You should be able to have this freedom in your classes. In some cases, the way in which a class is taught makes accommodations unnecessary. Accommodations change the situation, not the content of the instruction. However, accommodations on standardized tests must be connected to IEP's or 504 Plans.

May teachers give different assignments on the same content as a way to meet the needs of different learning styles without lowering standards?

Absolutely. The point is to remove the barrier of the disability; this is one way to accomplish that. Some teachers find they tap student knowledge best in active projects; others find that written work is best. Many secondary schools are using portfolios or performance activities to document student learning.

These assessment activities can be very compelling and they do tap different methods of expression. A student like Jim, for example, might communicate depth of understanding and analysis to a social studies debate with a disability in the area of speech or language might find barriers in the performance activities that do not exist on a paper-and-pencil task.

. . . educators should be willing and able to take barriers out of the school activities that prepare a student for the workplace.

What if accommodations are not implemented?

Since accommodations allow equal access, refusing to provide them can be viewed as discrimination. Individuals who knowingly refuse to implement accommodations make themselves personally liable for legal suit.

This sounds serious, and it is serious. Once the accommodations are found to be necessary, everyone must implement them in situations where the student's disability poses a barrier that prevents equal access.

If no barrier exists in your class, the accommodation is not necessary. No one has the option, however, of deciding not to implement a necessary accommodation. Telling students they could not wear glasses or use a hearing aid is unthinkable. Just as inappropriate is a decision not to allow Jim to use accommodations to remove the barrier posed by his disability, even though it means making some changes to your own work.

Questions About Specific Accommodations

Now that the issues underlying accommodations have been addressed, it is time to talk about frequently-encountered accommodations that raise questions and concern. All these questions have come from secondary school faculty members in a variety of school systems.

Why is it fair to read material aloud to some students?

Some students have a learning disability that makes it difficult for them to decode print. They can understand the concepts; they can comprehend the material when they hear it; they can reason through the material. They just can't turn print into meaning. If the task is to determine if the student can read, you already know they will have difficulty. If the task is to determine if the student has content knowledge, reading material aloud removes the barrier of the learning disability. Reading material aloud to a student who does not understand the material will not result in a higher grade.

Why is it fair to give some students extra time on tests?

Some students have motor difficulties that make writing an enormous challenge. They may not be able to form the letters correctly. They may not be able to monitor their thoughts while they work on the physical act of writing. They understand the material, and they know what they want to respond; it just takes longer to write the answer. If the task is to determine how quickly the student can respond, you already know they will have difficulty. If the task is to determine if the student has the knowledge, providing extra time removes the

barrier of the motor disability. Providing extra time to a student who does not understand the material will not result in a higher grade.

Why is it fair to permit some students to respond orally to tests?

Think about the example above. For some students, responding orally would be a comparable accommodation. In this case, allowing an oral response will not result in a higher grade if the student does not know the material.

A student with a disability in the area of speech or language might find barriers in the performance activities that do not exist on a paper-and-pencil task.

The Bottom Line

It all comes down to deciding what is important. Think about your assignment and expectations. Think about the disability. If the disability provides a barrier, the accommodation removes it. The accommodation does not release a student from participating or demonstrating knowledge—it allows the student to be able to participate and demonstrate knowledge. And isn't that what school is all about?

References

Americans with Disabilities Act of 1990, P.L. 101–336, 2, 104 Stat. 328.1991.

Individuals with Disabilities Education Act Amendments of 1997, P.L. 105–17, 20 U.S. Code Sections 1401–1486.

Livovich, Michael P. *Section 504 of the Rehabilitation Act of 1973 and the Americans with Disabilities Act. Providing access to a free appropriate public education: a public school manual.* Indianapolis, Ind.: 1996.

Vocational Rehabilitation Act of 1973, 29 U.S.C. 794.

*MaryAnn Byrnes (**byrnes@mediaone.net**) is assistant professor at the Graduate College of Education, University of Massachusetts-Boston.*

Chaos in the Classroom: Looking at ADHD

Diagnosing and helping students with ADHD requires the collaboration of parents, clinicians, teachers, and students.

Steven C. Schlozman and Vivien R. Schlozman

Students increasingly walk through the classroom door wearing invisible labels and prescriptions. A list of psychiatric and learning disorders that was intended to clarify the difficulties different students experience has instead bewildered teachers and administrators. Educators must make sense of their students' new diagnostic criteria and glean from this information the most effective ways to assist their pupils. Given the enormous increase in the diagnosis and treatment of attention deficit hyperactivity disorder (ADHD) among school-age children, neuropsychiatric problems characterized by inattention and hyperactivity are pressing classroom issues.

Students diagnosed with ADHD often arrive in the classroom with medication and teaching recommendations that are based on completed psychological testing. In spite of these recommendations, teachers frequently have little or no contact with their students' clinicians. Tight budgets, large classrooms, and often multiple students with the same diagnosis who require different teaching strategies substantially challenge the educator's primary objective: to teach and inspire every student dynamically and efficiently. Reaching that goal starts with an understanding of ADHD and how teachers can help students who have been diagnosed with the disorder.

Describing and Diagnosing ADHD

ADHD is a neuropsychiatric disorder that begins before 7 years of age (American Psychiatric Association, 1994). Problems in the three core domains of *inattention, hyperactivity*, and *impulsivity* characterize the disorder.

Clinicians define *inattention* as age-inappropriate poor attention span and *hyperactivity* as age-inappropriate

increased activity in multiple settings. For example, an inattentive child may pay poor attention to details or appear as though his or her mind is elsewhere. Often, the child has difficulty sustaining a single activity. One mother describes her son's bedtime difficulties: He starts to brush his teeth, follows the cat into the playroom while his mouth is full of toothpaste, notices the blocks and sits down to play, and in two minutes turns on the computer at the other end of the room.

Most children will occasionally display many of the aspects ascribed to ADHD, and this recognition may account for much of the controversy surrounding the disorder.

Hyperactive children may fidget excessively and have difficulties playing quietly. Children with ADHD display, sometimes paradoxically, a level of inflexibility that leads them to experience intense frustration when asked to break from one activity and move on to something new. The child will appear to have well-honed attentional skills, but his or her rigidity will increasingly lead to tantrums and agitation.

Impulsivity refers to the tendency to act rashly and without judgment or consideration. A child might frequently interrupt others, take other children's toys, or appear consistently impatient and frustrated.

As these descriptions suggest, the symptoms of ADHD exist along a spectrum. Most children will occasionally display many of the aspects ascribed to ADHD, and this recognition may account for much of the controversy surrounding the disorder. To standardize the diagnosis, the Diagnostic and Statistical Manual-IV (DSM-IV) lists formal criteria (American Psychiatric Association, 1994). ADHD can be characterized as three types: predominantly inattentive, predominantly hyperactive-impulsive, or a combination of the two types. To some extent, these differentiations account for the increasingly recognized population of children—often girls—who display what appear to be difficulties primarily with attention but who respond to conventional treatments.

The brief adolescent tantrum or the distraction of an 8-year-old before vacation does not constitute sufficient data for a diagnosis of ADHD.

Finally, one of the most difficult and important aspects of understanding ADHD is to consider the child's developmental expectations. Obviously, we don't expect the same judgment or attention span from a 6-year-old and a teenager. In addition, symptoms must persist over time and exist in more than one setting. The brief adolescent tantrum or the distraction of an 8-year-old before vacation does not constitute sufficient data for a diagnosis of ADHD.

In fact, the heterogeneity and developmental aspects of ADHD make the diagnosis of the disorder potentially quite complicated (Cantwell, 1996). Ideally, the clinician should take a very careful history from as many sources as possible and note such important factors as the persistence of the symptoms and the extent to which these symptoms cause problems. Because emotionally troubled children often appear inattentive or agitated, the clinician should ask about difficulties in the child's life that might account for a change in the child's behavior. We must also remember, however, that many children experience difficult life changes but do not display symptoms of agitation or inattention.

Although research addresses the efficacy of specific laboratory tests, the descriptive criteria of ADHD remain the most effective means of making an accurate diagnosis. Clinicians must take the time to speak with parents and teachers, noting that children with ADHD will often appear normal in a brief office visit or in a one-on-one situation. As evidence mounts of a strong genetic component to the disorder, clinicians should ascertain whether siblings, parents, or close relatives suffer similar symptoms. Because many parents were not diagnosed as children, simply asking whether they were diagnosed with something similar to ADHD is usually not sufficient (Biederman et al., 1992). The clinician must probe parents for their memories of their childhood behavior.

Do inattention and hyperactivity always equal ADHD? In addition to the heterogeneity of ADHD, we must note that other psychiatric processes may account for many of the disorder's symptoms. Children with intense anxiety or depression are particularly likely to have problems that appear similar to ADHD, and evidence also exists that suggests that symptoms of depression—as the child's self esteem suffers in the face of continuing social and developmental failures—can complicate ADHD (Zametkin & Monique, 1999). Clinicians should also screen for problems with substance abuse, Tourette's syndrome, and psychosocial stressors. Clinicians, parents, or teachers may mistakenly attribute symptoms of these conditions to ADHD, and the symptoms may complicate the course of a child who happens also to suffer from ADHD.

In general, younger children with ADHD are happy. The preteen diagnosed with ADHD who is not generally in good spirits should be carefully scrutinized for other or additional psychological problems. Conversely, as children with untreated ADHD age, they may develop significant self-image problems. These difficulties come about as the young people continually endure academic and social failures; simply treating their ADHD will often not meet all of their social, developmental, and learning needs.

Although we don't clearly understand the causes of ADHD, current research suggests evidence of potentially causative brain abnormalities. Many of these studies implicate problems with frontal lobe function (Rubia et al., 1999). In general, the frontal lobe region of the cerebral cortex allows for the planning and execution of complex and complicated tasks. We often refer to the activity of this portion of the brain as executive function, and we think that children with ADHD have deficits in executive functioning.

Evidence for these deficits has been generated both by neuropsychological testing and by neuroimaging studies, as well as by the observation that individuals with frontal lobe injuries display behavior similar to that of people with ADHD. As stated earlier, strong evidence for a genetic component of the disorder also exists (Biederman et al., 1992). Further, mounting evidence suggests that psychological and environmental stress can lead to the development of the syndrome (Weiss, 1996). Although we know of no clear cause for the disorder, most theorists would argue that both environmental and biological factors play substantial roles in the development of ADHD.

Treating ADHD

Treatments for ADHD include behavioral and medical therapies. Stimulants such as methylphenidate (Ritalin) and dextroamphetamine (Dexedrine) continue to be first-line medical treatments, with more than 40 years of experience confirming the relative safety and effectiveness of these medications. Although the number of stimulants on the market proliferates, response to a specific stimulant remains idiosyncratic; some children will do better on one stimulant than the other, and it is difficult to predict which medication will work best. In addition to the stimulants, tricyclic antidepressants such as desipramine can be very effective, though their use is somewhat limited in younger children. Medications such as clonidine (Catapress) and guanfacine (Tenex), both high blood pressure medications, appear to treat the impulsive symptoms of the syndrome, but are not effective for inattention.

In general, if medical therapies work and the child receives the appropriate dose and stimulant, the child's behavior should improve relatively quickly. If a child does not improve or improves only minimally, both the proposed treatment regimen (dose and/or medication) and often the diagnosis itself should be re-evaluated. Nevertheless, we need to understand the limitations of medical therapies. Although such symptoms as overactivity, attention span, impulsivity, aggression, social interaction, and academic performance will often improve, such specific skills as reading and such antisocial behavior as cheating or stealing may not show marked progress without additional interventions (Zametkin & Monique, 1999). Children still must master the fundamental developmental task of learning to focus on activities or subjects that are not of immediate interest. No medication can take the place of the mastery of skills and attainment of maturity necessary for academic and social success.

Behavioral treatments of ADHD include daily report cards, positive reinforcement, social skills groups, and individual therapy (Barkley, 1990). As the child matures, these treatments may also address the child's self-image. Although psychodynamic therapies (play or talk therapies) may not be directly effective, we have found that the relationship between a child and an effective therapist often ameliorates many of the problem behaviors associated with ADHD.

Finally, when deciding on treatment, the parents and the child must take part in the decision-making process. Some families prefer behavioral remedies; others may request medications. Attention to such details as the meaning of each treatment modality, as well as the hopes and concerns of both the parents and the child, will have enormous benefits. Adolescents may not wish to take medications, for instance, but may be willing to implement equally effective study and behavioral strategies. Conversely, both time and financial constraints may limit the efficacy of psychotherapy. Clinicians must educate families about ADHD and its treatment and help the families make informed decisions. Clinicians should leave time at the end of an appointment for questions—if families cannot ask questions, their understanding of and compliance with treatment is severely threatened.

The issue of alcohol and drug abuse and ADHD deserves special mention. Because stimulants are addictive substances, we often worry that prescribing these medications will predispose children to addictive problems. Although caution is always necessary when using stimulants, recent research suggests that, in fact, the number of children developing substance abuse problems is substantially higher in those with ADHD who do not receive adequate treatment (Biederman, Wilens, Mick, Spencer, &

Faraone, 1999). Nevertheless, in adolescents with pre-existing problems with substances, clinicians often prefer treatment with medications other than stimulants.

ADHD in the Classroom

Just as diagnosing and treating children with ADHD is complex, working with the inattentive and hyperactive child challenges all teachers. The problems that children with ADHD experience may lead to chaotic classrooms, missed and incomplete assignments, and miserable teachers and students alike. Educators have found, however, a number of useful classroom techniques.

To assist the student with ADHD, educators need to exercise caution, creativity, and vigilance.

First, teachers must view the child as a whole person. The child is not a person with ADHD, or an "ADHDer," but a complete and unique individual. Although seemingly obvious, teachers must resist the tendency to label a child with unfair expectations. Most important, teachers can remind students that they are capable of learning and of enjoying the learning process. Many students diagnosed with ADHD will arrive in the classroom severely demoralized, having gleaned from their parents and peers that they are unable to excel academically. On the other hand, telling students that they can learn as easily as students without attentional deficits might reintroduce a pattern of failure and disappointment.

Educators, therefore, should be proactive when they suspect a psychiatric reason for a student's difficulties. Studies have demonstrated that teachers are valuable sources of clinical information. At the same time, teachers should be aware of their own biases. Many of the studies, for instance, suggest that teachers frequently suspect ADHD in boys more often than in girls (Dulcan, 1997).

To assist the student with ADHD, educators need to exercise caution, creativity, and vigilance. Teachers must employ all of their professional skills to structure classrooms and make assignments clear. Educators should let students with ADHD know that they will work creatively with the students to explore learning and organization strategies. An honest relationship between teacher and student is essential.

To be most effective, teachers should discuss the strategies with the student outside of class so that the student understands the teacher's expectations and the kinds of support the teacher will offer. Specific strategies might include nonverbal reprimands for out-of-control behavior. A simple and silent hand on the student's shoulder inconspicuously tells the student that his or her behavior is inappropriate. Similarly, relying on such cues as lost eye contact between a student and teacher might help a teacher recognize wavering attention. If a child is persistently unable to focus, move his or her seat to a less distracting part of the room. Some other strategies include the following:

Require meticulously organized assignment books. For every class, the student with ADHD must have each day's homework recorded. When the teacher doesn't assign homework, the student writes "no homework" in the appropriate place. If the student fails to keep the log current, he or she must get the teacher's signature in the assignment book at the end of class. The teacher should also both write the assignment on the board and repeat the assignment aloud. This time-honored teaching technique of appealing to multiple senses works well for children with ADHD.

Teach students with ADHD to break down assignments into smaller, less overwhelming components. When reading textbooks, for example, we have found a variation of Robinson's SQ3R method to be effective (Robinson, 1961). The student surveys each section of the text by first reading the boldfaced print, looking at the visuals, and reading the captions under the visual displays. The student then generates a general statement about what he or she will be reading, allowing him or her to focus on the content of the reading material. After each section, the student stops to recap the main idea of the completed segment. This strategy helps the student become actively engaged with and focused on the text.

Use flash cards. After students give themselves a pretest to determine what they have already mastered, they make flash cards of all of the material that they don't know. They then can separate the cards into three piles: mastered material that they know without hesitation, material that they've guessed correctly but without confidence, and material that they don't know. In this way, the students gain a sense of control over the learning situation and learn to transfer these strategies to other academic and non-academic learning settings. The corresponding sense of accomplishment for both teacher and students can be enormously rewarding.

Experienced teachers will note that many of these strategies have been around for years—long before we reached our present understanding of ADHD. We know now that ADHD leaves the student with deficits in executive functioning and that the time-honored classroom techniques create for the student a kind of external frontal lobe. Good teachers have simply hit upon these techniques in their quests to engage and teach their students.

Teachers need not be overwhelmed by the growing complexity of psychiatric and psychological diagnoses that follow their beleaguered students. As always, good educators remain central to a child's development.

Teachers should never hesitate to contact a child's clinician. If a student appears different or suffers a behavioral change, a physician or psychologist will use this valuable information to determine a diagnosis and treatment. Although clinicians and teachers have just begun to work together, educational and clinical collaborations need to evolve and prosper. The teacher, the clinician, and most important, the student, will benefit enormously.

References

American Psychiatric Association. (1994). *Diagnostic and statistical manual for mental disorders* (4th ed.). Washington, DC: Author.

Barkley, R. A. (Ed.). (1990). *Attention deficit hyperactivity disorder: A handbook for diagnosis and treatment.* New York: Guilford.

Biederman, J., Faraone, S. V., Keenan, K., Benjamin, K., Krifcher, B., Moore, C., Sprich-Buckminster, S., Ugaglia, K., Jellinck, M. S., & Steingard, R. (1992). Further evidence for family-genetic risk factors in attention deficit hyperactivity disorder: Patterns of comorbidity in probands and relatives in psychiatrically and pediatrically referred samples. *Archives of General Psychiatry,* 49, 728–38.

Biederman, J., Wilens, T., Mick, E., Spencer, T., & Faraone, S. V. (1999). Pharmacotherapy of attention deficit hyperactivity disorder reduces risk for substance use disorder. *Pediatrics,* 104, e20.

Cantwell, D. P. (1996). Attention deficit disorder: A review of the past 10 years. *Journal of the American Academy of Child and Adolescent Psychiatry,* 35, 978–87.

Dulcan, M. (1997). Practice parameters for the assessment and treatment of children, adolescents and adults with attention deficit/hyperactivity disorder. *Journal of the American Academy of Child and Adolescent Psychiatry,* 36 (Suppl. 10), 85S–121S.

Robinson, F. P. (1961). *Effective study.* New York: Harper and Row.

Rubia, K., Overmeyer, S., Taylor, E., Brammer, M., Williams, S. C., Simmons, A., & Bullmore, E. T. (1999). Hypofrontality in attention deficit hyperactivity disorder during higher order motor control: A study with functional MRI. *American Journal of Psychiatry,* 156, 891–6.

Weiss, G. (1996). Attention deficit hyperactivity disorder. In M. Lewis (Ed.), *Child and adolescent psychiatry: A comprehensive textbook* (pp. 544–63). Baltimore, MD: Williams and Wilkins.

Zametkin, A. J., & Monique, E. (1999). Current concepts: Problems in the management of attention deficit hyperactivity disorder. *New England Journal of Medicine,* 340, 40–46.

Steven C. Schlozman, M.D., is Clinical Instructor in Psychiatry, Massachusetts General Hospital/Harvard Medical School, 15 Parkman St., WACC-725, Boston, MA 02114; and Lecturer in Education, Harvard Graduate School of Education; 617-724-6300, ext. 133-1114; sscholzman@partners.org. **Vivien R. Schlozman** is a private practice educator at the Pembroke Hill School. She may be reached at 6600 Overhill Rd., Shawnee Mission, KS 66208.

UNIT 10
Giftedness

Unit Selections

Key Points to Consider

- How can adults identify children with exceptional gifts and talents? What types of assessment are valid and reliable? What guidelines are important for their individualized education programs?

- Do children from minority cultures with exceptional gifts and talents hide their creative potentials? Why? How can their special gifts be identified and enhanced?

- How should gifted programs be assessed and how should schools change to meet the needs of high-ability students?

 Links: www.dushkin.com/online/
These sites are annotated in the World Wide Web pages.

The Council for Exceptional Children
http://www.cec.sped.org/index.html
National Association for Gifted Children (NAGC)
http://www.nagc.org/home00.htm

The individuals with Disabilities Education Act (IDEA) mandates special services for children with disabilities, but not for children with exceptional gifts or talents. The monies spent to provide special services for three children with high-cost disabilities could pay for accelerated lessons for a classroom full of college-bound students with intellectual giftedness. Should schools in the twenty-first century be more egalitarian? IDEA mandates appropriate education but not sameness of quantity or degree of knowledge to be imported to every child. Are we inclined to push compensatory education of students with shortcomings in learning, while leaving students with a gift for learning to cope for themselves to counterbalance the equation? Do we want educational parity?

Since many textbooks on exceptional children include children with special gifts and talents, and since these children are exceptional, they will be included in this volume. Instructors who deal only with the categories of disabilities covered by IDEA may simply omit coverage of this unit.

The Omnibus Education Bill of 1987 provided modest support for gifted and talented identification and the education of students with giftedness in the United States. It required, however, that each state foot the bill for the development of special programs for children with exceptional gifts and talents. Some states have implemented accelerated or supplemental education for the gifted. Most states have not.

Giftedness can be viewed as both a blessing and a curse. Problems of jealousy, misunderstanding, indignation, exasperation, and even fear are often engendered in people who live with, work with, or get close to a child with superior intelligence. Are children with giftedness at a disadvantage in our society? Do their powerful abilities and potentialities in some area (or areas) leave them ridiculed or bored in a regular classroom? Children with special gifts and talents are deprived of some of the opportunities with which less exceptional children are routinely provided.

Students who are gifted tend to ask a lot of questions and pursue answers with still more questions. They can be incredibly persistent about gathering information about topics that engage them. They may, however, show no interest at all in learning about topics that do not. They may be very competitive in areas where they are especially skilled, competing even with teachers and other adults. They may seem arrogant about their skills when, in their minds, they are only being honest.

Many children and youth with special gifts and talents have extraordinary sensitivity to how other people are reacting to them. As they are promoted through elementary school into middle school and high school, many such children learn to hide their accomplishments for the secondary gain of being more socially acceptable or more popular. Because they have not been challenged or have been discouraged from achieving at their highest potentialities, underachievement becomes a problem. They have poor study habits as a result of not needing to study. They are unmotivated, intensely bored, and discouraged by the educational programs available to them.

Researchers who have studied creative genius have found that most accomplished high achievers share one childhood similarity. Their parents recognized their special abilities early and found tutors or mentors who would help them develop their skills. This is true not only of mathematicians and scientists but also of world-class sports players, musicians, artists, performers, writers, and other producers of note.

Educational programs that refuse to find tutors or mentors, to encourage original work, or to provide special education in the skill areas of students with gifts are depriving the future of potential producers.

The earlier that children with special gifts and talents are recognized, the better. The sooner they are provided with enriched education, the more valuable their future contributions will become. Children from all ethnic backgrounds, from all socioeconomic levels, and from both sexes can have exceptional gifts and talents. Researchers have reported that parents of gifted children seldom have any special creative skills or talents of their own.

The assessment of children with special gifts and talents, especially in the early childhood years, is fraught with difficulties. Should parents nominate their own children when they see extraordinary skills developing? How objective can parents be about their child's ability as it compares to the abilities of other same-aged children? Should measures of achievement be used (recitals, performances, art, reading levels, writings)? Many parents are embarrassed by their child's extraordinary aptitudes. They would rather have a popular child or a child more like his or her peers.

The first article in this unit suggests resources for parents and teachers of young gifted children. Guidelines are given for understanding the uniqueness of each preschooler with special gifts and talents. They are often described as "4 going on 40." In fact, each one has different areas of acceleration. Helping them understand themselves and their environments can be a challenging task. Many people, unaccustomed to working with children with advanced talents, may misinterpret their unique behaviors. If unattended, they may learn to camouflage their giftedness in order to "fit in" with their peers. While peer tutoring can make children with advanced abilities feel needed, if used excessively it can lead to problems. Finding and reinforcing areas of giftedness, while attending to their social needs and their self-esteem, are areas addressed in this article.

The second article, "Cultivating Otherwise Untapped Potential" warns that allowing special talents to lie dormant may lead to their demise. Our society can benefit greatly from identifying creative potential and developing it early. The article includes a discussion of the pros and cons of acceleration for children with exceptional potential.

In the last article Susan Winebrenner gives strong arguments for spending the time, effort, and money to ensure that our children with gifts and talents get all the education they need. Many students with special gifts and talents become underachievers. They rarely are challenged to learn above their current abilities. Because they score high on achievement tests, it is assumed that they must be learning. An alternate explanation is that they already possessed these abilities. When they are not given a chance to pursue their special interests or are not requested to demonstrate increased excellence in an area, they lose confidence in their abilities to perform. This article urges that they be given a stimulating learning environment of their own.

Understanding the Young Gifted Child: Guidelines for Parents, Families, and Educators

Young children who are gifted or talented share special characteristics that impact on the way they learn and develop. Teachers and parents need to consider the unique needs of each child as they plan ways to nurture and educate these youngsters. Concerns such as uneven development, the need for acceleration and/or enrichment, appropriate socialization and peer interactions, and modification of the curriculum are some of the topics discussed. Suggestions for teachers and parents are included along with a variety of resources.

KEY WORDS: gifted; talented; acceleration; enrichment; socialization.

Jennifer V. Rotigel

INTRODUCTION

Much has been written about the development of children, and it is generally agreed that early development has profound consequences for later development. However, the social, emotional, and intellectual development of young *gifted* children has received little attention outside of the journals that deal specifically with gifted and talented children. The net result is that teachers and parents are often uninformed or misinformed regarding the social and emotional development of young gifted children, particularly in relation to intellectual development and schooling. This article describes characteristics of young gifted children, focuses on typical concerns voiced by parents and teachers, and provides suggestions for appropriately meeting the needs of the young gifted child through curricular modification and enhanced understanding.

WHAT DOES IT MEAN TO BE GIFTED AND TALENTED?

Gifted and talented children are usually identified by schools in the early grades when they are referred for evaluation by either the teacher or the parents. The child may be evaluated through the consideration of a constellation of factors, such as scores on an intelligence test, grades in school, classroom achievement, and teacher and parent input. For example, some schools require that the child demonstrate achievement of at least two grade levels above their current grade placement in reading or mathematics. The identification process varies from district to district and state to state, but the outcome should be that the gifted child receives necessary modifications to the school's curriculum so that she can be appropriately challenged in school.

It is important to realize that when a child is gifted and talented, all aspects of the child's experience are affected. Young gifted children are gifted all day, not just when they are in school or in a "pull-out" program. The cluster of traits that are characteristic of gifted and talented individuals encompasses intellectual, social, emotional, and physical aspects of the child's life. Not all gifted children demonstrate all traits, of course, but there is a commonality that allows for some description of the gifted individual. For example, gifted children often become deeply absorbed in a topic and need to know all there is to know about it, while high achieving children may be satisfied with a more superficial understanding and are then ready to move on. Gifted individuals are often perfectionists, and they grasp new information with little or no repetition. Many gifted children have advanced vocabularies and seek to understand and be involved in world events, even at a young age.

Research in the area of emotional and social adjustment of gifted children has produced overwhelmingly positive results. Children who are gifted are, in general, as well adjusted and emotionally mature as other students (Howley, Howley, & Pendarvis, 1995). As noted by Clark (1997), gifted children need to be given the opportunity to understand themselves and experience positive educational opportunities.

Helping young gifted children understand themselves and their world can be a challenging task for teachers and parents. Many gifted children strive to understand at an early age why they do not seem to fit in with their peers, and it is important that their questions be answered truthfully and carefully. Too many children misunderstand the interactions that they experience and draw conclusions that may be harmful to their development. For example, a young gifted child may be frustrated by his inability to guess the "right" answer that the kindergarten teacher is looking for. Often this is because he is thinking more deeply about a topic than the other children or than the teacher expects and therefore does not supply the simple answer to a simple question. Since he fails to have the answer that the teacher rewards, he may conclude that he is stupid or inadequate.

WHAT ARE TYPICAL CONCERNS REGARDING GIFTED YOUNG CHILDREN?

The information that a child has been identified as being gifted is not always welcomed by adults or even by the child. Teachers are sometimes intimidated by the news and fearful of the demands that may be made of them in terms of providing an appropriate education for the child. Teachers may lack specific information that would assist them in meeting the child's educational needs, and they may be uninformed regarding the social and emotional factors that must be considered in planning for the child. Teachers with little experience in educating gifted children may misinterpret a child's behavior. For example, at a meeting between the parents and the first-grade teacher of a gifted child, the teacher assured the parents that the child was being appropriately challenged in school. The parents reported that their daughter often complained that she was bored in school. The teacher countered with her observation that the child seldom participated in class, so she must not really know the material. When they got home, the parents asked their daughter about her reported lack of participation in class. She responded, "Well, I don't want the other kids to know that I know all of the answers. I do put up my hand when the teacher is really stuck, because I feel like I should help her out when no one else has the answer."

Schools that are already under fire for low performance in academic areas may not have the resources to devote to children who are already able to perform well on required state assessment tests. As school funding becomes increasingly problematic, programs for gifted children are among the first to go, thereby placing an increased burden on the classroom teacher.

Parents sometimes greet a diagnosis of giftedness with relief, as they may feel that there should be some explanation of their child's differences. Along with the information that the child is gifted, however, comes the expectation that somehow the child's educational experiences will improve. Unfortunately, this is not always the case, as school districts vary widely in their provisions for gifted children. This can lead to struggles between the school and the parents who advocate for their children. In many cases, the teachers and parents are in agreement regarding what would be best for the child, but the school administrators are unable to commit financial resources or are fearful of setting a precedent of service that they may not be able to provide for other gifted children.

Some parents, however, are upset by the news that their child is gifted, as they feel overwhelmed by the responsibility of raising a child who seems to be so different from anyone that they know. Many parents have little understanding of what giftedness really means and have heard some of the myths that surround giftedness. For example, on receiving the news of her 3-year-old child's high score on a screening test, a mother burst into tears because she believed that her child would grow up to be "weird" or "like Einstein." If parents are told that their child scored in the top 2% of the population, they may fear that they will need to send the child to a boarding school for very bright children.

Although to the uninitiated it might seem to be a blessing to be a gifted child, many children do not view their life experience as particularly lucky. Many will go to great lengths to camouflage their giftedness in order to "fit in" with their peers (Roedell, 1988). For example, one young gifted child who learned to read at an early age tried to hide this newfound skill from everyone. His mother overheard him confiding to his younger brother, saying, "It's not my fault that I can read, the words just keep jumping out at me!" This same child tried to conceal his reading abilities from his mother because he was afraid that she would stop reading aloud to him. He was, emotionally speaking, a young child who really enjoyed the closeness of the time that he spent each day sitting in his mother's lap as they shared books together.

HOW DO YOUNG GIFTED CHILDREN DEVELOP?

Gifted children sometimes demonstrate uneven development that can be problematic (Tolan, 1989). For example, gifted children often have interests that are unusual for their age. A 4-year-old who is interested in the Civil War is unlikely to find someone among his age mates who is interested in exploring this topic with him. Unfortunately, it is sometimes difficult to find reading material that is suitable for such a child and similarly difficult to find an adult who wants to discuss Civil War events with a young child.

Because of their advanced vocabulary skills and unusual interests, gifted children sometimes seem to be more mature than their age mates. In fact, since they spend so much time conversing with adults about their shared interests, these young gifted children may seem to be 4 years old, going on 40. This can lead to difficulties, as often there is a gap between their emotional development and their intellectual development that is not as obvious as is the difference between their physical and intellectual development.

There are many ways to describe the differential that may occur between the physical, intellectual, social, and emotional development of gifted children. Researchers have called this differential "internal dyssynchrony" and use the term to describe areas of development that are not "in sync" with other areas within a particular child (Callahan, 1997; Roedell, 1988). Internal dyssynchrony may be a significant problem for some gifted children, yet it is poorly understood and seldom addressed by parents or teachers. A young gifted child may be able to function intellectually at a much higher level than her age mates and thus finds that sometimes she needs to discuss ideas with older children or adults who share her interests. But if a 6-year-old child is able to read at the fourth grade level, it may be very inappropriate to place her in a fourth-grade class because of physical, social, and emotional factors.

The level of dyssynchrony varies with each individual and is felt more severely by highly gifted children. For example, the 7-year-old child who is interested in the war on terrorism and how it relates to his understanding of religion is likely to have difficulty engaging a classmate in a conversation of this type. On the other hand, he may not have the emotional development that would allow him to participate in viewing the CNN reports on this subject, so his information must come from secondary sources. This child may be very concerned about what he hears adults discussing but lack the social development to understand that this is not a topic that can be adequately addressed in school. With no one to help him make sense of this, the child may become frightened and withdrawn, unable to explore ideas that have captured his imagination.

One of the most important aspects of socialization for gifted children is having peers who share similar interests. Because of the dyssynchrony they experience, many gifted children will need several different peer groups. One group may satisfy their intellectual needs and be able to discuss topics of mutual interest. Another group may fit better emotionally, and yet a third group may be the social solution that the child needs. The gifted child may have to hide her intellectual ability from the social group and her emotional development from the intellectual group. This role-playing can be difficult for the young child to understand, and she will need to talk with understanding adults who can help her to cope.

Gifted children are sometimes teased about their abilities and interests. One of the most common strategies is for someone to ask a very difficult question of the child. If the gifted child admits that they do not know the answer, the person may respond, "What's the matter, you should know since you are so smart!" Such exchanges are bound to cause the gifted child to resolve that they will no longer appear to know the answers to anything, if that would be the way to avoid such cruel teasing. In this way, abilities that cause very bright children to be so out of step with their classmates can come to be regarded by the child a poor gift, indeed.

WHAT ARE THE IMPLICATIONS FOR TEACHING AND CURRICULUM?

Many people have criticized programs for gifted children on the grounds that providing programs for them is elitist, since the gifted and talented child already seems to have so much. Although it is certainly true that enrichment programs such as trips to the museum or the opera can and should be provided to all children who are interested in them and can benefit from them, it is equally true that gifted children deserve to learn something of value in school each and every day, just as we think all children should.

Gifted children are as different from the norm as are children with other special needs, and the range of abilities covered by the gifted label is wide. Gifted children are not necessarily gifted in all academic areas, either. The child who may absolutely zoom in math may be an average reader. Unfortunately, schools often attempt to treat gifted children as though they all possess the same strengths and weaknesses (Fiedler, 1993).

The curriculum in most schools is designed to meet the needs of the "average" student, so the assumption is made that most children benefit from that curriculum. However, many gifted children begin a school year having mastered most of the content that will be presented that year. Few schools provide routine pretesting of content mastery, so gifted children are expected to march in place for a large portion of their days, waiting for their classmates to grasp the material. This situation causes gifted children to waste much of their instructional time, unless their educational programs are modified to better meet their needs. Gifted children who are forced to waste much of their time in school sometimes resort to misbehavior in order to combat boredom. In addition, when schoolwork is always too easy, children do not learn how to study and are robbed of the opportunity to feel satisfaction in the accomplishment of a project that challenged them intellectually. Researchers have pointed out that when we reward children for doing tasks that are too easy, their self-esteem is not enhanced (Tomlinson, 1994).

For highly gifted children, the question of whether to provide acceleration or enrichment programs may come up very early in their schooling. Of course, the answer to this question is that both acceleration and enrichment should be provided as needed. According to Boatman, Davis, and Benbow, "the goal of acceleration is curricular flexibility or curricular access without regard to age" (1995, p. 1085). An appropriate education for gifted children is one that allows the learners to make progress at their own pace. Since one of the hallmarks of giftedness is an increased rate of acquisition, this means that children who are gifted and talented naturally accelerate themselves. Allowing a kindergarten child to have access to third-grade materials is appropriate if he is reading on the third-grade level and comprehending the content well.

If a young gifted child needs to receive modifications in the school program, it is important to explain to the child why this is being done. One young 6-year-old whom I met was upset when he was told that he had been chosen to attend the special class. He concluded that he must have fallen far behind his classmates if he needed so much special help.

One of the surest ways to foster an unrealistic view of the world is to isolate a gifted child in a classroom where he has no intellectual peers. It is very important for gifted children to interact with each other so they can see that they are not the only ones with lots of answers, lots of questions, and perhaps some unusual hobbies and interests.

One difficulty that is sometimes ignored is the problem of providing reading material of an appropriate social and emotional level for a precocious reader (Halstead, 1990). For example, a third grader who reads on the college level cannot be expected to read only the third-grade text and elementary level chapter books. But finding college-level novels that have an appropriate theme and content for a young child can be a challenge to teachers and parents. Young children should not be exposed to the inappropriate language and adult content that are so often found in popular literature. It is also essential that the child have someone with whom to discuss his reading, and this can be problematic. Gifted children have lots of time to read and often can read faster than the adults who are trying to keep up. Local reading groups seldom welcome a young gifted child since they may indulge in gossip or adult conversation along with their discussion of the book of the week. If a child has no one to share his reading with, it can reinforce his feelings of isolation and limit his understanding of the content.

One of the inappropriate solutions that are sometimes employed is giving children three books to read while the other students are only expected to read one. This is referred to as "more of the same, piled higher" and often serves to make gifted children feel that they are being punished for their ability, especially if all of the books are at an inappropriately low level. The curriculum needs to be modified to meet a gifted child's needs, and this can only be done by assessing the child's needs and carefully planning strategies and content that will allow her to interact with challenging and appropriately difficult materials.

In school, group work may be assigned with a mixed-ability group. Unfortunately, the gifted child sometimes ends up "carrying" the group. Even when gifted children resent this, they are often trapped because they do not want to receive a bad grade or disappoint the teacher or the other group members. Gifted children are often asked to teach other children. Within reason, this can be beneficial to both parties, but if the strategy is used excessively, it can lead to problems. For example, when does the gifted child get a chance to learn something new if his time is spent tutoring his classmates? Additionally, simply because someone has ability in a particular area or understands a concept does not mean that he will be able to teach it to classmates. Some children do not want to be viewed as the teacher's aide, or worse, the teacher's pet. The child is often asked to tutor others in an area of content in which he excels. If the gifted child's progress is hampered by too much time spent tutoring others, he may lose interest in the subject completely.

CONCLUSION

Parents and teachers need to develop a more complete understanding of the gifted child so that they can truly be helpful (Table I). Nurturing young gifted children requires sensitivity to the special challenges that gifted children face and a willingness to work together with other adults who are involved with the child. Adults must clearly define giftedness, understand how it develops in children, and recognize the impact that it has on curriculum and instruction. When all of this is in place, a gifted and talented child is not likely to say, as one 8-year-old did, "school must be made for someone else, because it just doesn't work for me."

Table I. How Can Teachers and Parents Help?

- View each gifted child as an individual. Make clear assessments of the child's social, emotional, physical, and educational needs.
- Group children according to ability, achievement, or interest. Flexible group strategies can be powerful tools in assisting children to find appropriate intellectual, social, and emotional peer groups.
- Guard against unrealistic and unfair expectations. Do not ignore the social and emotional development of the child when setting goals.
- Talk with children to discover their level of understanding regarding their giftedness. Children are not always able to articulate the reasons they do certain things.
- Ensure that the gifted child has intellectual peers who are also age mates.
- Encourage hobbies and interest. Mentors can be a wonderful help, as they can share their expertise in the area of interest.
- Remember that although children may interact with adults in a seemingly mature way, their emotional development may be more closely matched with that of their age mates.
- Make sure that the educational program is appropriate. Each gifted child needs to have an individual assessment and the curriculum needs to be modified in order to meet the child's needs.
- Do not expect the gifted child to spend too much time tutoring his classmates. All children need to be able to learn new things every day, not just repeat lessons already learned.
- Search out reading materials that are age appropriate as well as challenging, and make sure that the child has someone with whom to discuss his reading.

APPENDIX: RESOURCES FOR TEACHERS AND PARENTS

National Association for Gifted Children
http://www.nagc.org

American Association for Gifted Children
http://www.aagc.org/index.html

Hoagies Gifted Education Page
http://www.hoagiesgifted.org/

National Research Center on Gifted and Talented, University of Connecticut
http://www.gifted.uconn.edu

Gifted Development Center
http://www.gifteddevelopment.com

Gifted and Talented Resources
http://www.Gtworld.org/links.html

Center for Talent Development
Northwestern University
617 Dartmouth Place
Evanston, IL 60208
(847) 491-3782

The Council for Exceptional Children
1920 Association Drive
Reston, VA 22091-1589
(703) 620-3660

Gifted Child Society, Inc.
Ms. Gina Ginsberg Riggs, Ex. Dir.
190 Rock Rd.
Glen Rock, NJ 07452
(201) 444-6530

Institute for the Academic Advancement of Youth (IAAY)
Johns Hopkins University–IAAY
Office of Public Information
3400 N. Charles Street
Baltimore, MD 21218
(410) 516-0245

National Association for Gifted Children
Suite 550
1707 L Street, NW
Washington, DC 20036
(202) 785-4268

National Research Center on the Gifted and Talented
The University of Connecticut
2131 Hillside Road, Unit 3007
Storrs CT 06269-3007
(860) 486-4676

REFERENCES

Boatman, T. A., Davis, K. G., & Benbow, C. P. (1995). Best practices in gifted education. In A. Thomas & J. Grimes (Eds.), *Best practices in school psychology-III* (pp. 1083–1095). Washington, DC: The National Association of School Psychologists.

Callahan, C. M. (1997). Giftedness. In G. Bear, K. Minke, & A. Thomas (Eds.), *Children's needs II* (pp. 431–448). Bethesda, MD: National Association of School Psychologists.

Clark, B. (1997). *Growing up gifted* (5th edition). Upper Saddle River, NJ: Merrill.

Fiedler, E. (1993). Square pegs in round holes: Gifted kids who don't fit in. *Understanding Our Gifted, 5*(5A), 1, 11–14.

Halstead, J. W. (1990). *Guiding the gifted reader.* Reston, VA: ERIC Clearinghouse on Handicapped and Gifted Children.

Howley, C. B., Howley, A., & Pendarvis, E. D. (1995). *Out of our minds: Anti-intellectualism and talent development in American schooling.* New York: Teachers College Press.

Roedell, W. C. (1988). "I just want my child to be happy." Social development and young gifted children. *Understanding Our Gifted, 1*(1), 1, 7–11.

Tolan, S. S. (1989). Helping your highly gifted child (ERIC Digest #477). Reston, VA: ERIC Clearinghouse on Handicapped and Gifted Children. (ERIC Document Reproduction Service No. ED321482 90)

Tomlinson, C. A. (1994). The easy lie and the role of gifted education in school excellence. *Roeper Review, 16*(4), 258–259.

Jennifer V. Rotigel, Department of Professional Studies in Education, Indiana University of Pennsylvania.

Correspondence should be directed to Jennifer V. Rotigel, D.Ed., Professional Studies in Education, 312 Davis Hall, Indiana University of Pennsylvania, Indiana, PA 15705; e-mail: jrotigel@iup.edu.

From *Early Childhood Education Journal,* Summer 2003, pp. 209-214. © 2003 by Human Sciences Press.

Cultivating otherwise untapped potential

Psychologists are developing programs to identify gifted children earlier—and to ensure their success.

BY DEBORAH SMITH
Monitor staff

Psychologist Frank Worrell, PhD, has seen countless adolescents develop into highly talented college students in the Academic Talent Development Program at the University of California, Berkeley—a program that offers summer enrichment and acceleration classes to children in kindergarten through 11th grade. Students who struggle with introductory courses when they enter the program can earn As in the program's most difficult classes by the end, says Worrell, the program's lead researcher.

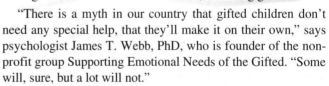

Dr. Frank Worrell is the lead researcher of the Academic Talent Development Program, which uses a broad range of assessments, such as teacher recommendations and work samples, to boost minority participation in its summer enrichment programs.

But that talent doesn't flourish on its own, he says: "People have talents in various areas, but if those talents aren't developed, they're not going to mean anything."

Without extra supports, many children with potential are left behind, agrees James Gallagher, PhD, professor emeritus at the University of North Carolina at Chapel Hill, who has written extensively on educating gifted children. "When you have a youngster brought up in poverty with no stimulation and little language development, you often will lose a youngster who might have been gifted," he explains. "With the proper environment and the proper education, you can increase the number of high-ability youngsters and adults."

Psychologists are working in schools and through their own independent programs to provide youth with that kind of environment. They're casting wide to find and nurture potentially gifted children and also increasing the achievement and creative productivity of exceptional performers, says Rena Subotnik, PhD, director of APA's Esther Katz Rosen Center for Gifted Education Policy.

"This second effort is viewed as more selective and elite, yet is also an essential component of gifted education," says Subotnik. The hope, she explains, is that students of all backgrounds will have equal access to the heights of talent development if schools do an effective job of nurturing potential talent.

However, some public schools' gifted supports are in danger, say psychologists in the field. In an era of mandated, high-stakes testing, schools with limited resources are being forced to focus on raising the scores of low performers—instead of on raising the achievement of all students, including gifted ones.

"There is a myth in our country that gifted children don't need any special help, that they'll make it on their own," says psychologist James T. Webb, PhD, who is founder of the nonprofit group Supporting Emotional Needs of the Gifted. "Some will, sure, but a lot will not."

"Students need to be in the right place at the right time. For some students, this means that high school would offer very little."

Nancy M. Robinson,
University of Washington

Indeed, gifted students may be teased for their abilities, hide their talents to avoid being singled out and have difficulty establishing true friendships. The problems arise when there is a mismatch between gifted students and the education system or family, says Webb. "There is really little inherent in being a gifted child that creates emotional problems," he explains.

Acceleration: Is moving ahead the right step?

When many people hear talk of a 15-year-old student heading to college, their gut reaction is to wonder how a teen could miss out on high school football games and dances, or how a teen could ever fit in with students so much older.

But some psychologists' research shows that acceleration—skipping grades or working ahead in a particular subject—can be one of the best methods to meet the needs of gifted youth. While not a panacea, acceleration gives students access to true peers and challenging work, say a number of experts.

"Students need to be in the right place at the right time," explains psychologist Nancy M. Robinson, PhD, of the University of Washington and former director of the Halbert and Nancy Robinson Center for Young Scholars. "For some students, this means that high school would offer very little."

However, many schools are hesitant to accelerate students out of concern for their emotional development. While research by Robinson and others finds accelerated students who receive appropriate support don't suffer adverse social or emotional effects from moving ahead, others note that most of this research has been conducted with gifted students who are already achieving—not underachieving or unidentified students. Indeed, says Robinson, students can struggle when they are accelerated without effective study habits, access to similarly talented peers and a supportive family or encouraging mentor, such as a teacher or counselor.

That's why acceleration decisions should be made on a case-by-case basis, say experts such as Susan Assouline, PhD, and Nick Colangelo, PhD, who have developed the Iowa Acceleration Scale, a tool to help parents and educators make such decisions.

For example, acceleration may not be right for a gifted student who is also a stand-out football player or isn't socially mature. And others may need acceleration in only one area, since many gifted children develop asynchronously.

Moreover, some caution against looking at acceleration as just moving ahead. Talented students—whether they skip grades, work ahead in one subject or stay with their peers—need enriching experiences, says Joseph S. Renzulli, EdD, director of the University of Connecticut's National Research Center on the Gifted and Talented.

"It's not just how far and fast one can run," he explains, "but rather what one can do to apply the material that one has learned in an environment that allows them to generate hypotheses, gather data, to write a play, poem or song."

But gifted students who don't receive some kind of enrichment—whether it's acceleration or a supplemental program—are less likely to excel. For instance, many gifted children spend 25 to 50 percent of class time waiting for other students to catch up. To make up for the boredom, gifted students may engage in self-stimulating behavior, such as counting their teeth with their tongue, tapping a foot or entertaining themselves by distracting other students—actions that look like problem behaviors to a teacher.

"From the child's point of view, it's an attempt to make an unendurable situation endurable," explains psychologist James T. Webb, PhD, founder of the nonprofit group Supporting Emotional Needs of the Gifted. "The very characteristics that make these children what they are—curiosity, advanced intellect, intensity, sensitivity—can become problems at school or at home if they're not understood."

When teachers, parents and even mental health professionals mistake common attributes of giftedness for social and emotional problems, students can end up with misdiagnoses of attention-deficit hyperactivity disorder, Asperger's disorder oppositional-disorder and other problems, instead of an enriching education, says Webb.

And boredom has other consequences. If gifted students never meet a challenge in school, they may not develop the coping skills necessary to persevere through challenges later in life, notes Paula Olszewski-Kubilius, PhD, director of the Center for Talent Development at Northwestern University.

—D. SMITH

Who is gifted?

Because the school environment plays such a key role in fulfilling the potential of gifted students, many psychologists are looking for different ways to identify talented students.

"We need to start working at the kindergarten level to start, in fact, preparing kids well so that those who do have potential gifts actually get those gifts developed sufficiently," says Worrell, who is also an associate school psychology professor at Penn State University.

For example, since an academic-achievement gap between whites and minorities still exists, Worrell's program recruits

youth from traditionally under-represented groups using a broad range of criteria: test scores, teacher recommendations, grades, interest inventories and a work sample of the student's choice, such as a short story.

Other psychologists are advocating for different kinds of tests to identify gifted students. For example, Jack Naglieri, PhD, of George Mason University, has developed tests to measure nonverbal reasoning ability without the influence of achievement or knowledge. Children who speak English as a second language or don't have the benefit of educated parents can still be smart, he reasons, but because they're not knowledgeable, they are often overlooked for gifted programs.

APA President Robert J. Sternberg, PhD, is studying how measures of creative and practical thinking, such as writing cartoon captions and doing practical math, in addition to the SAT, predict college students' success. He and his colleagues at Yale University have found that the tests predict freshman-year performance substantially better than the SAT alone, and also close the gap between ethnic groups.

Such efforts to close the gap are critical, many say, because gifted programs are taking a hit over diversity concerns. The reductions could be felt all the more sharply in the current economic climate as financial pressures will force many middle-class gifted children from more challenging private programs back into public school, say Subotnik and Nancy M. Robinson, PhD, professor emerita at the University of Washington and former director of the Halbert and Nancy Robinson Center for Young Scholars.

"Programs for gifted kids are being dropped or weakened in many cases because [they are] in many cases over-weighted with white and Asian middle-class-and-above kids," says Robinson. "But the fault doesn't lie with the programs nor with those kids. It lies within our society and the burdens that are put on families who don't have financial resources or who are marginalized."

The concern, say psychologists, is that children and adolescents who have great potential—whether they're unidentified minority students or attending a school that's cutting gifted programs—will flounder without support.

Gifted students with disabilities are especially at risk. It's not uncommon for these "multiexceptional" youth to be passed over for both gifted and academic support programs because their talents and disabilities often mask each other, says school psychologist Ron Palomares, PhD, of APA's Practice Directorate. For example, a girl's learning disability hides her math talent, and the math talent compensates for her learning disability—so she gets passing, but mediocre, math grades.

"To receive services, there has to be an education need, and when the issues are masked, they go without help," Palomares explains.

Developing talents

Because gifted students are a diverse group with varying needs, experts in the field agree that there's no one way to help them flourish.

"We need to be much more explicit about examining the individual child and his or her needs, and then structuring program services around those needs," says Richard Olenchak, PhD, president-elect of the National Association for Gifted Children and director of the Urban Talent Research Institute at the University of Houston. The institute's research has found

that gifted students' social and emotional adjustment is moderately correlated with whether they receive personalized program opportunities.

Psychologists are also working with educators and parents to provide gifted youth with a host of options that will develop their particular skills and abilities. Besides advanced placement courses, online classes and magnet schools, many students can enroll concurrently in a local community college or university. The program Worrell helps run at Berkeley offers students intensive summer programs and access to the university's libraries and laboratories.

Other programs provide students with year-round academics, substituting for all or part of high school and sending adolescents to college at 15 or 16 years old. For example, the Center for Talent Development at Northwestern University, directed by psychologist Paula Olszewski-Kubilius, PhD, supplements students' high school coursework by offering intensive courses that pack a typical year's worth of material into several weeks.

Mentoring from experts is another option. APA's Center for Gifted Education Policy teams talented adolescents with top thinkers in an array of fields, from music to psychology, through its Pinnacle Project and Young Scholars Social Science Summit. The programs also provide students with an opportunity to meet similarly talented peers.

"Kids who don't have access to true peers, particularly among the highly gifted, tend to have significant ongoing problems," says Montana clinical child psychologist Maureen Neihart, PhD, explaining that gifted children need interaction with others who share the same interests, abilities and drive—qualities they seldom find in 'normal' same-age peers.

FURTHER READING

- Friedman, R.C., & Rogers, K.B. (1998). *Talent in context: Historical and social perspectives on giftedness.* Washington, DC: American Psychological Association.
- Friedman, R.C., & Shore, B. (2000). *Talents unfolding: Cognition and development.* Washington, DC: American Psychological Association.
- Heller, K.A., Mönks, F.J., Sternberg, R.J., & Subotnik, R.F. (Eds.). (2000). *International handbook of giftedness and talent* (2nd ed.). Oxford, United Kingdom: Pergamon.
- Horowitz, F.D., & O'Brien, M. (Eds.). (1985). *Gifted and talented: Developmental perspectives.* Washington, DC: American Psychological Association.
- Neihart, M., Reis, S.M., Robinson, N.M., & Moon, S.M. (2002). *The social and emotional development of gifted children.* Waco, TX: Prufrock Press.

From *Monitor on Psychology*, May 2003, pp. 62-64. © 2003 by the American Psychological Association.

Gifted Students Need an Education, Too

Gifted children have the right to an education that takes into account their special needs. Here are suggestions for how to provide it.

Susan Winebrenner

Math time is beginning in Kate Ahlgren's primary grade classroom. Her objective is to teach several concepts relating to the base 10 method of counting and computing. Her first task is to assess her students' previous mastery of these concepts. She plans to allow those students who already have a clear understanding of this week's work to spend their math time applying what they have mastered about base 10 to learning about base 5.

Kate conducts a hands-on assessment by giving all students several tasks to complete with Cuisenaire rods. As she directs students to demonstrate what happens when they count past 10, she watches specifically for students who complete each directed task quickly and correctly. Fifteen minutes later, she has identified four children who clearly need more challenging content for the rest of this week's math work. She assigns a base 10 application task for most of the students to complete with partners and takes those four youngsters aside to briefly teach them the essential elements of base 5.

The four students practice excitedly for a few minutes under Kate's supervision. She explains that they will be working together for the rest of this week on learning about base 5 because that will challenge them. She assures them that all students should be working on challenging learning tasks.

Kate gives the four advanced students several tasks similar to those she has demonstrated. They practice together while she works with the rest of the students for the duration of the math period. Just before her instruction ends, she explains to the whole class that they will notice that not all students are working on the same tasks in math. She reassures them that this is perfectly all right and that her job is to make sure that all students are working on tasks that will help them move forward in their own learning. In this way, Kate makes differentiation the normal and acceptable condition of her classroom. She

knows that when her students know something is all right with her, it will generally be all right with them, too.

Differentiated learning for high-ability students in heterogeneous classrooms is as important as it is for other children, yet the needs of the gifted are often misunderstood. Here are reasons why and suggestions for how teachers and administrators can differentiate the prescribed grade-level curriculum to meet the needs of high-ability students.

Why Provide Differentiated Learning for Gifted Students?

For the past 10 years, students who were not learning successfully were targeted for special attention. Sadly, during that same time, the needs of our most capable students have been overlooked. One reason for this neglect is the ability of gifted students to score high on assessments, which has led to the erroneous assumption that they must be learning. Another reason for ignoring their needs is that many educational leaders have misunderstood research on role modeling to mean that some gifted students should be present in all classrooms to facilitate forward progress for other students. Although students who struggle to learn can benefit from mixed-ability classes, they have plenty of positive role models in students who function well at the appropriate grade level, who are capable but not gifted learners. The discrepancy in learning ability between students who struggle to learn and gifted students is simply too wide to facilitate positive role modeling (Schunk, 1987).

Consider the range of abilities present in most classrooms. Visualize that both extremes of a learning curve are equally far removed from the norm. Students who fail to achieve the designated standards have received unprecedented attention during the past several years. They are identified for special services before they start kindergarten, experience lower student-teacher ratios, and may even have a full-time aide assigned to them for the entire school day. School districts spend much more money educating this population than they designate for the usual per-pupil expenditure.

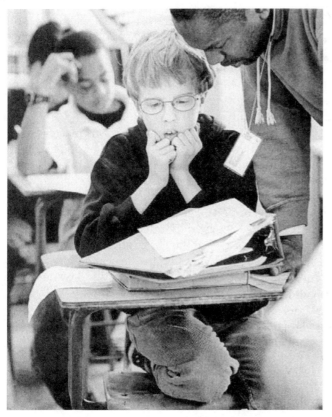

© SUSIE FITZHUGH

Teachers are expected to create numerous differentiation adjustments for low-achieving students by modifying the amount of work, depth, complexity, and content of the curriculum and by linking students' learning styles and interests to the prescribed learning tasks. Politicians, community members, and teachers avidly follow the progress of these students' learning for evidence that these students are indeed moving forward.

Contrast this with the situation for gifted students, whose natural learning abilities place them as far from average as their classmates who struggle to learn. In September, many of these youngsters could take the assessments that all students in their grade will take at the end of the year and still score at or above the 95th percentile. Simply in the interests of equity, these students are as entitled to receive the same types of differentiation so readily provided to the students who struggle to learn.

To assume that gifted students are learning because they achieve acceptable standards on state assessments is unrealistic. In Colorado, Oregon, and several other states,

educators have realized that the learning progress of gifted students cannot be adequately measured simply because the students meet or exceed minimum standards, so these states have specified learning expectations at exemplary levels. By setting exemplary standards, they can document the learning progress of gifted students.

Does the Promise of Education for All Apply to Gifted Students?

Every school district's mission statement promises its parents that "[a]ll students, including those who are exceptional, are entitled to a public-supported education in which instruction is geared to their needs, interests, and developmental levels" (Reis, Burns, & Renzulli, 1992, p. 3). Unfortunately, those at greatest risk of learning the least in classrooms are those at the top range of ability. Because a sense of confidence comes primarily from being successful at something perceived to be difficult (Rimm, 1990), gifted students who rarely undergo demanding learning experiences may lose confidence in their ability to perform well on challenging learning tasks. Many of these students learn to find the easiest way out, postponing their exposure to challenge in many patterns of underachievement (Rimm, 1990; Schmitz & Galbraith, 1985).

Either we must explain to parents that the promise of the school's mission statement does not apply to high-ability students, or we must commit ourselves to providing these students with appropriate and differentiated learning experiences. Whatever has been designated as suitable for students who are learning at a level commensurate with their age is not equally appropriate for students who learn at levels more typical of students several years older.

What Are the Characteristics and Needs of Gifted Students?

Gifted students learn differently from their classmates in at least five important ways. They learn new material in much less time. They tend to remember what they have learned, making spiral curriculums and reviewing previously mastered concepts a painful experience. They perceive ideas and concepts at more abstract and complex levels than do their peers. They become passionately interested in specific topics and have difficulty moving on to other learning tasks until they feel satisfied that they have learned as much as they possibly can about their passionate interest. Finally, gifted students are able to operate on many levels of concentration simultaneously, so they can monitor classroom activities without paying direct or visual attention to them.

Gifted students have already mastered much of the grade-level work, so they should have opportunities to function at more advanced levels of complexity and depth and to tie their own passionate interests into their schoolwork.

Why Are Many Educators Reluctant to Help Gifted Students?

Many teachers are reluctant to facilitate the needs of gifted students because of the lack of teacher training in this type of differentiation, a concern that other students or parents will accuse them of unfairness, or their belief that providing differentiation for this population is elitist.

Most preservice teachers take at least one course about meeting the needs of special–education students, but few states require teachers to take any courses in how to recognize and teach gifted students. Many teachers assume that gifted kids are highly productive, always complete their work on time, get consistently high grades, and will make it on their own without much assistance. Many educators believe that a student who is unproductive in school could not possibly be gifted.

Such misconceptions about how gifted students do their work are sources of great frustration for the students, their parents, and their teachers. Most teachers in my workshops are surprised when I tell them that gifted students often resist doing their assigned work because it is designed for age-appropriate learners and usually cannot provide the challenge and sense of accomplishment that would keep gifted learners motivated to work.

Another part of the problem is confusion about whether the mandated goals must actually be *taught* to students. Realistically, teachers are only required to demonstrate that all their students have *learned* the designated standards. Students who have already mastered the required content should be allowed to demonstrate their mastery before test-preparation sessions begin and to work on alternative activities because they already know the required content. When teachers learn how to plan and provide these alternative activities routinely to students who demonstrate prior mastery, these students can make progress in their own learning during more of their time in school.

How Can Teachers Provide Differentiation for Gifted Students?

The typical approach to differentiation for gifted students in heterogeneous classes has been to offer extra credit, an expectation that doesn't work because the only students eligible for extra credit are those who often have more than enough earned credit. The practice of offering extra credit should be replaced with approaches that can motivate gifted students to become enthusiastic learners.

Compact the curriculum. The most important needs of gifted students are to have regular opportunities to demonstrate what they already know, to receive full credit for

content they have already mastered, and to spend their own learning time on challenging activities that accelerate and enrich the regular curriculum (Reis, Burns, & Renzulli, 1992). Compacting the curriculum can answer these needs.

To ascertain who would benefit from a compacted curriculum for a specific topic, teachers will want to provide interested students with pre-assessment opportunities for all learning activities. Teachers should use the same methods of assessment that they plan to use at the end of a learning unit, including written tests or observed performance on designated tasks. Because the preassessment is open to all students, the learning task itself can identify those who could benefit from the specific differentiated tasks regardless of whether particular students have been designated as gifted.

Students who can demonstrate previous mastery of upcoming content are expected to pay attention to direct instruction only when instruction includes concepts they have not yet mastered. On days when the lesson content is based on what these students have already mastered, they work instead on extension activities provided by the teacher or suggested by the students themselves. They receive full credit for what they have already mastered and earn daily credit for following the teacher's expectations about on-task behavior and productivity and by developing alternative projects and activities.

Design alternative learning experiences. As part of their regular lesson planning, teachers design alternative learning experiences. These provide differentiation opportunities in terms of *content, learning processes, products, learning environment*, and *assessment*.

The *content* is different because it moves students beyond grade-level standards or is connected to students' passionate interests. The *learning processes* called upon are different because they provide depth and complexity appropriate to these students' learning abilities. *Products* differ in that they demonstrate the students' learning at advanced levels, moving beyond typical research activities to the development of individual students' talents and curiosities and the presentation of their findings to appropriate audiences. Sometimes the *learning environment* is also different; students may pursue interests outside the regular classroom, work more independently on self-directed projects, or collaborate with other students. Even the *assessment process* is different because students receive full credit for what they have already mastered and do not have to complete all the work assigned to the rest of the class.

One particularly striking opportunity to provide alternative learning experiences presented itself when I discovered that James, one of my exceptionally gifted 6th graders, was writing a book at home on the anatomy and physiology of the human body. I pretested him and other interested students at the beginning of all language arts, reading, and writing units. James experienced differentiation in *content* because he wrote his book in class, in *learning processes* because he used sophisticated writing techniques, and in *assessment* because his grades for each unit were earned at the time of the pretest rather than at the end of the unit, with an overall grade that included an evaluation of his on-task behavior and project.

Allow differentiated pacing. For a curriculum that cannot be assessed beforehand because it is unfamiliar to all, gifted students work at their own pace to learn the required concepts and spend more time developing an expertise on a related topic of their choice.

Agree on expectations. Teachers and students work together to set up standards for evaluating productivity, behavior, and differentiated products and then agree to these standards in writing. Teachers should arrange to spend time with these students. It is important that gifted students not feel abandoned by the teacher and that they learn that everyone needs help on challenging tasks.

What Can Administrators Do to Facilitate Differentiation for Gifted Students?

Acknowledge the needs of gifted students. Acknowledge that the precedent for differentiation has been firmly set by the differentiation opportunities always available for students who struggle to learn. Because gifted learners are just as far removed from average as are children with learning problems, the differentiation that gifted students need is highly defensible and equitable.

Facilitate gifted education training for staff. Any strategies teachers learn for the benefit of their gifted students are applicable to many other students and tend to raise the learning bar for all students. One strategy, for example, is to allow students to get credit for an entire assignment by answering correctly at least four of the five most difficult problems first. This challenge motivates many students to listen more carefully to instructions so they can also qualify.

Investigate cluster grouping. Look into the practice of cluster grouping for gifted students. Cluster grouping is the practice of purposefully placing four to six gifted students together in an otherwise heterogeneous class. Their teacher must have some training in how to differentiate the curriculum for students who demonstrate previous mastery or who can learn new content faster than their classmates. Studies have demonstrated that cluster grouping can lead to improved achievement for many

students at all levels of learning ability (Gentry, 1999; Winebrenner & Devlin, 1996).

Communicate your expectations. Make clear your pledge that all students, including the most capable, will be able to learn something new and challenging every day. Clarify your commitment to the goal that all students will be expected to make continuous progress in their own learning. To that end, expect gifted students to demonstrate competencies that exceed those designated as basic.

Keep the Promise

Parents of gifted learners have a right to expect that schools will fulfill the promise made to all students that children will have consistent and daily opportunities for challenging learning experiences and will demonstrate continuous forward progress in their learning. This expectation requires providing gifted students with differentiation of the regular curriculum. To complacently accept their performance at regular competency levels is to deny their equal right to an appropriate education.

References

Gentry, M. L. (1999). *Promoting student achievement and exemplary classroom practices through cluster grouping: A research-based alternative to heterogeneous elementary classrooms.* Storrs, CT: National Research Center on the Gifted and Talented.

Reis, S. M., Burns, D. E., & Renzulli, J. S. (1992). *Curriculum compacting: The complete guide to modifying the regular curriculum for high ability students.* Mansfield Center, CT: Creative Learning Press.

Rimm, S. (1990). *How to parent so children will learn.* Watertown, WI: Apple Publishing.

Schunk, D. H. (1987). Peer models and children's behavioral change. *Review of Educational Research, 57,* 149–174.

Schmitz, C., & Galbraith, J. (1985). *Managing the social and emotional needs of the gifted.* Minneapolis, MN: Free Spirit Publishing.

Winebrenner, S., & Devlin, B. (1996). *Cluster grouping of gifted students: How to provide full-time services on a part-time budget.* Reston, VA: ERIC Clearinghouse on Disabilities and Gifted Education (ERIC Digest Document Reproduction Service No. 397618).

Susan Winebrenner is an educational consultant and author of *Teaching Gifted Kids in the Regular Classroom* (Free Spirit Publishing, 2000). She may be reached at P.O. Box 398, Brooklyn, MI 49230–0398 (e-mail: ecsfirst @aol.com)

Educational Leadership, September 2000, pp. 52–56. © 2000 by the Association for Supervision and Curriculum Development. All rights reserved. Reprinted by permission.

UNIT 11
Transition

Unit Selections

Key Points to Consider

- What are some of the collaborative efforts needed to help students with severe disabilities make the transition from a sheltered setting to the outside world?

- What·services are needed to make the transition smoother from high school to postsecondary programs for students with disabilities?

- What are the eight curricular components of a self-determination curriculum?

 Links: www.dushkin.com/online/
These sites are annotated in the World Wide Web pages.

Building Partnerships Between Centers for Independent Living and Schools
http://cdrc.ohsu.edu/csd1/home/Projects_at_the_Center/Networks/BUILDING_PARTNERSHIPS

National Center on Secondary Education and Transition
http://www.ncset.org

Special educational services are now required by law for students from the completion of their public school education through age 21 if they have a diagnosed condition of disability. The U.S. Individuals with Disabilities Education Act (IDEA), when it was reauthorized in 1997, made transitional services mandatory. These additional benefits for students with exceptional conditions are to help them transfer from their relatively protected life as students into the more aggressive world of work, driven by forces such as money and power. The services that the educational system needs to give to students with disabilities to help them prepare for the world of work start with an assessment of their interests, abilities, and aptitudes for different types of work. Career counseling about what they need to do to prepare for such employment, and its feasibility, comes next. Counselors must remember to allow students to dream, to think big, and to have optimistic visions of themselves. They also need to inculcate the idea that persistence pays: It takes a lot of little steps to achieve a goal.

The implementation of transitional services has been slow. The U.S. government defined transitional services as outcome-oriented, coordinated activities designed to move students with disabilities from school to activities such as college, vocational training, integrated employment, supported employment, adult education, adult services, independent living, and community participation. Choices are not either/or but rather multiple: to help students with disabilities move from school to successful adulthood. While some students may only be able to achieve partial independence and supported employment, others may achieve professional degrees and complete self-sufficiency.

Every student with a disability should have an individualized transition plan (ITP) added to his or her individualized education plan (IEP) by age 16, the upper limit for beginning transition planning. Transitional services are more difficult to design than educational plans because of the nearly unlimited possibilities for the rest of one's life compared to the defined academic subjects it is possible to learn while in school.

The first step is to determine an appropriate individualized transition plan (ITP) for each unique student. Many teachers, special educators, vocational counselors, and employment mentors (job coaches) are not sure what kind of vocational preparation should be given in the public schools or when. Should children with disabilities start planning for their futures in elementary school, in middle school, in high school, throughout their education, or just before they finish school? Should there be a trade-off between academic education and vocational education for these students? Should each student's vocational preparation be planned to meet the kind of needs and abilities of the individual, with no general rules about the wheres and whens of transitional services? Should students with disabilities be encouraged to seek out postsecondary education? The choices are legion. The need to rule out some possibilities and select others is frightening. Nobody on a team wants to make a mistake. Often the preferences of the student are quite different from the goals of parents, teachers, counselors, or significant others. Compromises are necessary but may not please everyone, or anyone.

The transition to the world of work may take the form of supported employment (mobile work crew, clustered or enclave placement, on-site training and supervision by a job coach, group providing a specific service product) or sheltered employment (in a workshop). Many students with disabilities can make a transition from school to competitive employment. If they will eventually work side-by-side with nondisabled coworkers, they may need transitional services such as assertiveness training, conflict resolution, negotiating skills, and personal empowerment counseling.

Just a few years ago, adults with disabilities were expected to live in institutions or with parents, siblings, or extended family members. This is no longer considered appropriate. Each individual with a disability should be encouraged to be as autonomous as possible in adulthood. Self-sufficiency is enhanced by providing education in life skills such as meal preparation and cleanup, home deliveries (for example, mail) and delivery pickups (for example, trash), using money and paying bills, making household repairs, and following home safety precautions.

The transition from noncommunity participant to fully participating member of society requires ITP modifications quite different from IEP academic goals. Students with exceptional conditions may need more than the usual amount of assistance in learning to drive a car or to use public transportation. They need to know how to read maps and schedules. They must be able to assert their right to vote in secret (for instance, ballot in braille or computerized for their software) and to marry, divorce, reproduce, sue, defend themselves, or even run for public office. They should know social conventions (greetings, conversation skills, manners), grooming fashions, and clothing styles. They deserve to have the same access to health settings, religious locales, social activities, and information services (telephone, television, computer networks) as do persons without disabilities.

The first article in this unit offers insights into the collaborative efforts required of administrators, staff, regular and special education teachers, employment specialists, and students with severe disabilities. The authors emphasize the need for rigorous employment-training programs. Students who lack communication skills and academic skills pose special challenges. The development of partnerships with potential employers of disabled students in the area surrounding the school can make each ITP voyage a smoother sail.

In the second article, Jean Lehmann, Timothy Gray Davies, and Kathleen Laurin report on the transition needs of students with disabilities who go on to postsecondary institutions. Thirty-five such students attended a summit to discuss what would best meet their requirements in higher education. The ideas expressed most frequently were for more understanding of their disabilities, more services, more financial resources, and more self-advocacy training.

The last article in this transition unit deals with self-determination. This is one of the most important considerations for any ITP, yet one that is often forgotten as experts (parents, teachers, counselors, and so on) debate what would be most appropriate for a student with a disability. This selection describes a project whose goal was to promote each student's self-determination.

Transition Planning for Students with Severe Disabilities:

Policy Implications for the Classroom

CHRISTY HOLTHAUS STUART AND STEPHEN W. SMITH

The reauthorization of the Individuals with Disabilities Education Act Amendments (IDEA, 1997) is the cornerstone for disability legislation entitling students to a free appropriate public education. Within the law, students with disabilities are afforded an Individualized Education Program (IEP) that provides an appropriate education in the least restrictive environment. The reauthorization of IDEA included several specific components addressing transition issues (e.g., career planning, job training, functional skill development) beginning at age 14 for students receiving special education services. The transition components for students with disabilities included (a) a coordinated set of activities (e.g., real work experience) specific to the individual, (b) activities for movement from school to postschool environments (e.g., supported employment, adult services), (c) assessment of students' individual needs, (d) identification of student preferences and interests, and (e) development of employment objectives.

The IDEA transition components are intended for all students with disabilities; however, some professionals may disregard students with more severe disabilities, such as profound mental retardation and deaf-blindness. Under the Rehabilitation Act (1973), when students with severe disabilities leave school, they are entitled to continued services for supported living and employment services. The Rehabilitation Act promotes individuals with severe disabilities and their rights to gainful employment. Specifically, the Act defines *a person with a severe disability* as an individual whose ability to function independently in family or community or whose ability to become gainfully employed is limited due to the severity of his or her disability. Both the IDEA and the Rehabilitation Act are equally important in providing support, such as supported employment and educational training programs, for individuals with disabilities, yet for individuals with severe disabilities there continue to be significant problems.

Individuals with severe disabilities have unique learning characteristics, such as difficulty in generalizing learned skills to new work situations. Further, individuals with more significant disabilities learn more slowly, which in turn means that they learn less and have difficulty generalizing learned skills to other settings, putting together isolated activities that make a skill, and maintaining what they have learned over time (Ryndak & Alper, 1996). These learning characteristics may lead some people to believe that persons with severe disabilities are incapable of learning necessary job skills. Consequently, persons with severe disabilities are caught in a difficult cycle. They have difficulty learning the job skills, resulting in perceptions of being incapable of successful employment, which causes them to be further stigmatized and reduces the possibility that employers will hire them. Despite the legislative support that has evolved over the years, outcome data such as long-term employment continue to show poor results for individuals with severe disabilities.

Educator's General Role

Teachers of secondary students with severe disabilities play a significant role in developing and implementing effective transition plans to help students plan for the future and obtain gainful employment. For example, a student may indicate that following school, he or she wishes to live in an apartment with friends and have a job that involves sports. The student's interests can be gathered from a variety of sources, such as student, parents, and family members, and used as a stepping stone to prepare the student for the skills necessary to achieve future goals. Specifically, exposing the student to a variety of sport jobs (e.g., greeter/usher using a communication device or an equipment manager paired with a peer) and encouraging the student to develop goals assists the student in eventually maintaining employment and living as independently as possible. Because of poor outcomes, such as low full-time employment rates, and decreased competitive wages and hours, policymakers need knowledge and direction from practitioners at the implementation level (i.e., school-based vocational programs) to compose effective policies that, in turn, promote effective practice.

Promoting Employment Skills Through Transition Planning

Secondary educators must do their part in facilitating a meaningful transition for their students with severe disabilities to create a link between school setting services and services provided in the postschool employment setting. McDonnell, Mathot-Buckner, and Ferguson (1996) emphasized the need for an effective and rigorous

202

employment-training program that would identify the skills students need to participate successfully in the postschool employment setting. Students need

- work experience and work-related behaviors,
- work interests and preferences, and
- supports necessary to ensure success in employment settings.

Because common work and work-related behaviors are necessary for success in every job, the goal for every student during high school is to develop employment skills (e.g., manage one's time, stay on task, complete step-by-step directions), communicate effectively, demonstrate social and interpersonal skills, and tend to personal hygiene. The behaviors that accompany the skills are paired with a successful transition for the student with disabilities.

Employment training must incorporate a job sampling process that provides students with the basis for determining their work interests and preferences. Exposure to a wide range of employment options is a key component for the future job matching process (Chadsey-Rusch & Heal, 1995). Students with severe disabilities who may lack adequate communication and academic skills pose a special challenge because the information traditionally gathered (student interests and preferences) regarding career alternatives must be gathered from sources other than the student (e.g., parents, peers, service coordinators from agencies).

Identifying the nature and amount of supports depends on the individual needs of the student, but coordinating the supports to be as least restrictive as possible is the challenge. During the employment-training phase, a variety of supports can be tested. For example, a student with severe disabilities may respond more effectively with supports from a peer rather than a paraprofessional. This information may be used for future interactions with service agencies that use peers on the job versus job coaches from an agency.

Obtaining meaningful employment is crucial to the successful transition of students from school to community/employment life. This outcome is achieved most effectively when an educational program is designed to develop skills and routines that better prepare individuals with disabilities for life after school. It is up to secondary educators to develop and implement meaningful training programs that equip their students with skills and prepare them for employment and community involvement outside the educational arena. Several guidelines are recommended for secondary education teachers to follow while developing individual transition programs:

- Promote individual choice and self-determination activities (e.g., self-directed IEPs);
- include a variety of participants who have contact with the student (special education and general education) in the development of the transition IEP;
- develop partnerships with community establishments and potential job training or employment sites;
- extend agency collaboration as part of the transition process;

- make significant changes to traditional prevocational training programs to include job training in natural work environments and to include all students, especially those with the most severe disabilities in the program; and
- incorporate placement models at the secondary level to ease the transition to postschool employment activities (individual placement model, clustered placement model, mobile crew model, and the entrepreneurial model).

Summary

The increase in responsibility for educators to collaborate and develop effective transition plans should also empower educators to become stakeholders in the transition process (Kohler, 1998). As stakeholders, the secondary educators should be encouraged to

- participate in program-level planning;
- serve on curriculum development teams;
- participate in teacher or family training, technical assistance, and staff development activities; and
- play a role in strategic planning and resource allocation.

Although transition planning is to be included on a student's IEP, all professionals, otherwise known as stakeholders (general education teachers, special education teachers, transition specialists, employment specialists), need to be prepared to participate in an ongoing process that begins in secondary schools and continues in the postschool environment. This process needs to be collaborative in nature. Feedback from stakeholders proves to be an effective tool in making changes or improvements to current practices. The expertise of those individuals at the grass roots level, in this case the educators themselves, should prove to be a source of knowledge and information that will drive best practice in transition planning.

References

Chadsey-Rusch, J., & Heal, L. (1995). Building consensus from transition experts on social integration outcomes and interventions. *Exceptional Children, 62(3)*, 165–187.

Individuals with Disabilities Education Act Amendments of 1997, 20 U.S.C. § 1401 (26).

Kohler, P. D. (1998). Implementing a transition perspective of education. In F. R. Rusch & J. G. Chadsey (Eds.), *Beyond high school: Transition from school to work* (pp. 179–205). Boston: Wadsworth.

McDonnell, J., Mathot-Buckner, C., & Ferguson, B. (1996). *Transition programs for students with moderate/severe disabilities.* Baltimore: Brookes.

Rehabilitation Act of 1973, 29 U.S.C. § 701 *et seq.*

Ryndak, D. L., & Alper, S. (1996). *Curriculum content for students with moderate and severe disabilities in inclusive settings.* Boston: Allyn & Bacon.

Christy Holthaus Stuart, MS, is a doctoral candidate in the Department of Special Education at the University of Florida. **Stephen W. Smith**, PhD, is a professor in the Department of Special Education at the University of Florida. Address: Christy Holthaus Smart, Dept. of Special Education, G315 Norman Hall, University of Florida, Gainesville, FL 32611.

From *Intervention in School and Clinic*, March 2002, pp. 234–236. © 2002 by The Council for Exceptional Children. Reprinted by permission.

Listening to Student Voices About Postsecondary Education

Jean P. Lehmann • Timothy Gray Davies • Kathleen M. Laurin

Every year an increasing number of students with disabilities enter postsecondary education. Many of these students fail to successfully compete academically or simply leave before they complete their planned programs of study (Fairweather & Shaver, 1991; Wagner, 1989). In an effort to change the status quo, one community college and a university school of education program formed a collaborative support team to:

- Identify and systematically eliminate barriers to postsecondary education.
- Improve students' potential for having successful postsecondary experiences.

"Aiming for the Future," the project described here, is housed in a Midwestern community college in a rural area.

Using a systems-change model borrowed from Fullan (1993) that emphasizes the importance of listening to and acting on the ideas expressed by those most likely to be affected by change efforts, the collaborative support team sought information from the students' perspective. We asked students with disabilities currently attending postsecondary programs at the community college and university what they felt they needed to succeed. The process used to elicit these students' perceptions and ideas, which resulted in plans developed by the support team, is the focus of this article.

A Summit on "Aiming for the Future"

We invited 35 college students with a variety of disabilities—including hearing impairment, deafness, low vision, blindness, learning disabilities, traumatic brain injury, cerebral palsy, and paraplegia and quadriplegia—to attend a half-day focus group, which we called a *summit*. We asked the students to give us their perspectives on their personal and academic needs, barriers to their success, their support needs, and their visions for their future.

Using a nonthreatening group process designed to elicit a wealth of information in a short time, we ran-domly placed the students in seven groups of five people each. We then asked each group to discuss questions aimed at helping students identify the barriers they have experienced as they attempt to successfully complete their educational and career goals. Students considered barriers encountered with admissions, financial assistance, and classes. They were asked to answer the following three questions:

- What are the most substantial barriers to your college experience?
- Are there special problems for students whose disability is not identified until posthigh school?
- What problems are encountered when making the transition from one college/university setting to another or into a job?

As students discussed their experiences, it became evident that the first question was central to understanding the realities and hopes of students receiving postsecondary training. Students perceived similar problems regardless of when their disability was identified, their year in college, or if they had entered the job market.

Next, we asked students to browse through magazines we placed on their table and select pictures representing barriers to their success in their current postsecondary institutions. We also asked them to select a second group of pictures representing strategies to support them in reaching their academic and career goals. Finally, we asked them to arrange these pictures to form a collage communicating their thoughts and ideas. Each group chose a spokesperson who interpreted the collage to the entire summit audience.

Student Barriers

As the students explained the experiences represented in their collages, four dominant themes emerged (see "Theme" boxes).

1. The lack of understanding and acceptance concerning disabilities in general, and their disabilities in

particular, on the part of people in general, fellow students, staff, and even faculty.

2. The lack of adequate services to assist in tackling academic and nonacademic responsibilities.

3. The lack of sufficient financial resources and the knowledge of how to acquire them, to live a more self-sufficient life.

4. The lack of self-advocacy skills and training needed to live independently.

Lack of Understanding and Acceptance

All the student groups emphasized two elements: the lack of acceptance and the lack of understanding of those with disabilities. One group's members strikingly portrayed how they felt about this lack of acceptance by placing a large picture of Tom Hanks in a trendy two-piece dress suit in its collage. Rather than leave the familiar face in place, however, they replaced it with a head disproportionately smaller. According to students, this picture "represents for us the small-minded people, small-minded students on campus; and every once in a while you run into a professor like that, too."

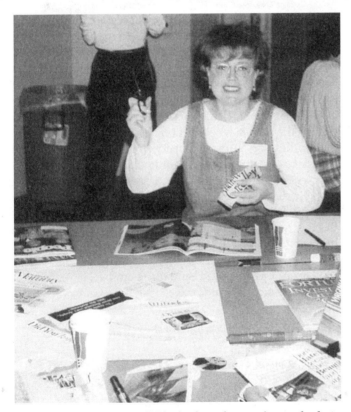

One member of the "summit" looks through magazines and selects pictures representing barriers to her success in her current postsecondary institution.

As groups shared their collages with other summit participants, they elaborated on their frustrations. For ex-

ample, another group shared that this lack of understanding and acceptance often resulted in a "crash and burn effect with the teachers; they don't understand you, and it gives you a sense of being out of order." Particularly troubling to students was the perception they had that society generally viewed disability to be associated with incompetence. Typifying this perception is the remark of one student, who stated: "Because of the problems we have, a lot of times people get mad that we are not doing things the way they do it and you always want to say, 'Yes, I will do it!'"

> ## Theme 1. The lack of understanding and acceptance concerning disabilities by fellow students, staff, and faculty
>
> - Small-mindedness.
> - Disability viewed as incompetence.
> - Instructor frustration.
> - Instructors can damage students.

Several groups of students expressed the difficulties they experience when instructors are not knowledgeable or experienced in modifying classroom environments, instructional strategies, or grading methods, For example, one group noted:

> We have to deal with professors, but they don't deal with us. They deal with the norm, and some are frustrated with us.

Another student expanded on this remark by saying: "Not only do we have a problem, we then have to alleviate accommodation anxiety [of instructors]." Perhaps the most poignant remark relative to this first barrier was from a student who stated:

> Some teachers and TA's [teaching assistants] don't have an understanding of students' needs. They cause damage to students with disabilities through their lack of understanding. It makes me think sometimes, so who has the real problem? Me or them?

Lack of Adequate Services

The second barrier identified by the students was the lack of adequate services available to assist them in tackling both academic and nonacademic challenges. These summit students realized that they were not alone in needing academic support outside the postsecondary classroom. Many of these students perceived that college educators and college-services staffs needed information, training, and ongoing support themselves to effectively teach students with disabilities. Perhaps that is why students expressed such disappointment in their traditional academic support laboratories, where tutoring in math, reading, writing, and computer literacy skills are available to all students. Their disappointments stem from the examples mentioned previously—that the staff and tutors knew little about these students' disabilities and thus could not communicate with them effectively.

Theme 2. The lack of adequate services to assist in tackling academic and non-academic responsibilities

- Teachers and support staff need information, training, and ongoing support themselves to effectively teach students with disabilities.
- Documentation of disability is not forwarded to postsecondary institutions.
- Students are unable to acquire medical and dental services because communication was difficult.
- Students felt need for increased access to transportation, buildings, and adaptive computers.

Further, students indicated that they literally were "searching for services" that were more appropriate to their needs but were beyond the scope of the support traditionally provided on campus. Examples of these needs included having adequate, reliable transportation to campuses, as well as on campus, and the need for networking and mentoring so that students could "learn from each other and reach their potential."

Theme 3: Lack of sufficient financial resources and the knowledge of how to acquire them to be self-sufficient

- Need reliable income to move out on their own and become more self-sufficient.
- Less on-campus opportunity to work compared to other students.
- Feeling insecure in their knowledge of time and money management.

Disabilities documentation was a major issue for many students. High school records of special education services received were not routinely given to students or passed along to the postsecondary institutions. Without this documentation, students were faced with several dilemmas, including having to prove their eligibility for postsecondary services. Often, students felt themselves to be unable to explain fully or even identify strategies previous educators had found to be helpful for enhancing their learning processes. Thus, students in several groups pointed out the need for more assessment opportunities at the postsecondary level so that incoming students could learn more about the extent of their disability and what assistance the support laboratories can provide on

an individual and group basis. Students reported that "disability changes the way you see life," but they needed to learn the accommodations and compensatory skills that might enhance their success.

It was not only the lack of academic support services and inadequate knowledge of their individual files that these students decried. For example, some students were upset at being unable to obtain service at local medical centers where neither doctors nor their staff could understand even basic signing, thus causing frustration and anxiety during examinations. Students said that there was no systematic career-services network to assist them in obtaining full-time employment. One student shared his appreciation for a counselor who was well connected with community employers; but when the counselor left, the contacts seemed to disappear.

Finally, students discussed the need for environmental support on campus and in the community so that they could more easily manage access to dependable transportation, buildings, restrooms, and adaptive computer technology on their campuses and at their banks.

Need for Financial Resources

The third barrier, insufficient financial resources, was a universal concern among students at the summit. They knew they needed a steady, reliable income for food, clothing, housing, transportation, and medical insurance so they could "move out on our own and be self-sufficient." Yet they were not sure they had the knowledge base to independently manage their time and budget their money effectively.

In addition, students' postsecondary experiences had taught them that, as students with disabilities, their opportunities for employment to work-study positions or student assistantships were limited and not on a par with their peers without disabilities. Further, the consequences of their disability often precluded the possibility of employment due to complicating factors of Social Security Disability Income (SSDI), Medicaid, or Vocational Rehabilitation Services. Often students' time was limited by constraints related to their disability, such as time scheduled for tutoring sessions and the need to reserve as much time as possible to studying.

Need for Self-advocacy Skills

The fourth barrier is a theme unto itself, yet is also a thread connecting the first three barriers. The students feel they lack self-advocacy skills. A constant cry from each of the groups at the summit was the need for respect: from their peers, their community, their professors, and from themselves. Students, however, also indicated that they had no training or experience in describing their disability to others. They wanted to learn how to advocate for themselves; to help educate their college community;

to be more assertive in gaining knowledge of their disability; to be forceful in communicating their strengths and weaknesses, abilities and inabilities; and to gain the necessary strength and courage to ask for what they needed to be able to succeed. In learning to advocate for themselves, they would continue to deepen their own self-understanding, increase their self-esteem and self-worth, and begin to develop "a positive attitude to live life to its potential!"

Theme 4. The lack of self-advocacy skills and training to live independently

- Need to gain respect from the college community.
- Need to learn to advocate for themselves.
- Need to be more assertive in gaining knowledge of their disability.
- Need to deepen their own self-understanding, self-esteem, and self-worth.

Visions for the Future

Although students expressed enormous frustration with the multiple barriers they encounter, they were positive in their outlook as they begin the "journey" to their futures. One student expressed this optimism by telling the group, "The dream begins as soon as you open the door." In describing their visions for the future, the students' statements signified the importance of self-advocacy skills. One group related that the key to breaking free of barriers was having "confidence, family, self-esteem, strength, and support." Another student stated that each day, "you get up in the morning, and you have to encourage yourself somehow." Other students discussed the importance of surrounding themselves with a supportive network of people. One student stated, "I didn't want to go to school, but I found out [that] more learning and knowledge make life easier."

Self-responsibility, interdependence, realistic goals, self-acceptance, positive self-esteem, knowledge of disability, communication skills, the ability to self-advocate, a supportive network of people, and a positive attitude—these were the elements that defined the students' perspective on self-determination.

Recommendations for Eliminating Barriers

In response to students' statements, the postsecondary education support team has planned a three-pronged approach that supports students, secondary teachers, and postsecondary faculty. The plan also addresses larger institutional issues regarding receptivity to recruiting and serving students with disabilities (see box, "Tips for Eliminating Barriers").

The support team provides tuition waivers (using federally granted funds) for students who need financial assistance. The team also provides students with more intensive academic and nonacademic support. Specifically, the support team holds workshops throughout the state to recruit students with disabilities and inform them about higher education requirements. These workshops, for students, secondary teachers, and parents, are held on college and community college campuses. The workshops also help students gain insight into their responsibilities as college students, help them explore their learning styles, and provide students with self-determination training.

Tips for Eliminating Barriers

- Ask students to conduct workshops that describe the nature of various disabilities to faculty and staff.
- Provide staff development to postsecondary faculty regarding adaptations and accommodations they can implement.
- Reward faculty who are willing to adapt instruction to address the learning needs of students.
- Evaluate transportation availability to campus and on campus.
- Inform students about the documentation requirements of local postsecondary institutions before their senior year at high school.
- Identify potential financial resources for students entering into postsecondary settings.
- Teach high school students time and money management skills.
- Tour the college campus with interested students during transition planning.
- Provide summer classes addressing compensatory strategies on college campuses for high school students interested in obtaining a postsecondary education.
- Role-play with students ways of communicating to college faculty about students' disability and learning needs.
- Encourage networking between college students via focus groups, student meetings, and information workshops.

The support team also invites high school and college faculty members to training sessions regarding laws and accommodations for students with disabilities. To remind and assist institutions of higher education about the level of their commitment to teaching students with disabilities, the team is developing an evaluation instrument for postsecondary faculty members to use. The instrument addresses accessibility in terms of attitudes and architecture of many aspects of higher education: the college admissions office, career center, housing office, library, financial aid office, and student centers.

To gather more information, the team holds focus groups with community members, secondary teachers, and families. We hope to learn more about the specific types of support that these stakeholders perceive they need.

Final Thoughts

Students' perceptions solicited in the summit are consistent with research reported in recent years. Students in studies by Finn (1998) reported that receiving accommodations in courses and during testing were most beneficial to their success in postsecondary education. Finn (1998) concluded, as a result of these findings, that both staff development and student training in self-advocacy were therefore necessary (see box, "Why Involve Students?"). Research regarding faculty attitudes confirms that there is, in fact, a lack of understanding on the part of instructors relative to issues of disabilities (Hill, 1996; West et al., 1993).

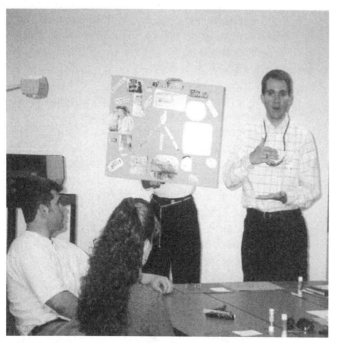

One member from each group presented a collage communicating his or her thoughts and ideas to the entire "summit" audience.

What is unusual about the "Aiming for the Future" project? From the beginning, the support team solicited students' concerns and then designed the project's interventions in accordance with project goals *and* student responses generated during the focus group activities. This approach to changing systems is consistent with national efforts to increase self-determination of students with disabilities.

Clearly, it is futile to create new student support services—or even enhance existing services—without gathering the opinions of all stakeholders, particularly students' opinions (Fullan, 1993). Excluding students from opportunities to articulate their needs is a recipe for failure. Not only do students lose a sense of ownership of the services (Smith, et al., 1995), but they also miss opportunities to practice self-determining skills, such a problem-solving and advocating for themselves (see box, "Why Involve Students?"). As noted by the students participating in the "Aiming for the Future" project, having a disability should not prevent you from having dreams and "going the distance."

Why Involve Students?

- *Increases knowledge of and ownership of the services offered.* According to Smith, Edelen-Smith, & Stodden (1995), excluding key participants in planning processes may increase resistance to ideas and decrease cooperation.
- *Enhances students' future success.* Reiff, Gerber, and Ginsberg (1997) found that successful adults with learning disabilities sought to and exerted control over their lives by making decisions about events in their lives. Further, Ward (1988) suggested that people who take control of their lives and can identify future goals will have greater future success.
- *Fosters high self-esteem.* Students whose opinions are valued, listened to, and acted upon become equal partners in the service delivery, thus increasing their sense of accomplishment and dignity (Lovett, 1996).
- *Provides students with opportunities to practice self-determination skills.* In a study by Lehmann, Bassett, and Sands (1999), students lack opportunities to engage in activities that facilitate the development of self-determination skills, such as articulating ideas, expressing needs, and acquiring leadership skills. Powers and her colleagues (1996) concluded that self-determination skills are learned and must be bolstered through application.
- *Encourages responsibility and decision-making skills.* Wehmeyer (1993) found that students who did not have opportunities to practice making choices tended to avoid making decisions and accepting responsibility.

References

Fairweather, J. S., & Shaver, D. M. (1991). Making the transition to postsecondary education and training. *Exceptional Children, 57,* 264–267.

Finn, L. (1998). Student's perceptions of beneficial LD accommodations and services at the postsecondary level. *Journal of Postsecondary Education and Disability, 13*, 46–67.

Fullan, M. (1993). *Change forces: Probing the depths of educational reform.* London: The Falmer Press.

Hill, J. L. (1996). Speaking out: Perceptions of students with disabilities regarding adequacy of services and willingness of faculty to make accommodations. *Journal of Postsecondary Education and Disability, 12*, 22–43.

Lehmann, J. P., Bassett, D. S., & Sands, D. J. (1999). Students' participation in transition-related actions: A qualitative study. *Remedial and Special Education, 20*, 160–169.

Lovett, H. (1996). *Learning to listen: Positive approaches and people with difficult behavior.* Baltimore: Paul H. Brookes.

Powers, L. E., Wilson, R., Matuszewski, J., Phillips, A., Rein, C., Schumacher, D., & Gensert, J. (1996). Facilitating adolescent self-determination: What does it take? In D. J. Sands, & M. L. Wehmeyer (Eds.), *Self-determination across the life span: Independence and choice for people with disabilities* (pp. 257–284). Baltimore: Paul H. Brookes.

Reiff, H. B., Gerber, P. J., & Ginsberg, R. (1997). *Exceeding expectations: Successful adults with learning disabilities.* Austin, TX: PRO-ED.

Smith, G. J., Edelen-Smith, P. J., & Stodden, R. A. (1995). How to avoid the seven pitfalls of systematic planning. A school and community plan for transition. *Teaching Exceptional Children, 27*(4), 42–47.

Wagner, M. (1989). *Youth with disabilities during transition: An overview of descriptive findings from the National Longitudinal Transition Study.* Menlo Park, CA: The National Longitudinal Study of Special Education Students.

Ward, M. J. (1998). *The many facets of self-determination: Transition summary.* Washington, DC: National Information Center for Children and Youth with Handicaps.

Wehmeyer, M. (1993). Perceptual and psychological factors in career decision-making of adolescents with and without cognitive disabilities. *Career Development for Exceptional Individuals, 16*, 135–146.

West, M., Kregel, J., Getzel, E. E., Zhu, M., Ipsen, S. M., & Martin, E. D. (1993). Beyond Section 504: Satisfaction and empowerment of students with disabilities in higher education. *Exceptional Children, 59*, 456–467.

Jean P. Lehmann, *Associate Professor,* **Timothy Gray Davies**, *Associate Professor, School of Education, Colorado State University, Fort Collins, Colorado;* **Kathleen M. Laurin**, *Project Coordinator, Department of Health and Human Services, The University of Northern Colorado, Greeley, Colorado.*

Address correspondence to Jean P. Lehmann, School of Education, Colorado State University, Fort Collins, CO 80523-1588 (e-mail: lehmann@CAHS. colostate.edu).

Preparation of this article was funded in part through the support of Grant HO78C60015 from the U.S. Department of Education, Office of Special Education and Rehabilitation Services. The contents of this article do not necessarily reflect the policies of the funding agency.

Choosing a Self-Determination Curriculum

PLAN *for the Future*

David W. Test • Meagan Karvonen • Wendy M. Wood • Diane Browder • Bob Algozzine

Self-determination. In almost every special education publication, conference, or inservice workshop, someone mentions "self-determination." The popularity of this term is not surprising, considering the urgent need to improve postsecondary outcomes for students with disabilities (see box, "What Does the Literature Say About Self-Determination?"). Self-determination is certainly a factor in the success of all students.

This article describes a project to help educators improve the self-determination of students with disabilities. We conducted this project with support from the U.S. Department of Education, Office of Special Education Programs, to gather, evaluate, and disseminate information about curriculum/ assessment materials and strategies on promoting self-determination. In addition, we suggest a process other educators can use to select materials and curricula.

The Self-Determination Synthesis Project

The Self-Determination Synthesis Project (SDSP) has the objective of synthesizing and disseminating the knowledge base and best practices related to self-determination for students with disabilities. To this end, the purpose of the project was to improve, expand, and accelerate the use of this knowledge by the professionals who serve children and youth with disabilities; parents who rear, educate, and support their children with disabilities; and the students themselves.

We found 60 curricula designed to promote self-determination skills.

As part of the SDSP effort, we have conducted a comprehensive literature review of self-determination interventions research, visited school systems that exhibited exemplary self-determination outcomes, and gathered and catalogued published self-determination curricula. For more information on our exemplary sites and literature review visit our Web site at http://www.uncc.edu/sdsp.

Existing Self-Determination Curricula

To identify existing self-determination curricula, we reviewed the literature, conducted Web searches, asked experts in the area, and advertised in newsletters and at conferences. As a result, we found 60 curricula designed to promote self-determination skills. Table 1 shows a sampling of these curricula; other reviews are available from the authors (see Table 1). We compiled the name of each curriculum, the publisher, telephone number, and cost information for each curriculum. Further, we identified, for each curriculum, which of the eight self-determination components the curriculum included, based on the most commonly identified components of self-determination found in the literature (e.g., Field & Hoffman 1994; Mithaug, Campeau, & Wolman, 1992; Ward, 1988; Wehmeyer, 1996). The eight curricular components are as follows:

- Choice/decision-making.
- Goal setting/attainment.
- Problem-solving.
- Self-evaluation, observation, and reinforcement.
- Self-advocacy.
- Inclusion of student-directed individualized education programs (IEP).
- Relationships with others.
- Self-awareness.

Finally, we listed the materials included in each curriculum and the appropriate student audience identified by the author, and noted whether the curriculum had been field-tested.

Table 1. A Sample of Self-Determination Curricula and Components
(For a complete listing, see http://www.uncc.edu/sdsp)

TITLE	Choice/ Decision Making	Goal Setting/ Attainment	Problem Solving	Self Eval	Self Advocacy	IEP Plan	Relationships w/Others	Self Awareness
Next S.T.E.P.: Student transition and educational planning **Product Info:** Pro-Ed (800) 897-3202 Price: $144	X X	X		X		X		X
Contents: Video, Teacher manual, Student workbook **Audience:** Transition aged students with and without disabilities, and students at-risk **Other:** Adjustment, Employment, Education, Housing, Daily living, Community _Field Test_ X								
Self-advocacy strategy for education and transition planning **Product Info:** Edge Enterprises (785) 749-1473 Price: $15	X X				X	X		X
Contents: Instructor's manual **Audience:** Audience: Primary and secondary students with mild disabilities, and high risk students **Other:** Employment, Education, Housing, Daily living, Personal, Community _Field Test_ X								
Take action: Making goals happen [Choicemaker] **Product Info:** Sopris West Inc. (800) 547-6747 Price: $95	X X	X	X					
Contents: Teacher's manual, Reproducible lesson masters, Video **Audience:** Not specified **Other:** Adjustment, Employment, Education, Housing, Daily living, Personal, Community _Field Test_ X								
TAKE CHARGE for the future **Product Info:** OHSU Center on Self-Determination (503) 232-9154 Price: $45	X X	X		X	X	X		X
Contents: Student guide, Companion guide, Parent guide, Class guide **Audience:** Sophomores and juniors with disabilities **Other:** Adjustment, Employment, Education, Housing, Daily living, Personal, Community _FieldTest_ X								
Whose future is it anyway? A student-directed transition process **Product Info:** The Arc National Headquarters (888) 368-8009 Price $20	X X	X		X	X	X		X
Contents: Student manual with coach's guide **Audience:** Middle school and transition aged students with mild to moderate cognitive, developmental, or learning disabilities **Other:** Employment, Education, Housing, Daily living, Personal, Recreation, Community _Field Test_ X								

Choosing the Right Curriculum

We found many curricula that address the different components of self-determination. Some curricula teach specific skills, such as decision making or goal setting. Others include content intended to increase students' knowledge about their disabilities or about disability rights. Still others include learning approaches or processes by which students take greater ownership of their IEP planning process. With the variety of materials available, how do teachers know what will be most effective for use with their students? We suggest that the process begin with a careful review of the sampling in Table 1 to become familiar with the variety of resources that are available. In addition, you might want to gather other published descriptions/reviews of self-determination curriculum (see Field, 1996; Field et al., 1998).

What Does the Literature Say About Self-Determination?

Here are the current trends in self-determination research:

- Current research has referred to self-determination as the ultimate goal of education (Halloran, 1993).
- Research has demonstrated a positive relationship between self-determination and improved postsecondary outcomes. These outcomes include a higher rate of employment and higher wages 1 year after graduation for students with mild mental retardation and learning disabilities (Wehmeyer & Schwartz, 1997).
- Classroom teachers are recognizing that self-determination is an important skill to teach students (Agran, Snow, & Swaner, 1999; Wehmeyer, Agran, & Hughes, 2000).

Definition of Self-Determination. Beginning with the "normalization" movement in the early 1970s, many researchers, educators, and self-advocates have developed definitions of self-determination. According to a consensus definition by Field, Martin, Miller, Ward, and Wehmeyer, 1998, self-determination is

a combination of skills, knowledge, and beliefs that enable a person to engage in goal-directed, self-regulated, autonomous behavior. An understanding of one's strengths and limitations together with a belief in oneself as capable and effective are essential to self-determination. When acting on the basis of these skills and attitudes, individuals have greater ability to take control of their lives and assume the role of successful adults. (p. 2)

Conceptual models of self-determination have included knowing and valuing oneself (Field & Hoffman, 1994); skills and knowledge on topics such as choice and decision making, goal setting and attainment, problem-solving, and self-advocacy (Martin & Marshall, 1995; Wehmeyer, 1999); and recognition of the environment's role in supporting self-determination for people with disabilities (Abery & Stancliffe, 1996).

Need for Instruction in Self-Determination. Unfortunately, so far all the rhetoric, research, and recognition is not being translated into classroom instruction. For example, Agran et al. (1999) found that whereas over 75% of middle and secondary teachers rated self-determination skills as a high priority, 55% indicated that self-determination goals were either not included in their students' IEPs or only in some students' IEPs. This finding is supported by: (a) Wehmeyer and Schwartz (1998) who found no self-determination skills in 895 IEP transition goals; and (b) Wehmeyer et al. (2000) who found 31% of secondary-level teachers reported writing no self-determination goals in student IEPs, 47% reported writing self-determination IEP goals for some students, and only 22% reported writing self-determination IEP goals for all students.

Although many explanations may exist for why self-determination skills are not included in student IEPs, we believe a major reason is that teachers are unaware of what resources exist to help with the task. This is supported by Wehmeyer et al. (2000), who reported that 41% of teachers with secondary-aged students indicated that they did not have sufficient training or information on teaching self-determination, and 17% were unaware of curriculum/assessment materials/strategies.

Promoting self-determination also requires training those without disabilities to encourage and respect the decisions made by self-determining individuals with disabilities.

Figure 1 shows a curriculum materials review checklist that we have found useful when deciding what curriculum might be most appropriate. The information included in Figure 1 is summarized in the following set of questions:

Does the intended audience match my students?

Are the materials age-appropriate? Are they designed for use with students who have mild, moderate, or severe disabilities? Some materials that may have been originally designed for use with a specific group of students may have to be modified for use with other groups (including students without disabilities). Check the introductory section of the teacher's manual to see what the authors say.

Do the skills covered in this curriculum meet my students' needs?

You may find that your students are perfectly capable of setting goals, but they do not know enough about their rights under current legislation such as the Individuals with Disabilities Education Act or the Americans with Disabilities Act to be able to ask for reasonable accommodations in their postsecondary setting, or maybe they need a better understanding of how to run their IEP meeting. In some cases, the introduction or overview section of the teacher's manual will state the goals of the curriculum. For example, the Take Action curriculum states: "Students learn to act on their plans, evaluate their plan and results, and make any necessary adjustments" (Marshall, et al., 1999, p. 9). Do the goals of the curriculum match your instructional objectives?

Does the curriculum require prerequisite skills?

Some curricula may require relatively sophisticated reading levels, or assume that the students will already understand how to make choices for themselves. Both the teacher's manual and the student activities will give you a sense of what skill level is required for students to begin using the curriculum.

Figure 1. Curriculum Materials Review Checklist

CURRICULUM MATERIALS REVIEW CHECKLIST

Title:_____

Author:_____

Publisher's name contact/information:_____

Date of publication:_____ Cost of materials:_____

For what type of student is the curriculum designed (e.g., age, disability)?

_____

What types of materials are included (e.g., instructor manual, student workbook, video, alternate formats)

_____

Do the components of self-determination match my students' needs

Students' Needs	Included in Curriculum		Comments
Choice-making	YES	NO	
Decision-making	YES	NO	
Goal setting/attainment	YES	NO	
Problem solving	YES	NO	
Self-evaluation	YES	NO	
Self-advocacy	YES	NO	
Self-awareness	YES	NO	
Person-centered IEP Planning	YES	NO	
Relationship with Others	YES	NO	

Other:_____

Rate each of the following on a scale from 1 (Excellent) to 4 (Poor) based on your students and yourself as a teacher.

	1 Excellent	2 Good	3 Fair	4 Poor	5 Can't tell
How easy is it to get materials?					
How well do the cost of materials fit my budget?					
Are the materials available in alternative formats?					
Are support materials provided?					
Are the instructions "teacher friendly"?					
Are the prerequisite skills delineated?					
Are there sufficient opportunities for practice?					
How relevant/motivating is the content for my students?					
How age-appropriate is the content for my students?					
How well do the materials match the academic level of my students?					
Is a system for assessing student progress included?					
Is the content based on research/field testing?					
How appealing are the videos and other materials?					
How well does the instructional time (number and length of sessions) fit with my schedule?					
Additional Comments:					

What types of materials are provided?

If you work with students who are visually or hearing impaired, does the curriculum have audiotape, closed-captioned, or Braille formats? Are the materials durable and easy to use? Do they provide enough variety or hold the interest of students? Is an assessment tool included?

How easy is it to follow the lesson plans?

Are the objectives for each lesson clearly stated? Is it easy to tell what materials you will need and how much time each lesson will require? Is the text formatted so you can easily find prompts? Is there flexibility in the order of the lesson plans?

Were the materials field-tested?

Has anyone collected information about whether students who used this curriculum improved their self-determination knowledge, skills, or behaviors? Just because someone is selling a product doesn't mean that it works. Many of the curricula we listed have been field-tested, but not all of them report the results of those tests. Sometimes authors report field-test results in a journal article or book chapter instead of the manual.

What are the time and financial obligations associated with this curriculum?

The costs of materials sampled in Table 1 range from nothing to more than $1,000. The time commitments also vary extensively. Is the financial cost of the curriculum appropriate to the length of instructional time you have available to teach the skills?

Important questions include: Are the materials age-appropriate? Are they designed for use with students who have mild, moderate, or severe disabilities? Do they provide enough variety or hold the interest of students? Is an assessment tool included?

Sample Curricula

We have selected five curricula which have published research documenting their effectiveness to describe in more detail here.

The Self-Advocacy Strategy for Education and Transition Planning

This curriculum was developed using a modified version of the Strategies Intervention Model (Ellis, Deshler, Lenz, Schumaker, & Clark, 1991) at the University of Kansas. The

Self-Advocacy Strategy is a motivation strategy that teachers can use to help students prepare for any type of educational or transition planning meeting. The strategy, called I-PLAN, consists of five steps:
- *Inventory* your strengths, areas to improve, goals, needed accommodations, and choices for learning.
- *Provide* your inventory information.
- *Listen* and respond.
- *Ask* questions.
- *Name* your goals.

The instructor's manual contains step-by-step lesson plans and cue cards that you can use as transparencies, handouts, or worksheets. Finally, the Self-Advocacy Strategy has been field-tested with students with learning disabilities ages 14–21 (Van Reusen & Bos, 1994; Van Reusen, Deshler, & Schumaker, 1989).

Next S.T.E.P. (Student Transition and Education Planning)

Developed by Andrew Halpern and his colleagues at the University of Oregon, the purpose of the Next S.T.E.P. curriculum is to teach high school students how to begin planning for their lives after they leave school. Materials include a teacher's manual with lesson plans and necessary forms, a student workbook, and a videotape that contains an overview of the curriculum, as well as vignettes that address important issues from specific lessons. The Next S.T.E.P. curriculum has been field-tested with students with mild mental retardation ages 14–19 (Zhang, 2000).

Take Action: Making Goals Happen

Take Action is the last of the three strands of the Choice-Maker Self-Determination Curriculum designed by Laura Huber Marshall and Jim Martin and their colleagues at the University of Colorado at Colorado Springs. The first two strands are Choosing Goals and Expressing Goals (or Self-Directed IEP). Take Action is designed to provide teachers with a set of lessons to teach students a generalizable process for attaining their goals. Materials include a teacher's manual with reproducible lesson masters and a student instructional video. Take Action was field-tested with six students with mild or moderate mental retardation ages 16 to 18 (Jerman, Martin, Marshall, & Sale, 2000). Results indicated that all six students accomplished all goals set during maintenance.

TAKE CHARGE for the Future

This multicomponent curriculum was designed by Laurie Powers and her colleagues at Oregon Health Sciences University to assist students to become more involved in their transition planning process. The four components are coaching, mentorship, parent support, and staff training. Materials include a student guide, companion guide, parent guide, and class guide. TAKE CHARGE for the Future was field-tested with 43 students with specific learning disabilities, emotional disabilities, other health impairments, or orthopedic impairments ages 14–17 years (Powers, Turner, Matuszewski, Wilson, & Phillips, in press). Results indicated significant differences in education planning, transition awareness, family empowerment, and student participation in transition planning.

41% of teachers with secondary-aged students indicated that they did not have sufficient training or information on teaching self-determination.

Whose Future Is It Anyway? A Student-Directed Transition Planning Process

Developed by Michael Wehmeyer and his colleagues at the Arc National Headquarters, this curriculum is designed for middle school and transition-aged students with mild or moderate disabilities. The curriculum consists of a student manual, which includes a cut-out Coach's Guide. While the manual is written for students to read and work through at their own pace, the teacher's role is three part:

- To facilitate student success.
- To teach information requested by students.
- To advocate for a successful transition for students.

This curriculum was field-tested with 53 students with mild or moderate mental retardation ages 15–21 (Wehmeyer & Lawrence, 1995). Results indicate significant increases in self-efficacy and outcome expectancy measures.

For more information on our exemplary sites and literature review visit our World Wide Web site at http://www.uncc.edu/sdsp.

Final Thoughts

Self-determination develops over the life span as students gain self-awareness and learn to make increasingly important decisions about their lives with the guidance of their parents, teachers, and other adult mentors. Because traditionally other people (professionals) have made most major life decisions for them, students with disabilities often require instruction on the skills needed to be self-determining citizens. Promoting self-determination also requires training those without disabilities to encourage and respect the decisions made by self-determining individuals with disabilities.

Fortunately, many self-determination curricula are available from which to choose. We hope that the suggestions provided in this article will help you decide which

Article 35. Choosing a Self-Determination Curriculum

curriculum will best promote self-determination for your students.

References

Abery, B., & Stancliffe, R. (1996). The ecology of self-determination. In D. J. Sands & M. Wehmeyer (Eds.), *Self-determination across the lifespan: Independence and choice for people with disabilities* (pp. 111–145). Baltimore: Paul H. Brookes.

Agran, M., Snow, K., & Swaner, J. (1999). Teacher perceptions of self-determination: Benefits, characteristics, strategies. *Education and Training in Mental Retardation and Developmental Disabilities, 34*, 293–301.

Ellis, E. S., Deshler, D. D., Lenz, B. K., Schumaker, J. B., & Clark, F. L. (1991). An instructional model for teaching learning strategies. *Focus on Exceptional Children, 23*(4), 1–24.

Field, S. (1996). Self-determination instructional strategies for youth with learning disabilities. *Journal of Learning Disabilities, 29*, 40–52.

Field, S., & Hoffman, A. (1994). Development of a model for self-determination. *Career Development for Exceptional Individuals, 17*, 159–169.

Field, S., Martin, J., Miller, R., Ward, M., & Wehmeyer, M. (1998). *A practical guide for teaching self-determination*. Reston, VA: Council for Exceptional Children.

Halloran, W. D. (1993). Transition service requirements: Issues, implications, challenge. In R. C. Eaves & P. J. McLaughlin (Eds.), *Recent advances in special education and rehabilitation* (pp. 210–224). Boston: Andover.

Jerman, S. L., Martin, J. E., Marshall, L. H., & Sale, P. R. (2000). Promoting self-determination: Using *Take Action* to teach goal attainment. *Career Development for Exceptional Individuals, 23*, 27–38.

Marshall, L. H., Martin, J. E., Maxson, L., Hughes, W., Miller, T., McGill, T., & Jerman, P. (1999). *Take action: Making goals happen*. Longmont, CO: Sopris West.

Martin, J. E., & Marshall L. H. (1995) Choicemaker: A comprehensive self-determination transition program. *Intervention in School and Clinic, 30*, 147–156.

Mithaug, D., Campeau, P., & Wolman, J. (1992). *Research on self-determination in individuals with disabilities*. Unpublished Manuscript.

Powers, L. E., Turner, A., Matuszewski, J., Wilson, R., & Phillips, A. (in press). TAKE CHARGE for the future: A controlled field-test of a model to promote student involvement in transition planning. *Career Development for Exceptional Individuals*.

Van Reusen, A. K., & Bos, C. S. (1994). Facilitating student participation in individualized education programs through motivation strategy instruction. *Exceptional Children, 60*, 466–475.

Van Reusen, A. K., Deshler, D. D., & Schumaker, J. B. (1989). Effects of a student participation strategy in facilitating the involvement of adolescents with learning disabilities in Individualized Education Program planning process. *Learning Disabilities, 1*, 23–34.

Ward, M. J. (1988). The many facts of self-determination. *NICHCY Transition Summary: National Information Center for Children and Youth with Disabilities, 5*, 2–3.

Wehmeyer, M. L. (1996). Self-determination in youth with severe cognitive disabilities: From theory to practice. In L. E. Powers, G. H. S. Singer, & J. Sowers (Eds.), *On the road to autonomy: Promoting self-competence for children and youth with disabilities* (pp. 17–36). Baltimore: Paul H. Brookes.

Wehmeyer, M. L. (1999). A functional model of self-determination: Describing development and implementing instruction. *Focus on Autism and Other Developmental Disabilities, 14,* 53–61.

Wehmeyer, M. L., Agran, M., & Hughes, C. A. (2000). A national survey of teachers' promotion of self-determination and student directed learning. *The Journal of Special Education, 34,* 58–68.

Wehmeyer, M., & Lawrence, M. (1995). Whose future is it anyway? Promoting student involvement in transition planning. *Career Development for Exceptional Individuals, 18,* 69–83.

Wehmeyer, M. L., & Schwartz, M. (1997). Self-determination and positive adult outcomes: A follow up study of youth with mental retardation or learning disabilities. *Exceptional Children, 63,* 245–255.

Wehmeyer, M. L., & Schwartz, M. (1998). The self-determination focus of transition goals for students with mental retardation. *Career Development for Exceptional Individuals, 21,* 75–86.

Zhang, D. (2000). The effects of self-determination instruction on high school students with mild disabilities. *Louisiana Education Research Journal, 25*(1), 29–54.

David W. Test *(CEC Chapter #147), Professor, Special Education Program;* **Meagan Karvonen***, Project Coordinator, Special Education Program;* **Wendy M. Wood***, Associate Professor, Special Education Program;* **Diane Browder***, Snyder Distinguished Professor, Special Education Program; and* **Bob Algozzine***, Professor, Department of Educational Administration, Research, and Technology, College of Education, University of North Carolina at Charlotte.*

Address correspondence to David Test, Special Education Program, University of North Carolina at Charlotte, 9201 University City Blvd., Charlotte, NC 28223 (e-mail: dwtest@email.uncc.edu; URL: http://www.uncc.edu/sdsp).

From *Teaching Exceptional Children,* November/December 2000, pp. 48-54. © 2000 by The Council for Exceptional Children. Reprinted with permission.

Index

Index

Test Your Knowledge Form

We encourage you to photocopy and use this page as a tool to assess how the articles in *Annual Editions* expand on the information in your textbook. By reflecting on the articles you will gain enhanced text information. You can also access this useful form on a product's book support Web site at *http://www.dushkin.com/online/*.

NAME: _____ DATE: _____

TITLE AND NUMBER OF ARTICLE: _____

BRIEFLY STATE THE MAIN IDEA OF THIS ARTICLE:

_____

LIST THREE IMPORTANT FACTS THAT THE AUTHOR USES TO SUPPORT THE MAIN IDEA:

_____

WHAT INFORMATION OR IDEAS DISCUSSED IN THIS ARTICLE ARE ALSO DISCUSSED IN YOUR TEXTBOOK OR OTHER READINGS THAT YOU HAVE DONE? LIST THE TEXTBOOK CHAPTERS AND PAGE NUMBERS:

_____

LIST ANY EXAMPLES OF BIAS OR FAULTY REASONING THAT YOU FOUND IN THE ARTICLE:

_____

LIST ANY NEW TERMS/CONCEPTS THAT WERE DISCUSSED IN THE ARTICLE, AND WRITE A SHORT DEFINITION:

We Want Your Advice

ANNUAL EDITIONS revisions depend on two major opinion sources: one is our Advisory Board, listed in the front of this volume, which works with us in scanning the thousands of articles published in the public press each year; the other is you—the person actually using the book. Please help us and the users of the next edition by completing the prepaid article rating form on this page and returning it to us. Thank you for your help!

ANNUAL EDITIONS: Educating Exceptional Children 04/05

ARTICLE RATING FORM

Here is an opportunity for you to have direct input into the next revision of this volume.
We would like you to rate each of the articles listed below, using the following scale:

1. **Excellent: should definitely be retained**
2. **Above average: should probably be retained**
3. **Below average: should probably be deleted**
4. **Poor: should definitely be deleted**

Your ratings will play a vital part in the next revision.
Please mail this prepaid form to us as soon as possible.
Thanks for your help!

RATING	ARTICLE	RATING	ARTICLE
	1. Standards for Diverse Learners		24. Making Inclusion a Reality for Students With Severe Disabilities
	2. Trends in the Special Education Teaching Force: Do They Reflect Legislative Mandates and Legal Requirements?		25. Training Basic Teaching Skills to Paraeducators of Students With Severe Disabilities
	3. What's Good? Suggested Resources for Beginning Special Education Teachers		26. Using Technology to Construct Alternate Portfolios of Students With Moderate and Severe Disabilities
	4. An Interview With Dr. Marilyn Friend		27. Mobility Training Using the MOVE® Curriculum: A Parent's View
	5. Music in the Inclusive Environment		28. Accommodations for Students With Disabilities: Removing Barriers to Learning
	6. Language Flowering, Language Empowering: 20 Ways Parents and Teachers Can Assist Young Children		29. Chaos in the Classroom: Looking at ADHD
	7. The Itinerant Teacher Hits the Road: A Map for Instruction in Young Children's Social Skills		30. Understanding the Young Gifted Child: Guidelines for Parents, Families, and Educators
	8. Providing Support for Student Independence Through Scaffolded Instruction		31. Cultivating Otherwise Untapped Potential
	9. Graphic Organizers to the Rescue! Helping Students Link—and Remember—Information		32. Gifted Students Need an Education, Too
	10. Successful Strategies for Promoting Self-Advocacy Among Students With LD: The LEAD Group		33. Transition Planning for Students With Severe Disabilities: Policy Implications for the Classroom
	11. Don't Water Down! Enhance: Content Learning Through the Unit Organizer Routine		34. Listening to Student Voices About Postsecondary Education
	12. For the Love of Language		35. Choosing a Self-Determination Curriculum
	13. Language Differences or Learning Difficulties		
	14. Young African American Children With Disabilities and Augmentative and Alternative Communication Issues		
	15. The Secrets of Autism		
	16. Citizenship and Disability		
	17. Inscrutable or Meaningful? Understanding and Supporting Your Inarticulate Students		
	18. Wraparound Services for Young Schoolchildren With Emotional and Behavioral Disorders		
	19. Making Choices—Improving Behavior—Engaging in Learning		
	20. Homeless Youth in the United States		
	21. Classroom Problems That Don't Go Away		
	22. A Half-Century of Progress for Deaf Individuals		
	23. Seeking the Light: Welcoming a Visually Impaired Student		

(Continued on next page)

ANNUAL EDITIONS: EDUCATING EXCEPTIONAL CHILDREN 04/05

BUSINESS REPLY MAIL
FIRST-CLASS MAIL PERMIT NO. 84 GUILFORD CT

POSTAGE WILL BE PAID BY ADDRESSEE

NO POSTAGE
NECESSARY
IF MAILED
IN THE
UNITED STATES

McGraw-Hill/Dushkin
530 Old Whitfield Street
Guilford, Ct 06437-9989

ABOUT YOU

Name   Date

_____   _____

Are you a teacher? ❑   A student? ❑
Your school's name

_____

Department

_____

Address   City   State   Zip

_____

School telephone #

_____

YOUR COMMENTS ARE IMPORTANT TO US!

Please fill in the following information:
For which course did you use this book?

_____

Did you use a text with this ANNUAL EDITION?   ❑   yes ❑   no
What was the title of the text?

_____

What are your general reactions to the *Annual Editions* concept?

_____

Have you read any pertinent articles recently that you think should be included in the next edition? Explain.

_____

Are there any articles that you feel should be replaced in the next edition? Why?

_____

Are there any World Wide Web sites that you feel should be included in the next edition? Please annotate.

_____

May we contact you for editorial input?   ❑   yes ❑   no
May we quote your comments?   ❑   yes ❑   no